plus 1/6
cost of procuring

PUBLISHED FOR

JUDAICA RESEARCH AT YALE UNIVERSITY

on the

LOUIS M. RABINOWITZ FOUNDATION

YALE JUDAICA SERIES

Volume III

THE CODE OF MAIMONIDES

(*MISHNEH TORAH*)

BOOK FOURTEEN

The Code of Maimonides

BOOK FOURTEEN

THE BOOK OF JUDGES

TRANSLATED FROM THE HEBREW BY

ABRAHAM M. HERSHMAN, D.D., D.H.L.

NEW HAVEN

YALE UNIVERSITY PRESS

LONDON · GEOFFREY CUMBERLEGE · OXFORD UNIVERSITY PRESS

1949

Printed in the United States of America

CONTENTS

INTRODUCTION

Book XIV and the Treatises It Comprises

The last book of the *Mishneh Torah,* denominated by Maimonides "The Book of Judges," is made up of five treatises, arranged in the following sequence: Sanhedrin, Evidence, Rebels, Mourning, and Kings and Wars.

Sanhedrin. This term usually signifies in rabbinical literature the superior courts of seventy-one and twenty-three. However, in the treatise under consideration, the appellation embraces, as it does in the mishnaic Tractate *Sanhedrin,* the entire judiciary, ranging from the Supreme Court to a court of three laymen, indeed, to a court of one well-qualified judge. The treatise deals with the composition, functions, and powers of the courts and the ethical standards to which the incumbents thereof are to conform; the rules—substantive and procedural—governing civil, ritual, and criminal cases; [1] offenses punishable by death, offenses punishable by flagellation, and the regulations for the administration of these penalties; adjudication of monetary suits by law and settlement of those suits by arbitration.

Evidence. This treatise has as its central theme the examination of witnesses. It brings out with notable clearness the distinction between inquiry and query, wherein these differ from cross-examination or investigation; describes the rules in case of a discrepancy in answers given to questions coming under the categories of inquiries and queries, on the one hand, and the rules in case of a discrepancy in the answers given in the course of cross-examination, on the other; and treats of enactments by the Rabbis looking to leniency in monetary disputes, in order to facilitate credit. It sets forth the grounds on which witnesses are disqualified from giving testimony, some by scriptural law, others on rabbinical authority, and the difference between these two classes of ineligibles; the distinc-

1. It is well to bear in mind that the Jewish law prescribes penalties for willful transgression of purely ritual laws.

tion between refuted evidence and contradicted evidence; and the procedure followed in the case of plotting witnesses.

Rebels. This treatise describes the primacy of the Great Sanhedrin, the legislative body, and court of highest instance on legal and ritual questions, detailing the circumstances under which the Supreme Court of a later day may reverse decisions and measures of an earlier Supreme Court. It defines, moreover, three kinds of "rebels," each of whom incurs the penalty of death: a sage who gives a practical ruling which is in conflict with the one given by the Great Sanhedrin; a son or daughter who curses or strikes a parent; and a stubborn and rebellious son.

Mourning. This treatise discusses the time when mourning begins; those for whom mourning is to be observed by biblical law and those for whom it is to be observed on rabbinical authority; for whom a priest is bound to defile himself; the Jewish practice with respect to the dead and their burial; the things forbidden to a mourner during the "seven" days and the things forbidden to him during the "thirty" days; the law of "recent" information and that of "deferred" information; how and when a rent in a garment (made for a deceased kin) may be mended; the effect of the Sabbath or a festival on the "seven" and "thirty" days of mourning; funeral services, orations, and dirges; comforting mourners; the mourner's meal; and the Mourner's Benediction.

Kings and Wars. In I Sam. 8:11–17 is set forth "the manner of the king." According to some rabbinical authorities (B. San 20b), the section describes the royal prerogatives, the power vested in the king by the law; according to others (*ibid.*), it forecasts the abuse of power on the part of the king, and forewarns the people of the high-handed methods the monarch will be tempted to employ in the exercise of his authority. Maimonides favors the first view. He stresses, however, the duty of the king to make himself worthy of the exalted position he occupies, to prove "loyal to the royal" in him. In order that he live up to the responsibilities his office involves, he is bidden carry a copy of the scroll of the Law about him. The treatise dwells upon the honor due to the king; and reproduces the contents of I Sam. 8: 11–17, the section referred to above, adding, however, that the king must compensate his subjects for whatever he takes from them. It differentiates between a war for a religious cause and an optional war. It also treats of the Noachian commandments, that is, commandments enjoined upon mankind at large. The last two chapters describe the "Messianic age" and the consequences it will bring in its wake—namely, the liberation of Israel and the ultimate transformation of human nature.

Four of the treatises in Book XIV readily fall under the general title, *The Book of Judges*. "Sanhedrin" has as its basic theme the administration of the law. "Evidence" forms a natural sequel to "Sanhedrin," for it is on the testimony given by witnesses that judgment is rendered. "Rebels" describes the position of unique importance held by the Great Sanhedrin, and is, moreover, concerned with offenders who incur the penalty of death. "King and Wars" links up with "Sanhedrin," because one of the prime functions of the king was to administer justice (see v, iv, 10). More than this: according to Maimonides, the king was empowered to execute murderers whom the religious courts, by reason of technical restrictions, could not convict (v, iii, 10; see below, "State Courts," p. xviii f).

While the over-all title *The Book of Judges* covers the above-mentioned treatises, it has no bearing whatever on "Mourning," the fourth treatise embodied in Book XIV. The subsumption by such a master systematizer as Maimonides of purely ritual laws under "the judiciary" is an anomaly. The sole link between the treatise on Mourning and that on Sanhedrin—according to the author himself [2] (iv, preamble)—is that just as it is mandatory to bury one who was convicted by the court on the day of execution, so it is mandatory to bury one who dies a natural death on the day of the demise (see i, xv, 8). The connection between the two treatises is a flimsy one.

2. This is the only instance in the *Mishneh Torah* where Maimonides finds it necessary to offer an explanation why he included a given treatise in a given Book.

Scriptural Basis

The basic source of the *Mishneh Torah* is the Bible—the cornerstone on which the edifice of Judaism rests. The *Sefer ha-Miṣwoṯ* (Book of Commandments), which contains a tabulation of the positive and negative precepts of the Torah, was designed by Maimonides as an introduction to the Code (see SM, ed. Heller, p. 3). To be sure, those precepts were to be followed in accordance with the interpretation handed down by tradition. The *Mishneh Torah,* we are told by its author, was to be a crystallization of the scriptural and rabbinical laws that enter into the substance of Judaism (*ibid.*). For to Maimonides the rules enunciated in the Bible and those enunciated in postbiblical sources represented an organic unity.[3] The latter was a concomitant of the former. For all that, however, the Bible is the fountainhead, the primordial source from which Jewish law has sprung.

In strict consistency with this appraisal of the Scriptures, each treatise in the Code is prefaced with a list of biblical commandments, positive and negative, which may be said to be the nuclei of what is contained therein. Each treatise opens with a scriptural passage or passages, setting forth the precepts which are at the core of what follows. Hence Maimonides seizes every opportunity to seek a warrant for statements made by him in this ultimate source—the Bible. Thus in describing benevolent deeds which the Rabbis characterize as "bestowal of loving kindness in person," he says (IV, xiv, 1): "Although all these commands are only on rabbinical authority, they are implied in the precept: *And thou shalt love thy neighbor as thyself* (Lev. 19: 18)." His sole authority for the greater part of Chapter iv in Treatise V is I Sam. 8: 11–17.

Small wonder, therefore, that in citing scriptural sources, he feels free to choose any passage which in his opinion furnishes the strongest proof for the point made by him. Not only does he at times in support of a ruling or a statement quote a biblical verse used in the Palestinian Talmud in preference to one used in the

3. See C. Tchernowitz, *Tolĕḏoṯ ha-Posĕḳim,* I, 198.

Babylonian Talmud (see iv, vi, 1) but he does not hesitate to base conclusions upon passages which according to the Talmud do not bear out those conclusions (see i, ii, 1; i, v, 1, *passim*). Sometimes he disregards altogether a biblical citation given in the Talmud and substitutes for it another, not utilized, so far as we know, in any of the sources that have come down to us (see v, i, 2; cf. LM *ad loc.*).

Book XIV and the Mishnah

The Book of Judges covers part of *Nĕzikin,* the fourth of the Six Orders into which the Mishnah is divided, and the major part of chapter 3 of *Mo'eḏ Ḳaṭan,* a tractate which belongs to the Second Order known as "Seasons." But as we shall presently see, these mishnaic sources do not exhaust the contents of the book.

Sanhedrin. This treatise comprises, as the title indicates, the laws contained in the mishnaic tractate which bears this name. But it includes much more. Besides material culled from tractates in other orders, it comprehends most of chapter 3 of *Makkoṭ,* the chapter which deals with the rules touching corporal punishment (flagellation).

Evidence. This treatise draws largely upon the above-named two tractates and takes in a considerable amount of legal matters found in Tractates *Šĕḇu'oṭ, Baḇa Baṭra,* and *Kĕṭubboṭ,* the last of which is an integral part of the Third Order of the Mishnah.

Rebels. The rules laid down in this treatise are derived from several tractates. The rules in Chapters i, iii, iv, v, and vii are based on Tractate *Sanheḏrin;* those in Chapter ii on *'Eḏuyyoṭ* and *'Aḇoḏah Zarah;* those in Chapter vi on *Ḳiddušin* in the Third Order.

Mourning. The legal matters discussed in this treatise are for the greater part taken from *Mo'eḏ Ḳaṭan* in the Second Order.

Kings and Wars. This treatise has as its main source Tractate *Sanheḏrin.* But it includes, in addition to material gathered from other sources, much that is contained in chapter 8 of Tractate *Soṭah* in the Third Order.

Nomenclature. Of the five treatises of which Book XIV consists, only the first, "Sanhedrin," retains the mishnaic designation. The title "Evidence" (Treatise II) was borrowed from *Hălaḵoṯ Gĕḏoloṯ* (a work composed in the ninth century). The appellation "Rebels" (Treatise III) was coined by Maimonides by adding the plural ending to the word denoting "rebel" (see Deut. 9:7), the opprobrious epithet applied to an elder who defies the authority of the Supreme Court, the author using the plural because the treatise is concerned also with the rules bearing upon a son or daughter who treats either parent contumaciously, and upon a stubborn and rebellious son. The title "Mourning" (Treatise IV) was derived from the name of the Minor Tractate *'Aḇel Rabbaṯi*, "Great Tractate of Mourning," which supplied much of the material contained in Treatise IV. The name "Kings and Wars" (Treatise V), sometimes called "Treatise on Kings," or "Laws Concerning Kings," was probably formed after the biblical expression in I Sam. 8:11, usually rendered "the manner of the king" (I. Herzog, *The Main Institutions of Jewish Law,* I, Intro. p. xxiii), Maimonides replacing the term translated "the manner of" with the word which has the definite connotation of "laws concerning."

Codification of Postmishnaic Laws. In addition to the many older sources upon which Maimonides draws freely, he has made full use of the entire postmishnaic law down to his own time. The rules formulated by the *'Amora'im* in the Gemara, Babylonian and Palestinian, the decisions reached by the Geonim, the opinions given by Alfasi[4]—all this immense accumulation of legal matters, representing the growth and expansion of Jewish law of nearly a thousand years, is restated in the *Mishneh Torah,* which was intended by the author to be *the* code, the ultimate word on Jewish law. To quote Maimonides: "I have entitled this work *Mishneh Torah* ("Repetition of the Law") for the reason that

4. The Geonim are mentioned only twice in Book XIV (I, v, 10; IV, v, 14); the name of Alfasi does not occur at all. We know, however, that many of the rulings by the Geonim and by Alfasi have been incorporated in the Book of Judges. In XIII, II, v, 6, Maimonides cites a ruling by Rabbi Joseph Hallevi (Ibn Migas).

one who first reads the Written Law and then this compendium will know from it the entire Oral Law, without having to consult any other book" (Preface).

Points of Special Interest

a. Historical

1. King Jannaeus and the Sanhedrin. Treatise I, ii, 5, contains a ruling to the effect that the kings of Israel (i.e., kings who are not of the House of David, though they reign in Judea) can neither judge nor be judged, because to sit in judgment on them might lead to untoward consequences. This ruling is repeated in V, iii, 7. The "untoward consequences" cautioned against refer to the following incident related in B. San 19a: A slave of King Alexander Jannaeus (103–77 B.C.E), charged with murder, was sent by his master to be tried by the Sanhedrin. The latter, however, demanded that the king appear in person in compliance with the law that, if a slave committed murder, the master too must be present at the trial. The king came and sat down. Thereupon Simeon ben Sheṭaḥ, the president of the Sanhedrin, said to him: "King Jannaeus, stand on thy feet, and let the witnesses testify against thee, as it is said: *Then both men between whom the controversy is, shall stand . . . before the judges*" (Deut. 19:17). In reply, the king said that he would stand up only at insistence of the other members of the Sanhedrin. Overawed, the others did not utter a word. Turning to his colleagues, Simeon rebuked their pusillanimity and warned them that they would pay dearly for it. They died shortly thereafter.[5] It was then enacted that the kings of Israel neither judge nor be judged.

5. The talmudic account of the incident concludes thus: "Gabriel (the angel) struck them down, and they died."

By the expression "untoward circumstances," Maimonides has reference not so much to the physical danger to which judges would expose themselves were they to sit in judgment on the king, as to the moral danger which might ensue, i.e., the failure of judges to assert the supreme authority of the law. Afraid to brave the anger of the king, they might be tempted to render an unjust decision. Hence in V, iii, 7, he says: ". . . the cause of religion would suffer."

2. Revival of the System of Ordination. A noteworthy statement made by Maimonides in his Mishnah Commentary, San 1:3, recurs in 1, iv, 11. In his opinion, the scholars of Palestine may by unanimous consent confer ordination upon one of the members of the academy; and the one thus ordained may, by associating two others with himself, ordain others and revive the Great Sanhedrin. "Otherwise," he adds in the Mishnah Commentary, "the restoration of the Supreme Court will never be possible." In 1538 the Academy at Safed proceeded to act upon this suggestion. It ordained Rabbi Jacob Beraḇ, who in turn ordained four of his disciples. A heated controversy ensued. Some scholars headed by Rabbi Levi ben Jacob Haḇiḇ, Chief Rabbi of Jerusalem, vehemently protested against the action taken by the Academy at Safed. Radbez too, who at that time lived in Egypt, strenuously opposed it. One of the reasons for his objections was that Maimonides himself was undecided on this point; for, while in his Mishnah Commentary he affirmed the right of Palestinian scholars to renew the system of ordination, in his Code (1, iv, 11), he says that this innovation requires careful reflection (cf. Radbez *ad loc.;* see Graetz, *History of the Jews,* IV, 351–356).

3. Karaites. It is interesting to note Maimonides' attitude toward the Karaites of his day. In his view, they were to be regarded as "forced converts," who abjured Judaism under duress; i.e., they had been raised by Karaite parents and reared in their religion. He urged that they be befriended by Jews, so that they return to the Jewish fold (III, iii, 3).[6]

4. State Courts. From several statements in the *Mishneh Torah* (XI, v, ii, 4; XIV, 1, xviii, 6; XIV, v, iii, 8, 10) we gather that, according to Maimonides, state or secular courts existed by the side of religious courts.

The main function of the courts set up by the government was to try offenders against the State or the king (XIV, v, iii, 8; see B. San 49a). This, however, did not exhaust the scope of their jurisdic-

6. The Venice edition has "heretics" instead of "Karaites." But Maimonides' argument in favor of friendly relations with those who were brought up by heretic parents applies also to descendants of Karaites. See, however, Radbez *ad loc.*

tion. They dealt also with matters that were within the province of the Sanhedrin—matters affecting the social welfare—such as murder; but they were not hemmed in by the regulations governing the religious courts in the administration of criminal law. Thus in the case of a person charged with homicide, if the evidence was not sufficiently conclusive to warrant conviction, or the accused had received no warning, or if there was only one witness to testify against him, or if he killed accidentally one whom he disliked, the Sanhedrin was not empowered to pass the death sentence upon the accused. The maximum penalty within its jurisdiction to impose upon him in the second instance mentioned was imprisonment for life on bread and water (XI, v, iv, 8; see also XIV, I, xviii, 5). The state courts could, if in their opinion conditions demanded it, put the accused to death (XIV, v, iii, 10).

Nor were the secular courts bound by the statute forbidding the religious courts to execute more than one offender on one day or by that forbidding them to let the body of the executed remain hanging overnight. It was within their prerogative to try and execute many offenders on one day and suffer their bodies to remain hanging for a long time (XIV, v, iii, 10). There were only two limitations imposed upon the state courts: a. they could employ only one mode of death: "decapitation" (XIV, v, iii, 10); b. they were denied the right to confiscate the possessions of an offender (XIV, v, iii, 10).

b. Cultural

1. Maimonides was unalterably opposed to anything that smacks of superstitious belief. His position on this point is made clear in I, IV, xi, 16, where he says "These practices (witchcraft and demonology) are all false and deceptive. Whoever believes in these and similar things is nothing but a fool." Hence he avoids all mention of what savors of superstition. Thus with reference to admonition required in the case of an offender, he declares: "Once warning was given him . . . even if the warning was uttered by himself—he is put to death" (I, xii, 2). This ruling is based on B. Mak 6b

where it is added: "even if the admonition comes from a demon." Maimonides omits this phrase.

2. In stressing the duty of visiting the sick, he says: "He who visits the sick is as though he would take away part of his sickness and lighten his pain" (IV, XIV, 4). The statement in B. Ned 39b is: "He takes away a sixtieth part of his pain."

Another point of special interest and significance is Maimonides' formulation of the Golden Rule. Much has been said to explain why Hillel phrased the famous precept: *And thou shalt love thy neighbor as thyself* (Lev. 19:18) in the negative form: "Do not unto your neighbor what you would not have him do unto you" (B. Shab 31a). It would seem that Maimonides did not recognize any distinction between the positive and the negative form. In IV, XIV, 1, he interprets the rule in Lev. 19:18 affirmatively.

c. Lexicographical

Book XIV contains a goodly number of words and expressions to which Maimonides attaches meanings somewhat different from the usual and accepted ones. To cite some examples:

1. *dine mamonoṯ*—literally: "civil suits," "monetary cases." In I, VI, 1, the phrase refers to all noncapital cases, including what is forbidden and what is permitted, what is impure and what is pure. In I, XX, 4, it means suits arising from commercial transactions, as distinct from suits involving fines.

2. *hiḇṭiaḥ*—literally: "promised." In III, I, 1, it means "bids us trust" (see Ps. 22:10).

3. *naḥaṯ ruaḥ*—literally: "satisfaction." in II, XVI, 1, it signifies "preference," "finding it easier."

4. *šĕʾar dine mamonoṯ*—literally: "other civil suits." In I, V, 8, it denotes "nontortious cases," i.e., cases distinct from torts, such as larceny, assault, and battery.

5. *peleʾ*—literally: "marvelous," "unknown." In III, VI, 3, it signifies "uncommon," "unusual" (see Judg. 13:8).

6. *yiṯʿaššĕru*—literally: "they will grow rich." In II, XV, 3, it means "they will get a liberal share."

The Translation

It has been the aim of the translator to present the Book of Judges in clear, intelligible English, without destroying its original coloring. To achieve this objective, he has endeavored to steer a middle course between two extremes, between too literal and too free a translation. A verbal rendering would do violence to the English idiom and make the translation incomprehensible to the reader. On the other hand, a mere paraphrase would fail not only to preserve the flavor and spirit of the original but also to convey the exact shades of meaning. In the interest of clarity, the translator has taken the liberty to insert here and there a word, phrase, or sentence, and in rare instances to transpose a sentence (e.g., II, i, 1; V, vii, 11), but not at the cost of fidelity to the Hebrew text. Maimonides' style is lucid; but as a rule his sentences are long, sometimes extending over an entire section or the major part of it (e.g., I, vi, 2; II, xiv, 3). At times his statements are too brief, requiring amplification (e.g., II, viii, 4; III, iv, 2). In the former case it has been deemed necessary to split up the sentences into shorter ones; in the latter, it has been found expedient to clarify the wording. Words and sentences which do not occur in the original have been enclosed in parentheses.

Broadly speaking, the technical terms in Book XIV are of two descriptions: those that can be adequately covered by English equivalents (e.g., the terms rendered "a well-qualified judge," "query," etc.), and those that cannot be converted into another tongue without a somewhat lengthy explanation which would interrupt the continuity of the subject. Technical terms of the first description have been translated in the text; those of the second have been left untranslated and, with the sole exception of the names of Jewish months, explained in the notes. All of them—even those that have been rendered into English, if the Hebrew term also occurs (in transliteration) in the text—have been included in the Glossary, where some have been given more space than in the notes.

The sources are as a general rule given in the first note of a section. They are meant to cover every statement contained therein. E.g., Treatise IV, xiii, 10, consists of four parts: 1. "One should not weep for the deceased more than three days . . ." 2. "This obtains only in the case of ordinary people, but in the case of scholars, the length of the period of weeping and lamentation is in proportion to their wisdom." 3. "But the weeping should not last longer than thirty days . . . nor are memorial services to be held after twelve months." 4. "So too, if the news of the demise of a sage is received after twelve months (of his death), no lamentation is made for him." The source for (1) is B. MḲ 27b; for (2) B. Meg 6a; for (3) B. Ket 103a; for (4) B. Yeb 78b, 79a. All these sources are mentioned in the first note of xiii, 10.

The text of Book of Judges, like that of the *Mishneh Torah* in general, presents a variety of problems. It suffers from omissions, misplacement of words and sentences, insertions of marginal glosses, variant readings, possibly combinations of variant readings, and emendations. Most of these defects have been taken note of. Manuscripts and old editions, which Professor A. Marx was good enough to make available to me, proved helpful in the preparation of the work. I may say in this connection that the Oxford Codex, photostats of which were furnished to me by the Judaica Research Committee at Yale University through the kind offices of Professor Julian J. Obermann, offered much help. Thus, e.g., an additional word which occurs in the Codex in the latter part of I, ix, 3 throws new light upon the meaning of that section.

There are, however, two points to which the attention of the reader should be called:

1. Treatise V, xi, bears marks of deletion on the part of the censor (see n. 3 in that chapter). In manuscripts and some of the early printed editions, there is toward the end of Sec. 4 a long passage concerning the founder of Christianity, the contention that the commandments of Scripture have become obsolete, and the part which Christianity and Islam have played in the higher education of the human race, i.e., in the propagation of the God idea, the Messianic doctrine, etc. In the Venice edition and the Oxford Codex the greater part of the passage has been expunged. I hope to discuss

this passage at some length in a special article on the textual problems of Book XIV. For the present the mere rendering of the passage may suffice. It reads as follows:

But if he does not meet with full success, or is slain, it is obvious that he is not the Messiah promised in the Torah. He is to be regarded like all the other wholehearted and worthy kings of the House of David who died and whom the Holy One, blessed be He, raised up to test the multitude, as it is written *And some of them that are wise shall stumble, to refine among them, and to purify, and to make white, even to the time of the end; for it is yet for the time appointed* (Dan. 11: 35).

Even of Jesus of Nazareth, who imagined that he was the Messiah, but was put to death by the court, Daniel had prophesied, as it is written *And the children of the violent among thy people shall lift themselves up to establish the vision; but they shall stumble* (Dan. 11: 14). For has there ever been a greater stumbling than this? All the Prophets affirmed that the Messiah would redeem Israel, save them, gather their dispersed, and confirm the commandments. But he caused Israel to be destroyed by the sword, their remnant to be dispersed and humiliated. He was instrumental in changing the Torah and causing the world to err and serve another beside God.

But it is beyond the human mind to fathom the designs of the Creator; for our ways are not His ways, neither are our thoughts His thoughts. All these matters relating to Jesus of Nazareth and the Ishmaelite (Mohammed) who came after him, only served to clear the way for King Messiah, to prepare the whole world to worship God with one accord, as it is written *For then will I turn to the peoples a pure language, that they may all call upon the name of the Lord to serve Him with one consent* (Zeph. 3: 9). Thus the messianic hope, the Torah, and the commandments have become familiar topics —topics of conversation (among the inhabitants) of the far isles and many peoples, uncircumcized of heart and flesh. They are discussing these matters and the commandments of the Torah. Some say, "Those commandments were true, but have lost their validity and are no longer binding"; others declare that they had an esoteric meaning and were not intended to be taken literally; that the Messiah has already come and revealed their occult significance. But when the true King Messiah will appear and succeed, be exalted and lifted up, they will forthwith recant and realize that they have inherited naught but lies from their fathers, that their prophets and forbears led them astray.

2. Most of the imperfections in the original are due to carelessness on the part of medieval copyists. Some, however, are the effect of liberties taken with the text. At times copyists unable to apprehend the meaning of the text emended it to suit themselves. The following is a most glaring instance of tampering with a text:

In III, ii, 9, occurs the statement: "The Bible says: *Thou shalt not seethe a kid in its mother's milk* (Exod. 23: 19). We have it on tradition that this verse prohibits the cooking or eating of flesh with milk, be it the flesh of a domestic animal or of a beast of chase; that the flesh of fowl with milk is permitted by biblical law." In other words, Maimonides asserts that the cooking or eating of the flesh of a beast of chase with milk is forbidden by biblical law. This contradicts what he says in V, II, ix, 4, where he states "Likewise, the flesh of a beast of chase or of a fowl is not forbidden by biblical law to be eaten with the milk of either a domestic animal or of a beast of chase." The commentators are at a loss to harmonize these contradictory statements. Maimonides himself—we are told by R. Joshua Hannaḡiḏ, a great-grandson of his—was asked to explain this inconsistency (see David S. Sassoon, *Notes on Some Rambam Manuscripts, Moses Maimonides Eighth Centenary Memorial Volume* [London, 1935], p. 221). The answer given by him was that the copying was incorrect. Sec. 9 (III, ii) originally read "We have it on tradition that this text prohibits the cooking or eating of flesh with milk, whether it be the flesh of an ox or of a sheep, but the flesh of fowl with milk is permitted by biblical law. Should the court permit the flesh of (an ox) or of a sheep with milk," etc. The copyist, as Radbez (LhR [Venice, 1743], p. 10) shows, did not grasp the full import of the argument in the passage that follows. He took it upon himself to emend the first part of the original, and transmitted a corrupt text.

I gladly take this opportunity to record my deepest thanks to Professor Julian J. Obermann, director of Judaica Research at Yale University, under whose supervision this work was done. He made many a valuable suggestion by which this volume has profited. I am also indebted to Professor Alexander Marx who generously supplied me with manuscripts and rare editions for use in connection with the translation. Finally, I deem myself most fortunate in having had the benefit of the counsel of Professor Louis Ginzberg, the Nestor of Rabbinics. I sought his advice on particular points and the information received from him was of inestimable advantage to me.

THE BOOK OF JUDGES

COMPRISING FIVE TREATISES IN THE FOLLOWING ORDER

I. LAWS CONCERNING THE SANHEDRIN AND THE PENALTIES WITHIN THEIR JURISDICTION

II. LAWS CONCERNING EVIDENCE

III. LAWS CONCERNING REBELS

IV. LAWS CONCERNING MOURNING

V. LAWS CONCERNING KINGS AND WARS

Open thy mouth, judge righteously, and plead the cause of the poor and needy (Prov. 31: 9.)

TREATISE I

LAWS CONCERNING THE SANHEDRIN AND THE PENALTIES WITHIN THEIR JURISDICTION

Involving Thirty Commandments

Ten Positive and Twenty Negative

To Wit

1. To appoint judges;
2. Not to appoint a judge who is not conversant with judicial procedure;
3. To follow the majority, when the judges disagree;
4. Not to execute the accused unless there is at least a majority of two for conviction;
5. That, in capital cases, one who has argued for acquittal shall not again argue for conviction;
6. To put to death by stoning;
7. To put to death by burning;
8. To put to death by beheading with the sword;
9. To put to death by strangling;
10. To hang *;
11. To bury the body of the executed person on the day of his execution;
12. Not to let the body remain overnight;
13. Not to suffer a sorcerer to live;
14. To flog the wicked;

* That is, the bodies of some of the executed; the blasphemer and the idolater are hanged after they have been stoned. See below, xv, 6.

15. Not to exceed the number of stripes (prescribed);
16. Not to punish one who has committed an offense under compulsion;
17. Not to condemn to death on mere presumption;
18. Not to spare one who slays another person, or inflicts physical injury upon him;
19. Not to show pity at a trial for one who is poor;
20. Not to show favoritism at a trial to one who is great;
21. Not to render an unjust verdict against one who is addicted to transgression, even though he is a sinner;
22. Not to pervert judgment;
23. Not to wrest the judgment of a stranger or an orphan;
24. To judge righteously;
25. When trying a case not to be afraid of a man of violence;
26. Not to take a bribe;
27. Not to curse judges;
28. Not to heed a baseless report;
29. Not to curse the *Naśi* †;
30. Not to curse any worthy Israelite.

An exposition of these commandments
is contained in the following chapters.

† *"Naśi"*—the Head of the State (king, ruler), or the Head of the Great Sanhedrin (president, patriarch); see below, xxvi, 1.

CHAPTER I

1. It is a positive biblical command to appoint judges and executive officials in every city and every district, as it is said: *Judges and officers shalt thou make thee in all thy gates* (Deut. 16:18). *Judges* refers to the magistrates assigned to the court, before whom litigants appear. *Officers* refers to those who wield the rod and the lash. They stand before the judges; they make their rounds to the markets, squares, and shops, fixing prices, regulating weights, and correcting abuses. Their work is directed by the judges. Any person they find guilty of a misdemeanor is taken by them to court, and punishment corresponding to his offense is inflicted upon him.

2. The duty to set up courts in every district and every city is limited to Palestine; outside Palestine it is mandatory to set up courts [only] in every district, as it is said: *Judges . . . shalt thou make thee in all thy gates which the Lord giveth thee.*

3. How many regular tribunals are to be set up in Israel? How many members is each to comprise? First there is established a Supreme Court holding sessions in the sanctuary. This is styled "the Great Sanhedrin" and consists of seventy-one elders, as it is said: *Gather unto Me seventy men of the elders of Israel* (Num. 11:16), with Moses at their head, as it is said *that they may stand there with thee* (*ibid.*), thus making a tribunal of seventy-one. The one who excels in wisdom is appointed head of the tribunal. He is the presiding officer of the college and is always designated by the Sages as *Naśi*. He occupies the place of Moses, our teacher. The most distinguished of the seventy is next in rank. He is seated to the right of the Naśi and is known as *'Aḇ beṯ din*. The other members are seated with them according to age and standing. The greater the knowledge a member possesses, the closer to the left of the Naśi is the seat assigned to him. They sit in the form of a semicircular threshing floor, so that the Naśi and 'Aḇ beṯ din may see all of them.

In addition (to the Great Sanhedrin), two other tribunals, each numbering twenty-three members, are set up (in Jerusalem), one sitting at the entrance of the Temple Court and the other at the entrance of the Temple Mount.

Moreover, in each town with a population of one hundred and twenty and upward there is set up a Small Sanhedrin, meeting at the gate of the town, as it is said: *And establish justice in the gate* (Amos 5:15). How many are to make up the Small Sanhedrin? Twenty-three. The most learned among them is the presiding judge; the others are seated in the form of a semicircular threshing floor, so that the presiding judge is able to see them all.

4. If a town has a population of less than one hundred and twenty, a court-of-three is set up there. There can be no tribunal of less than three members, for there must be a majority and a minority in case a difference of opinion arises on a question of law.

5. No city, even if its population reaches into the thousands, can qualify for a Sanhedrin unless it has two great scholars—one competent to teach the whole Torah and to decide questions within its entire domain, and the other who understands (the whole Torah) and is able to discuss learnedly (all legal questions).

6. A Sanhedrin which includes two such men—one who is at home (in the whole Torah) and one who is competent to speak with authority (on all questions of law)—is a qualified Sanhedrin. If it includes three such men, it is an average Sanhedrin. If it counts four who are able to speak with authority, it is a wise Sanhedrin.

7. Facing each Small Sanhedrin are three rows of scholars, each row numbering twenty-three. Those in the first row are seated directly in front of the Sanhedrin, those in the second behind the first, those in the third behind the second. They are assigned seats in each row according to their degree of knowledge.

8. If the members of the Sanhedrin disagree and it becomes necessary to ordain a new member to serve as judge, the most eminent disciple in the first row is ordained. Thereupon the first in the second row takes the last seat in the first row to fill the vacancy, the first in the third row takes the last seat in the second, and another member of the congregation is chosen to occupy the last seat in the third row. The same procedure is followed if

it becomes necessary to ordain a second or a third disciple.

9. Each Sanhedrin is provided with two clerks, one standing to the right of the judges, and the other to the left; one records the arguments of those who are for conviction, and the other the arguments of those who are for acquittal.

10. Why is no Sanhedrin established in a locality with a population of less than one hundred and twenty? The community must be large enough to supply twenty-three men, making up the Sanhedrin; three rows of disciples, each comprising twenty-three; ten men of leisure to attend services at the Synagogue; two clerks; two court attendants; two litigants; two witnesses; two to refute the witnesses; two to rebut the refuters; two collectors of charity; one more in addition to the two collectors to constitute a commission of three for the distribution of charity; an expert surgeon; a scribe; and a schoolteacher. Hence the total population must be (at least) a hundred and twenty.

CHAPTER II

1. Only those are eligible to serve as members of the Sanhedrin—whether the Great or a Small Sanhedrin—who are wise men and understanding, that is, who are experts in the Torah and versed in many other branches of learning; who possess some knowledge of the general sciences such as medicine, mathematics, (the calculation of) cycles and constellations; and are somewhat acquainted with astrology, the arts of diviners, soothsayers, sorcerers, the superstitious practices of idolaters, and similar matters, so that they be competent to deal with cases requiring such knowledge.

Moreover, those who would qualify for membership in the Sanhedrin must be priests, levites, and (lay) Israelites of good birth, worthy to marry (their daughters) into the priesthood, as it is said *that they may stand there with thee* (Num. 11:16), implying, like thee in wisdom, reverence, and lineage.

2. It is desirable that the Great Sanhedrin should have among its members priests and levites, as it is said: *And thou shalt come*

unto the priests the Levites (Deut. 17:9). If there are no priests and levites available, the entire membership may be drawn from (lay) Israelites.

3. Neither a very aged man nor a eunuch is appointed to any Sanhedrin, since these are apt to be wanting in tenderness; nor is one who is childless appointed, because a member of the Sanhedrin must be a person who is sympathetic.

4. The king of Israel is not given a seat on the Sanhedrin, because it is forbidden to differ with him or to rebel against his word. But the High Priest may be given a seat, if he is fit for the office by reason of scholarship.

5. Although the kings of the House of David may not be given seats on the Sanhedrin, they judge others and are judged in a suit against them. But the kings of Israel may neither judge nor be judged, because they do not submit to the discipline of the Torah. (To sit in judgment on them) might lead to untoward consequences.

6. Just as the members of the court must be free from all suspicion with respect to conduct, so must they be free from all physical defects.

Every conceivable effort should be made to the end that all the members of that tribunal be of mature age, imposing stature, good appearance, that they be able to express their views in clear and well-chosen words, and be conversant with most of the spoken languages, in order that the Sanhedrin may dispense with the services of an interpreter.

7. In the case of a court-of-three, all the above-mentioned requirements are not insisted upon. Nevertheless it is essential that every one of the members thereof possess the following seven qualifications: wisdom, humility, fear of God, disdain of gain, love of truth, love of his fellow men, and a good reputation. All these prerequisites are explicitly set forth in the Torah. Scripture says *wise men and understanding* (Deut. 1:13), thus stating (that those chosen) must be men of wisdom; *and beloved of your tribes* (*ibid.*), that is, men with whom the spirit of their fellow creatures is pleased. What will earn for them the love of others? A good eye,

a lowly spirit, friendly intercourse, and gentleness in speech and dealings with others.

Elsewhere it is said *men of valor* (Exod. 18:21), that is, men strong in the performance of the commandments, and strict with themselves, men who control their passions, whose character is above reproach, aye, whose youth is of unblemished repute. The phrase *men of valor* implies also stoutheartedness to rescue the oppressed from the hand of the oppressor, as it is said: *But Moses stood up and helped them* (Exod. 2:17). And just as Moses, our teacher, was humble, so every judge should be humble. *Such as fear God* (Exod. 18:21)—this is to be understood literally; *hating gain* (*ibid.*), that is, they are not anxious about their own money and do not strive to accumulate wealth, for he that hastens after riches, want shall come upon him; *men of truth* (*ibid.*), that is, they pursue righteousness spontaneously and of their own accord; they love the truth, hate violence, and flee anything that savors of unrighteousness.

8. It is stated by the Rabbis that the Great Sanhedrin used to send messengers throughout the Land of Israel to examine (candidates) for the office of judge. Whoever was found to be wise, sin-fearing, humble and contrite, of unblemished character, and enjoying the esteem of his fellow men was installed as local judge. From the local court, he was promoted to the court situated at the entrance of the Temple Mount; thence to the court situated at the entrance of the Court; thence to the Supreme Court.

9. A court-of-three, one of whose members is a proselyte, is not competent unless the proselyte's mother is a Jewess by descent. If one of them is a bastard, indeed, even if all three are bastards, it is still competent. So too, if all are blind in one eye, it is competent; but these are barred from membership in the Sanhedrin. One who is blind in both eyes is ineligible for any court.

10. Although there can be no court of less than three, according to biblical law even one man may try a case, as it is said: *In righteousness shalt thou judge thy neighbor* (Lev. 19:15). On the authority of the Scribes, however, there must be three to try a case. If two try a case, their decision is not valid.

11. One who is recognized by the public as well qualified, or has obtained authorization from the court, may judge alone. In some respects, however, he cannot be said to constitute a court. And though he has the right to act as sole judge, the Rabbis enjoin upon him the duty of associating others with himself. They said: *Judge not alone, for none may judge alone save One* (Ab 4:8).

12. A man may take the law into his own hands, if he is in a position to do so; since he acts according to the law, he need not go to the trouble of appearing in court, even if the delay involved in taking the case to court would cause him no loss. Therefore, if his opponent protests and takes him to court, and the latter, after careful investigation, finds that the defendant has acted according to the law, and that the judgment he has rendered in his own interests is correct, the judgment is not reversed.

13. Although a court-of-three constitutes a full court, the larger the number (of those who participate in the deliberations) the better. It is more desirable that judgment be rendered by eleven men than by ten. It is essential therefore that those who (at the invitation of the judges) participate in the deliberations be learned and competent.

14. A scholar is forbidden to sit in judgment unless he knows those who are to sit with him, lest those associated with him be not qualified, and he would thus be not a member of a tribunal but a party to a confederacy of faithless men.

CHAPTER III

1. During what hours do the judges hold sessions? The Small Sanhedrin and the court-of-three meet from the time when the morning prayers are over until the end of the sixth hour of the day. The Great Sanhedrin meets from the time of the morning *tamiḏ* (daily burnt offering) until the evening tamiḏ is slaughtered. Sabbaths and festivals they spend in the House of Study, located in the Temple Mount.

2. It is not necessary for all the seventy-one members of the Great Sanhedrin to be in their places in the sanctuary all the time,

Only when the occasion demands it, do they all convene. At other times, whoever has a business matter requiring his attention may leave, take care of it, and return, provided that during the sessions no less than twenty-three are present. If one has to leave, he should make sure that there are twenty-three without him; if there are not, he must wait till one of the absentees returns.

3. No trial is to be begun at night. By tradition it has been learned that the rule applying to cases of leprosy applies also to lawsuits, as it is said: *According to their word shall every controversy and leprosy be* (Deut. 21:5). Just as leprosy must be examined by day only, so controversies must be tried in the daytime only.

4. Likewise, no evidence is accepted nor are documents attested at night. In civil cases, a trial begun in daytime may be concluded at night.

5. The rule applying to lawsuits applies also to cases of legacies, as it is said (concerning legacies) *a statute of judgment* (Num. 27:11). Therefore no assignment of estates is to take place at night.

6. If two men come to visit a sick person and he makes his last will in their presence, they may record the will but cannot execute it. In case three visit him, it is left to their option whether to record it or to execute it. This rule obtains only if the will is made in the daytime; if it is made at night, they may record it but not execute it.

7. The Divine Presence dwells in the midst of any competent Jewish tribunal. Therefore it behooves the judges to sit in court enwrapped (in fringed robes) in a state of fear and reverence and in a serious frame of mind. They are forbidden to behave frivolously, to jest, or to engage in idle talk. They should concentrate their minds on matters of Torah and wisdom.

8. A Sanhedrin, or king, or exilarch, who appoints to the office of judge one who is unfit for it (on moral grounds), or one whose knowledge of the Torah is inadequate to entitle him to the office, though the latter is otherwise a lovable person, possessing admirable qualities—whoever makes such an appointment trans-

gresses a negative command, for it is said: *Ye shall not respect persons in judgment* (Deut. 1:17). It is learned by tradition that this exhortation is addressed to one who is empowered to appoint judges.

Said the Rabbis: "Say not, 'So-and-so is a handsome man, I will make him judge; So-and-so is a man of valor, I will make him judge; So-and-so is related to me, I will make him judge; So-and-so is a linguist, I will make him judge.' If you do it, he will acquit the guilty and condemn the innocent, not because he is wicked, but because he is lacking in knowledge. Therefore Scripture says: *Ye shall not respect persons in judgment.*"

The Rabbis said, furthermore, that he who appoints a judge who is unfit for his vocation is as though he had set up a pillar, for it is said: *Neither shall thou set thee up a pillar, which the Lord thy God hateth* (Deut. 16:22). And if such an appointment is made in a place where scholars are available, it is as though he had planted an asherah, for it is said: *Thou shalt not plant thee an asherah of any kind of tree beside the altar of the Lord thy God* (Deut. 16:21).

Moreover, the injunction *Thou shalt not make with Me gods of silver or gods of gold* (Exod. 20:20) has been interpreted by the Sages to mean: gods who come into being through the influence of silver or gold, that is, a judge who owes his appointment to his wealth only.

9. It is forbidden to rise before a judge who procured the office he holds by paying for it. The Rabbis bid us slight and despise him, regard the judicial robe in which he is enwrapped as the packsaddle of an ass.

10. It was the habit of the early Sages to shun appointment to the position of judge. They exerted their utmost endeavors to avoid sitting in judgment unless they were convinced that there were no others so fit for the office as they, and that were they to persist in their refusal, the cause of justice would suffer. Even then they would not act in the capacity of judges until the people and the elders brought pressure upon them to do so.

CHAPTER IV

1. No one is qualified to act as judge, whether of the Great or a Small Sanhedrin or even of a court-of-three, unless he has been ordained by one who has himself been ordained. Moses, our teacher, ordained Joshua by laying his hands upon him, as it is said: *And he laid his hands upon him, and gave him a charge* (Num. 27:23). He, likewise, ordained the seventy elders, and the Divine Presence rested upon them. The elders ordained others, who in turn ordained their successors. Hence there was an uninterrupted succession of ordained judges, reaching back to the tribunal of Joshua, indeed, to the tribunal of Moses, our teacher. It matters not whether one is ordained by the Naśi, or by a judge who has himself been ordained though he has never served as a member of the Sanhedrin.

2. What has been the procedure through the generations with regard to ordination? It has been effected not by the laying of hands upon the elder but by designating him by the title "Rabbi" and saying to him: "Thou art ordained and authorized to adjudicate even cases involving fines."

3. The ordination must be conferred by three men, (at least) one of whom has himself been ordained, as was stated before.

4. No tribunal can be dignified with the title *'Ĕlohim* unless the members thereof have been ordained in Palestine. They are the scholars who, on being examined by (the messengers of) the Great Sanhedrin, are found competent and are thereupon ordained and installed in the office of judge.

5. At first every teacher who had been ordained, ordained his disciples. Later, however, as a mark of respect for (the House of) Hillel the Elder, it was enacted that no one be ordained without authorization from the Naśi; (it was also enacted) that the Naśi ordain no one save in the presence of the 'Aḇ beṯ din and that the 'Aḇ beṯ din ordain no one save in the presence of the Naśi. As for the other members of the Sanhedrin, every one had the right to ordain, if he obtained the sanction of the Naśi, provided that there

were two others with him, for ordination requires the presence of three judges.

6. Ordination cannot be conferred outside Palestine, even if the ordainers were ordained in Palestine. It cannot be conferred even if the ordainers are in Palestine and the candidate is outside Palestine. Needless to say this stricture also applies if the ordainers are outside Palestine and the candidate is in Palestine. If both are in Palestine, ordination may be conferred, even if they do not live in the same locality. In the last instance, the candidate is advised either by a messenger or by a written communication that he has been ordained and given authorization to adjudicate cases involving fines, since both ordainer and ordained are residents of the Land of Israel. Every part of Palestine occupied by those who came up from Egypt is an integral part of the area where ordination may be conferred.

7. Ordainers may confer ordination even on one hundred candidates at one time. Thus David ordained 30,000 in one day.

8. It is within the jurisdiction of ordainers to grant only partial authorization to a candidate, provided that he is competent to perform all the functions of a judge. Thus in the case of an outstanding scholar, fully qualified to decide all questions of law, the court has the right to ordain him, giving him authorization to decide civil cases but not questions of ritual, or questions of ritual but not civil cases; or licensing him to decide both civil cases and ritual matters but not to adjudicate cases involving fines; or to adjudicate cases involving fines, but not to declare blemished first-born animals permissible (for slaughter); or limiting the authorization to the absolution of vows, or the examination of stains, or similar matters.

9. It is within the jurisdiction of ordainers to grant authorization for a limited period, to say to the recipient of the ordination, "You have permission to decide civil cases or questions of ritual till the Naśi arrives here," or "as long as you are not with us in this province," or to attach any similar condition to the authorization.

10. In the case of an outstanding scholar who is blind in one

eye, no ordination is conferred upon him, not even ordination limited to the adjudication of civil cases; for, though he is eligible to try civil suits, he is ineligible to exercise other judicial functions. This applies also to those disqualified for a like reason.

11. If there should be in all Palestine but one man competent to confer ordination, he could invite two others to sit with him and proceed to ordain seventy men, either en masse or one after the other. He and the other seventy men would then constitute the Supreme Court and would thus be in a position to ordain other tribunals.

It seems to me that if all the wise men in Palestine were to agree to appoint judges and to ordain them, the ordination would be valid, empowering the ordained to adjudicate cases involving fines and to ordain others. If what we have said is true, the question arises: Why were the Rabbis disturbed over the matter of ordination, apprehending the abolition of the laws involving fines? Because Israel is scattered and agreement on the part of all is impossible. If, however, there were one ordained by a man who had himself been ordained, no unanimity would be necessary. He would have the right to adjudicate cases involving fines because he would be an ordained judge. But this matter requires careful reflection.

12. If the members of a court who were ordained in Palestine go abroad, they may adjudicate even there cases involving fines, just as they adjudicate those cases in Palestine, for the Sanhedrin has competence both within and without the Land of Israel, provided the members thereof have been ordained.

13. The exilarchs of Babylon stand in the place of the king. They exercise authority over Israel everywhere and sit in judgment over the people, with or without the consent of the latter, as it is said: *The sceptre shall not depart from Judah* (Gen. 49:10). This refers to the exilarchs of Babylon.

14. Therefore any competent judge, who has been authorized by the exilarch to exercise judicial functions, may act as judge everywhere, in or outside Palestine, even if the litigants are un-

willing to accept him (as judge), though he is denied the right to adjudicate cases involving fines.

Any competent judge who has obtained authorization from the court in Palestine may exercise his mandate throughout Palestine and the cities situated on the border, even if the litigants are unwilling to accept him. But outside Palestine the authorization does not confer upon him the right to compel litigants (to submit their cases to him). Though he is empowered to adjudicate outside Palestine cases involving fines, he is denied the right to coerce parties to a suit to appear before him for trial, unless he has been invested with authority by the exilarch.

15. If a man who is not qualified to discharge judicial duties, either because of lack of adequate knowledge or because of unseemly conduct, has been clothed by the exilarch with authority to act as judge, in disregard of the would-be incumbent's unfitness, or has obtained authorization from the court, the latter having been ignorant of his unfitness, the authority vested in him is of no avail. It is as though one would dedicate to the altar a blemished animal, in which case no sacredness attaches to it.

CHAPTER V

1. A king can be appointed only with the approval of the court of seventy-one. A Small Sanhedrin for each tribe and each city can be set up only by the court of seventy-one. A tribe, the entire membership of which has been seduced to idolatry, a false prophet, and a High Priest in a capital case can be tried only by the Supreme Court; in a civil case, however, the High Priest is tried by a court-of-three. An elder is not declared rebellious, unless he defies a decision by the Supreme Court. A city is not pronounced condemned, nor is a woman who is suspected by her husband of infidelity subjected to the ordeal of drinking the bitter waters, except by the decision of the Supreme Court. No additions are made to the city (of Jerusalem) or the Courts of the Temple, nor are the people sent forth to an optional war, nor are the cities in the vicinity of the spot where a slain body is found measured, save with the sanction

of the Supreme Court, as it is written *Every great matter they shall bring to thee* (Exod. 18:22).

2. Capital cases cannot be tried by less than twenty-three, that is, the Small Sanhedrin. This rule holds good in cases involving the life of a beast as well as in cases involving human life. Therefore sentence of death by stoning on an ox (that killed a human being), or sentence of death on a beast that was covered by a man or that covered a woman, can be passed only by a court of twenty-three. Even if a lion, a bear, or a hyena—animals which can be tamed and have owners—kills a person, the death sentence can be passed only by twenty-three. But if a serpent kills a person, anyone may kill it.

3. If one spreads an evil report about his wife, the case must be tried at the very outset by a court of twenty-three, since it may involve a capital offense, for should infidelity be proved the woman would be stoned. If the charge turns out to be baseless, and the father (of the woman) comes to claim the fine due to him, the case is tried by three.

Whence do we learn that capital cases cannot be tried by a tribunal of less than twenty-three? Although this is a law which has come down to us by tradition, there is a scriptural warrant for it, for it is said *The congregation shall judge . . . the congregation shall deliver* (Num. 35:24–25)—one congregation judges and another congregation delivers; the congregation that judges represents those who are for condemnation, the congregation that delivers represents those who are for acquittal. No congregation consists of less than ten men, thus we have twenty. Three more are added that the court should not be of an even number and should, moreover, have a majority that can be followed.

4. Cases involving the penalty of flogging are tried by three judges, although there is the possibility that the culprit may die as a result of the flogging.

5. The breaking of the heifer's neck requires the presence of five judges.

6. The intercalation of the month is effected by three judges.

7. The intercalation of the year is effected by (no more than)

seven judges. In all the above-enumerated cases, it is required that the tribunal consist of ordained judges, as was stated before.

8. Cases involving fines, such as larceny, mayhem, claims for twofold or fourfold or fivefold restitution, for rape or seduction, or claims of a similar nature, are adjudicated by three well-qualified judges, i.e., judges who received their ordination in Palestine. But cases that do not involve action in tort, such as admission of indebtedness and transaction of loans, do not require for their adjudication three well-qualified judges. Three laymen or even one well-qualified judge may try them. Therefore cases of admission and transaction of loans and the like may be tried even outside Palestine, for although no tribunal outside Palestine can be designated as 'Ĕlohim, it acts merely as agent for the court of Palestine. It is denied, however, the power to act as agent for the court of Palestine in matters involving fines.

9. A court outside Palestine may try only cases that are of frequent occurrence and entail a loss of money, such as admission of debts, transaction of loans, and damage done to property. But it is not within the competence of that court to try cases that are of infrequent occurrence, though they involve a loss of money, such as when a beast inflicts physical injury upon another beast; or cases that are of frequent occurrence, but do not entail a monetary loss, such as twofold restitution. So too, judges outside Palestine are not empowered to collect the fine imposed by the Rabbis in case one strikes another on the back with a clenched fist or slaps his face with the palm of his hand, or the like; nor is it within their competence to collect the half damage, to which the injurer is liable, except the half damage to be paid in the case of "pebbles," for the payment of half damage caused by pebbles is due indemnity and is not to be regarded as penal.

10. Compensation, the amount of which is determined by valuing the injured person as if he were a slave, is not collected by judges outside Palestine. Therefore if one inflicts a wound upon another, damages for injury, pain, and degradation, for which the offender is liable, are not collected by judges outside Palestine; but payment for loss of time and for medical expense is collected, be-

cause these represent an actual monetary loss. This is the decision of the Geonim. They said that collection of payment for loss of time and healing expense was a matter of daily occurrence in Babylon.

11. Payment for injury caused by a beast to a man is not collected by judges outside Palestine, because such a case is of infrequent occurrence. But if a man injures the beast of another man, he pays everywhere full damage, as though he had torn his garment, broken his vessels, or cut down his plants. Likewise, damage caused by the tooth or foot of a beast is collected outside Palestine, because the owner always stands "forewarned" with respect to such damage—such damage being of frequent occurrence. The owner is liable whether the beast harms another beast by rubbing itself against the other, or consumes fruit which is natural for it to consume, or causes similar injury. He is liable whether it spoils food or breaks vessels, occasioning injury of the kind for which he has to make full restitution. In all these instances, payment is collected by judges outside Palestine.

But if the beast was a *tam* and the owner was forewarned and later it causes damage by biting, or pushing, or lying down, or kicking, or goring, it is not within the jurisdiction of judges outside Palestine to collect the full damage, because the law of "forewarning" (with regard to a goring ox) does not obtain outside Palestine. Even if the owner was forewarned in Palestine, and he goes abroad, where the beast causes damage, payment is not collected, because such an instance is of infrequent occurrence.

12. Why does the law of "forewarning" not obtain outside Palestine? Because the warning must be given in the presence of a court, and no judges outside Palestine constitute a competent court unless they received their ordination in Palestine. Hence if a Palestinian tribunal happens to be outside Palestine, it is within its province to have the owner of the beast warned before it, just as it is within its competence to adjudicate there cases involving fine.

13. In the case of theft or robbery, judges outside Palestine collect the principal but not the additional amount (prescribed in the Torah).

14. Not in every instance when one is bound to pay compensation on one's own admission are judges outside Palestine authorized to collect payment. Thus a person has to pay compensation for blemish and degradation, if he says, for example, "I seduced So-and-so's daughter"; so too, he must pay ransom if he says, "My ox killed So-and-so." In neither of these instances have judges outside Palestine the right to collect payment.

15. Cases of damage caused indirectly, unlike those involving fines, are tried and collected outside Palestine.

16. Likewise, it is within the province of judges outside Palestine to compel one responsible for the delivery of a fellow Jew's money into the hands of heathens to make good the loss, although the culprit has committed no overt action.

17. It has been the practice of the academies outside Palestine, in lands where no fines are imposed, to place the offender under ban, which lasts until he has satisfied his opponent or has gone with him for trial to Palestine. As soon as he has given the claimant what is due to him, the ban is removed, whether or not the claimant is satisfied. If the plaintiff seizes chattel of the defendant in the amount due to him, he is not dispossessed of it.

18. In case one man acts as sole judge, even if he is recognized by the public as fully qualified and is thus authorized to try civil cases by himself, an admission (of a claim) made before him is not tantamount to an admission made in court, though he is an ordained judge. But in case of a court-of-three, even if the members thereof are laymen, that is, they are not ordained, and cannot be designated as 'Ĕlohim, the admission (of a claim) made before them has the force of an admission before a court. So too, if one denies a claim in their presence and subsequently witnesses come (and establish the claim), he is adjudged a liar and cannot change his plea, as has already been stated. The general principle is: with respect to admission (of claims) and transaction of loans and similar matters, a court of three (laymen) has the status of an ordained court in every respect.

CHAPTER VI

1. In the event a judge gave an erroneous decision in a non-capital case, if his error is one with regard to a matter that is obvious and well known, that is, an error in a law that is explicitly stated in the Mishnah or the Gemara, the decision is revoked, the case reconsidered, and decided according to the law. If reversal is impossible, as for instance, when the plaintiff, after obtaining unlawfully the money claimed by him, has gone abroad, or is a man of violence, or the judge has pronounced unclean what is clean or has declared unfit for consumption what is fit and ordered it to be given to dogs, or in similar cases, he is exempt from making good the loss, for, though he caused the loss, he did it unintentionally.

2. In case of an error due to a wrong decision between two opposing opinions, that is, when the judge erred in a matter concerning which there is a controversy between *Tanna'im,* or between *Amora'im,* and it is not explicitly stated with whom the law rests, and he acted according to the opinion of one (authority), not knowing that the prevailing practice favors the contrary opinion—in such a case, the following distinctions are to be observed:

If the judge is well qualified and holds authorization from the exilarch, or was accepted by the litigants and does not hold authorization from the exilarch, his decision is revoked, since he is a well-qualified judge. But if revocation is impossible, he is exempt from making good the loss. The authorization obtained either from the exilarch or from the court in Palestine is effective in Palestine; but outside Palestine, authorization received from the court in Palestine is not effective, as has already been stated.

3. In the event the judge who gave a wrong decision is well qualified but did not receive authorization and the litigants did not accept him (as judge); or in the event he is not well qualified but the litigants did accept him, with the understanding that he would decide the case according to the law, and he erred in a

decision between two conflicting opinions, if he implemented his decision by taking from one and giving to the other with his own hand, his decision stands, but he must make good the loss by paying for it out of his own pocket. If he did not implement his decision by taking from one and giving to the other with his own hand, the decision is revoked. If revocation is impossible, he must pay out of his own pocket.

4. But if he is not well qualified and the litigants did not accept him, even though he received authorization, he is to be classed not as a judge but as a man of violence. Therefore the decisions he has rendered, whether erroneous or correct, are void. The litigants may reject his verdicts and take the cases to court. If he erred and implemented a decision by taking from one and giving to the other with his own hand, he is liable to pay out of his own pocket and be reimbursed by the litigant to whom he unlawfully awarded the claim. [But if he did not implement his decision by taking from one and giving to the other with his own hand, the defendant may recover from the plaintiff what he has given him.] If the plaintiff is unable to reimburse him, or the judge has pronounced unclean what is clean or ordered what is fit for consumption to be given to dogs, the judge must make restitution, as is the law in the case of one who intentionally causes damage, for it was his intention to cause monetary loss.

5. If a judge had mistakenly imposed an oath upon a litigant who, according to the law, was not required to take it and the litigant, in order to avoid the oath, effected a compromise with his opponent and subsequently became aware that he was not subject to an oath, the compromise is void, even if the litigant had obligated himself by a *ḳinyan* to abide by it. His purpose in agreeing to pay the claim or to waive it was to be released from the oath mistakenly imposed upon him, and every agreement made in error, even if it is confirmed by a ḳinyan, is of no validity. This applies also to similar instances.

6. If two parties to a suit are in violent disagreement with respect to the place where their lawsuit is to be tried, one saying,

"Let us go to the local court"; the other saying, "Let us repair to the Supreme Court, lest the local judges err and unlawfully exact payment of the claim," he (the latter) is compelled to appear before the local court. If he (subsequently) says, "State in writing the ground on which you have made your decision against me, because it is possible that your decision is wrong," his request is complied with, a copy of the statement is given him and payment is exacted from him. If it becomes necessary to consult the Supreme Court in Jerusalem, a written communication is forwarded and the local court follows the instructions it receives from that tribunal.

7. The preceding rule holds good in cases where both litigants appear as claimants, as well as in cases where the creditor insists that the suit be tried by the local court and the debtor demands that it be tried by the Supreme Court. But if the creditor is the one who demands that the suit be taken to the Supreme Court, the debtor must comply with his demand, for it is said: *And the borrower is servant to the lender* (Prov. 22:7). So too, if one who was injured or robbed desires to have his case tried before the Supreme Court, the local court compels the defendant to acquiesce. This applies also to similar cases.

8. What has been said before obtains only if the robbed or injured person or creditor has witnesses or proof (to substantiate his claim), but if his claim is unsupported, the defendant is not compelled to have the case tried outside his home town. He takes an oath in the local court and is exonerated.

9. What has been said before holds good even at the present time, when the Supreme Court is no longer in existence. There are, however, places which can point to great scholars in their midst, recognized by the public as well-qualified judges, while other places have scholars who are not the peers of the former. If, therefore, the creditor says, "Let us go to such-and-such a place, in such-and-such a province, to So-and-so, who is renowned for his greatness and submit our suit to him," the borrower is compelled to do so. This was a daily practice in Spain.

CHAPTER VII

1. If one of the parties to a suit says, "Let So-and-so try my case," and the other says, "Let So-and-so try my case," the two judges—each chosen by one of the litigants—jointly select a third and the three try the suit, for in this way a correct judgment will be rendered. Even if the judge chosen by one of the parties is a great scholar and ordained, the litigant who selected him has no right to force him upon his opponent. The latter, too, can choose whomsoever he wishes.

2. If a litigant accepts as judge or witness a kinsman or a person who is otherwise ineligible—even if he accepts a person who is disqualified on the ground of religious delinquency to act as two competent witnesses or as a court of three fully qualified judges—and confirms the acceptance by a ḳinyan, he cannot retract. This obtains whether he is the plaintiff and agrees to remit his claim, or he is the defendant and agrees to pay the claim, on the evidence or the decision of the disqualified person. But if he does not confirm the acceptance by a ḳinyan, he may retract, as long as the verdict has not been rendered. Once, however, the verdict has been given and, as a result of the evidence or decision of the disqualified person, he has been ordered to pay the claim, he can no longer retract.

3. So too, if a litigant is under the obligation of an oath to his opponent and the latter says to him, "Swear unto me by the life of your head and you will be exempt from paying my claim," or "Swear unto me by the life of your head and I will make good your claim," if the opponent pledges himself by a ḳinyan (to be satisfied with this minor oath), he cannot retract. If he does not pledge himself by a ḳinyan, he may retract so long as the verdict has not been rendered. Once, however, the verdict has been announced and the oath has been taken, it is as though he had stated explicitly that he could not retract and therefore must pay the claim.

4. The same law applies to one who was under obligation to take a consuetudinal oath but transferred it (to his opponent). If he pledged himself by a ḳinyan (to be content with the oath taken by

the other party), or if he to whom the oath had been transferred has already taken it, no retraction is possible.

5. The same law is operative in the case of one who is under no obligation to take an oath, but who of his own accord says, "I will swear to it." If he confirms his offer by a ḳinyan, he cannot retract. But if there is no such confirmation, although he has made the offer in court, he may retract until the verdict has been announced and he has taken the proffered oath.

6. If the court has given an adverse decision to one of the contesting parties and the latter subsequently produces witnesses or proof favorable to him, the decision is set aside and the case is reconsidered. Even if the verdict has already been announced, as long as he produces proof, it is set aside. If the judges had said, "Bring whatever proof you have within thirty days," even if he brought it after the thirty days, the ruling is reversed. For what is he to do who did not find proof within the specified time but found it later?

7. But if he has declared his arguments closed, the decision is not set aside. Thus, if the judges had asked him, "Can you produce witnesses?" and he said, "I have no witnesses"; "Can you bring proof?" and he said, "I have no proof," and thereupon they passed sentence on him, declaring him guilty, and on hearing the sentence, he says, "Admit So-and-so and So-and-so, who will testify in my behalf," or he produces documentary proof from his wallet, no attention is paid to his witnesses or proof.

8. The ruling just given obtains only if the documentary proof was in his possession or the witnesses were within his reach; but if he had said, "I have no witnesses, no proof," and subsequently witnesses arrived from overseas, or someone in whose keeping the father of the litigant had left his dispatch bag came with the bag containing documentary proof, the decision is set aside. Why? Because he can say, "The reason for my previous statement that I had no witnesses, or proof, is that these were unavailable to me." As long as he can offer unavailability as a reason for maintaining that he had neither witnesses nor proof, or give some other valid reason, he has not closed his arguments and the decision is set

aside. Therefore if he has stated explicitly, "I have no witnesses either here or overseas, no proof either in my possession or in the possession of anybody else," the decision is not set aside.

9. What has been said before applies only to an adult who had declared his arguments closed, and, after sentence had been passed on him, brought witnesses to testify in his favor. It is different in the case of an heir who was a minor when his father died. If after he came of age, a plaintiff appeared, seeking from him recovery of a claim against his father, and, since he had neither witnesses nor documentary proof, the court adjudged him liable, and subsequently some men came to him saying, "We are in possession of evidence favorable to your father—evidence which will reverse the decision," or someone said, "Your father has left in my keeping this documentary proof"—in either of these cases the evidence or documentary proof is produced forthwith and the decision is set aside; for the heir who was a minor (at the time his father died) is in no position to know of all the proofs his father possessed.

10. In the event the defendant said—confirming his statement by a ḳinyan—that if he did not appear in court on a certain day to take an oath, the plaintiff's claim should be conceded, entitling him to collect the full amount without an oath; or in case the plaintiff said—confirming his statement by a ḳinyan—that if he failed to appear in court on a certain day to take an oath, the claim should be remitted and his opponents be relieved from responsibility, and he does not appear on the day set by him, the condition stipulated is enforced and he forfeits his right. But if he can prove that he was unavoidably prevented from coming on that day, the ḳinyan is not binding, and when his opponent summons him to court, he takes an oath as if the stipulation had never been made. This applies also to similar cases.

CHAPTER VIII

1. If the court is divided, some voting for acquittal and others for conviction, the majority opinion is followed. This is a positive

biblical command, as it is said *to incline after the many* (Exod. 23:2). It applies to civil cases, to matters pertaining to what is forbidden and what is permitted, to what is clean and what is unclean, and to other noncapital cases. But in capital charges, in the event opinions differ as to whether the accused is liable to death, if the majority is for acquittal, he is acquitted; but if the majority is for conviction he is not put to death unless those who are for conviction exceed those who are for acquittal by at least two. It has been learned by tradition that this is what the Law meant by the injunction *Thou shalt not follow a multitude to do evil* (*ibid.*), that is, if the multitude is leaning toward what is unfavorable, i.e., toward executing the accused, do not follow it, unless it comprises a clear-cut majority, exceeding those who are for acquittal by (at least) two, as it is said *to side with a majority that can decide* (*ibid.*); for a favorable verdict a majority of one is sufficient, for an unfavorable verdict a majority of two is required. These interpretations have come down to us by tradition.

2. In case a court-of-three disagrees, two finding the defendant not guilty and one finding him guilty, he is declared not guilty. If two find him guilty and one finds him not guilty, he is declared guilty. If one finds him not guilty, one finds him guilty, and one has formed no opinion, or two find him not guilty or guilty and one has formed no opinion, two more judges are added. There are thus five judges deliberating the case. If three find him not guilty and two find him guilty, he is pronounced not guilty. If three find him guilty and two find him not guilty, he is pronounced guilty. If two find him not guilty, two find him guilty, and one has formed no opinion, two more judges are added. But if four find him not guilty or guilty and one has formed no opinion, or three find him not guilty, one guilty, and one has formed no opinion, the majority opinion prevails. It matters not whether the one who has formed no opinion is a member of the original court-of-three and was undecided at the outset (of the trial), or is one of the judges that have been added.

If they are evenly divided and one has formed no opinion, two more judges are added. This process of increasing the number of judges continues as long as there is no majority opinion, until the tribunal comprises seventy-one men. When this (maximum) number is reached and thirty-five find the defendant guilty, thirty-five not guilty, and one has formed no opinion, they argue the case with the latter until he is won over to one side or the other and there are thirty-six for acquittal or for condemnation. Should he, however, hold out and no other member of the tribunal change his vote, the case is undecided and the money remains in the possession of its owner.

3. The judge who has formed no opinion does not have to give a reason for his inability to arrive at a decision, whereas the judge who declares for acquittal or for condemnation is bound to state the ground on which his opinion is based.

CHAPTER IX

1. If in trying a capital case all the members of the Sanhedrin forthwith vote for conviction, the accused is acquitted. Only when some cast about for arguments in his favor and are outvoted by those who are for conviction is the accused put to death.

2. In case there is a difference of opinion among the Small Sanhedrin with respect to a capital charge, twelve voting for acquittal and eleven for conviction, the accused is acquitted. If twelve vote for conviction and eleven for acquittal, or eleven for acquittal, eleven for conviction and one is undecided, even if twenty-two vote for acquittal or for conviction and one is undecided, two more judges are added. The one who is undecided is as though he were nonexistent because he cannot afterward argue for conviction. There are therefore, after the addition has been made, twenty-four judges besides the one who is undecided. If thirteen vote for acquittal and twelve for conviction, he is acquitted. If eleven vote for acquittal and thirteen for conviction, he is convicted, even if one of the original twenty-three is undecided, because there is a majority of two for conviction. If, however, twelve are for acquittal, twelve for conviction, and one is undecided, two more judges are added. This process of increasing the

number of judges goes on, until those who are for acquittal constitute a majority of one, in which case the accused is acquitted, or until those who are for conviction constitute a majority of two, in which case the accused is convicted. If the vote is tied, while one judge is undecided, the number of judges is increased, until the tribunal comprises seventy-one.

When this number is reached and thirty-six are for acquittal and thirty-five for conviction, the accused is acquitted; if thirty-six are for conviction and thirty-five for acquittal, the two sides argue the case until one changes his opinion and the accused is either acquitted or convicted. If no one changes his opinion, the presiding judge announces, "We have reached an impasse," and the accused is acquitted. If thirty-five are for conviction, thirty-five for acquittal, and one is undecided, he is acquitted. If thirty-four declare for acquittal, thirty-six for conviction, and one is undecided, the accused is convicted, because there is a majority of two for conviction.

3. If a difference of opinion arises among the members of the Supreme Court—whether the difference is one bearing on a capital charge, or on a monetary matter, or on any question of law—the number of judges is not increased. They argue the case one with the other and the decision favored by the majority is followed. If the difference is one with respect to a capital charge, the same procedure is followed until the accused is either acquitted or convicted.

CHAPTER X

1. Any judge in a capital case, whose vote—either for acquittal or for conviction—voices not his own carefully considered opinion but that of a colleague, transgresses a negative command. Concerning him Scripture says: *Neither shalt thou bear witness in a cause to turn aside* (Exod. 23:2). It has been learned by tradition that this injunction means, "Do not say when the poll is taken, it is good enough if I follow So-and-so; but give expression to your own opinion."

2. This negative command also forbids the judge who argued in favor of acquittal to argue later for conviction, as it is said: *Neither shalt thou bear witness in a cause to turn aside*. This rule holds good only as long as the case is still in the stage of discussion. But at the time when the verdict is about to be handed down, he who argued for acquittal may change his opinion and vote for conviction.

3. If one of the disciples who has spoken in favor of the accused dies, he is regarded as (though alive and) standing by his opinion.

4. If one of the disciples says: "I have a statement to make in favor of the accused," and then becomes speechless, or dies before he makes his statement and gives the reason for his opinion, his declaration is disregarded.

5. If two judges deduce the same argument from two scriptural verses, they are counted as one only.

6. It has been learned by tradition that in capital charges we do not begin with the opinion of the most prominent judge—lest the others not considering themselves competent to differ with him accept his opinion. It is mandatory that everyone should voice his own view.

7. Moreover, in capital cases, the opening statement (of the judges) must be one of encouragement and not of discouragement; that is, the judges say to the defendant, "If you have not committed the offense with which you are charged by the witnesses, you have no cause to fear the outcome."

8. If in a capital charge one of the disciples says, "I have a statement to make against the accused," he is silenced. But if he says, "I have a statement to make in his favor," he is brought up and seated among the Sanhedrin. If there is substance in his argument, he is listened to [and is allowed to vote], and he does not descend from there any more. If there is no substance in his argument, he does not descend from there all that day. Even if the accused himself says, "I have a statement to make in my favor," he is listened to, provided there is anything of substance in what he says.

9. If the court has erred in a capital case, declared guilty one who

is not guilty, and rendered a verdict for conviction, and later discovers a reason for setting aside the decision—a reason which would give the accused a chance to clear himself—it revokes its decision and tries him again. But if it has erred in that it acquitted one who is liable to death, its decision is not revoked and the case is not reconsidered. This applies only to an error in a law which the Sadducees do not admit. But if the court has erred in a law which even the Sadducees admit, the decision is reversed for condemnation. Thus if the court has declared not culpable one who has had unnatural intercourse with a relation in a forbidden degree, the verdict is reversed and the offender is put to death. But if it has declared not culpable one guilty of the first stage of illicit intercourse in an unnatural way, the decision is not reversed. This applies also to similar cases.

CHAPTER XI

1. In what respects do civil cases differ from capital cases? Civil cases are tried by three judges, capital cases by twenty-three. In civil cases, the judges open the debate with either a favorable or an unfavorable statement; in capital cases they open the debate with a favorable statement, not with an unfavorable one, as has already been stated. In civil cases, the decision either for acquittal or for conviction is by a majority of one; in capital cases by a majority of one for acquittal, by a majority of (at least) two for conviction. In civil cases the verdict may be reversed either for acquittal or for conviction; in capital cases only for acquittal but not for conviction, as has already been stated. In civil cases, both the judges and the disciples may argue either for acquittal or for conviction; in capital cases, all may argue for acquittal, but only the judges may argue for conviction. In civil cases, the judge who has argued for conviction may subsequently argue for acquittal and the judge who has argued for acquittal may subsequently argue for conviction; in capital cases the judge who has argued for conviction may afterward argue for acquittal, but the judge who has argued for acquittal may not afterward argue for conviction, except at the time

when the verdict is about to be pronounced, when he has the right to range himself on the side of those who are for conviction, as has been stated before. In civil cases the trial is held in daytime and the verdict may be reached at night; in capital cases the trial is held in daytime and the verdict must be reached in daytime. In civil cases the verdict, whether of acquittal or of conviction, may be reached on the same day; in capital cases the verdict of acquittal may be reached on the same day, but a verdict of conviction may not be reached until the following day.

2. Therefore, capital cases are not tried on the eve of a Sabbath or on the eve of a festival, for should the accused be found guilty, he could not be executed the following day, and it is forbidden to delay execution of the sentence until after the Sabbath. Therefore, he is kept in prison till Sunday, when his trial begins.

3. According to biblical law, civil suits may be tried any day, as it is said *And let them judge the people at all seasons* (Exod. 18:22). The Rabbis, however, ordained that no trials be held on Fridays.

4. The rules obtaining in capital cases obtain also in cases involving flogging and those involving banishment. The only respect in which a case involving flogging differs from a capital charge is that the former is tried by three judges. None of these rules is operative in the trial of "an ox to be stoned" save that it is tried by a tribunal of twenty-three.

5. The rules followed in other capital cases are not followed in the case of an enticer. In his case, witnesses are put in hiding. No forewarning, required in other cases of those who are put to death by order of the court, is required. If the court has pronounced him not guilty, and someone says, "I have a statement to make against him," the enticer is brought back (to court). If he has left the court adjudged guilty, and someone says, "I have a statement to make in his favor," he is not brought back. There is no plea made on his behalf. On the tribunal trying his case are appointed a very aged man, a eunuch, and a childless man, because these are not likely to show him compassion. For stern treatment, meted out to those who mislead the people to go after things of nought, is

clemency to the world at large, as it is said *that the Lord may turn from the fierceness of his anger, and show thee mercy* (Deut. 13:18).

6. In monetary matters and cases of uncleanness and cleanness, the court begins with the opinion of the most eminent judge, hearing what he has to say. But in capital cases, the court begins with the opinion of those on the side (benches) and the opinion of the most distinguished is heard last.

7. In monetary matters, and in cases of uncleanness and cleanness, a father and his son, or a teacher and his disciple count as two; but in capital charges, cases of flagellation, the sanctification of the new moon, and the intercalation of the year a father and his son, or a teacher and his disciple, count as one only.

8. The ruling that a son may be associated with his father in a legal procedure, the two counting as one in some matters and as two in others, obtains only if one of them is a member of the Sanhedrin and the other is a disciple (and the trial is still in the stage of discussion). If, in such an event, the disciple says that he has a statement to make either for or against the defendant, the court gives him a hearing, discusses the question with him, and grants him the right to vote.

9. But at the time when the verdict is announced, kinsmen are barred from participation, for men who are related to each other are disqualified from acting as judges, as will be stated later.

10. If the disciple is wise and resourceful but is deficient in knowledge of traditional law, his teacher transmits to him the traditional laws required for application to a capital case under consideration, and the disciple pronounces judgment with him.

11. All are qualified to try civil cases, even a proselyte, provided that his mother is a Jewess by descent. Even if his mother is not Jewish, a proselyte may try a case in which a fellow proselyte is involved. A bastard, or one who is blind in one eye, is eligible to serve as judge in civil cases. But capital charges can be tried only by priests, levites, and (lay) Israelites worthy to marry (their daughters) into the priesthood, provided that none of the members thereof is blind in one eye, as has already been stated.

CHAPTER XII

1. What is the procedure in capital charges? When the witnesses appear in court, stating, "We saw So-and-so commit such-and-such a transgression," the questions are put to them, "Do you know him (the accused)?" "Did you warn him?" If they say, "We do not know him," or "We are in doubt as to his identity," or if they did not warn him, he is exonerated.

2. Whether the accused be a scholar or an ignorant man, forewarning is a prerequisite, as the purpose of warning is to make it possible to distinguish between the unwitting and the presumptuous transgressor, for there is the possibility that the accused committed the offense unwittingly.

How is he warned? He is told: "Abstain, or Refrain, from doing it, for this is a transgression carrying with it a death penalty," or, "the penalty of flagellation." If he abstains, he is exonerated. So too, if he remains silent, or nods his head, he is exonerated. Even if he says, "I know it," he is not culpable, unless he surrenders himself to death, saying, "I know full well (the nature of the offense and the penalty it involves), nevertheless I will commit it." If such be the case, he is put to death. Moreover, he is not liable unless the offense is committed by him immediately after the warning, that is, within an utterance. But if the interval is longer than an utterance, another warning is required. Once warning was given him—whether by one of the witnesses or by someone else in the presence of witnesses, even if the admonitor was a woman or a slave, aye, even if he heard the admonition but did not see the admonitor, even if the warning was uttered by himself—he is put to death.

3. Once the witnesses say: "We gave him due warning and we know him," the court gives them a solemn charge. How are they charged in a capital case?

The court addresses them thus: "Perhaps what you are about to say is mere conjecture or hearsay, based on secondhand information, on what you heard from a trustworthy person. Perhaps you are unaware that we will in the course of the trial subject you to inquiry and query. Know that capital cases are unlike monetary cases. In a monetary case, one may make restitution and his offense is expiated; but in a capital case (the witness) is accountable for the blood of the man and the blood of his (potential) posterity until the end of time. Thus with respect to Cain it is said: *The voice of thy brother's bloods crieth* (Gen. 4:10)—that is, his blood and the blood of his (potential) descendants. For this reason, but a single man was created, to teach us that if any man destroys a single life in the world, Scripture imputes it to him as though he had destroyed the whole world; and if any man preserves one life, Scripture ascribes it to him as though he had preserved the whole world. Furthermore, all human beings are fashioned after the pattern of the first man, yet no two faces are exactly alike. Therefore, every man may well say, 'For my sake the world was created.' And perhaps you will say, 'Why borrow this trouble?' It is said: *He being a witness, whether he hath seen or known, if he do not utter it, then he shall bear his iniquity* (Lev. 5:1). And perhaps you will say, 'Why should we incur guilt for the blood of this man?' It is written: *And when the wicked perish, there is joy* (Prov. 11:10)."

If the witnesses stand by their evidence, the oldest of them is called and is subjected to inquiry and query, as will be set forth in the Treatise on Evidence. If his testimony is unshaken, the second is called and examined likewise. Even if there are a hundred witnesses, each is subjected to inquiry and query. If their evidence tallies, the debate is opened with words of encouragement (to the accused), as has already been stated. He is advised not to be afraid of what the witnesses have said, if he knows that he is not guilty. Then the trial proceeds. If he is found not guilty, he is set free. If he is found guilty, he is held in custody till the following day. In the meantime the judges meet in pairs to study the case, eat but little and drink no wine at all; all night each judge discusses the case with his colleague or deliberates upon it by himself. The following day, early in the morning, they come to court. He who was in favor of acquittal says, "I was for acquittal and I hold to my opinion"; he who was for conviction says, "I was for conviction and hold to my opinion," or "I changed my opinion and am now for acquittal." Should there be any mistake as to the identity of those who were in favor of conviction or of acquittal for the same argument (deduced from two scriptural verses), in which case the two count only as one, as has already been stated, the judges' clerks, who have a record of the reason given by each for his vote, call attention to this fact. The discussion is renewed. If (after the final vote is taken), the accused is found not guilty, he is set free. If it becomes necessary to add to the judges, the addition is made. If those for conviction are in the majority and the accused is pronounced liable, he is led forth to be executed.

The place of execution was outside the court, far away from it, as it is said: *Bring forth him that hath cursed without the camp* (Lev. 24:14). It seems to me that it was approximately six miles distant from the court, corresponding to the distance between the court of Moses, our teacher—the court located at the entrance of the Tent of Meeting—and the [outer limit of the] camp of Israel.

4. Once the verdict of conviction has been rendered, the culprit is executed on the same day without delay. Even if the culprit is a pregnant woman, it is not permitted to wait until she has given birth. She is struck against the womb so that the embryo is killed first. But if she had already sat on the birth stool, the execution is delayed until she has given birth.

If a woman is put to death, use may be made of her hair.

5. Whoever is led forth to death when the offering he brought was already slaughtered is not executed until the blood of his sin offering or guilt offering has been sprinkled. But if the offering has not been slaughtered at the time when the verdict is announced, the execution is not put off till it is slaughtered, because it is not permitted to delay execution of the sentence.

CHAPTER XIII

1. He who is condemned to death is led forth from the court while one with a signaling flag is stationed at the door of the court and another, at some distance from him, is mounted on a

horse. A herald precedes the culprit, announcing, "So-and-so is going forth to be executed by such-and-such a death, because he committed such-and-such an offense in such-and-such a place at such-and-such a time, and So-and-so and So-and-so are the witnesses against him. Whoever knows anything in his favor, let him come forward and state it." If one says, "I have something to say in his behalf," the signalman waves his flag, and the horseman runs and brings the culprit back to court. If he is found not guilty, he is set free; otherwise, he is led forth to be executed. Should the accused himself say, "I have something to say in my favor," although there may be no substance in what he has to say, he is returned once, aye, even a second time, because it is possible that, overwhelmed by fear, he was unable to marshal his arguments and that on being brought back to court (once again), he might regain his composure and offer a plausible plea. If after he has been returned to court no substance is found in what he said, he is once more led to the place of execution.

Should he assert a third time that he has a statement to make in his own behalf, if there is some cogency in his statement, he is brought back. This is done even many times. For this reason two scholars accompany him that they may listen to what he says. If they find that there is substance in his statement, he is brought back; otherwise, he is not brought back. If nothing is found in favor of acquittal, the execution is carried out. The duty of executing the culprit by the mode of death prescribed for him rests upon the witnesses. But in case of one convicted of murder, if the witnesses do not put him to death, others are bound to do so.

When he is about ten cubits away from the place of execution, he is told to make confession, for it is incumbent on all who are condemned to death to make confession. Everyone who does so has a portion in the world to come. If he knows not how to confess, he is instructed: "Say, 'May my death be an expiation for all my sins.'" Even if he knows that the evidence on which he is convicted is false, he uses this form of confession.

2. After he has confessed, he is given a cup of wine containing a grain of frankincense to induce a state of stupor and then he is

executed by the mode of death prescribed for the offense of which he is guilty.

3. The wine, the frankincense, the stone with which the culprit is stoned, the sword with which he is beheaded, the cloth with which he is strangled, the tree on which he is hanged, the flags which are waved in the case of those who are executed by order of the court, the horse which runs that he might be delivered (from death)—all these are provided out of public funds, but if any individual offers to donate them, his offer is accepted.

4. The members of the tribunal must not follow the bier of one who is condemned to death. They are forbidden to eat food on the day of the execution. The latter prohibition is included in the injunction *Ye shall not eat with the blood.* (Lev. 19:26). Neither is a meal of comfort prepared for the near of kin of one who is executed by order of the court, because of the negative command *Ye shall not eat with the blood.* These things are forbidden; but the disregard of them does not involve the penalty of flagellation.

5. If one charged with a capital offense is found guilty on any of the intermediate days of a festival, the judges study carefully his case, eat and drink (all that day), give their final decision when the sun is about to set, and have him put to death.

6. No mourning is observed for those who are executed by order of the court. After the execution, the relatives come and greet the witnesses and the judges, as if to say that they harbor no ill feeling against them, for the judgment given by them was a true judgment. But though they do not observe mourning rites, they grieve for the executed, for grief is a matter of the heart.

7. If one escapes after death sentence has been passed upon him and he (subsequently) comes before another court, the verdict is not set aside. Wherever two men rise up and say: "We testify that So-and-so was adjudged to be executed in such-and-such a court and So-and-so and So-and-so were the witnesses," the culprit is put to death. This applies only to one who was condemned to death on a murder charge. But one who was adjudged to death on any other charge is not executed unless the original witnesses appear

and testify that the death verdict has been pronounced upon him, and they slay him with their own hands, provided they give evidence before a tribunal of twenty-three.

8. If one who has been condemned to death by a court outside Palestine escapes to Palestine and is brought before a court there, his verdict may, under all circumstances, be set aside. But if the Palestinian tribunal is the tribunal that has convicted him outside Palestine, the verdict is not set aside, although it has pronounced sentence upon him outside Palestine.

CHAPTER XIV

1. The court is empowered to inflict four modes of death: stoning, burning, slaying by the sword, and strangulation. The penalties of stoning and burning are expressly stated in the Bible. By a tradition reaching back to Moses, our teacher, it has been learned that whenever the Bible decrees the death penalty without specifying the mode, strangulation is meant, and that one who slays another is put to death by decapitation, as are the inhabitants of a seduced city.

2. It is a positive command to inflict upon the offender the death to which he is liable. The State, however, has no right to employ any mode of execution other than that by the sword.

3. A tribunal that does not execute an offender who has incurred the death penalty by decree of the court, violates a positive command, but does not thereby transgress a negative command, save in the case of a sorcerer. Failure to execute the latter entails the transgression of a negative command, as it is said *Thou shalt not suffer a sorceress to live* (Exod. 22:17).

4. Death by stoning is a severer punishment than death by burning, that by burning is severer than that by beheading, death by beheading is severer than that by strangulation. Any person liable to two death penalties is punished by the severer one—whether he committed two transgressions one after the other or one transgression which carries with it two death penalties. Even if sentence of death by a lighter mode had been passed on him and subsequently

he committed another transgression, carrying with it death by a severer mode, and sentence was passed upon him, the severer one is imposed upon him.

5. Both man and woman are subject to the four modes of death.

6. If offenders liable to different modes of death became mixed up with one another, each one is executed by the lighter mode.

7. If a person sentenced to death was mixed up with others and he cannot be identified, or if one upon whom the death sentence had already been passed was mixed up with other culprits who have not yet been sentenced and the first cannot be identified, all are set free, because no one can be condemned except in his presence.

8. If the convicted person offers resistance and the court is unable to put him in prison pending preparation for his execution in the manner prescribed for him, the witnesses put him to death by any means possible, since sentence has already been passed on him. But the initiative in the matter of execution cannot be taken by others. Therefore, if the hands of the witnesses were cut off, the convicted is set free. But if they were without hands at the outset of the trial, the execution is carried out by others.

The rule (that the initiative in carrying out the death sentence be taken by the witnesses) applies to all who are liable to death by order of the court save one convicted on the charge of murder. In the latter case, if sentence has been pronounced upon him, it is incumbent upon all men to use every means at their disposal to pursue him and put him to death.

9. Those executed by order of the court are not buried in their ancestral tombs among other Israelites. Two burial places are provided by the court, one for those who are stoned or burned, and the other for those who are beheaded or strangled. This ordinance has come down to us by tradition.

When the flesh has been completely decomposed, the bones are gathered and buried in the ancestral tomb. It is the duty of the kinsmen to procure for them a coffin and a shroud.

10. It is the duty of the court to be deliberate in capital cases, to exercise caution and patience. Any court that condemns to death one man in seven years is (branded as) destructive. Nevertheless,

if it becomes necessary to execute culprits every day, the court must do so. However, no two offenders are to be tried on the same day, but one on one day, and the other the following day. If, however, both are implicated in the same transgression and are liable to the same death penalty, as is the case with an adulterer and his paramour, they are tried on the same day. It follows therefore that if one committed adultery with the daughter of a priest, they are not executed on the same day, since he is punished by strangulation and she by burning.

11. Capital charges are tried only while the Temple is in existence, provided that the Supreme Court meets in the Hall of Hewn Stones in the sanctuary, as it is said concerning the defiant elder *in not hearkening unto the priest that standeth to minister there before the Lord thy God* (Deut. 17:12). By tradition it has been learned that capital offenses are tried only when the priests bring offerings on the altar, provided that the Supreme Court is in its right place.

12. Originally, when the sanctuary was built, the Supreme Court sat in the Hall of Hewn Stones in the Court of the Israelites. The place where it met was not holy, for none but the kings of the House of David were permitted to sit in the other part of the Court. But when the conduct of the Israelites deteriorated, the Supreme Court was exiled from place to place, ten in all, the last of which was Tiberias and since that time it has ceased to exist. But there is a tradition to the effect that it will be re-established in Tiberias and that thence it will be transferred to the sanctuary.

13. Forty years prior to the destruction of the Second Temple, the right of Israel to try capital cases ceased, for, though the sanctuary still existed, the Sanhedrin was exiled and no longer held sessions in the place assigned to it in the sanctuary.

14. As long as capital cases are tried in Palestine, they are also tried outside Palestine, provided that the members of the Sanhedrin were ordained in Palestine, for the Sanhedrin has competence within and without Palestine, as was stated before.

CHAPTER XV

1. How is the ordinance of death by stoning carried out? When the culprit is four cubits from the place of stoning, he is stripped of his garments, only his nakedness in front being covered. In case the culprit is a woman, she is not stoned naked but is clad in one shirt. The place of stoning is twice a man's height. With his hands manacled, the condemned and the witnesses ascend there. One of the witnesses pushes him over from behind on his loins, so that he is turned over falling on his heart. If death ensues, the duty (of the witness) is fulfilled, as it is said: *He shall surely be stoned or cast down* (Exod. 19:13). Scripture thus likens death resulting from the stone falling upon the convicted to death resulting from his falling upon the ground, consequent on being hurled down. If the hurling does not result in death, the witnesses lift the stone lying there for this purpose—a stone which it takes two men to carry—the second witness lets his hand go and drops the stone on the heart of the culprit. If death ensues, his duty is done; if not, the culprit is stoned by all Israel, as it is said *The hands of the witnesses shall be first upon him to put him to death, and afterward the hand of all the people* (Deut. 17:7).

2. If one worshiped an idol, he is stoned at the gate (of the city) where he worshiped. If the majority of the inhabitants are idolaters, he is stoned at the entrance of the courthouse. It has been learned by tradition that *unto thy gates* (Deut. 17:5) refers to the gates (of the city) where the idol was worshiped, not where the trial was held.

3. The procedure in the case of one condemned to death by burning is as follows: he is lowered knee-deep in dung, then a hard cloth placed in a soft one is wound around his neck, the two witnesses pull the two ends in opposite directions until he opens his mouth, tin or lead or other (inflammatory) material is melted and thrown into his mouth, so that it goes down his body and burns his bowels.

4. The ordinance of decapitation is carried out by cutting off the

head of the culprit with a sword—the mode of execution employed by the government.

5. The procedure in the case of one condemned to death by strangulation is as follows: he is lowered knee-deep in dung, then a hard cloth placed in a soft one is wound around his neck, the two witnesses pull the ends of the cloth in opposite directions until the culprit dies.

6. It is a positive command to hang the blasphemer and the idolater, as it is said: *He is hanged because of a curse against God* (Deut. 21:23). The punishment of the blasphemer is thus stated; with reference to an idolater, it is said: *The same blasphemeth the Lord* (Num. 15:30). A man is hanged, but not a woman, for it is said *And if a man have committed a sin worthy of death, he shall be put to death, and thou hang him* (Deut. 21:22).

7. How is the ordinance of hanging carried out? After the culprit has been stoned, a post with a piece of wood projecting from the top is sunk into the ground; his two hands are brought together and in this manner he is hanged just before sunset and the body is taken down at once. If it remains there overnight, a negative command is transgressed, as it is said: *His body shall not remain all night upon the tree* (Deut. 21:23).

8. It is a positive command to bury those convicted by the court on the day of the execution, as it is said: *But thou shalt surely bury him the same day* (*ibid.*). This command applies not only to those who are executed by order of the court, but also to those who die a natural death. Whoever lets his dead lie overnight transgresses a negative command. Should one, however, keep the body overnight because of the honor due to the deceased, i.e., to procure for him a coffin and a shroud, no transgression is committed thereby.

9. The culprit is not hanged on a growing tree but on a detached one, so that no felling is needed; for the tree on which he is hanged is buried with him, in order that it should not serve as a sad reminder, people saying: "This is the tree on which So-and-so was hanged." So too, the stone with which the condemned is stoned, the sword with which he is beheaded, or the cloth with which

he is strangled—all these are buried in the earth surrounding the corpse, but not in the grave itself.

10. Those condemned to death by stoning are eighteen in number. They comprise the following: he who has intercourse with his mother, his father's wife, his daughter-in-law, a betrothed maiden, a male, or a beast; a woman who has connection with a beast; a blasphemer; an idolater; he who gives of his seed to Molech; a necromancer; a wizard; an enticer; a seducer; a sorcerer; he who desecrates the Sabbath; he who curses his father or his mother; and a stubborn and rebellious son.

11. Those condemned to death by burning are ten in number. They comprise the following: the married daughter of a priest who commits adultery; one who has intercourse with his daughter, his daughter's daughter, his son's daughter, his wife's daughter, her daughter's daughter, her son's daughter, his mother-in-law, his mother-in-law's mother, or his father-in-law's mother. In the last (six) instances he is liable only if he has connection with any of them during his wife's lifetime, but intercourse with any of them after the death of his wife comes under the category of those illicit connections which are punishable by excision (*ḳareṯ*).

12. Those executed by decapitation are two in number: a murderer and the inhabitant of a seduced city.

13. Those condemned to strangulation are six in number. They are as follows: one who has intercourse with a married woman, one who strikes his father or his mother, one who kidnaps a Jew, an elder who rebels against the decision of the Court, a false prophet, and one who prophesies in the name of an idol. Thus the number of those who are executed by order of the court totals thirty-six.

CHAPTER XVI

1. Just as it is mandatory to inflict the penalty of death upon him who incurred it, even so it is mandatory to inflict the penalty of flagellation upon him who incurred it, as it is said *The judge shall cause him to lie down, and to be beaten before his face*

(Deut. 25:2). Although cases involving flagellation are tried by three, flagellation is deemed a substitute for death.

2. According to scriptural law flogging is imposed everywhere even at the present time, but only in the presence of three ordained judges, not in the presence of three laymen.

3. The flogging imposed everywhere (nowadays) by judges outside Palestine is to be regarded as "beating for disobedience."

4. No man is liable to flogging unless there are witnesses and there has been due warning. The witnesses are subjected to inquiry and query as witnesses are in cases involving capital charges. If a person contravened a prohibition transformed into a positive command, after due warning had been given him, the admonitors saying to him: "Refrain from doing it, for if you will do it and subsequently neglect to take the action designed as a corrective measure you will render yourself liable to the penalty of flogging," and he, in disregard of the warning, violated the command and failed to make amends by fulfilling the attendant positive command, he is punished by flogging. It is true that the warning in this case was a qualified warning, for had he subsequently taken the action required to repair the wrong done by him, he would not have been liable. But a qualified warning is considered a warning.

5. In the event a man committed a transgression involving the penalties of flagellation and death by order of the court, as when, e.g., he sacrificed an animal and its young to an idol, if the warning had been given with respect to the death penalty, he is stoned but not flogged, since he incurred a severer punishment; but if the warning has been only with respect to the penalty of flogging, he is flogged.

6. The two witnesses, on whose evidence the accused is flogged, are required to testify that they saw him commit the forbidden act; but only one witness is needed to certify to the prohibited character of the act itself. To cite a concrete example: if one had said to him, "The fat before you is the fat of kidney," "The fruit before you is of mixed seed in the vineyard," "This woman is a divorced woman," or "a harlot," and he ate (the fat or fruit) or had connection with the woman in the presence of two men after

due warning had been given him, he is flogged, although the fact of the prohibition was established only by one witness. This ruling obtains only if the offender did not contradict the admonitor when the admonition was given. But if he said to the admonitor: "This is not forbidden fat" (or "forbidden fruit"), "This is not a divorced woman," or "a harlot," and he ate (the fat or fruit) or had connection with the woman after denying the statement (of the admonitor), he is not flogged—unless the prohibition had been established by two witnesses.

7. If at the time when the witness affirmed that the act was forbidden the offender remained silent, but after committing the transgression, following due warning given him, he contradicted the statement, no heed is paid to what he says, and the penalty of flogging is inflicted upon him.

8. How is the penalty of flagellation carried out? The culprit's hands are tied to a post on either side of it and the synagogue attendant lays hold on his garments—if they are rent they are rent, if they are ripped open they are ripped open—until his chest is bared, so that the strokes fall upon the naked body, not upon the clothes, as it is said *And he shall beat him* (Deut. 25:2)—*him,* not his clothes. Behind the offender a stone is placed on which the attendant stands, holding in his hand a strap of calf's hide, which is first folded into two, then into four, with two (other) straps of asshide going up and down through it. The width of the strap is one handbreadth; as to its length, the top must reach the navel; the haft by which it is held is one handbreadth in length.

9. The functionary charged with administering the scourging must be a man of more than ordinary intelligence and of less than common physical strength. He raises the strap with both hands, and strikes with one hand with all his might. He administers one third of the lashes in front, [on the chest] between the nipples, and two thirds behind, one third on each shoulder.

10. While the flogging is administered the culprit is to be neither standing nor sitting but bent low, as it is said *that the judge shall cause him to stoop; and have him beaten* (Deut. 25:2).

Before his face (*ibid.*), this implies that the eyes of the judge should be focused on him, that he should not look at something else while the flogging is on. We infer therefore that two offenders should not be flogged at the same time.

11. While the lashes are being administered, the most prominent of the judges recites the scriptural verses *If thou wilt not observe to do . . . then the Lord will make thy strokes extraordinary* (Deut. 28:58–59). He should so time the recital that it end when the scourging is done. If the scourging is not over, he goes back to the beginning of the verses until the scourging is finished. The second judge counts the strokes; the third says to the attendant, "Strike"; the latter continuing to strike as long as he is directed to do so.

12. If the culprit died under the hand of the attendant, the latter is exempt. But if the attendant inflicted upon him one stroke more than the estimated number, and the offender died, he goes into banishment; if the offender did not die, the attendant has transgressed a negative command, for it is said: *He shall not exceed* (Deut. 25:3).

Similarly, any man who smites another contravenes a negative command. For if this man (the attendant) who is invested by the Torah with the authority to inflict corporal punishment is enjoined from beating the offender [in excess of] the measure of his wickedness, is it not an argument from the minor to the major that the prohibition applies to other men? Therefore whoever strikes another man, even if he strikes a slave a blow which is estimated (in damage) at less than a *pĕruṭah,* is flogged. But if the damage is estimated at a pĕruṭah, he is not liable to flogging, since he is bound to make compensation for the injury, for no one who is liable to pay compensation is flogged, as has been stated many times.

CHAPTER XVII

1. How many stripes are inflicted upon one who is liable to flogging? As many as he can endure, as it is said: *to be beaten*

. . . *according to the measure of his wickedness by the number estimated* (Deut. 25:2). As to the word *forty* (Deut. 25:3), it is to enjoin the court from adding to that number, even if the offender be as strong and hale as Samson. But the number is reduced in the case of a frail man, for if he be given a heavy beating, death is certain to ensue. Therefore the Rabbis said that even the most robust shall not be given more than thirty-nine stripes, so that if by a miscount another stripe be added, the offender will have received no more than the forty he really deserved.

2. When the number of stripes that the offender can endure is estimated, it must be a number divisible by three. If it is estimated that he can stand twenty stripes, the court does not say that he should receive twenty-one, a number divisible by three; but he is given no more than eighteen. If it was estimated that he could bear forty stripes, but after administering some it is found that he is weak and it is decided therefore that he is incapable of enduring more than the nine or twelve already inflicted upon him, he is exempt from the rest. If it was estimated that he was capable of standing twelve stripes and after administering the number decided upon, it is found that he is physically strong, capable of bearing more, he is exempt and is not given more stripes than the number originally estimated.

3. If on the day set for the flogging it was estimated that the offender was physically fit to stand twelve stripes and the flogging was deferred till the following day, when it is found that he is fit to receive eighteen stripes, only twelve are inflicted. But if the flogging was set for the next day and he was estimated to be capable of receiving twelve lashes, but the flogging was postponed to the day after the next, when it is found that he is strong enough to stand eighteen, eighteen stripes are inflicted upon him. For at the time of the first estimate, it was understood that the flogging was to take place later. This applies also to other estimates.

4. In case the offender is liable to many floggings, either as a result of the violation of several prohibitions or of one prohibition carrying with it several floggings, if one estimate was made for all of them, he is administered the estimated number of stripes and

is exempt from more; but if not, he is flogged for one transgression, is allowed to recover and is then flogged again. Thus if he was liable to two floggings, and it was estimated that he could endure forty-five stripes, as soon as the forty-five stripes have been inflicted upon him, he is exempt. But if the estimate had been only with respect to the first flogging, and he was administered three or nine or thirty stripes according to the estimate, he is permitted to recuperate, then another estimate is taken with regard to the second flogging until he has been flogged for every offense of which he is guilty.

5. If after the estimate was taken and the flogging has begun, the offender, in consequence of the violence of the strokes inflicted upon him, befouls himself either with excrement or urine, the flogging is discontinued, for it is said: *Then thy brother should be dishonored before thine eyes* (Deut. 25: 3); since he has been dishonored, he is discharged. But if as a result of fright he befouls himself before the flogging has begun, even if he befouls himself on leaving the court to be flogged, aye, even if the befouling occurs on the night before, the estimated number of stripes is inflicted upon him. If an estimate was taken with respect to two floggings and he befouls himself, whether this occurs during the first or the second flogging, he is exempt from the rest of the stripes.

If the strap snaps during the second flogging, he is discharged. If this happens during the first flogging, he is exempt from more stripes for the first, but the estimated number of stripes for the second flogging is inflicted upon him.

6. If after he has been tied to the post, he breaks the rope and escapes, he is exempt (on being captured) and is not brought back (to be flogged).

7. After the offender has received the penalty of flogging, he is restored to his former status, as it is said: *Then thy brother should be dishonored before thine eyes* (Deut. 25: 3)—once he has been flogged, he is (again) they brother. So too, all who have incurred the penalty of excision, obtain remission from this penalty as soon as they have been flogged.

8. If the High Priest commits a sin, he, like any other man, is

adjudged by a court-of-three to be flogged and is reinstated.

9. But if the Head of the College commits a sin, he is flogged, and is not reinstated. He cannot even serve as a member of the Sanhedrin, on the principle that we may promote to a higher degree of dignity, but we cannot demote to a lower degree.

CHAPTER XVIII

1. The following incur the penalty of flagellation: one who transgresses a negative command involving the punishment of excision but not death by the court, as when one eats fat, or blood, or leavened bread on the Passover; one who transgresses a negative command carrying with it the penalty of death by divine intervention, as when one eats *ṭeḇel,* or when a priest while unclean eats of clean heave offering; one who transgresses a negative command involving a tangible action, as when one eats meat with milk, or wears a garment made of wool and linen—all these are subject to flogging. But a negative command, which does not involve tangible action, such as tale carrying, revenge taking, grudge bearing, or spreading a false report, does not entail the penalty of flogging.

2. One who transgresses a negative command, involving no tangible action, is not punished by flogging save in the following instances: one who takes an oath and does not fulfill it, one who exchanges a beast (set aside for sacrifice), and one who curses by the Name. Any negative command which is intended as a warning that the violation thereof involves a death sentence by the court, such as the injunctions *Thou shalt not commit adultery* (Exod. 20:13) and *Thou shalt not do (any manner of) work* (Exod. 20:10) on the Sabbath, does not carry with it the penalty of flogging; neither is there flogging for a negative command, the breach whereof renders the offender liable to compensation, such as the injunctions *Nor shalt thou rob him* (Lev. 19:13), and *Thou shalt not steal* (Exod. 20:13); nor is there flogging for a negative command transformed into a positive command, such as the injunctions *Thou shalt not take the dam with the young* (Deut.

22:6), and *Thou shalt not wholly reap the corner of thy field* (Lev. 19:9), unless the offender subsequently fails to carry out the act enjoined in the positive command. Nor is there flogging for the contravention of a comprehensive negative command. But the infraction of any other negative scriptural command entails the penalty of flogging.

3. What is meant by a comprehensive negative command? It is a negative command which implies several prohibitions of different categories such as the injunction *Ye shall not eat with the blood* (Lev. 19:26). It comprises, moreover, a negative command (that includes several forbidden acts belonging in the same category), as when Scripture says, "Thou shalt not do this *and* that." Since there is no special injunction interdicting each single act the violation of the command does not entail the penalty of flogging for each act comprised therein, unless there are other negative commands which single out one or more of the acts, or there is a tradition to the effect that each be treated separately. Thus the Bible says *Eat not of it raw, nor sodden* (Exod. 12:9). If one eats of it raw *and* sodden he is flogged but once. On the other hand, concerning the new produce, it is said *And ye shall eat neither bread, nor parched corn, nor fresh ears* (Lev. 23:14). If one eats all three, he is liable to three floggings, for we learn by tradition that the word *wĕ-ḳali,* "nor parched corn," indicates that the eating of each constitutes an infraction. Likewise, it is said *There shall not be found among you anyone that maḳeth his son or his daughter to pass through the fire, one that useth divination, a soothsayer, or an enchanter* (Deut. 18:10); although these interdictions are included in one negative command, there are other injunctions which deal with (some of) them separately. Thus it is said *Neither shall ye practice divination, nor soothsaying* (Lev. 19:26). We infer, therefore, that any of the practices enumerated in the verse from Deuteronomy is a contravention of a specific negative command. This applies also to similar negative commands.

4. In case a man was flagellated in court for a transgression involving the penalty of excision, and was later flagellated again for

the repetition of the same transgression, as when, for instance, he ate fat once and was scourged, ate it again and was scourged again, if he eats it a third time, he is not flogged, but is put in a prison cell—a narrow place of the offender's height, with no room to stretch out—and is fed on bread of adversity and water of affliction until his intestines shrink and he wastes away, then he is fed on barley until his stomach bursts.

5. If a man commits a transgression involving the penalty of excision or that of death by order of the court and due warning was given him but he nodded his head or remained silent, i.e., he did not (explicitly) accept the warning, he is not put to death, as was already stated, nor is he flogged. If he commits the transgression a second time, after due warning was given him and he nodded his head or remained silent, he is not put to death, nor is he flogged. If he commits the transgression a third time after due warning, even if he nodded his head or remained silent, he is put in a prison cell and kept there until he dies.

All who refuse to accept warning incur the penalty of disciplinary beating, for, at all events, they are guilty of a transgression. Even one who disregards a rabbinical prohibition suffers beating for disobedience.

6. If one steals service vessels from the sanctuary or curses God by the name of an idol or cohabits with a heathen woman, he is not punished by the court. Zealots deal with him, and he who kills him acquires merit. So too, if an unclean priest performs the Temple Service, his brother priests do not bring him to court, but the young priests take him outside the Temple Court and split his brain with clubs.

It is a scriptural decree that the court shall not put a man to death or flog him on his own admission (of guilt). This is done only on the evidence of two witnesses. It is true that Joshua condemned Achan to death on the latter's admission, and that David ordered the execution of the Amalekite stranger on the latter's admission. But those were emergency cases, or the death sentence pronounced in those instances were prescribed by the State law. The Sanhedrin, however, is not empowered to inflict the penalty of death or of flagellation on the admission of the accused. For it is possible that he was confused in mind when he made the confession. Perhaps he was one of those who are in misery, bitter in soul, who long for death, thrust the sword into their bellies or cast themselves down from the roofs. Perhaps this was the reason that prompted him to confess to a crime he had not committed, in order that he might be put to death. To sum up the matter, the principle that no man is to be declared guilty on his own admission is a divine decree.

CHAPTER XIX

1. Negative commands, the breach of which involves the penalty of excision, but not execution by the court, and renders the transgressor liable to flagellation, are twenty-one in number. The following violate those commands: (1) one who cohabits with his sister; (2) with his father's sister; (3) with his mother's sister; (4) with his wife's sister; (5) with his brother's wife; (6) with the wife of his father's brother; (7) with a woman during the period of her menstruation; (8) one who eats (forbidden) fat; (9) who eats blood; (10) who eats what is leavened during the Passover; (11) who eats on the Day of Atonement; (12) who does work on the Day of Atonement; (13) who eats what is left (of the sacrificial meats); (14) who eats of sacrifices that are loathsome; (15) an unclean person who eats holy meat; (16) an unclean person who enters the courtyard (of the sanctuary); (17) who slaughters sacrifices outside (the sanctuary); (18) who offers up sacrifices outside (the sanctuary); (19) who compounds oil (in the manner prescribed for the sanctuary); (20) who anoints himself with anointing oil; (21) who compounds incense (in the manner prescribed for the sanctuary).

2. Negative commands involving tangible action, the contravention of which is punishable by divine intervention and renders the transgressors liable to flagellation are eighteen in number. The following violate those commands: (1) a lay person who eats of the great heave offering, whether it be undefiled or defiled; (2) a

lay person who eats of the tithe of the tithe; (3) a lay person who eats of the first fruits, after they have been brought to Jerusalem; (4) a lay person who eats of the *ḥallah;* (5) one who eats of the yields of the harvest before the heave offering or the tithe of the tithe has been separated; (6) who eats dough from which the ḥallah has not been separated; (7) a priest who while unclean eats of the heave offering that is undefiled; (8) a priest who enters the Holy of Holies at a time when he does not perform service there; (9) a priest who leaves the sanctuary during service; (10) a levite who performs the service assigned to priests; (11) a nonpriest who ministers in the sanctuary; (12) a priest who ministers while lacking the priestly garments (prescribed for him), in which case he is regarded as a nonpriest who is subject to flogging; (13) a priest who ministers while he is unclean; (14) a priest who ministers while he is intoxicated; (15) a priest who ministers on the day he has taken a ritual bath (before sundown); (16) a priest who ministers while lacking the atonement prescribed for him; (17) a priest who ministers while his hair is overgrown; (18) a priest who ministers with torn garments.

3. But a priest who performs service without having washed his hands and feet, though he incurs thereby the penalty of death (by divine intervention), is not flogged, because this is a positive command (Exod. 30:19). So too, a prophet who suppresses his prophecy, a prophet who acts contrary to his own words, and one who disregards the words of a prophet, are not liable to flogging—though these three offenders incur the penalty of death (by divine intervention)—because the prohibition they transgress is derived by implication from a positive command, as it is said: *Unto him ye shall hearken* (Deut. 18:15) and a negative command derived by implication from a positive command is treated as a positive command, the violation of which does not entail the penalty of flogging.

4. Negative biblical commands, the infraction of which involves neither the penalty of excision nor death by the court (nor death by divine intervention), but renders the transgressor liable to flogging are 168 in number. The following violate those com-

mands: (1) one who makes an idol; (2) who makes an idol for ornament; (3) who turns to idolatry by an overt act; (4) who sets up a pillar (for worship); (5) who plants a tree in the sanctuary; (6) who places a figured stone (for worship); (7) who vows by the name of an idol; (8) who swears by it; (9) who makes use of it; (10) who rebuilds a city that has been declared condemned; (11) who makes use of the property thereof; (12) who adopts the customs of idolaters; (13) who practices divination; (14) who practices soothsaying; (15) who practices enchantment; (16) who practices the art of the charmer; (17) who practices necromancy; (18) who erases the (divine) Name, or is guilty of similar desecration, such as removing a stone from the altar or kindling firewood belonging to the sanctuary; (19) who extinguishes the fire on the altar; (20) who goes up to the altar by steps; (21) who enters the courtyard (of the sanctuary) with unclean garments; (22) who, suffering from a flux or similar impurity, enters the Temple Mount; (23) who removes the stakes from the Ark; (24) who loosens the breastplate from the Ephod; (25) who rends the High Priest's robe; (26) who offers a sacrifice upon the golden altar; (27) a priest who enters the sanctuary at a time when he does not perform service there; (28) a priest with a physical blemish who enters there; (29) an intoxicated priest who enters there; (30) a priest with a physical blemish who ministers (in the sanctuary); (31) an uncircumcised priest who performs service; (32) a priest who performs service assigned to levites; (33) a priest who enters the sanctuary with overgrown hair; (34) a priest who enters the sanctuary with torn garments; (35) a person who sets apart a blemished beast (for sacrifice); (36) who slaughters a blemished beast (as sacrifice); (37) who sprinkles the blood thereof (upon the altar); (38) who burns the limbs thereof (upon the altar); (39) who offers up blemished beasts (even) if they are presented by non-Israelites; (40) who inflicts a blemish on a beast set apart for sacrifice—at the time when the sanctuary stands; (41) who does work with cattle set apart for sacrifice; (42) who shears them; (43) who offers up leaven or honey; (44) who allows the remainder of the meal offerings to become leavened; (45) who offers up (any offering) unsalted; (46) who brings a sacrifice out of the hire of a harlot, or the price of a dog; (47) who puts oil in a sin offering made of flour; (48) who puts frankincense on it; (49) who puts oil in the (meal) offering of a woman suspected of infidelity; (50) who puts frankincense on it; (51) who severs completely the head of a fowl offered up as a sin offering; (52) who exchanges a beast set apart for the altar; (53) who eats of hallowed flesh that has become unclean; (54) who eats of the flesh of beasts set apart for sacrifices that have become unfit for sacrificial purposes; (55) a priest who eats of the flesh of the most holy sacrifices outside the courtyard (of the sanctuary); (56) a lay person who eats of the flesh of the most holy sacrifices after the blood has been sprinkled (on the altar); (57) a lay person who eats of the flesh of an (unblemished) firstling; (58) a priest's daughter who after her marriage to a nonpriest eats of the breast or of the shoulder (of peace offerings), even if she eats it after her husband's death; (59) a *ḥălalah* who eats of the heave offering; (60) one who eats of the flesh of sacrifices that are holy in a lesser degree outside (the walls) of Jerusalem; (61) who eats of sacrifices that are holy in a lesser degree before the blood has been sprinkled (on the altar); (62) a priest who eats of the (unblemished) firstling outside Jerusalem; (63) who eats the second tithe outside Jerusalem after it has been brought within the walls of Jerusalem; (64) a priest who eats of the first fruits after these had been brought within the walls of Jerusalem but were not set down yet in the courtyard (before the altar); (65) a priest who eats of the first fruits outside Jerusalem after these have been set down in the courtyard (before the recital of the Declaration over them); (66) one who eats of the second tithe that has become unclean and has not been redeemed, even if he eats of it in Jerusalem; (67) one who while unclean eats of the second tithe that is clean, even if he eats of it in Jerusalem; (68) who eats of the second tithe or of other holy things, when he is in mourning; (69) an uncircumcised priest who eats of hallowed flesh, or of heave offerings; (70) one who eats of the meal offering brought by the priest or of any sacrifice that is to be wholly burnt (upon the altar); (71) who eats of the flesh of sin offerings which are to be entirely burnt or of any other sacrifice that is to be entirely burnt; (72) who slaughters the Paschal lamb while there is leaven in the home; (73) who breaks a bone thereof, whether the lamb is brought on the First or on the Second Passover; (74) who carries off the flesh thereof from the place where his group is assembled; (75) who eats of it outside his group; (76) who eats it raw or sodden; (77) who makes use of any of the holy things presumptuously; (78) who eats of the yield of the annual harvest from which any of the tithes has not been separated, even if it be the tithe of the poor, although the heave offerings have been separated; (79) who eats of the flesh of an animal that has been condemned to be stoned, although it was slaughtered according to the law; (80) who eats the flesh of an unclean beast; (81) who eats the flesh of an unclean fowl; (82) who eats unclean fish; (83) who eats winged insects; (84) who eats things that creep upon the earth; (85) who eats things that swarm in the water; (86) who eats things that swarm upon the earth, however tiny they be; (87) who eats worms found in fruit, after they have emerged; (88) who eats of the flesh of a *nĕḇelah;* (89) who eats of the flesh of a *ṭĕrefah* animal; (90) who eats a limb removed from a living beast; (91) who eats the sinew of the thigh vein which shrank; (92) who eats milk with meat; (93) who boils meat with milk; (94) who eats of the new grain before the *'omer* (of barley) has been offered up; (95) who eats of the fruit of a tree during the first three years; (96) who eats of the produce of mixed seed in the vineyard; (97) who eats on Passover any food containing a mixture of leaven; (98) who eats leavened bread after midday; (99) who keeps leaven in his premises (and is guilty of a tangible act), as when he causes the dough to leaven; (100) one who drinks forbidden wine; (101) a nazarite who eats aught made of grapevine; (102) a nazarite who cuts his hair; (103) a nazarite who defiles himself for a dead person; (104) one afflicted with leprosy (of the head or of the beard) who shaves off the hair of the scall; (105) who plucks out the marks of leprosy or cauterizes them; (106) who plows the rough valley, in which the heifer's neck was broken; (107) who sows a field in Palestine in the Sabbatical year; (108) who prunes trees in the Sabbatical year; (109) who reaps the aftermath in the usual way; (110) who gathers fruit (in the Sabbatical year) in the usual way, (111) who sows in the Jubilee year; (112) who in the Jubilee year reaps the aftermath in the usual way; (113) who gathers fruit in the Jubilee year in the usual way; (114) who reaps the entire corner of the field and neglects (subsequently) to give it to the poor; (115) who gathers the defective clusters of his vineyard, and neglects (subsequently) to give them to the poor; (116) who gathers the gleanings and neglects (subsequently) to give them to the poor; (117) who gathers the clusters of the grapes that have dropped to the ground, and neglects (subsequently) to give them to the poor; (118) who returns to take a forgotten sheaf, and neglects (subsequently) to give it to the poor; (119) who takes the mother bird with the young, and neglects (subsequently) to let the mother go; (120) who sows different kinds of seed together (in one field) in Palestine; (121) who sows divers seed in a vineyard in Palestine; (122) who grafts trees of different kinds in any land; (123) who anywhere mates animals of different species; (124) who anywhere drives animals of different species; (125) who anywhere muzzles a beast while it is at work; (126) who anywhere slaughters an animal and its young on the same day; (127) who takes a pledge from a debtor by force, and (subsequently) fails to return it to him; (128) who takes a pledge from a widow, and (subsequently) fails to return it to her; (129) who takes in pledge implements needed for preparation of food; (130) who gives evidence which is refuted in a case where he is not liable to the payment of compensation; (131) who strikes another, inflicting upon him an injury estimated at less than a pĕruṭah; (132) the wayward and rebellious son on the evidence submitted at the first trial; (133) who spreads an evil report, which (on investigation) proves to be false; (134) who curses a fellow Jew by the Name (of God); (135) who swears falsely; (136) who swears needlessly; (137) who violates a vow; (138) who walks on the Sabbath beyond the prescribed limits; (139) who does work on a festival; (140) who rounds the corners of the head; (141) who rounds (removes) the corner of the beard; (142) who gashes himself for the dead; (143) who makes a bald spot on his head for the dead; (144) who tattoos himself; (145) who wears garments of wool and linen; (146) who cuts down a fruit tree in sheer wantonness; (147) a man who wears a woman's attire; (148) a woman who wears a man's attire; (149) a priest who defiles himself for a dead body; (150) a priest who marries a harlot and consummates the marriage; (151) a priest who marries a divorced woman and consummates the marriage; (152) a priest who marries a ḥălalah and consummates the marriage; (153) a High Priest who cohabits with a widow, even without marriage; (154) one who remarries his divorced wife, who after her divorce had been betrothed to another man; (155) one who marries a widow who is bound to her husband's brother; (156) who cohabits with a harlot; (157) a bastard who marries the daughter of an Israelite, and consummates the marriage; (158) a eunuch who marries the daughter of an Israelite and consummates the marriage; (159) one who castrates a man or the male of any species, be it cattle, beast of chase, or fowl; (160) who divorces the maiden he has ravished and refuses to take her back; (161) who divorces his wife concerning whom he has spread an evil report and refuses to take her back; (162) who indulges in familiarities with a close relative in ways that may lead to incest—even though he has had no connection with her—because he is suspected of unchastity; (163) who intermarries with idolaters; (164) an Ammonite proselyte who marries the daughter of an Israelite and consummates the marriage; (165) a Moabite proselyte who marries the daughter of an Israelite and consummates the marriage; (166) a king who marries an excessive number of wives; (167) a king who acquires an excessive number of horses; (168) a king who amasses an excessive quantity of silver and gold.

Thus the total number of those who are liable to flogging is two hundred and seven.

CHAPTER XX

1. The court does not impose the penalty of death on mere conjecture but on the conclusive testimony of witnesses. Even if the witnesses saw him (the assailant) chasing the other, gave him warning, and then lost sight of him, or they followed him into a ruin and found the victim writhing (in death agony), while the sword dripping with blood was in the hands of the slayer, the court does not condemn the accused to death, since the witnesses did not see him at the time of the slaying. Concerning this and similar cases, Scripture says: *And the innocent and righteous slay thou not* (Exod. 23:7).

Likewise, if two witnesses testify that the accused committed idolatry but one of them avers that he saw him worship the sun and gave him warning, the other declares that he saw him worship the moon and gave him warning, their evidence is not combined, as it is said: *And the innocent and righteous slay thou not,* since there is a possibility of clearing him of the charge and thus proving him innocent, slay him not.

2. If one was coerced to commit an offense punishable by death by order of the court, the court does not impose upon him the death penalty even in those instances when it is his duty to suffer death rather than commit a transgression. For although he has desecrated the Name (of God), he has acted under duress and is therefore not put to death, as it is said: *But unto the damsel thou shalt do nothing* (Deut. 22:26). This is an admontion to the court not to inflict punishment upon one who commits a transgression under compulsion.

3. Any man who was forced to have connection with a woman of one of the forbidden degrees is guilty of a mortal offense, for erection is a voluntary act. But a woman who had illicit relations under duress, even if she said after force had been used against her: "Let him alone," is exempt from punishment, because she was overpowered by passion.

4. The court is forbidden to spare a murderer. It should not say, "This one is already slain; what good will it do to execute the

other?" and thus prove lax in the duty of putting the murderer to death. For Scripture says: *And thine eye shall not pity him, but thou shalt put away the blood of the innocent from Israel* (Deut. 19:13). So too, the court is forbidden to show pity for one who is liable to payment of fine. It should not say: "This man is poor, he did it unintentionally." Payment is to be exacted from him to the limit of his ability, not allowing pity (to interfere with the law), as it is said: *And thine eye shall not pity* (Deut. 19:21).

Likewise, in cases that do not involve action in tort, no compassion is to be shown to one who is poor. Say not: "This man is poor, his opponent rich. Since I and the rich man are under obligation to support him, I will give judgment in his favor and he will be able to maintain himself honorably." Therefore the Torah admonishes: *Neither shalt thou favor a poor man in his cause* (Exod. 23:3), and it is said: *Thou shalt not respect the person of the poor* (Lev. 19:15).

It is forbidden to show respect (at a trial) to a great man. For instance, if two litigants come before you for trial, one of whom is a great scholar, and the other is an ordinary man, do not greet the great man first, showing him friendliness and esteem. The outcome of such partiality will be that the other will find it impossible to marshal his arguments. The judge should therefore maintain an attitude of neutrality until the verdict is reached, as it is written: *Nor favor the person of the mighty* (*ibid.*). Said the Rabbis, "Say not, 'This man is rich, this one is well connected. How can I put him to shame and see him humiliated?' " Therefore it is said: *Nor favor the person of the mighty* (Sif Lev. 19:15, p. 351a).

5. When two litigants come before you, one of whom is a worthy person, and the other wicked, do not say, "Since this one is wicked, the presumption is that he is lying and the other is truthful, I will therefore turn the verdict against the wicked." It is concerning such an instance that it is said: *Thou shalt not wrest the judgment of thy poor in his cause* (Exod. 23:6), although he is poor religiously, do not wrest his judgment.

6. *Ye shall do no unrighteousness in judgment* (Lev. 19:15). This refers to the judge who perverts judgment, acquits the guilty

and condemns the innocent. It also refers to the judge who delays judgment, who discusses at undue length things that are obvious in order to annoy one of the parties to the suit. He too is included among the unrighteous.

7. A judge who is arrogant in decision, who hastens to give judgment before weighing it carefully in his mind, so that it be as clear to him as the sun, is foolish, wicked, and haughty. Therefore the Rabbis enjoined, "Be deliberate in judgment," (Ab 1:1). So too, Job said: *And the cause of him that I knew not I searched out* (Job 29:16).

8. Any judge who, when a suit is brought before him, seeks to deduce the decision in the case from an analogous case concerning which the law is known to him, and though there is in the vicinity a greater scholar than he, refuses to go to consult him—such a judge belongs to the category of the wicked who are arrogant in decision. Touching such a judge, the Rabbis said: *Evil upon evil will come upon him* (B. Yeb 109b). For this and like attitudes betoken haughtiness and will lead to perversion of judgment.

For she hath cast down many wounded (Prov. 7:26); this refers to a disciple who is not qualified and nevertheless renders decisions. *Yea, a mighty host are all her slain* (*ibid.*); this refers to a scholar who is qualified and refrains from rendering decisions. The last statement applies only to one whose services are indispensable to the community. If, however, he refrains from rendering decisions because he knows that there is another man in the city who is competent to act as judge, he is praiseworthy. He who shuns the office of judge avoids enmity, robbery, and false swearing; and he who is arrogant in decision is foolish, wicked, and haughty.

9. A disciple is forbidden to give decisions in the presence of his teacher, unless there is a distance of three Persian miles between them—a distance corresponding to the space occupied by the camp of Israel.

10. Think not that the foregoing rules apply only to a case involving a large sum of money to be taken from one (litigant) and given to the other. At all times and in all respects, regard a suit

entailing one thousand *maneh* and one entailing a pĕruṭah as of equal importance.

11. Judges do not meet to try a suit involving less than the value of a pĕruṭah. But, if they have met to consider a case involving the value of a pĕruṭah, the trial is completed even if the claim is reduced to less than the value of a pĕruṭah.

12. The judge who perverts judgment due to an Israelite transgresses one negative command, as it is said: *Ye shall do no unrighteousness in judgment* (Lev. 19: 15). If the one thus wronged is a stranger, the judge transgresses two negative commandments, as it is said: *Thou shalt not pervert the justice due to the stranger* (Deut. 24: 17). If the one wronged is an orphan, the judge transgresses three negative commands, as it is said: *Thou shalt not pervert the justice due to . . . the fatherless* (*ibid.*).

CHAPTER XXI

1. A positive command enjoins upon the judge the duty to judge righteously, as it is said: *In righteousness shalt thou judge thy neighbor* (Lev. 19: 15). What is meant by a righteous judgment? It is a judgment marked by perfect impartiality to both litigants, not permitting one to state his case at length and telling the other to be brief, not to show courtesy to one, speaking softly to him, and frown upon the other, addressing him harshly.

2. If one of the parties to a suit is well clad and the other ill clad, the judge should say to the former, "Either dress him like yourself before the trial is held or dress like him, then the trial will take place."

3. One of the litigants must not be allowed to be seated and the other kept standing; but both should be standing. It is, however, within the discretion of the court to permit both to be seated. But one must not occupy a higher seat and the other a lower one; they are to be seated side by side. The latitude given to the judges to seat both litigants holds only while the case is still in the stage of discussion; once the case is completed, both must stand, for it is said: *And Moses sat to judge the people; and the people stood*

about Moses (Exod. 18:13). When is the case to be regarded as completed? When the judges announce their decision saying, "So-and-so, you are innocent; So-and-so, you are guilty." This applies only to the litigants, but the witnesses must stand, as it is said: *Then both the men . . . shall stand* (Deut. 19:17).

4. If a scholar and an ignorant person come to court for a trial, the scholar is seated and the ignorant person is asked to take a seat. If the latter declines, the court does not insist (that he be seated). The scholar should not, however, come first and sit down before his teacher as though he would state his case to him. But if he has a set hour for study with him, he may come at the appointed time.

5. Since the close of the Talmud, it has become the practice of all courts associated with the academies to permit the parties to a lawsuit and the witnesses to be seated, in order to obviate strife. For we are powerless to maintain intact all the requirements of the law.

6. If the court has many cases on the docket, the case of an orphan is tried before that of a widow, as it is said: *Judge the fatherless, plead for the widow* (Isa. 1:17), the case of a widow comes before that of a scholar, a scholar's before an illiterate's, the suit of a woman before that of a man, for the humiliation is greater in the case of a woman.

7. The judge is forbidden to hear the arguments of a litigant, aye, even a single statement made by him, before his opponent appears, or in the absence of his opponent, for it is said. *Hear the causes between your brethren* (Deut. 1:16). The judge who hears only one side, transgresses a negative command, as it is said: *Thou shalt not accept a false report* (Exod. 23:1). This negative command implies also an admonition against listening to slander, indulging in it, and giving false testimony.

The litigant also is warned not to state his case to the court before his opponent arrives. Even to this and similar matters applies the injunction *Keep thee far from a false matter* (Exod. 23:7).

8. The judge shall not hear the arguments from the mouth of

an interpreter unless he knows the language spoken by the litigants and understands their arguments. If he is unable to speak their language fluently enough to address them, he may appoint an interpreter to advise them of the decision and to set forth the reason for pronouncing one guilty and the other innocent.

9. It is imperative that the judge after hearing the arguments of both parties to the suit should repeat those arguments, as it is written: *And the king said: The one saith, "This is my son that liveth, and thy son is dead"* (I Kings 3:23). He must be satisfied in his mind that the decision he reached is correct and then give it.

10. How do we know that the judge should not express approval of the arguments of a litigant? It is said: *Keep thee far from a false matter* (Exod. 23:7). He should give his opinion and keep silent. Nor should he suggest to either suitor a line of argument. Even if he (the plaintiff) brought but one witness, the judge should not say to him, "We do not accept the testimony of one man." But he should address the defendant thus: "This man has testified against you." Perhaps the defendant would then admit the claim, saying, "The evidence given by him is true." The judge must therefore wait until the *defendant* says, "There is but one witness. I do not deem him trustworthy." This applies also to similar cases.

11. In the event the judge sees a point in favor of a litigant and finds that the latter is trying to bring out the point but is unable to formulate it, or the judge finds that the litigant is at pains to defend himself by a sound argument but that, agitated by fierce anger, the argument escapes him, or finds that as a result of an inferior mentality the litigant is confused, he is permitted to assist him somewhat by giving him a lead, in compliance with the exhortation *Open thy mouth for the dumb* (Prov. 31:8). But this matter requires due deliberation, for the judge must not appear as one who "plays the part of an advocate."

CHAPTER XXII

1. When two litigants come before you, one of whom is gentle, the other hard, before you have heard their statements, or even after you have heard them, so long as you are uncertain in whose favor the verdict will be, you have a right to say to them, "I am not bound to decide your case," lest the hard man be found guilty and persecute you. Once, however, you have heard their statements and know in whose favor the verdict will be, you no longer have the right to say, "I am not bound to decide your case," for it is written: *Ye shall not be afraid of the face of any man* (Deut. 1:17). Say not, "So-and-so is wicked, he may slay my son, set fire to my shock of grain, or cut down my plants." But if he has been appointed to act as judge, he is bound to try all cases.

2. So too, if a disciple sitting before his master sees a point in favor of a poor man as against a rich man and remains silent, he transgresses the command *Ye shall not be afraid of the face of any man*. Concerning such a disciple it is said: *Keep thee far from a false matter* (Exod. 23:7).

How do we know that a judge should not permit an uncultured disciple to sit before him? It is written: *Keep thee far from a false matter.*

3. How do we know that a disciple, on finding that his master is in error on a point of law, should not say, "I will wait until he gives his opinion, then upset it, and give a contrary decision, so that the decision be credited to me"? Because Scripture says: *Keep thee far from a false matter.*

4. It is commendable at the outset of a trial to inquire of the litigants whether they desire adjudication according to law or settlement by arbitration. If they prefer arbitration, their wish is granted. A court that always resorts to arbitration is praiseworthy. Concerning such a court, it is said: *Execute the justice of . . . peace in your gates* (Zech. 8:16). What is the kind of justice which carries peace with it? Undoubtedly, it is arbitration. So too, with reference to David it is said: *And David executed justice and charity unto all his people* (II Sam. 8:15). What is the kind of

justice which carries charity with it? Undoubtedly, it is arbitration, i.e., compromise.

What has been said holds good only as long as the verdict has not yet been announced, in which case even if the judge has already heard the arguments of the litigants and knows in whose favor the verdict will be, it is commendable to effect an arbitration. But if the verdict has already been announced and the judge said: "So-and-so, you are not guilty; So-and-so, you are guilty," he is not permitted to advise arbitration, but the law must take its course.

5. Even if both litigants have consented to arbitration by the court, they have the right to change their minds and demand a decision by legal procedure, unless both have pledged themselves by a ḳinyan to abide by the outcome of the arbitration.

6. The power of arbitration is greater than that of adjudication. For if two ordinary men try a case, their decision is not valid and the litigants may reject it; whereas if two arbitrate a case and the litigants have obligated themselves by a ḳinyan to abide by the decision, they cannot repudiate the decision.

7. A judge is forbidden to say, on leaving court, "I voted for acquittal, or for condemnation, but my colleagues differed with me. And what could I do, seeing that they were in the majority?" If he speaks in this wise, he belongs to those concerning whom it is written: *He that goeth about as a talebearer revealeth secrets* (Prov. 11:13). It happened once that a disciple divulged things that had been said (confidentially) in the House of Study twenty-two years before, and the court expelled him from the House of Study, announcing publicly, "This man revealeth secrets."

8. If one of the parties to a suit asks for a transcript of the legal decision, it is worded thus: "So-and-so appeared in such-and-such a court with So-and-so, his opponent, who advanced the following claim against him and the defendant was found liable" or "not liable." He is handed a transcript of the decision from which the names of those who found him not liable and those who found him liable are omitted, stating only, "By the verdict of such-and-such a court So-and-so was acquitted."

9. This was the practice of the judges of Jerusalem. First the litigants were admitted and their statements and arguments heard, then the witnesses were admitted and their evidence heard. All were then told to leave and the judges discussed the case, until a decision was reached. Thereupon the litigants were readmitted and the chief justice announced, "So-and-so, you are not liable; So-and-so, you are liable." In this way neither litigant knew who had voted for him and who had voted against him.

10. A judge who knows his colleague to be dishonest or wicked is forbidden to join him, for it is said: *Keep thee far from a false matter* (Exod. 23:7). The pure minded in Jerusalem were wont to act thus: they would not sit in judgment unless they knew who was to sit with them; they would not sign a deed unless they knew who would sign with them; and they would not sit at the table to dine unless they knew who would dine with them.

CHAPTER XXIII

1. *Thou shalt take no gift* (Exod. 23:8). The purport of this prohibition is not to caution the judge against accepting a gift with the intention of perverting justice. Its purpose is to warn him not to accept a bribe even if he proposes to acquit the innocent and condemn the guilty. He who does it transgresses this negative command. To him too is addressed the admonition *Cursed be he that taketh a bribe* (Deut. 27:25). He is bound to return the bribe if the giver demands it.

2. The giver of a bribe, as well as the receiver, contravenes a negative command, as it is said: *Nor put a stumbling block before the blind* (Lev. 19:14).

3. Any judge who stays at home and magnifies his greatness in order to increase the perquisites of his attendants and clerks is classed with those who turn aside after gain. The sons of Samuel did it. Therefore it is written concerning them: *And they turned aside after lucre and took bribes* (I Sam. 8:3). Not only is a bribe of money forbidden but also a bribe of words.

It happened once that a judge was crossing a river on a small fishing boat, when a man stretched forth his hand and helped him get ashore. That man had a lawsuit, but the judge said to him, "I am disqualified from acting as judge in your suit."

It also happened that a man once removed a bird's feather from a judge's mantle; another man once covered spittle in front of a judge. In each of these instances, the judge said, "I am barred from trying your case."

There is also an incident on record of a man who presented to a priest, who was also a judge, a gift due to the priest. The judge said to the man, "I am ineligible to act as judge in your suit."

There is still another incident of a tenant farmer who, on Fridays used to bring to the owner figs from the garden he was cultivating. On one occasion, however, he brought the figs on Thursday, because he had a lawsuit. The judge, however, said, "I am barred from acting as judge in your case," for though the figs were his, since the tenant brought them ahead of time, he was ineligible to try the case.

4. A judge who borrows things from others is ineligible to try a suit in which the man he borrows from is involved. This applies only to a judge who has nothing to lend in return. If, however, he is in possession of things to lend to others, he is qualified, for the man from whom he borrows may borrow things from him.

5. If a man takes payment for acting as judge, his decisions are null. This ruling obtains only if it is evident that the payment represents compensation for judicial services. But if he has an occupation in which he is engaged and two men come before him with a lawsuit, and he says to them, "Either procure me one who will attend to my work until I shall have adjudicated your case or remunerate me for loss of time," he is permitted to do so, provided that it is obvious that the payment is for loss of time only and no more and that the fee he receives is contributed equally by both parties to the suit and is given him in the presence of both. Under these circumstances he is permitted to accept payment.

6. A man is forbidden to act as judge for a friend even though the latter was not his groomsman, or is not his most intimate friend. Nor is he to act as judge for one whom he dislikes, although he is

not his enemy, seeking his harm. It is essential that both parties to the suit should be alike in his estimation and affection. The judge who does not know either litigant and the life he leads is in the best conceivable position to render a righteous judgment.

7. Two scholars who dislike each other are forbidden to sit together in judgment, for this might lead to the rendering of a perverted judgment. Prompted by hostility, each will be inclined to refute the arguments of the other.

8. At all times a judge should think of himself as if a sword were suspended over his head and Gehenna gaping under him. He should know whom he is judging and before Whom he is judging, and Who will call him to account if he deviate from the line of truth, as it is written: *God standeth in the congregation of God, in the midst of the judges* (Ps. 82:1); and it is also written: *Consider what ye do; for ye judge not for man, but for the Lord* (II Chron. 19:6).

9. A judge who does not render an absolutely true judgment causes the Divine Presence to depart from Israel. If he unlawfully expropriates money from one and gives it to another, the Holy One, blessed be He, will exact his life from him, for it is written: *And the Lord will despoil of life those that despoil them* (Prov. 22:23). A judge who, even for a single hour, renders absolutely true judgments is as though he had (helped to) set the world in order and cause the Divine Presence to dwell in Israel, as it is written: *God standeth in the congregation of God* (Ps. 82:1).

Lest the judge say, "Why should I subject myself to this anxiety?" It is written: *He is with you in giving judgment* (II Chron. 19:6); the judge is to be guided only by what he sees with his eyes.

10. At all times while the litigants are before you regard them as guilty, on the presumption that there is no truth in the statements made by either of them, and be guided by what appears to you from the general drift of the arguments to be true. But when they have departed from your presence, regard them both as innocent, since they have acquiesced in the sentence passed by you, and judge each of them by the scale of merit.

CHAPTER XXIV

1. In monetary matters, the judge should act in accordance with what he is inclined to believe is the truth when he feels strongly that his belief is justified, though he has no actual proof of it. It is hardly necessary to say that if he is certain that the opinion he has formed is correct, he should act upon it. The following are cases in point.

If the court imposes an oath upon the defendant and a person whom the judge regards as trustworthy and by whose opinion he sets much store tells him that the defendant is suspected of perjury, it is the duty of the judge to transfer the oath to the claimant, and the latter swears and recovers his due. This ruling holds good even if the informant be a woman or a slave; since the suspicion has a firm hold on him he may rely upon the informant and act accordingly. It goes without saying that he is to follow this course if he himself knows that the suspicion is warranted.

So too, if a note of indebtedness is produced in court and a person who enjoys the confidence of the judge, even if that person is a woman or a kinsman, says to him, "This note is paid up," since the judge trusts that person, he is to advise the defendant not to pay it, unless the claimant takes an oath. If in addition to the impaired note an unimpaired note is produced against the same defendant by another claimant, the judge is to order payment of the unimpaired one, and put away (undisposed) the one that according to his informant is impaired, or throw it out of court, as the judge sees fit.

Similarly, in case a person appears before the judge claiming that he had entrusted a (valuable) object to the safekeeping of one who has since died intestate, and identifies the object by unmistakable marks, and it is known that he was not a frequent visitor at the house of the deceased, if the judge knows that the departed was not wealthy enough to own such a costly object and is satisfied in his mind that it did not belong to him, he takes it away from the heirs and gives it to the claimant who is a man of means and has identified it by unmistakable marks. This applies to like cases. Matters of this kind are matters committed to the heart of the judge, who in pronouncing judgment is to be guided by what appears to him to be a true judgment.

If this be so, why does the Torah require two witnesses? The answer is: when two witnesses give testimony, the judge is bound to decide on their evidence, although he does not know whether the evidence submitted by them is true or false.

2. What has been said before constitutes a fundamental of (Jewish) law. But with the increase of courts whose members are lacking the requisite moral qualifications, and when even those whose conduct entitles them to the office do not possess adequate knowledge and understanding, most courts have decided not to transfer an oath (from the defendant to the plaintiff), unless there is clear evidence (to warrant such a procedure), nor to impair a note causing it to lose its validity on the evidence of a woman or otherwise ineligible witness.

So too with reference to other legal matters (it was decided) that the judge should not be guided by his own opinion or that of one in whom he reposes confidence, lest any mediocre judge will say, "I believe it is so"; or "I put credence in this man."

Likewise, it was decided not to take away things from orphans —unless there is ample warrant for such seizure—on the strength of an opinion formed by the judge or on an estimate of the wealth of the deceased or of the claimant.

Nevertheless, if a trustworthy person testifies concerning any of these matters, and the judge feels that he speaks the truth, he will deliberate before giving his opinion, will not disregard the evidence, but will discuss the matter with the litigants until they acknowledge the truth of the statement made by the informant, or will have the suit arbitrated; else he will withdraw from the case.

3. Whence do we derive that a judge who has reason to suspect one of the litigants of misrepresentation should not say, "I will decide the case according to the evidence and let the witnesses bear the responsibility"? Because it is said: *Keep thee far from a false matter* (Exod. 23:7). How is he to proceed in such a case?

Let him sedulously investigate the witnesses with the inquiries and queries to which witnesses in capital offenses are subjected. If after this thoroughgoing examination, he concludes [that there is nothing fraudulent about the suit, he gives his decision on the basis of the evidence. But if he has any scruples about it,] suspecting dishonesty, or has no confidence in the witnesses, although he has no valid ground on which to disqualify them, or he is inclined to believe that the litigant is a subtle fraud, that the witnesses are honest men, giving their evidence in all innocence, but were led astray by the litigant, or if it appears to him from the whole tenor of the proceedings that some information is withheld, not brought into the open—in any of these or similar circumstances—the judge is forbidden to render a decision. He should withdraw from the case and let another judge, who can without qualms of conscience pronounce judgment, handle it. For matters of this nature are committed to the heart, and Scripture says: *For the judgment is God's* (Deut. 1:17).

4. The court is empowered to flog him who is not liable to flagellation and to mete out the death penalty to him who is not liable to death. This extensive power is granted to the court not with the intention of disregarding the Law but in order to build a fence around it. Whenever the court sees that a command has fallen into general disuse, the duty devolves upon it to safeguard and strengthen the command in any way which in its judgment will achieve the desired result. But whatever measure it adopts is only a temporary one and does not acquire the force of a law, binding for all time to come.

Thus we are told that a man was flogged for cohabiting with his wife under a fig tree. There is also the incident of a man who, during the days of the Greeks, rode a horse on the Sabbath and was brought before the court and stoned. There is also the incident of Simeon son of Sheṭaḥ (at whose instance) eighty women were hanged on the same day at Ashkelon, without the legally prescribed inquiry and query, due warning, and conclusive evidence. He (Rabbi Simeon son of Sheṭaḥ) felt that the emergency of the hour demanded drastic action.

5. So too, the court may in all places and at all times flog a man whose reputation is unsavory, about whom the people are talking, accusing him of immoral conduct, provided that the rumor with respect to him is persistent, as has already been stated, and that he has no avowed enemies who spread an evil report about him. Similarly, a person of evil repute may be despised, and she that bore him reviled in his presence.

6. Likewise, the judge may at all times expropriate money from its owner, destroy it, or give it away, disposing of it in any way which in his judgment will halt the breakdown of religion, repair its breaches, or bring to terms the defier of the Law. Thus it is written in the Book of Ezra (10:8): *Whosoever come not within three days, according to the counsel of the princes and the elders, all his substance should be forfeited.* From this we infer that it is within the jurisdiction of the court to confiscate property.

7. So too the judge may lay the ban and invoke the major excommunication upon him who is not liable to these penalties in order to check the breakdown of religion, if in his opinion these disciplinary measures will achieve the desired end or meet the exigency of the hour. He shall say that he bans or excommunicates him by his authority, and make public the details of the offense, as it is written: *Curse ye Meroz, said the angel of the Lord, curse ye bitterly the inhabitants thereof, because they came not to the help of the Lord* (Judg. 5:23).

8. So too, the judge may quarrel with him who deserves to be quarreled with, curse him, smite him, pluck his hair, and compel him to take an oath that he will desist from committing the offense again or that he has not committed it, as it is written: *And I contended with them, and I cursed them, and smote certain of them, and plucked off their hair, and made them swear by God* (Neh. 13:25).

9. Likewise the judge may fetter the hands and feet of the offender, imprison him, knock him down, and drag him on the ground, as it is written: *Let judgment be executed upon him with all diligence, whether it be unto death, or to be banished, or to confiscation of goods, or to imprisonment* (Ezra 7:26).

10. With regard to all these disciplinary measures, discretionary power is vested in the judge. He is to decide whether the offender deserves these punishments and whether the emergency of the hour demands their application. But whatever the expedient he sees fit to resort to, all his deeds should be done for the sake of Heaven. Let not human dignity be light in his eyes; for the respect due to man supersedes a negative rabbinical command. This applies with even greater force to the dignity of the children of Abraham, Isaac, and Jacob, who adhere to the True Law. The judge must be careful not to do aught calculated to destroy their self-respect. His sole concern should be to enhance the glory of God, for whosoever dishonors the Torah is himself dishonored by men, and whosoever honors the Torah is himself honored by men. To honor the Torah means to follow its statutes and laws.

CHAPTER XXV

1. It is forbidden to lead the community in a domineering and arrogant manner. One should exercise one's authority in a spirit of humility and reverence. The man at the head of the congregation who arouses excessive fear in the hearts of the members thereof for any but a religious purpose will be punished. It will not be given to him to have a son who will be a scholar, as it is written: *Men do therefore fear him; he will not see any* (sons) *that are wise of heart* (Job. 37:24).

2. He is also forbidden to treat the people with disrespect, though they be ignorant. He should not force his way through the holy people (to get to his seat), for though they be uninformed and lowly, they are the children of Abraham, Isaac, and Jacob, of the hosts of God, brought forth out of Egypt with great power and with a mighty hand. He should bear patiently the cumbrance and burden of the community, as did Moses, our teacher, concerning whom it is said: *as a nursing father carrieth the sucking child* (Num. 11:12). It is also said: *And I charged your judges* (Deut. 1:16). This is an exhortation to the judge to bear patiently with the congregation, as does a nursing father bear with a sucking child.

Consider Moses, the master prophet! We are told that no sooner did the Holy One, blessed be He, send him to Egypt than *He gave them* (Moses and Aaron) *a charge unto the children of Israel* (Exod. 6:13), which sentence is interpreted by tradition that God said to Moses and Aaron, *"You are to command Israel with the understanding that they will curse you, and cast stones at you"* (Sif Num. 11:11, p. 23a [45]).

3. Just as the judge is bidden to observe this command, so is the congregation bidden to accord respectful treatment to the judge, as it is said: *And I commanded you* (Deut. 1:18). This is an exhortation to the congregation to regard the judge with a feeling of reverence. The judge therefore must not make himself contemptible or indulge in frivolity.

4. As soon as a man is appointed leader of the community, he is forbidden to do (menial) labor in the presence of three men, lest he lose their respect. If he is forbidden to do menial labor in public, how much more so is he forbidden to eat, drink, and get intoxicated in the presence of many, or attend assemblies of ignorant people or social parties. Woe unto those judges who make a practice of such indulgences for (their) contempt of the Torah of Moses. They despise its judgments, lower its standards, bring it down to the dust, and cause evil to themselves and their children's children in this world and in the world to come.

5. It is forbidden to treat contemptuously a messenger of the court. In the matter of the imposition of a ban, his evidence is as valid as that of two witnesses. If he says, "So-and-so has reviled me," or "has reviled the judge," or "has refused to come to court," that person is banned (orally) on the evidence of the messenger. However, no writ of the ban is issued unless two witnesses come and testify that the summons was disobeyed.

6. In reporting insolent behavior toward him, the messenger of the court is not guilty of slander. In case a man annoys its messenger, the court has the right to inflict disciplinary flogging upon him.

7. If the messenger summons a person to court, saying, "So-and-so (of the judges) has sent me," thus speaking in the name

of only one of the judges, and the person refuses to appear, no writ of the ban is issued—unless the messenger conveys the summons in the name of all three. This ruling obtains only if the messenger delivers the summons on a day not known to be court day. But if he delivers it on a court day, since it is a matter of common knowledge that the judges hold sessions on that day, even if he speaks in the name of one judge only, it is as though he spoke in the name of all three.

8. If a man summoned by the court fails to put in an appearance, the court imposes the ban upon him, issues a writ of the ban and the man cited pays the clerk's fee. When he answers the summons, the writ is torn up. If the writ was issued because of his refusal to accept the decision (of the court), as soon as he says, "I accept it," the writ is destroyed.

If the court had set a day for his appearance and he did not attend on that day, the writ is issued in the evening. This ruling holds good only if he was in town (on that day), and defied the order of the court. But if he was then in the neighboring villages, coming in and going out, the court cites him to appear on Monday, then on Thursday, and then on the following Monday. If the second Monday passes and he does not attend, the writ is issued the following day.

9. No court days are set during the months of Nisan and Tishri, because during these months the people are busy preparing for the festivals; nor is court held on the eve of the Sabbath or of a festival. But summonses may be served during Nisan, citing a litigant to appear after Nisan, and during Tishri citing him to appear after Tishri. But no summons is delivered on Friday for appearance in court after the Sabbath, for all are busy on the eve of the Sabbath.

10. If the litigant is in town and the messenger calls to see him but cannot find him, no date is fixed for his appearance until the messenger locates him and delivers the summons. In case he is out of town, in one of the neighboring villages, if he is used to return on the same day, the messenger asks one of the neighbors, even if the neighbor be a woman, to inform him on his return

that the court has appointed a date for his appearance. If he fails to appear, he is placed under the ban in the evening. This ruling obtains only if the road on his way home does not take him to the courthouse. If it does, he is not put under the ban until the messenger has advised him of the summons. For it is possible that the neighbor has not delivered the message to him, supposing that since he had passed the courthouse en route to his home he must have called there and attended to the matter. Likewise, if he did not return till the following day, the neighbors cannot be depended upon. They might have forgotten to convey the message to him.

11. If the litigant appears in court, accepts the decision, and is ordered to pay (the claim against him) but fails to do it, he is not placed under the ban until he is warned on Monday, then on Thursday, and again on the following Monday. Thereafter he is put under the ban which lasts until he pays what he owes. But if he has waited thirty days without asking that the ban be removed, the major excommunication is imposed upon him.

CHAPTER XXVI

1. He who curses a Jewish judge transgresses a negative command, for it is said: *Thou shalt not revile the judges* (Exod. 22:27). So too, he who curses the Naśi, whether it be the head of the Great Sanhedrin or the king, transgresses a negative command, for it is said: *Nor curse a ruler of thy people* (*ibid.*); aye, he who curses any Israelite is flogged, for it is said: *Thou shalt not curse the deaf* (Lev. 19:14). Why does Scripture single out the deaf? To teach that cursing even one who neither hears nor is pained when cursed carries with it the penalty of flogging. It seems to me that he who curses a minor sensitive to affront is flogged, (for he is like the deaf.)

2. He who curses a dead person is not liable. Since one who curses any Israelite suffers the penalty of flogging, why is there a special prohibition for cursing a judge and another for cursing a Naśi? In order to make the offender liable on additional counts.

Hence we learn that one who curses any Israelite, whether the cursed be a man or a woman, an adult or a minor, is flogged once; if he curses a judge, twice; a Naśi, thrice. If the son of a Naśi curses his father, he is flogged on four counts, to wit, three floggings to which anyone who curses a Naśi is liable and a fourth flogging for cursing his father.

3. He who curses himself is liable to flogging—the penalty incurred when one curses his neighbor—for it is said: *Only take heed to thyself and guard well thy life* (Deut. 4:9).

Whether he curses himself or another Israelite or the Naśi or a judge, he is not subject to flogging unless he curses by one of the special Names (of God), such as *YH, 'Ĕlohim* (God), *Shaddai* (Almighty), or the like, or by any of the attributes (of God), such as the Merciful, the Jealous, or the like. Since cursing by any of the attributes entails the penalty of flogging, it follows that if one curses by the Name (of God) in any language, he is subject to flogging, for the names by which non-Israelites refer to God belong to the category of attributes.

The word *'arur* (cursed be) implies an oath, a curse, and a ban.

4. He who curses is not liable to flogging unless he has received due warning in the presence of witnesses, as is required in the case of all who transgress negative commands. But if there has been no previous warning, or if he curses not by any of the (special) Names or by any of the attributes, as when, for example, he says, "Cursed be So-and-so," or if the curse is only implied in the words he uses, as when he says, "Let So-and-so not be blessed of the Lord," or "God shall not bless him," or like expressions, he is not flogged.

5. Although he who reviles a scholar does not incur the penalty of flogging, he is placed under the ban. It is within the discretion of the judges to administer to the offender a disciplinary beating and fine him, because he has abused a sage. If he reviles an ignorant man, the judges fine him, taking into account the need of the hour, and the standing of the reviler and the reviled.

6. Although the judge or the Naśi may forego the honor due

him, it is not within his power to forgive a curse flung at him. This holds good even if the cursed is one of the rank and file; even if he is willing to forgive the offender, the latter is flogged because he has sinned and has rendered himself liable to this penalty. But if one has incurred the penalty of the ban for disrespect shown to the court, and the members thereof desire to forgive him and not invoke the ban upon him, they are at liberty to do so, provided that the affront does not affect the honor of God, as is the case when the people rebel against the commandments of the Torah and the judges. Whenever the people defy the Law, it is incumbent upon the judges to strengthen it and to punish the offender as they may see fit to do.

7. Whoever submits a suit for adjudication to heathen judges in their courts, even if the judgment rendered by them is in consonance with Jewish law, is a wicked man. It is as though he reviled, blasphemed, and rebelled against the Law of Moses, our teacher, for it is said *Now these are the ordinances which thou shalt set before them* (Exod. 21:1)—*before them,* not before heathens, and not before ordinary men. If the hand of the heathens is powerful and his opponent is a man of violence and the claimant is unable to recover what is due to him through the Jewish court, he must first summon him to appear before Jewish judges; if his opponent refuses to appear, the plaintiff obtains permission from the court to recover his claim through the heathen court.

TREATISE II

LAWS CONCERNING EVIDENCE

Involving Eight Commandments

Three Positive and Five Negative

To Wit

1. That one who is in possession of evidence should testify in court;
2. That witnesses should be subjected *to inquiries and queries;*
3. That one who has given evidence in a capital case shall not act as judge in it;
4. That no decision shall be made on the evidence of only one witness;
5. That a transgressor shall not be eligible as witness;
6. That a relative shall not testify;
7. That one shall not give false testimony;
8. To do unto the false witness as he had purposed to do to the accused.

An exposition of these commandments is contained in the following chapters.

CHAPTER I

1. It is the duty of him who is in possession of evidence to testify in court, whether the evidence will lead to condemnation or vindication, as it is said: *He being a witness, whether he hath seen or known, if he do not utter it, then he shall bear his iniquity* (Lev. 5:1). In monetary matters, this duty devolves upon him only if he is asked to give evidence.

2. If the man in possession of evidence is a great scholar and the members of the tribunal are his inferiors in wisdom, seeing that it is beneath his dignity to appear before them as witness, he need not testify. The positive command to pay respect to the Torah (and its exponents) takes precedence of the negative command. This applies only to monetary cases; but in the case of a prohibition the infraction of which his testimony would avert, or in cases involving either capital or corporal punishment, it is his duty to appear in court and testify, as it is written: *There is no wisdom, nor understanding, nor counsel against the Lord* (Prov. 21:30). Whenever there is a profanation of the Name (of God), the honor due to a teacher is disregarded.

3. The High Priest is under no obligation to act as witness save in a suit involving the king of Israel, in which case he repairs to the Supreme Court and testifies. In all other suits, he is exempt from giving evidence.

4. It is a positive command to subject the witnesses to inquiry and query, to examine them exhaustively, to scrutinize their evidence in detail, leading them in the course of interrogation from point to point, so that if there is any flaw in their testimony they will either remain silent or retract, as it is said: *Thou shalt inquire and make search, and ask diligently* (Deut. 13:15). When they examine the witnesses, the judges must be on their guard, lest through the examination the witnesses learn to lie.

The judges put to the witnesses the following seven queries (*ḥăḳirot*). In what week of years was the crime committed? In what year? In what month? On which day of the month? On what day? At what hour? In what place? Even if the witnesses say, "He has killed him today," or "He killed him last night," they are asked, "In what week of years? In what month? On what day of the month? On what day? At what hour?"

In addition to these seven queries directed to witnesses in all capital charges, there are also other queries which are put to them. If they testify that the accused committed idolatry, they are asked: "What did he worship?" and "How did he worship it?" If they testify that he desecrated the Sabbath, they are asked, "What kind of work did he do? How did he do it?" If they testify that he partook of food on the Day of Atonement, they are asked, "What did he eat? How much did he eat?" If they testify that he killed a person, they are asked, "With what did he slay him?" These and similar questions come under the head of queries.

5. The queries and inquiries are the pivotal questions put to the witnesses. The acquittal or condemnation of the accused depends upon the answers given to them. Their purpose is to determine the act, the time, and the place. The answer to the last two questions will decide whether those who have given evidence are plotting witnesses. For witnesses cannot be found guilty of conspiracy unless they state the precise time and place (of the act).

6. The witnesses are also made to undergo a cross-examination bearing upon aspects of the evidence which are not pivotal to the testimony and do not affect its validity. This is styled *bĕḏiḳoṯ* (cross-examination, investigation). The more numerous the bĕḏiḳoṯ, the more praiseworthy is the judge. To illustrate what is meant by bĕḏiḳoṯ: After the witnesses who testified that the accused had killed a person were subjected to the seven queries enumerated before—queries relating to the exact time and place of the crime—and to the inquiries relating to the act itself, and answered correctly (the questions belonging to the category of queries, as well as those that come under the head of inquiries), establishing the act and stating precisely the weapon used, they are held for further examination. They are asked, "What clothes did the slain or the slayer wear? Were they white or black? Was

the dust of the earth where the slaying occurred white or red?" These and similar questions comprise bĕḏiḳoṯ.

Once witnesses testified that the accused had slain a person in a certain place under a fig tree. On cross-examination the witnesses were asked, "Were the figs black or white? Were the stalks long or short?" The more numerous the questions asked in the cross-examination, the more praiseworthy is the judge.

CHAPTER II

1. In what respect do queries and inquiries differ from cross-examination? If to any of the queries or the inquiries one witness gives a definite answer and the other says, "I do not know," their evidence is void; but if to any of the questions in the course of the cross-examination even both witnesses say, "We do not know," their evidence is valid. Yet if they contradict each other even during the cross-examination, their evidence is void. To illustrate the point of difference between them: if two testify that the accused killed a person and, in answer to the queries put to them, one says "It occurred in such-and-such a year of the Jubilee, in such-and-such a year, in such-and-such a month, on such-and-such a day of the month, on the fourth day of the week, during the sixth hour of the day, at such-and-such a place," and in answer to the inquiry, "With what weapon did the accused slay the victim?" he says, "with a sword"; and the second witness gives a definite answer to all queries and inquiries except the one relating to the hour of the day, saying, "I do not know what time it was," or he does state the hour but says, "I do not know with what he slew him, I did not notice the weapon in his hand"—in this case their evidence is void. If, however, they give definite answers to all the queries and inquiries put to them, but in reply to the question, "Were his clothes black or white?" they say, "We do not know; we took no notice of such an inconsequential matter," their evidence is valid.

2. If one of the witnesses says, "His clothes were black," and the other says, "It is not true, his clothes were white," their testimony is void. It is as if one had said, "It occurred on Wednesday,"

and the other, "on Thursday," a discrepancy which renders the testimony null, or as if one had said, "He killed him with a sword," and the other, "with a spear," in which case the evidence is invalid, for it is written *The thing is certain* (Deut. 13:15). Since the witnesses contradict each other, even though the contradiction is only with regard to answers given to questions asked in the course of the cross-examination, the thing is not certain.

3. If there are more than two witnesses, two of whom give definite answers to the queries and inquiries, and the third says, "I do not know," the evidence is established through the two and the accused is condemned to death. But if the third contradicts the two, even if he contradicts them in the course of the cross-examination, their testimony is void.

4. If one witness says, "The slaying occurred on Wednesday, the second day of the month," and the second says, "on Wednesday, the third day of the month," their evidence is valid, since one may have known that the month was intercalated and the other did not know it. This assumption holds good only in a discrepancy in date during the first half of the month. But if the discrepancy is with regard to a date after the first half of the month—for example, if one says, "It happened on the sixteenth day of the month," and the other, "on the seventeenth," although they agree on the day of the week—their evidence is void, because by the time that half the month has passed, everybody knows when the new moon occurred.

5. If one says, "(It happened) on the third day of the month," and the second, "on the fifth day," their evidence in null. If one says, "(It happened) during the second hour" and the other says, "during the third hour," their testimony is valid, for people are apt to err in the matter of one hour. But if one says, "during the third hour," and the second says, "during the fifth hour," their evidence is null. If one says, "(It happened) before sunrise" and the other says, "after sunrise," their evidence is null, for though the interval between the two is slight, the difference is evident to all. So too, if the discrepancy in the testimony is in the matter of time before or after sunset, their evidence is null.

CHAPTER III

1. Both civil and capital cases require inquiry and query, as it is said: *Ye shall have one manner of law* (Lev. 24:22). The Rabbis, however, said that in order not to shut the door to borrowers, witnesses who testify in monetary suits are not subjected to inquiry and query. Thus if the witnesses say, "So-and-so lent So-and-so one hundred *zuz* in our presence in such-and-such a year," although they do not specify the month (when the loan was made), or the place where it was made or the coinage of the maneh loaned, their evidence is valid.

2. The aforementioned enactment applies only to cases of admission and transaction of loans, gifts and sales, and the like. But in cases involving fines, and certainly in cases involving flogging or banishment, inquiry and query are required. So too, if the judge finds that the case before him bears evidence of trickery and he is troubled about it, the witnesses must undergo inquiry and query.

3. Although witnesses in civil cases are not subject to inquiries and queries, if they contradict each other in their answer to any of the inquiries and queries, their evidence is void. But if they contradict each other in their answer to questions put to them in the course of the cross-examination, their evidence is valid. To cite concrete examples: if one says, "The loan was made in Nisan," and the other says, "No! It was made in Iyyar," or one says "(It was made) in Jerusalem" and the other says, "No! It was made in Lydda," their evidence is null. (They contradict each other in their answer to one of the queries). So too, if one testifies to (a loan of) a barrel of wine and the second to a barrel of oil, their evidence is void. They contradict each other in their answer to one of the inquiries. But if one says that the maneh was black (old) and the second, that it was white (new), or if one asserts that the lender and the borrower were in the upper story when the loan was made and the second declares that they were in the lower story, their evidence is valid. Even if one maintains that it was a loan of one maneh and the second that it was a loan of two hundred zuz (two maneh), the defendant must pay the plaintiff a hundred

zuz, since one hundred is included in two hundred. Likewise, if one says that the defendant owes the claimant the value of a barrel of wine, and the other, that he owes him the value of a barrel of oil, the defendant must pay the lesser of the claims. This applies also to like cases.

4. According to scriptural law, no testimony, whether in civil or capital cases, is admitted, unless it is given orally, as it is said: *At the mouth of two witnesses shall the matter be established* (Deut. 19:15), that is, their oral, not written, testimony. The Scribes, however, enacted that monetary cases are to be decided on documentary evidence, although the witnesses are no longer living, in order not to shut the door to borrowers. Cases involving fines, however, and especially cases involving flagellation or banishment, are not decided on documentary evidence. In such cases, the testimony must be oral, not written.

5. Whether in monetary or capital cases, a witness whose evidence was examined by the court cannot retract. To illustrate the ruling: if the witness says, "I was misled, I had erred and later reminded myself that I was wrong," or he says, "My testimony was prompted by fear of him (the litigant)," the court pays no attention to his words, although he gives a reason for what he says. Nor is he permitted to add to his previous testimony the statement that there was a verbal condition attached to the transaction concerning which he has given evidence. The general principle is: once the evidence of a witness has been probed, no attention is paid to any further statement by him, whether the statement would have the effect of nullifying his testimony or of adding a rider to it.

6. If witnesses have signed a document, their (signed) evidence is as valid as evidence that has been examined by the court. They cannot therefore retract. This holds good only if the genuineness of the document can be established independently of the signatories, either by other witnesses who identify the signatures or by a comparison of the handwriting (on the document under consideration) with their handwriting on other documents. But if it is impossible to confirm the document without the signatories and the latter say, "It is our handwriting, but we acted under compul-

sion," or "We were minors," or "We were kinsmen," or "We were misled," they are believed, and the document is not valid.

7. If the witnesses say, "We were ineligible as witnesses on the ground of religious delinquency," or "We were bribed to give testimony," they are not believed, unless there are witnesses to testify that they are transgressors, for no man can incriminate himself.

So too, if they say, "The note of indebtedness was signed by us on trust," no credence is given to their statement, for if any man subscribes a note on trust, it is as though he would give false evidence.

8. If witnesses who signed a deed of sale say, "We signed it after the owner had entered a verbal protest before us against the sale," credence is given to their statement even if their signatures can be identified by comparing them with their signatures on other documents.

9. In the event the witnesses say, "(We signed the deed of sale but the sale) was made dependent upon a condition," if their handwriting can be identified by comparing it with the handwriting on other documents, no credence is put in their statement. If, however, the genuineness of the deed cannot be established without the signatories, they are believed. The court says to the purchaser, "Fulfill the condition and come to argue your case."

10. If one of the witnesses says that there was a condition attached to the sale and the other says that there was not (and the deed cannot be authenticated without the signatories), there is one witness to the sale.

11. Even in monetary suits, evidence is not accepted save in the presence of the defendant. If the plaintiff is ill, or the witnesses were preparing to go abroad and the other party to the suit was sent for by the court but failed to appear, evidence is accepted in his absence. This applies only to testimony given orally; but in case of documentary evidence, the document is confirmed in the absence of the opposing party; even if the latter protests vehemently, saying, "This document is forged, they who attested it are false witnesses," or "religiously delinquent witnesses," no attention

is paid to his protest. But if he brings proof to invalidate it, the document is invalidated.

12. If a litigant has witnesses to prove his case, it rests with him to find them and produce them in court. But if the court knows that his opponent is a difficult man and the plaintiff maintains that the witnesses are afraid to give evidence against him, the court compels the defendant to produce witnesses. The same procedure is followed in all cases where one of the litigants is a man of violence.

CHAPTER IV

1. In capital cases it is required that the witnesses should see the culprit simultaneously, while he is committing the offense. They must testify at the same time and in the same court. This is not so in civil cases. To elucidate this ruling: if, while the culprit was committing the offense, one witness saw him from one window and the other from another window, as long as the witnesses saw each other, their evidence is combined; otherwise, it is not combined. If the admonitor saw the witnesses and the witnesses saw him, although they did not see each other, the admonitor links their evidence together. If both witnesses were in the same house and one of them stuck his head out of the window, saw the offender doing work on the Sabbath while the admonitor was giving him warning, then withdrew his head from the window, and the second stuck his head out of that window and saw him working, their testimony is not combined—unless both saw him simultaneously.

In case two witnesses saw him from one window and two saw him from another, while one standing midway gave him warning, if two of them, (one on each side) saw each other, the testimony given by both pairs is counted as a single body of evidence. But if they did not see each other and the admonitor did not link their evidence together, their testimony counts as two bodies of evidence. Therefore, if one pair are found to be false witnesses, the accused and they are put to death; he is convicted on the evidence of the other pair.

2. In monetary cases, however, even if the witnesses did not see one another, their evidence is combined. Thus if one says, "The claimant made a loan to the defendant in my presence on such-and-such a day," or "The defendant admitted in my presence the loan made to him," and the second witness says, "I too declare that the loan was transacted in my presence," or "that the defendant admitted in my presence the loan made to him," stating, however, that it (the loan or admission) was made on another day, their evidence is combined.

3. So too, if one witness says, "The loan was contracted in my presence," and the second says, "The defendant admitted the loan in my presence," or the first states, "The defendant made the admission in my presence," and the second testifies some time later, "The loan was contracted in my presence," their evidence is combined.

4. The rule holds good also with reference to the time when the testimony is given. If one appears in court one day, his evidence is heard, and if the second appears at a later date, his evidence is heard, and their evidence is combined, and the plaintiff recovers his claim on the combined evidence.

5. So too, the signed evidence (on the bond) of one witness and the oral evidence of another are combined. If the one who gives oral testimony says, "The defendant obligated himself by a *ḳinyan* to pay the note, but the plaintiff did not ask me to set down the obligation in writing," their evidence is combined to give the loan the force of an obligation attested by a note signed by two witnesses, and the debtor cannot maintain that he paid it.

6. If one witness has given evidence in one court and the second in another, the two courts meet and combine the evidence. So too, if two witnesses have testified in one court, and then in another, [and still later in a third court, and two judges of each court have gone abroad], the remaining (three) get together and jointly consider the evidence submitted to them. But one of the witnesses and one of the judges before whom the witnesses have testified cannot jointly act as witnesses.

7. Although the evidence (of two witnesses) is combined in monetary matters, as has already been set forth, it is imperative that the evidence of each should be complete. But if each of them gives only partial evidence, the testimony is not confirmed by combining the evidence, as it is said: *At the mouth of two witnesses shall a matter be established* (Deut. 19:15). To illustrate this ruling: if one witness declares that so-and-so had the use of a field in such-and-such a year, and another testifies to his use of it the second year, and still another to his use of it the third year, the court does not combine the evidence of the three men, concluding that he enjoyed the use of it for three (successive) years, because each gives only partial evidence.

Similarly, if one says, "I saw one hair on his right side," and the other avers, "On that very day I saw one on his left side," the court does not combine the two statements, reasoning that both testify that on such-and-such a day he attained maturity, because each testifies only to one sign of puberty. This rule obtains even if two testify that they saw one hair, and two others that they saw another, since each pair of witnesses gives only partial evidence, which cannot be considered (satisfactory) evidence. But if one witness testifies that he saw two hairs on the right side, another that he saw two hairs on the left side, their evidence is combined. This holds good in like cases.

CHAPTER V

1. Neither in civil nor in capital cases is a legal decision given on the evidence of one witness, as it is said: *One witness shall not rise up against a man for any iniquity, or for any sin* (Deut. 19:15). By tradition it has been learned that he "rises up" (against a man) in a suit involving an oath, as has been stated in the Treatise on Pleading.

2. In two instances the Torah accepts the testimony of one witness: a woman suspected of marital infidelity is not made to drink of the water of bitterness; and the neck of a heifer is not broken,

as has already been stated. Moreover, on the authority of the Rabbis, a woman is permitted to remarry on the evidence of one witness that her husband is dead.

3. Whenever the evidence of one witness answers the legal requirement, a woman or any person (otherwise) ineligible may act as witness, except in a case requiring an oath. For an oath can be imposed only on the evidence of a competent witness, one qualified to be associated with another witness, so that on their combined evidence, the defendant—now ordered to take an oath—would be liable to payment of compensation.

At the mouth of two or three witnesses (Deut. 19:15). (If the evidence can be established by two, why does the Bible add "three"?). To indicate that what applies to two witnesses applies also to three. Just as in the case of only two witnesses, if one of them is found to be a kinsman or (otherwise) ineligible, the evidence is void, so it is in the case of three witnesses, aye, even in the case of a hundred witnesses. If one of them is found to be a kinsman or (otherwise) ineligible, the evidence, whether in civil or in capital cases, is void.

4. This rule obtains only if all of them intended to act as witnesses. But if not all of them intended to give evidence, what are two brothers to do who find themselves in the midst of a crowd witnessing one man slaying another, or inflicting physical injury upon him, or snatching an object from him?

5. How is their intention ascertained? When many witnesses constituting one group appear in court, they are asked, "When you came to the scene of the murder, or of the assault, was it with the intention of giving evidence or for the purpose of looking on?" Those who reply that they had come with the crowd as mere spectators are placed on one side; those who declare that it was their purpose to act as witnesses, to give accurate information, are placed on another side. If among the would-be witnesses is one who is a kinsman or ineligible for other reasons, the entire evidence is null.

This obtains only if among the would-be witnesses is one who is a kinsman or ineligible for other reasons, but if all are eligible, even those who did not intend to testify are included among the witnesses and the case is decided on their evidence, seeing that they have been eyewitnesses of what has taken place and are in a position to give accurate evidence, and the culprit has received due warning. This applies to both civil and capital cases.

6. In case a deed was signed by many witnesses and it is found that one of them is a kinsman or (otherwise) disqualified, or that two of them are related to one another, and the witnesses to be consulted about the matter are no longer living, if there is conclusive evidence that they all sat down at the same time to sign, thus signifying their intention to act as witnesses, the deed is null; otherwise, it is certified by the other (eligible) witnesses. Why is the deed permitted to be certified by the others? We assume that the competent witnesses signed it, leaving space for a prominent man to sign, and that this kinsman or otherwise disqualified person came instead and signed without their knowledge.

7. Even if the disqualified witness is the first signatory, the deed is valid.

8. One who has given evidence in a capital charge is not to act as one of the judges in the case. He is not to argue either for or against the accused. If he says, "I see a point in favor of the accused," he is silenced, for it is said: *But one witness shall not testify against any person that he die* (Num. 35:30), whether his testimony will lead to acquittal or condemnation. What does the text mean by the phrase "that he die"? It means that once the witness has given evidence calculated to condemn a person to death, he shall refrain from making any further statement, that is, he gives evidence and keeps his peace.

In monetary matters, however, he may argue either for acquittal or for condemnation. But he cannot be included among the judges in the case, on the principle that no witness can serve in the capacity of judge—a principle which applies also to monetary cases.

9. The above-cited principle applies only to a matter which, according to Scripture, requires witnesses and trial judges. But in a matter which is of rabbinical origin, a witness may act as judge. Thus if a man brings a bill of divorce and says, "It was written and signed in my presence," he and two others may hand it over to the

woman, and it is as though she received it from a court-of-three. This applies to like cases.

CHAPTER VI

1. We have already stated that the certification of documents is a rabbinical ordinance (enacted) for the benefit of those in need of credit. Nevertheless, the certification must be before a court of three men, even if all the three be ordinary men, because it is a judicial procedure. Therefore, documents cannot be certified in the nighttime, as was already stated.

2. Documents are certified in one of the following five ways: (a) by the court, provided that the judges are able to identify the handwriting of the witnesses and say, "This is the signature of So-and-so, and this of So-and-so"; (b) by the signatories, who write their names in the presence of the judges; (c) by the signatories, who appear in court, each saying, "This is my signature and I attest the transaction recorded in the document"; (d) by other witnesses who, in case the signatories are no longer living or reside in another city, come and identify their handwriting; (e) by other documents attested by the same signatories. The judges compare the handwriting of the witnesses on the document (under consideration) with their handwriting on other documents and find a marked correspondence between them, so that it is evident to all of them that the signatures are identical.

3. A document certified by a comparison of signatures is valid only if the signatures are compared with those on deeds of sale of two fields, the use of which was enjoyed by the possessor for three consecutive years, in a truly public manner, without fear or apprehension of any claimant, in the fashion that owners enjoy the produce of their fields; or if the signatures are compared with their counterparts on two marriage contracts. Such comparison is valid only if the other documents are produced by a person other than the one who desires to certify the document under consideration; otherwise, there is the possibility that he has forged the signatures on the three documents.

So too, a document may be authenticated (by a comparison of the signatures thereon with those) on another which had been contested and was declared valid by the court. Authentication by means of only one document of the latter description is as valid as authentication by means of two deeds of sale or two marriage contracts.

4. If the court sets forth in writing, "We were in a session of three judges and the document was certified in our presence," the certification is valid, even though it does not specify in which of the five ways it was certified. There need be no apprehension that the court erred. However, it has been the practice of all courts that we have seen and heard of to state the way in which the document was certified by them.

5. It is not within the jurisdiction of one court to scrutinize the action of another court. It should be assumed that the members thereof are experts and did not err. The court has the right, however, to scrutinize the testimony of witnesses.

6. If three met to confirm a document and one of them died, they (the surviving two) must state in the writ of certification, "We were in a session of three, and one is no more." If they fail to do so, one who will see the writ might say that the document was confirmed by only two judges. Even if the phrase "in court" is inserted, one might say that the two were of the opinion that two men constitute a court. But if there is any indication in the writ that originally there were three, it is unnecessary to make reference to the demise of the third.

7. In case three met to confirm a document and two witnesses came and objected to one of them, accusing him of robbery or charging him with a like offense, and two others appear testifying that he has returned in repentance, if the testimony of the latter pair is given before the two judges have signed the writ of certification, the third too may sign it, because there are three (competent) judges (when the two sign the writ). If the testimony is given after the two have signed the writ, he is not permitted to sign, for it is as though he was nonexistent at the time when the other two signed it.

This holds good only if his eligibility was challenged on the ground of improper religious conduct; but if it was challenged on the ground of family blemish—as, for example, the witnesses asserted that his mother was not emancipated and that therefore he is a slave, or that his mother did not accept the Jewish religion and that therefore he is a heathen—and after the two others have signed the writ of certification it is ascertained that his family was unblemished and that he is eligible, he may add his signature to the writ. In this case the testimony (of the latter pair) discloses his status at the outset.

8. It is permitted to write out the writ of confirmation before the signatures on the document have been attested, for what really counts is the signing of the writ, not the writing thereof. The judges are not required to read the document which they confirm, because it (the document) is attested by the signatories thereof, although the judges do not know its contents.

CHAPTER VII

1. One may testify to the signature of one's kinsman. Thus, if a document bears the signatures of A and B who died or have gone abroad, and A's son comes and says, "This is my father's handwriting," and B's son comes and says, "This is my father's handwriting," they are deemed competent witnesses, as though they were not related to the signatories; and if a third is added to them, who testifies to the handwriting of both signatories, the document is certified.

2. Among the things to be believed, when those who attain their majority testify to what they saw while they were yet minors, is the following: one who has come of age is believed when he says, "This is my father's handwriting," "This is my teacher's handwriting," "This is my brother's handwriting," "I knew their handwriting while I was yet a minor," provided, however, that he associates with himself another who knew their handwriting when he was already mature.

3. If a document bears the signatures of A and B, and two wit-

nesses come and testify to their handwriting, the document is certified. But if one of them identifies the handwriting of A and the other the handwriting of B, the document is not certified, for two witnesses are required to identify the handwriting of each signatory. If, however, there is a third witness who identifies both signatures, the document is certified.

4. If the first witness says, "This is my handwriting," and he and another attest the handwriting of the second signatory (who is not available), the bond is not certified, because the collection of three quarters of the amount named in the bond depends on the testimony of the first witness. So too, if the handwriting of the second is identified by the brother or the son of the first and by another, the bond is not certified because the collection of three quarters of the amount depends on the testimony of kinsmen.

5. If one of two witnesses signed on a bond died, two witnesses are required to identify the handwriting of the deceased. If only one is available besides the surviving signatory, the latter writes his signature, even on a piece of clay, in the presence of two witnesses and places it before the court, so that the court knows his signature, making it unnecessary for him to identify it, and he and the other testify to the handwriting of the deceased. His own is identified without him (by the court).

6. If three meet to confirm a bond, two of whom know the handwriting of the witnesses and one does not, before they sign the (writ of certification) the two may testify before the third that they identify the signatures, and he too signs, because as was already stated, in any matter which is of rabbinical derivation, witnesses are qualified to act as judges. But after they (the two judges) have signed (the writ), they cannot testify before him (the third) in order to make it possible for him to affix his signature to it, (because at the time when they signed it, only two could authenticate the handwriting) and no bond can be confirmed unless all the judges are able to identify the signatures or unless witnesses testify to the handwriting before every member of the court.

7. If two witnesses signed on a bond died, and two others come

and say, "This is their handwriting, but they acted under compulsion," or "They were minors," or "They were (otherwise) ineligible," the bond is not certified. It is invalidated even if there are other witnesses who identify the signatures, or even if their handwriting can be compared with their handwriting on a bond that had been contested and subsequently declared valid. We set the two witnesses on the bond against the two who testify to their ineligibility, and the creditor does not collect his claim.

CHAPTER VIII

1. If a person signed on a bond comes to court to identify his signature and he is certain that the handwriting is his but does not remember the evidence (embodied in the bond) and has not the faintest recollection of the transaction of the loan recorded therein, he is forbidden to testify to his handwriting. The reason for requiring a witness to identify his handwriting is not that he authenticate his signature, but that he authenticate the obligation contained in the bond, of which his signature is to remind him, and since he does not recall it, he is not permitted to give evidence.

2. Whether he remembers the evidence, or recalls it on seeing his signature or on being reminded of it by others—aye, even if the one who brings it back to his memory is the second witness—as long as he is able to recall it, he may testify. But if the plaintiff reminds him, he is not permitted to testify, even if as a result of the reminder he now recalls the transaction, because it will give the plaintiff the impression that he is giving false evidence, testifying to a matter about which he does not know anything.

3. Therefore if the plaintiff is a scholar and reminds the witness (of the transaction) and the latter now recalls it, he may testify, for the scholar knows that but for the fact that the memory of the witness is now revived, he would not give evidence. For in monetary matters, the rabbinical rule is lenient. Even if the witness has for a long time forgotten the transaction, as long as the bond brings it back to his mind, he is permitted to give evidence.

4. Since the sole significance attaching to the identification of signatures on the part of those who are signed on it is the confirmation of the transaction recorded therein, if a bond is produced in court and the signatories say, "It is our handwriting but we have no knowledge of having acted as witnesses, we do not recall the loan or the sale it records," the bond is not certified. Those witnesses are to be classed with deaf-mutes, unless they recall their evidence. He who does not follow this ruling cannot discern between his right hand and his left hand.

But if their handwriting can be verified by comparing it with their handwriting on other documents, or if there are witnesses to identify their signatures, the bond is certified, and no heed is paid to their statement that they do not recall the evidence. For it is possible that they have retracted (their evidence) in order to render the bond void. It is as though they argued, "We were minors," or "We were (otherwise) ineligible," in which case they are not believed, since the bond can be authenticated without them.

For this reason all documents (produced in court) are certified and the appearance of the (original) witnesses, for questioning whether they remember the evidence, is not required. For even if they do appear in court and say, "We do not remember," no attention is paid to them, since the document can be confirmed without them.

5. Whether the witness set down his testimony in the bond (produced in court), or entered in his handwriting in a notebook the item, "So-and-so called on me on such-and-such a day to testify in his behalf (with regard to a loan) in such-and-such an amount," if he remembers (the transaction), or recalls it on being reminded of it by others, he may give evidence. If he does not remember or recall it, he is forbidden to give evidence, because his position is analogous to that of a man who is told by a reliable person, "So-and-so owes So-and-so such-and-such an amount of money," and he gives evidence to this effect, while he knows nothing about it—save what he heard from another.

CHAPTER IX

1. There are ten classes of ineligibles, and whoever belongs to any of them is disqualified from giving evidence. They are as follows: women, slaves, minors, the mentally deficient, deaf-mutes, the blind, transgressors, the self-abased, kinsmen, and interested witnesses—ten in all.

2. Women are disqualified as witnesses by biblical law, as it is said *At the mouth of two witnesses* (Deut. 19: 15). The text employs the masculine, not the feminine gender.

3. So too, a *ṭumṭum* and a hermaphrodite are disqualified, because their sex is doubtful. Anyone whose eligibility is doubtful is disqualified, for it is on the evidence given by the witness that money is transferred and the sentence of conviction is passed, and according to biblical law no money is to change hands, nor is punishment to be inflicted, in a case of doubt.

4. Slaves are ineligible as witnesses by biblical law, as it is said: *Then shall ye do unto him as he had purposed to do unto his brother* (Deut. 19: 19). This implies that his status must be that of the one against whom he testifies; just as the latter is a son of the Covenant, he too must be a son of the Covenant. This stricture applies with even greater force to a heathen, for if a slave who is bound to observe some of the commandments is disqualified, it stands to reason that a heathen should all the more be disqualified.

5. One who is half slave and half free is ineligible.

6. A slave who has been manumitted but has not yet received his writ of emancipation is ineligible. His testimony is admissible only after he has obtained his writ of emancipation and has become a full son of the Covenant.

7. Minors are disqualified as witnesses by biblical law, as it is said *Then both the men . . . shall stand before the Lord* (Deut. 19: 17)—*men,* not minors. Even if the minor is discreet and intelligent, he is ineligible until he has grown two hairs after the completion of thirteen years. If, on reaching the age of twenty, he has not grown two hairs and shows any of the symptoms of a eunuch,

he is reckoned as a eunuch and is eligible to testify. But if he shows none of those symptoms, he may not give evidence until he has passed the greater part of the ordinary term of life, as was stated in the Treatise on Marriage.

8. In the case of a minor who has reached the general age of maturity, if the upper tokens of adolescence appeared, no further investigation is required; otherwise his evidence is inadmissible till further investigation. If one who is thirteen years and one day old has grown two hairs but does not know anything about business, his evidence pertaining to immovable property is not accepted, since he is unable to exercise due care in regard to matters with which he is unfamiliar. But his evidence with regard to movable property is accepted, because he is mature.

9. The mentally deficient is incompetent by biblical law, because he is not subject to the commandments. By "mentally deficient" is to be understood not only one who walks around naked, breaks things, and throws stones, but anyone who is confused in mind, invariably mixed up with respect to some matters, although with respect to other matters he speaks to the point and asks pertinent questions; nevertheless his evidence is inadmissible and he is included among the mentally deficient.

In case of an epileptic, during a fit he is ineligible; in the interval (between fits), he is eligible, whether the paroxysm occurs periodically or at irregular intervals, provided that he is not mentally disordered all the time, for there are epileptics who are always confused in mind. The question of the admissibility of the evidence of epileptics requires careful consideration.

10. The inordinately foolish, who are unable to discriminate between contradictory matters and do not comprehend things as normal people do, also those who are impulsive and hasty in judgment and act like madmen, are classed with the mentally deficient. Discretionary power is vested in the judge in this matter, as it is impossible to lay down detailed rules on this subject.

11. The status of the *ḥereš* (the deaf-mute) is that of the mentally deficient, because he is not of sound mind and is not bound

to observe the commandments. This applies also to the speaking deaf and the hearing mute; although the evidence of either of the last two may be convincing and the mind of the witness sound, it is required that he give oral testimony, and that he be able to hear the judges and the charge addressed to him.

So too, if the witness has lost his speech and presents his evidence in writing, his testimony is invalid, although he was tested (as to his competence) in the manner in which he would be tested if he were to divorce his wife and his evidence was found to be correct. The only instance when his testimony is accepted is in the case of an *'ăgunah,* in which event the Rabbis favor leniency.

12. The blind, though they recognize voices and thus identify persons, are ineligible by biblical law, as it is said *he being a witness, whether he hath seen* (Lev. 5:1), only one who can see may give evidence. The blind in one eye is eligible as witness.

CHAPTER X

1. Transgressors are ineligible as witnesses by biblical law, for it is said *Put not thy hand with the wicked to be an unrighteous witness* (Exod. 23:1). The traditional interpretation of this injunction is: "Accept not the wicked as a witness." Aye, if a competent witness knows that his fellow witness is a transgressor, but the judges do not know it, he is forbidden to join with him, even if the evidence is true, for by thus associating with him, the latter's testimony is accepted and the religiously competent man is in league with the wicked. It is hardly necessary to state that if the eligible witness knows that the other is a false witness, he is forbidden to give evidence, as it is said: *Put not thy hand with the wicked.*

2. Who is a transgressor? Whoever violates a negative command carrying with it the penalty of flogging is a transgressor and is therefore ineligible. For Scripture denominates him who is punished by flogging "wicked," as it is said *then it shall be, if the wicked man deserve to be beaten* (Deut. 25:2). It goes without saying, that whoever has incurred the sentence of death by the

court is ineligible, as it is said *that he is wicked deserving of death* (Num. 35:31).

3. If one transgresses a negative command punishable, by the law of Scripture, by flogging, he is ineligible by biblical law. If he disregards a rabbinical enactment, the violation whereof is punishable by disciplinary flogging, he is ineligible on the authority of the Rabbis. To cite concrete examples: if one eats the meat of a beast with milk, or eats nĕḇelah or reptiles or the like, whether he eats any of these things to satisfy his appetite, or in a spirit of defiance; or if he desecrates the first day of a festival, or wears *ša'aṭnez*—that which is *šua'* (hackled), *ṭawuy* (spun), and *nuz* (woven)—if he commits any of these transgressions, he is disqualified by biblical law. But if he eats the meat of a fowl with milk or desecrates the second day of a festival—the day observed in the Diaspora—or wears a woolen garment wherein a linen thread is woven and its place is not known, or the like, he is disqualified by rabbinical law.

We have already enumerated all the transgressions punishable by flogging. We have also stated in connection with each precept which is forbidden by the Bible, and which is forbidden by rabbinical authority.

4. There are also other transgressors who, though they have to make reparation and are (therefore) not liable to flogging, are nevertheless ineligible as witnesses. In view of the fact that they have taken by force money that does not belong to them, they are disqualified, as it is said *if a witness of violence rise up against any man* (Deut. 19:16). Among transgressors of this description are thieves and robbers; even if they have made restitution, they are disqualified from the time that they had stolen or robbed.

So too, one who was proved a plotting witness in a monetary case, although he has made restitution, is disqualified by biblical law from acting as witness in any suit. When does his disqualification begin? From the time that he had given (false) evidence in court, although he was not confuted till after the lapse of a long time.

So too, in case of a loan on interest, both lender and borrower are disqualified. If the interest charged was direct, they are ineligible by biblical law; if indirect, they are ineligible on the authority of the Rabbis. So too, whoever is guilty of what according to the Rabbis is robbery is barred by rabbinical authority from giving evidence. To cite a case in point: those who coerce a sale, that is, seize land or chattel against the desire of the owner, although they pay for it, are disqualified by rabbinical law.

In like manner, herdsmen, whether of small cattle or large, are disqualified if the cattle are their own, because the presumption is that they stretch out their hands after robbery, allow their cattle to graze in fields and vineyards belonging to others. Therefore, as a general rule, herdsmen are ineligible. Those who breed small cattle in Palestine are ineligible; those who breed them outside Palestine are eligible. It is permissible, however, to breed large cattle everywhere.

So too, tax farmers in general are ineligible. The presumption is that they exact (from the community) a sum in excess of that allowed them by the government, and appropriate the surplus. Tax collectors in general are eligible; if, however, it is discovered that they have collected, even once, more than what they are entitled to, they are disqualified.

So too, pigeon fowlers in populous areas are ineligible, because the presumption is that they decoy pigeons that belong to others without paying for them. Traders in the seventh year produce—that is, those who are usually idle but when the Sabbatical year comes round traffic in crops—are ineligible, because the presumption is that they gather the crops of the seventh year and trade in them.

A dice player is disqualified if he has no other occupation. In view of the fact that he contributes nothing to the welfare of society, the presumption is that he makes his living out of dice playing, which is a form of robbery. The rule holds good not only for those who play dice, but also for those who play with nutshells and pomegranate peels. Likewise, the ineligibility predicated of pigeon fowlers extends to those who indulge in the racing of cattle, beasts of chase, or birds, stipulating that the owner of the one that passes or overcomes the other shall get both, or any similar agreement made with regard to this sport, provided that the person under consideration has no other occupation. All these are disqualified on rabbinical authority.

5. A tenant farmer who takes a small quantity of the produce that ripens during the months of Nisan and Tishri before his work is completed, though he does it without the knowledge of the owner, is not deemed a thief and is eligible to be a witness, because the owner does not mind his taking it. This rule applies to similar cases.

CHAPTER XI

1. Whoever has no knowledge of the Scriptures, the Mishnah, and right conduct has the status of a (potential) sinner and is, by rabbinical authority, ineligible as witness. The presumption is that a person on such a low level will commit most of the transgressions that assail him.

2. Therefore an *'am ha-'areṣ* is not invited as witness, nor is his testimony accepted. If, however, he is known to be a person who is engaged in religious acts and the practice of benevolence, and leads a righteous life, so that "right conduct" may be ascribed to him, his testimony is accepted, even though he is ignorant, i.e., is devoid of knowledge of the Scriptures and the Mishnah.

3. It follows therefore that every scholar is to be deemed eligible, unless he is found to be ineligible, and that every ignorant person is to be regarded as ineligible, unless it is known that he walks in the way of the righteous.

4. Whoever, therefore, accepts the evidence of an ignorant man before the latter has established his eligibility or before witnesses come and testify that he is engaged in religious acts and that his conduct is ethical, is a *heḏyoṭ*. He will be called to account for causing loss of money to an Israelite on the evidence of an unrighteous man.

5. Likewise the self-abased are disqualified on the authority of the Rabbis. These comprise men who walk in the street eating in

the sight of the public, and those who walk about naked in the street while they are engaged in a repugnant occupation, and those who do similar things indicative of a lack of sense of shame. They are on a level with dogs and will not hesitate to give false evidence. Included in this class are those who publicly accept charity from heathens when it is possible for them to accept it privately. They thus demean themselves and have no compunction in doing it. All these are disqualified by rabbinical law.

6. What is the difference between one who is ineligible by biblical law and one who is ineligible by rabbinical authority? In the case of one who is ineligible by biblical law, his testimony is void, even if his ineligibility has not been announced in the Synagogues and Houses of Study; in the case of one who is ineligible by rabbinical authority, public announcement of his ineligibility is required. Therefore, all the evidence given by the latter before public proclamation was made is accepted, so that those in whose behalf he has testified do not forfeit their rights. They were unaware of his disqualification, since he is disqualified by rabbinical authority only.

7. In ritual matters one witness is believed, even if he be one who is ineligible in other matters. For if a person who is religiously delinquent slaughters an animal, his act is valid. He is believed when he says, "I slaughtered it according to the law." However, if he is suspected of disregarding a religious command, he is not deemed trustworthy if the matter involving the command concerns him (his interests), but he is deemed trustworthy if it concerns others.

8. It follows therefrom that one who is suspected of disregarding a certain religious command may act as judge or witness in a matter involving that command if it concerns others. The presumption is that no man will sin that others might benefit thereby. For example, an 'am ha-'areṣ is believed when he says, "The crops sold by So-and-so are fit for use"; one who is suspected of selling the flesh of a firstling is believed when he says, "The flesh sold by So-and-so is ordinary flesh." This applies also to other ritual

matters. For in ritual matters transgressors will be deterred by fear, but not so in monetary matters.

9. The kings of Israel may neither testify nor be testified against, because they resort to violence and do not submit to the authority of judges. But a High Priest may be testified against, and he may testify before the Supreme Court in a suit that concerns the king, as was stated before.

10. As to informers, epicureans, and apostates, the Rabbis did not deem it necessary to include them among the ineligibles, because they enumerated only the wicked among the Israelites. But these rebellious disbelievers are on a lower level than heathens. In the case of heathens, we are bound neither to rescue them (from the pit) nor cast them (into it), and the pious among them are assured of a portion in the world to come. The above mentioned, however, are to be cast into the pit, but not rescued, and they have no portion in the world to come.

CHAPTER XII

1. If two witnesses testify that a person committed a certain transgression, although he had received no warning and is therefore not liable to flagellation, he is nevertheless disqualified to be a witness. He becomes ineligible by reason of religious delinquency. This applies only to acts the sinfulness of which is well known to Israelites, such, for instance, as swearing falsely or needlessly, robbing or stealing, eating nĕbelah, and transgressions of a like character. But if there is any likelihood that the offense with which he is charged was committed by him in error, he must be warned first, and then he becomes ineligible. To cite a few examples: if the witnesses saw him making a knot or untying it on the Sabbath, it is imperative that they remind him that this constitutes a violation of the Sabbath, because most people are unaware of it.

So too, if they saw him doing work on the Sabbath or on a festival, they should remind him that it is the Sabbath (or a festival), because he may have forgotten it. So too, in the case of a habitual dice player, or tax farmer, or tax collector—who exacts a higher rate than he is entitled to and turns it to his own use—it is the duty of the witnesses to inform the offender that he who indulges in any of these practices is unfit to give evidence, for most people do not know that these things are forbidden. So it is with practices of a like nature.

The general principle is: if the transgression is such as to make it clear to the witnesses that the offender knew that he was a transgressor and committed it wantonly, he is disqualified, though he had not been given warning and is not subject to flogging.

2. No man becomes ineligible on his own admission of religious delinquency. For example: if a person appears in court and says that he has stolen or robbed, or loaned money on interest, although he has to make restitution on his own admission, he is not disqualified as witness. Likewise, if he says that he has eaten nĕḇelah or cohabited with a woman forbidden to him, he is not disqualified —unless there are two witnesses who testify against him—for no man can incriminate himself.

Therefore, if A testifies that B loaned money on interest, and C testifies, "He [B] made a loan to me on interest," B is disqualified on the evidence of A and C. As to C, though he admits that he contracted a loan on interest, he cannot incriminate himself. He is accounted trustworthy with regard to B, but not with regard to himself.

So too, if one testifies that So-and-so committed sodomy with him (the witness), whether (the offense was committed) against his will or with his consent, his evidence and that of another are combined to put the accused to death. If he declares, "So-and-so committed adultery with my wife," his evidence and that of another are combined to condemn the adulterer to death, but they are not combined to convict *her*. This applies also to similar cases. If he says, "So-and-so committed an unnatural crime with my ox," his evidence and that of another are combined to condemn the ox to death, for a man is not a relative to his property.

3. If two witnesses testify that a certain man is ineligible because

he committed one of the aforementioned transgressions and two others come and testify that he has repented and undergone a reformation, or that he was flogged, he is eligible. But if the latter set of witnesses contradict the former, asserting that he did not commit the offense and is therefore not disqualified, his status is doubtful and he is ineligible. Hence his testimony is not admissible, money is not made over on his evidence, and he cannot act as judge until it becomes definitely known that he has repented.

4. Whoever commits an offense punishable by flogging regains his status of eligibility as soon as he repents or is flogged; but those who are disqualified by reason of extortion or robbery, even if they subsequently make restitution, are not reinstated until they have repented, and remain ineligible until it is ascertained that they have reformed from their evil ways.

5. When may usurers be considered to have repented? When they tear up their notes of their own accord and undergo a thorough reformation so that they will not advance money on interest even to a heathen.

6. When may dice players be deemed to have repented? When they voluntarily break their blocks of wood and undergo a complete reformation, desisting from playing even as a pastime.

7. When may pigeon fowlers be considered to have repented? When they break up the receptacles wherein they trap them (the pigeons) and undergo a change of heart, refusing to indulge in this practice even in the wilderness.

8. When may traffickers in the produce of the Sabbatical year be said to have repented? When another Sabbatical year comes round and they are put to the test. Moreover, a mere verbal repentance is unsatisfactory. They must obligate themselves (to make restitution), setting down in writing, "I, So-and-so, the son of So-and-so, have amassed two hundred zuz by trading in the seventh-year crop; they are made over by me to the poor as a gift."

9. When may a perjurer be deemed to have repented? When he comes to a court where he is unknown and says, "I am suspected

of perjury," or when a court, where he is unknown, imposes upon him an oath in a suit involving a considerable sum of money and he pays rather than take the oath.

So too, if a slaughterer, who himself does (the slaughtering) and inspecting of the meat which he sells, has passed ṭĕrefah as ritually fit for consumption, which puts him in the class of those who eat ṭĕrefah and are ineligible as witnesses, he is barred from giving testimony until it has become evident from the life that he lives that he has repented of the evil (he has done). Let him don black garments, and wrap himself up in black garments, and repair to a place where he is unknown and look for an opportunity of restoring (to the owner) a lost article of appreciable value, or of pronouncing ṭĕrefah meat of considerable value.

10. Likewise a false witness who goes to a place where he is unknown and is offered an appreciable sum of money to give false testimony, but refuses the offer, gives evidence of genuine repentance, and is therefore rehabilitated. This applies also to similar cases.

CHAPTER XIII

1. By scriptural authority, kinsmen are ineligible to act as witnesses, as it is said: *The fathers shall not be put to death for the children, neither shall the children be put to death for the fathers* (Deut. 24:16). It is learned by tradition that included in this negative command is the exhortation not to condemn fathers to death on the testimony of their sons, nor sons on the testimony of their fathers. This applies also to other relatives. By biblical law only paternal relatives are disqualified, to wit: father, son, and son's son; brothers by the same father; sons of brothers (by the same father); uncles and brothers' sons. By rabbinical authority, even maternal relatives and relatives by marriage are ineligible to testify concerning one another.

2. The law of disqualification on the ground of kinship does not apply to proselytes. Even in the case of two twin brothers who have embraced the Jewish religion, one may testify with respect

to the other. For the status of a proselyte who accepts Judaism is like that of a newborn child.

3. Brothers, whether by the same mother or the same father, are relatives in the first degree; their sons are relatives in the second degree; their grandsons in the third degree.

4. Certain it is that a relative in the third degree and one in the first degree, and it goes without saying that a relative in the third degree and one in the second degree, may testify with respect to one another. But relatives in the second degree, and, it goes without saying, a relative in the second degree and one in the first degree, are ineligible to testify with respect to one another.

5. A father and son are considered relatives in the first degree. It follows therefore that a grandfather and his son's son are ineligible to testify with respect to one another; that a great-grandfather and his great-grandson, who is of the fourth generation, may testify one with respect to the other, their relationship being that of one in the third degree and one in the first degree. The same holds good if the consanguinity is in the female line. Thus two sisters, or a brother and a sister, whether by the same father or the same mother, are relatives in the first degree; their children, whether male or female, are relatives in the second degree; their sons' sons or daughters' daughters are relatives in the third degree. The procedure in determining the degree in the female line is identical with that in determining the degree in the male line.

6. Whoever is ineligible to testify with respect to the wife is also ineligible to testify with respect to the husband, for the husband is as his wife. Anyone who is ineligible to testify with respect to the husband is also ineligible to testify with respect to the wife, for the wife is as her husband.

7. In the case of two women who are relatives in the second degree, their husbands may testify with respect to one another. But if the relationship (of the women) is one of the first degree as is the case if one of them married the mother, and the other the daughter, the husbands are ineligible to testify one with respect to the other.

8. Likewise, the husbands of two sisters are ineligible to testify one with respect to the other, for the kinship of their wives is one in the first degree.

9. Neither may a man testify concerning the son of his wife's sister, or concerning the husband of his wife's sister's daughter; but he may testify concerning the son of his wife's sister's husband, if the son is by another wife.

10. While one may not testify concerning a kinswoman's husband, one may testify concerning his relatives, as, for instance, his son or his brother. So too, while one may not testify concerning a kinsman's wife, one may testify concerning her relatives.

11. The father of the bride and the father of the groom may testify with respect to one another.

12. Stepbrothers, who have a brother in common, may testify with respect to one another, because they are in no way related to each other. For example: if Rachel, the wife of Joseph, had a son by him by the name of Reuben, and Joseph was also the father of Manasseh born to him by another wife, then Joseph died and Rachel married again, giving birth to a son called Judah, Manasseh and Judah may testify concerning one another.

13. Husband and wife stand to each other in the relation of one in the first degree to one in the first degree. Therefore, he may not testify concerning her son, her son's wife, her daughter, her daughter's husband, her father, her mother, her stepfather or her stepmother.

14. One's betrothed wife, although the marriage has not yet been consummated, is with respect to the matter of testimony as one's married wife. This applies only to testimony concerning her. But if he gave evidence concerning her relatives, such as her sister's husband, her son, her daughter, or the like, it is not invalidated.

15. The disqualification by Scripture of kinsmen from testifying concerning one another is not to be accounted for on the presumption that they love one another, for one may not testify either for or against a relative. The disqualification is a biblical decree. Therefore both friend and foe are eligible to act as wit-

nesses, though not as judges. For the decree of Scripture is restricted to relatives.

CHAPTER XIV

1. In case ineligibility to act as witness is due to kinship with the wife, if she died, even if she left children, the kinship is severed and evidence is admissible.

2. If a person was in possession of evidence concerning another to whom he was not related, and subsequently became the latter's son-in-law; or if he was in possession of evidence when he had the faculty of hearing and subsequently became deaf; or when he had the faculty of sight and later became blind, though he is still able to determine the area and define the boundaries of the land with respect to which he is ready to testify; or (he was in possession of evidence) when he was sane and later became demented—in all these instances, he is barred from giving testimony. But if he was in possession of evidence concerning a man to whom he was unrelated, then became his son-in-law, and subsequently his daughter died; or when he had the faculty of hearing, then became deaf, and subsequently regained his hearing; or when he had the faculty of sight, then lost it, and subsequently regained it, his evidence is admissible.

The general rule is: evidence which the witness is eligible to give at the beginning and at the end is admissible even though there is an interval during which he is disqualified. If he is ineligible at the beginning, even though he becomes competent at the end, his evidence is inadmissible. Therefore if a minor is in possession of evidence which he offers on coming of age, it is not valid.

3. There are, however, matters in regard to which credence is put in the testimony given by a man come of age to what he saw while he was a minor—matters bearing upon ordinances instituted by the Rabbis. They are as follows:

A person is believed when he says, "This is the handwriting of my father," or "of my teacher," or "of my brother," because the confirmation of documents is a rabbinical enactment. (He is believed when he says,) "I remember that at the marriage of that woman all the customs in vogue at the weddings of virgins were followed," because most women are virgins at marriage and the *ḳĕṯubbah* is of rabbinical origin. (He is accounted trustworthy when he says,) "This is the place of a grave area," because the uncleanness attaching to a grave area is a rabbinical ordinance. (He is accounted trustworthy when he says,) "Thus far we used to walk on the Sabbath," because the restriction of the Sabbath limit to two thousand cubits is of rabbinical derivation. (He is believed when he says,) "So-and-so used to go from school to take a ritual bath in order to eat of the heave offering in the evening"; or "He used to share the heave offering with us"; or "My family used to send by me *ḥallah* or other gifts to So-and-so, the priest"; or "I have it from my father that this (priestly family) is unblemished and that family is blemished"; or "We partook of the refreshments served at the severance party of So-and-so given by his brothers in order to make public that their brother So-and-so married a woman who was unsuited to him." For these testimonies (the last five) have no other purpose than that of either confirming or denying the right of the priest to eat of the heave offering instituted by the Rabbis.

4. While evidence with regard to the aforementioned matters is admitted if an adult testifies that he saw them when he was a minor, it is not admitted if a proselyte or an emancipated slave testifies that he saw them prior to his conversion or his emancipation.

5. If a man in possession of evidence concerning another turns robber, his evidence with reference to his signature is not admitted. But if the court knew before he turned robber that his signature was affixed to the document, the document is valid.

If one who is in possession of evidence concerning another becomes the son-in-law of the latter, he is barred from identifying his signature; others, however, may, and the document is valid, even if the court did not know before he became the other man's son-in-law that his signature was affixed to it. There is no analogy between one who is incompetent on the ground of religious delinquency and one who is incompetent by reason of kinship, for one who is incompetent on the ground of religious delinquency is suspected of forgery.

6. A deed which is signed by only two witnesses who are related to each other or one of whom is incompetent by reason of religious delinquency is worthless, even if it is delivered in the presence of two competent witnesses, because it bears its own disqualification.

7. If a person assigns all his possessions to two men and the deed is signed by two witnesses who are related to one of the recipients and not to the other, the deed is invalid, because there is but one body of testimony. But if he states in the deed, "I assign this field to A and that field to B," and the witnesses are related to one and not related to the other, the gift bestowed upon the one who is not related is made over to him, for these are two independent testimonies, although the two gifts are embodied in one deed. This is analogous to the case of one who says to two men, "Be my witnesses that I have bestowed upon A such-and-such an amount of money and upon B such-and-such an amount, and that I have borrowed from C such-and-such an amount"; although all is incorporated in one document and the assignor is the same, the case is nevertheless one which presents three bodies of independent testimony.

CHAPTER XV

1. Any evidence from which the witness may derive benefit is inadmissible, for it is as though he would testify in his own behalf. Therefore if the right of a community to its bathhouse or town square is contested, none of the residents is eligible to testify or to act as judge, unless one renounces one's interest in it by a perfect ḳinyan, in which case one may testify or act as judge.

2. If a scroll of the Law belonging to a community has been stolen, none of the judges thereof may try the culprit, nor may any of the residents of the town give evidence against him, be-

cause the scroll of the Law is for public reading and no one can relinquish his duty of listening to the reading of the Law. The same applies to similar objects.

3. If a man says, "I bequeath a maneh to the poor people of the city," the judges of the community are ineligible to try the case, nor are the residents eligible to give evidence. This rule obtains only if the poor depend for their support upon the townsfolk, who are assessed for charity, in which case even if two of the people say, "We will contribute our rate of the tax and testify," no notice is taken of their offer. For since the poor depend upon the community for their maintenance, those who make the offer will derive satisfaction from the fact that their wards will receive more than the share usually allotted them. This rule applies also to similar cases.

4. If a parcel of land is jointly owned by two men and the title of one of them is contested, his partner is not eligible to testify for him, unless he relinquishes his share in it, declaring by a ḳinyan that he has made it over to the other and that he will pay him the value thereof in the event a creditor of his should seize it for a debt. If he fulfills this requirement, he may testify in his partner's behalf. This holds good in similar cases.

5. If one's title to a field is contested, as long as the produce thereof has not yet been gathered, the tenant farmer may not testify for the possessor because he would prefer that the field remain in the hands of its present possessor in order that he get his share of the crop. But if the crop has already been removed, he may testify. In the case of a lessee, however, if he brings the rent and says, "Whoever is declared the owner of the field may have it," he is qualified to testify. But if he has already paid the rent to the possessor of the field, he is barred from giving evidence, for should the field be awarded to the contestant, he would have to pay rent for all the years that he has occupied it. The same rule obtains in similar cases.

6. If A contracts a debt, B acting as his surety, and C comes and contests A's title to a field in his possession, seeking to take it away from him, then B, the surety, is eligible to testify that the field

belongs to A, provided that A also owns another field, which can be distrained for the payment of the debt he owes. In this case, B has nothing to gain (by his testimony), for should the field (in question) be given to C, there is another field left to settle the debt.

So too, if one sells a field to one man and later sells another field to another man, the buyer of the first is qualified to testify in favor of the second, provided that the seller owns an unencumbered field, worth the price of the first. The purchaser of the first has nothing to gain if the (contested) field remains in the possession of the purchaser of the second. For should the field of the first be seized by the seller's creditor, he could come back to the seller, who still has another field, and be compensated for his loss.

CHAPTER XVI

1. If A robs B of a field or a garment and C comes and contests A's right to it, claiming that it is his, B is not qualified to testify that the field or garment does not belong to C, because he is likely to prefer that the field or garment be retained by A, who has robbed him of it, in the hope of retrieving it. There is the possibility that the evidence on which he expects to recover it from A will not enable him to recover it from C.

So too, if A sells or bequeaths to C the field of which he has robbed B, and D contests C's right to it, B is not eligible to testify that it does not belong to D. His reason for doing so may be that he will find it easier to recover the field from C.

2. If A robs B of a garment and sells it to C, and D challenges the purchaser's right to it, and A dies in the meantime, B may testify that it does not belong to D, because under these circumstances B can never recover the garment, since the purchaser has acquired it by the (owner's) abandonment of hope of recovery and change of ownership, and now that A is dead there is no one to refund him the money he paid for it. But if A is still living, B is ineligible to give evidence, even though (the object concerning

which he is to testify) is a garment, because it is to his advantage that the garment should not be turned over to D. He can then bring evidence that A has robbed him of it, and will be indemnified by the latter.

So too, if the garment is in the possession of A's heirs, B may not testify (against D), because if it remains in the possession of the heirs, it will eventually be restored to him. This applies also to similar cases.

3. If A sells a field to B without a guarantee and C contests B's right to it, seeking to take it away from him, A is ineligible to testify for B. For though he is not responsible to him for it, A would prefer that it remain in the possession of B, so that if a creditor (of A) seize it in payment of a debt due to him, he be not branded as one to whom may be applied the scriptural words *A wicked man borrows and does not repay* (Ps. 37:21).

4. If A sells a cow or a garment to B and C disputes B's right to it, seeking to take it away from him, A is eligible to testify that it belongs to B, because even if B retains possession of it, A's creditor cannot seize chattel in payment of a debt due to him, even if the debtor has given it as security. This ruling obtains only if B affirms that he knows, beyond the shadow of a doubt, that A, the seller, was the original and lawful owner of the cow or the garment. But if B does not make such a positive statement, A is barred from giving evidence prejudicial to C, for should the cow or garment be taken away from B, the latter would come back to A, and claim the money he has paid him, saying, "You sold me what did not belong to you, for there are witnesses who testify that it belongs to C."

Furthermore, A is permitted to give evidence prejudicial to C, thus confirming B's right to retain the chattel in dispute only if there are witnesses to the effect that A never owned any landed property. But if there are no such witnesses, his evidence even with regard to the cow or garment is not admissible. Why is his evidence inadmissible? There is the possibility that A mortgaged the cow or the garment along with landed property, and inserted in the note the phrase, "Whatever I shall acquire," in which case the creditor is entitled even to the cow or garment. Therefore, in these circumstances A is ineligible to give testimony, because it is to his interest that the chattel remain in the possession of B, that his creditor may seize it in payment of his debt. The same rule applies to similar cases.

All such matters depend upon the judgment and the reasoning power of the judge, his grasp of the fundamental rules of evidence, his ability to know and discern the effect which any situation is likely to produce. If in his opinion the witness stands to gain, even in a remote and indirect way, by the evidence to be given by him, he should not permit him to testify.

Just as the person in question is disqualified from being a witness because he might be an interested party, even so he is disqualified from acting as judge in the case. This applies also to other ineligibles. Whatever precludes one from acting as witness precludes one from acting as judge.

5. Therefore two men who are related to each other cannot be ordained to serve in the same Sanhedrin—whether it be a Small or the Great Sanhedrin. It seems to me, however, that in the case of the intercalation of the year, if it becomes necessary to appoint additional judges to form the maximum number of seven—as was set forth in the Treatise on the Sanctification of the New Moon—and among those appointed are some who are related to one another, it does not matter.

6. Whoever is competent to judge is also competent to testify. There are, however, those who are competent to testify but are not competent to judge. The latter class includes a friend, a foe, a proselyte, and an emancipated slave. One advanced in age, a eunuch, a bastard, and one who is blind in one eye are eligible to testify but are ineligible to try capital cases, as has already been stated.

CHAPTER XVII

1. If a person is advised by others that So-and-so has transgressed such-and-such a negative command, or that So-and-so has bor-

rowed money from So-and-so, even if his informants be many in number and great in wisdom and fear of God, and he believes what they tell him as though he had witnessed it himself, he is not permitted to give evidence. He may testify only if he saw it with his own eyes, or if the borrower personally admitted the loan to him, saying to him, "Bear testimony that So-and-so has loaned me a maneh," as it is said *he being a witness, whether he hath seen it or known* (Lev. 5:1). There is no testimony that can be established by seeing (without knowing) or knowing (without seeing) but testimony relating to a monetary transaction. One who bases his testimony on what others have told him is a false witness and transgresses a negative command, as it is said: *Thou shalt not bear false witness against thy neighbor* (Exod. 20:13).

2. Therefore even in civil cases words of admonition are addressed to the witnesses. How are they admonished? They are cautioned in the presence of all (who are in court) of the far-reaching consequences of false evidence and the degradation both in this world and in the world to come attendant upon him who is guilty of it. Then all the people, with the exception of the oldest of the witnesses, are sent out of court. The judges address him, saying, "Tell us, how do you know that So-and-so is in debt to So-and-so?" If his reply is, "He himself told me that he is in debt to the claimant," or "So-and-so informed me that the defendant is in debt to So-and-so," his evidence is of no account. His evidence is considered only if he declares, "The defendant admitted in our presence that he is in debt to the claimant." Then the second witness is called in and is similarly examined. If their statements tally, the judges discuss the case and render a decision.

3. If the claimant puts his witnesses in a hiding place, and they overhear the defendant admit the loan to the claimant privately, saying, "It is true that I owe you such-and-such an amount, but I am afraid to admit it (in the presence of witnesses), lest you compel me to go to court," the evidence is disregarded. The admission must be made in the presence of witnesses.

4. Whether the borrower avows the claim in the form of an admission, declaring in the presence of witnesses, "I owe the claim-

ant such-and-such an amount," or he says (to the men present), "You are my witnesses," or "Be my witnesses," aye, even if the lender invites them to act as witnesses and the borrower remains silent in a manner indicative of good faith, they are accepted as witnesses. It is needless to state that if the borrower confirms his admission by a ḳinyan, or if he says, "Indite a note that I owe the lender such-and-such an amount," or says something else to the same effect, it constitutes an admission, and on the strength thereof the witnesses are permitted to give evidence.

5. In the event a teacher says to his disciple, "You know that if I were given all the money in the world, I would not tell a lie; now, So-and-so owes me one maneh, and I have only one witness against him, go and join him," if the disciple joins the other he is a false witness.

6. If a teacher says to his disciple, "Stand by the witness (I have); you need not give testimony; the borrower, on seeing you, will think that there are two witnesses against him and, prompted by fear, will of his own accord admit my claim," the disciple is forbidden to stand by, creating the impression that he is a witness, even though he does not give evidence. Concerning this and like instances, it is said *Keep thee far from a false matter* (Exod. 23:7).

7. Whoever hires false witnesses to testify against a person is exempt from the judgment of the court but is liable to the judgment of Heaven. So too, in a case where there is but one witness and he, suppressing the evidence he possesses, fails to give it, he is exempt from the judgment of the court but is liable to the judgment of Heaven.

CHAPTER XVIII

1. Whoever gives evidence which is refuted by witnesses is called a plotting (false) witness. It is a positive command to do unto him as he purposed to do unto the man against whom he testified. If the offense with which the accused is charged involves death by stoning, all who testify against him and are found to be plotting witnesses are stoned; if it involves death by burning, they are

burned. The same applies to the other modes of execution. If their evidence against him entails the penalty of flogging, each of them is flogged like all offenders who incur the penalty of flogging; the physical endurance of each is determined and he is flogged accordingly. If they testify against him in a case which renders him liable to compensation, the amount involved is divided among them, taking into account the number of witnesses, and each pays his proportionate share. But no flogging is inflicted upon the witnesses in cases where they have to pay compensation.

2. The foregoing rule applies only to witnesses who are found plotting. But if two sets of witnesses contradict each other, the evidence of neither (set) is accepted, and neither suffers punishment, because there is no way of knowing which is giving false evidence.

How is contradicted evidence to be distinguished from refuted evidence? The former affects the evidence, to wit: one set affirms, "It did happen"; the other asserts, "It did not happen," or the evidence of the latter *implies* that it did not happen. Refuted evidence incriminates the witnesses, to wit: those who refute the first witnesses do not know whether or not the thing did take place.

To illustrate the difference: if witnesses come and say, "We saw that the defendant killed a person," or "that he borrowed money *from* So-and-so on such-and-such a day and in such-and-such a place," and following the questions put to these, two other witnesses appear, saying, "On that very day and in that very place, we were together with you and with the principals all day. What you say is not true. The accused did not kill that person," or "the claimant did not advance a loan to the defendant," this is an instance of contradicted evidence. So too, if the second set say, "How could you testify the way you did? On that day the alleged murderer—or the murdered person, or the borrower, or the lender—was with us in another province," this is another instance of contradicted evidence, for what they (the witnesses of the second set) say amounts to an assertion that the accused did not slay the victim or that the alleged creditor did not make the loan to the defendant, because they spent the day "with us." The slaying or the transaction could therefore not have taken place. The same is true of similar evidence.

But if they (of the second set) say, "We do not know whether the accused killed the victim on that day in Jerusalem, as you aver, but we do testify that you yourselves were with us on that day in Babylon," the first witnesses are thus proved to be plotting witnesses and are put to death, or ordered to pay compensation. The witnesses who refute the evidence are not concerned at all with the evidence to affirm or deny it.

3. As to why the Law accepts the evidence of the second witnesses rather than that of the first, this is a decree of Scripture. Even if the first group comprises a hundred witnesses and two come and refute their evidence, saying, "We testify that the hundred of you were all with us on such-and-such a day, in such-and-such a place," all of them are punished on the evidence of the two, for the testimony of two is as valid as that of a hundred and the evidence of a hundred is no more valid than that of two. Likewise, if two sets of witnesses contradict each other, we do not follow the one that comprises the larger number, but disregard the evidence of both.

4. No previous warning is required for the conviction of plotting witnesses. Witnesses whose evidence is first contradicted and later refuted are executed, or flogged, or ordered to pay compensation, because counterevidence is an initial step culminating in refutation.

5. The evidence of witnesses cannot be refuted save in their presence, but it may be contradicted in their absence. However, evidence refuted in the absence of the witnesses is accounted contradicted evidence. Therefore if the plotting witnesses died before their testimony was refuted in their presence, there is no evidence in the case, since the two sets of witnesses contradicted each other.

6. Witnesses in a capital charge whose evidence is contradicted but not refuted are not subject to the penalty of flagellation, even if the alleged victim appears in court hale and sound, because the negative command (contravened by the witnesses) is one intended as a warning that the breach thereof involves a death sentence by the court and the violation of such a command does not carry with

it the penalty of flogging. The court may, however, inflict upon them a disciplinary flogging; the number of strokes to be administered is left to its discretion.

7. In case witnesses are found plotting, public announcement must be made of the fact. How is it done? A proclamation is issued and dispatched to all cities: "So-and-so and So-and-so, having given such-and-such evidence, were proved plotting witnesses. We therefore put them to death," or "flogged them" or "ordered them to pay so many *denar,*" for it is written: *And those that remain shall hear, and fear* (Deut. 19:20).

8. Compensation which plotting witnesses are bound to pay in cases involving such penalty is to be regarded as a fine. It follows therefore that they are not made to pay it on their own admission (of guilt). Thus, if, after submitting their testimony which was examined by the court, they say, "We have given false testimony, the defendant owes nothing to the claimant," or they say, "We testified that the defendant owes such-and-such an amount to the claimant, but our evidence was refuted," they are exempt from paying compensation. But if they say, "We had testified against the defendant and our evidence was refuted in such-and-such a court and we were ordered to pay such-and-such an amount," they are bound to pay, for since sentence has already been passed on them, their admission is one with respect to indemnity. If only one of the witnesses makes this admission, he pays his proportionate share.

CHAPTER XIX

1. In the event two witnesses testify that So-and-so killed So-and so, at such-and-such an hour on the eastward side of the citadel, and two others come and say to the first two, "At that hour you were with us at the westward side of the citadel," if while standing on the westward side, it is possible to see what is going on in the eastward side, they are not accounted plotting witnesses; if it is impossible to see (what is taking place in the eastward side), they are adjudged plotting witnesses. It is not to be assumed that

they have a stronger eyesight and can see farther than others.

Similarly, in case two testify, "So-and-so killed So-and-so in Jerusalem in the morning," then two others come and say to them, "In the evening of that day you were with us in Lydda," if it is possible to get, even by horse, from Jerusalem to Lydda between morning and evening, they are not convicted as plotting witnesses; otherwise, they are convicted as plotting witnesses. It is not to be assumed that they chanced to find a specially fast camel which made the distance in half the (usual) time. We rather calculate (the time it takes to cover a distance) by a conveyance which is accessible and familiar to all. Therefore they are accounted plotting witnesses.

2. If two witnesses affirmed that the accused had killed a person on Sunday in a certain place, and two others come and say, "On that day you were with us in another place, far (from the one named by you); the accused did indeed kill the person but that was on Monday," aye, even if the latter witnesses assert that the killing occurred several days before, both the slayer and the first two witnesses are condemned to death, because the evidence of the first two is refuted and, at the time when they testified to the slaying, the death sentence had not yet been passed upon the slayer. But if two witnesses came on Tuesday, asserting that the accused had been condemned to death on Sunday, and then two others come and say, "On Sunday you were with us in such-and-such a place, which is a long way (from the place you named); it is true that the accused was convicted but that was on Friday" or "Monday"—in this instance the witnesses found plotting are not put to death, for whatever the actual day of the conviction, at the time when the first witnesses testified (Tuesday), the slayer had already been sentenced to death.

The same rule obtains in cases involving fines. Thus if two witnesses came on Tuesday and said that So-and-so had stolen and killed or sold an animal on Sunday and sentence was pronounced upon him, and then two others come saying, "On Sunday you were with us in a place considerably distant (from the one you stated); sentence was passed on him Friday"; even if the latter witnesses declare that the accused stole and killed or sold on Sunday, but that the conviction was on Monday, the witnesses found plotting are exempt from making restitution, because, whatever the actual day of the verdict, at the time when the first witnesses testified, the accused had already been sentenced to make restitution. This rule holds good in similar cases.

3. Witnesses signed on a bond cannot be proved guilty of plotting unless they declare in court, "This bond was written, without delay, on the date it bears." As long as they do not make such a declaration, the bond is valid and the witnesses retain their competence, even if it is dated the first of Nisan and the place named is Jerusalem, while other witnesses testify that on that day the signatories were with them in Babylon. For it is possible that they postdated the bond, that they were in Jerusalem on the first of Adar and while there wrote the bond, giving it a later date, i.e., the first of Nisan. In case they insist that it was written on the day it is dated and their statement is refuted, if there are witnesses who know the day when the (plotting) witnesses signed it, or who saw the bond and the signatures on a certain day, the signatories are disqualified (as witnesses) since they were proved plotting witnesses.

Their disqualification is retroactive, that is, from the day that, according to the refuting witnesses, they signed the bond, for the signature of witnesses on a bond is accounted evidence that was confirmed by the court at the time that their signatures were affixed to it. But if there are no witnesses who had seen their signatures or the bond before (they were proved plotting witnesses), the disqualification begins from the time that they testified to their handwriting, declaring that the bond was written on the date it bears. For it is possible that the bond had been prepared years before, and they signed it on the day when they gave evidence, and that they were lying when they said, "We wrote it on the date it bears."

CHAPTER XX

1. Witnesses guilty of plotting are neither put to death, nor flogged, nor ordered to pay compensation, unless both of them are eligible and both are found plotting and the plotting is detected after sentence has been passed. But if only one of them is found plotting, or even if both are found plotting before judgment has been rendered, aye, even if both are found plotting after judgment has been rendered and it is discovered that one of them is a kinsman or disqualified by reason of religious delinquency, no punishment is inflicted upon them, although their evidence is refuted and they become ineligible to give evidence in all cases where Scripture requires evidence.

2. If the accused was put to death on the evidence given against him and the evidence is refuted, the (plotting) witnesses are not executed on the strength of a logical deduction, for it is said *Then shalt thou do unto him as he had purposed to do* (Deut. 19: 19), *purposed,* but has not yet done it. This ruling has come down to us by tradition. But if the accused was flogged on the evidence against him, the witnesses are flogged. Likewise, if on the evidence given by them, money was made over from the defendant to the claimant, it is returned to the defendant and the (plotting witnesses) are bound to make restitution to the defendant.

3. If three, or even a hundred, witnesses testify, and some of them are found guilty of plotting, none of them is punished. Punishment is inflicted only if all of them are found guilty of plotting. This rule holds good only if the witnesses follow one another in close succession so that the interval between the evidence given by each pair is no longer than "an utterance," that is, the length of time it takes a disciple to greet his master. But if the interval between the testimony given by the first two and those who follow them is longer than "an utterance," the continuity of the evidence is interrupted. Therefore the first two, who are found guilty of plotting, suffer punishment, but the other two who testify after the interval are exonerated, although the entire evidence is void, since all who give testimony constitute one set of witnesses and if

the evidence of some is invalidated, the evidence of all is null.

4. If one witness testifies and his evidence is examined, then the second witness says, "I too (heard or saw) thus," or he says "Yea," or uses a similar expression, and both are proved plotting witnesses, both are executed, flogged, or ordered to pay compensation. For any witness who follows another (on the stand), declaring "Yea," is regarded as though he has been examined and given full evidence, as was the case with the one that preceded him.

Witnesses who are guilty of plotting cannot plead error as an excuse, because the offense they are charged with does not involve action. Therefore in their case no previous warning is required, as has already been stated.

5. Just as two witnesses can prove a hundred, who testify simultaneously, guilty of conspiracy, so they can prove guilty of conspiracy even fifty sets of witnesses who testify one after the other in pairs. Thus, if one set testify that A has killed B in Jerusalem and two witnesses refute their evidence, and then a second set appear and confirm the statement that A has killed B in Jerusalem and the same two refute the evidence of the second, the third, the fourth, etc., even as many as a hundred (sets), all are executed on the evidence of these two.

6. If one pair of witnesses testify that A has killed B in Jerusalem, and a second pair come and refute the evidence of the first, the plotting witnesses are put to death and A is acquitted. If a third pair come and refute the evidence of the second, the second pair as well as A are put to death and the first are acquitted. If a fourth pair appear and refute the evidence of the third, the first and the third are put to death, and A and the second pair are acquitted. This procedure holds good even if there are a hundred sets, one refuting the evidence of the preceding, one pair following the other.

7. If witnesses testify that one who is suffering from a fatal disease has killed a person, and they are found guilty of plotting, they are not put to death, for even were they to slay him with their own hands, they would not be executed, since he is afflicted with an incurable ailment.

Likewise, if witnesses suffering from a fatal illness testify with respect to an offense which involves death by the court and are found guilty of plotting, they are not executed; for should the evidence of those who confute them be rebutted, the latter would not suffer death, because they would refute the evidence of those who are fatally ill.

8. If witnesses testified against a person, preferring against him an accusation which entails neither the penalty of flagellation, nor that of death, nor that of payment of compensation, and their evidence is refuted, they are flogged, although their evidence was not designed to render the accused liable to flogging or payment of compensation.

To illustrate this ruling: if they testified concerning a priest that he is ineligible to serve as priest, declaring that in their presence his mother was divorced or released from levirate marriage by *ḥălîṣah,* in such-and-such a place, on such-and-such a day, and their evidence is refuted, the witnesses are flogged.

Likewise, if they testified that a person had slain another man accidentally and their evidence is refuted, they are flogged and not banished (to a city of refuge). If they testified that someone's ox had killed a person and their evidence is refuted, they are flogged and do not pay the (prescribed) ransom. If they testified concerning a person that he had been sold as a slave and their evidence is refuted, they are flogged. These four things (with reference to plotting witnesses) have come down to us by tradition.

9. The following tradition has been received by the Sages: if two witnesses gave evidence designed to vilify the innocent and exculpate the wicked and subsequently two other witnesses come and refute their evidence, thus justifying the innocent and condemning the wicked, the first two witnesses are flogged even if their indictment (of the accused) did not contemplate the penalty of flogging. But if they testified that the accused had eaten meat with milk or had worn garments of wool and linen, they are flogged on the authority of Scripture, as it is said: *Then shall ye do unto him, as he had purposed to do* (Deut. 19:19).

10. If two testified that A had committed adultery with the daughter of a priest and A was sentenced to death by strangulation and the adulteress to death by burning, and later their evidence is refuted, the first witnesses are executed by strangulation, not by burning. This ruling has come down to us by tradition.

CHAPTER XXI

1. If witnesses testify that So-and-so divorced his wife and has not paid her kĕṯubbah, and their evidence (with regard to the divorce) is refuted, they do not have to pay the full amount stipulated in the kĕṯubbah, since it is possible that today or tomorrow the husband will have to pay it, in the event she is divorced. It is estimated how much one would be prepared to offer for it and how much she would be willing to accept in consideration of the benefit of having the money in her possession, and the plotting witnesses are ordered to pay that amount. In appraising the selling price, account is taken of the facts relating to the woman and the amount of the kĕṯubbah. If the woman is ill, or old, or lives in peace with her husband, the price which her kĕṯubbah will fetch is less than that of a woman who is well and young but lives in discord with her husband, in which case divorce is more likely than death.

So too, we take into consideration the amount of the kĕṯubbah. One with a large (marriage) settlement will command, in return for her satisfaction of the benefit of converting it into cash, a proportionately higher price than one with a small settlement. Thus if the kĕṯubbah provides for a thousand zuz, it may sell for 100 zuz, whereas if it provides for 100 zuz, it will sell not for ten zuz but for less. These appraisals are left to the discretion of the judges.

2. If witnesses testify that the defendant owes the claimant 1,000 zuz with the condition that he shall pay the same within thirty days, while the borrower contends, "within five years after the lapse of thirty days," and their evidence is refuted, it is estimated how much one would be willing to pay for having in his posses-

sion 1,000 zuz for five years, and the plotting witnesses are ordered to pay this amount. This applies also to like cases.

3. If they testify that someone's ox has gored another ox, and their evidence is refuted, they pay half damages. If the ox is not worth half the damage (caused), they pay no more than the value of the ox, because half damage is paid only from its own body. But if they testify that the ox has consumed fruit or broken vessels as it went along (and their evidence is refuted), they pay full damage. This obtains also in like cases.

4. If they testify that So-and-so had knocked out his slave's tooth and then blinded his eye, and their evidence is refuted, they are ordered to pay to the master the value of the slave and the value of the eye. If they testify that he had first blinded the slave's eye and then knocked out his tooth, and their evidence is refuted, and subsequently it is found that he had first knocked out his tooth and later blinded his eye, the plotting witnesses have to compensate the slave for the loss of his eye. The same principle obtains in similar cases.

5. If witnesses testify that a jealous husband has warned his wife (whom he suspects of infidelity), or that she has secreted herself (with her paramour), and their evidence is refuted, they incur the penalty of flogging. If one witness comes and testifies that she committed adultery after the husband's warning and her seclusion, and his evidence is refuted, he is ordered to pay her the amount named in the kĕṯubbah. If there are two witnesses who testify to the warning given by the husband, her seclusion, and her defilement, and their evidence is refuted, each pays his share of the amount to which the kĕṯubbah entitles her, but they are not subject to flagellation. Why are they not put to death? Did they not testify that she had defiled herself? Because they had not given her due warning.

6. If two testify that a man has stolen (an ox or a sheep) and killed or sold it, and their evidence is refuted, they must pay in full. If two testify that he has stolen an ox or a sheep and two others testify that he has killed or sold it, and the evidence of both pairs

is refuted, the first (pair) must make twofold restitution, and the second, twofold or threefold restitution. If only the second pair are proved plotting witnesses, the thief must make twofold restitution to the owner and the second pair must make twofold or threefold restitution to the thief. If one of the second pair is proved a plotting witness, the evidence of the second pair is null. But if one of the first pair is proved a plotting witness, the entire evidence in the case becomes null, for since the testimony with regard to the theft is not established, the killing or selling does not render the accused liable to any payment.

7. If two testify that So-and-so has had the use of a field for three (successive) years, and they are proved plotting witnesses, they must make full restitution to the owner. But if two testify to his use of it for the first year, two for the second, and two for the third, and they are all proved plotting witnesses, payment of restitution is divided among them, for although with respect to the title (to the field) the evidence furnished by them constitutes three independent testimonies, for the purpose of proving them plotting witnesses it is regarded as one testimony. Therefore if three brothers give evidence that So-and-so has had the use of a field for three years, each of the brothers testifying for one of the years only, and another witness for all the three years, their evidence is deemed three distinct testimonies, whereby the possessor's title (to the field) is established, but is accounted only one testimony in the matter of proving them plotting witnesses. If all of them are found to be plotting witnesses, the three brothers pay half the value of the field, and the other witness who joined them pays the other half.

8. If an ox is declared "forewarned" on the evidence of three sets of witnesses, and the first and second sets are proved plotting witnesses, they (both sets) are exempt from paying compensation. If the third set too are proved plotting witnesses, each set is ordered to pay (one third of the additional half of) the damage. As to the first half of the damage, he (the owner) would have to pay it (even without the evidence of the first two sets). This rule holds only if the three sets are motioning to one another, or if

they appear simultaneously, or if they know the owner but cannot identify the ox that did the goring. Otherwise the first and second sets are exempt from paying compensation. They have a right to say, "Our testimony was intended to make the owner liable for half the damage only. We did not know that another pair of witnesses would appear to declare him 'forewarned.'"

9. The foregoing principle obtains also in the case of a stubborn and rebellious son. If two testify to his first offense and two others come and testify to his second offense, and both pairs are proved plotting witnesses, the first two are flogged but not executed, because they can plead, "Our testimony against him involved only the penalty of flogging," but the second pair are put to death, since the accused would have been condemned to death solely on their evidence. If the second set consists of four witnesses, two of whom aver, "He stole from his father in our presence," and the other two declare, "He indulged in gluttony in our presence," and all of them are proved plotting witnesses, all of them are put to death.

If two testify that a certain person has kidnaped a Jew and sold him, and they are found to be plotting witnesses, they are liable to death by strangulation. If two testify to the kidnaping and two others to the selling, and one pair are found to be plotting witnesses, they are put to death, whether they be those who testified to the abduction or those who testified to the selling, because abduction is the first step toward the conviction of the accused. If two testify to the selling of a Jew and they are found to be plotting witnesses and there are no witnesses to testify to abduction, they are not culpable, for even if they were not proved plotting witnesses, the accused would not be executed, because he could say, "I sold my own slave." If after the refutation of the evidence given by those who testified to the selling, witnesses appear and testify to the abduction, they are not put to death, even if they made signs to one another.

10. If a defaming husband produces witnesses that his wife has committed adultery during her betrothal period and the father brings witnesses who refute the evidence of the first, the husband's

witnesses are condemned to death. If the husband then produces other witnesses who refute the evidence given by the father's witnesses, the latter are condemned to death and ordered to pay the fine to the husband. They are put to death because the death sentence has already been pronounced upon the husband's first witnesses on their evidence; they pay the fine because the fine sentence has already been imposed upon the husband on their evidence—death in retaliation for death intended to one party (the witnesses), and compensation for the loss intended to another (the husband).

Likewise, if two witnesses testify that a person committed adultery with a betrothed woman and their evidence is refuted, they are liable to death but are exempt from paying the fine. If, however, they testify that a person committed adultery with the betrothed daughter of So-and-so and their evidence is refuted, they are put to death and ordered to pay the fine. If they testify that one committed an unnatural crime with an ox and their evidence is refuted, they are condemned to death by stoning, but do not have to pay compensation; if, however, they name the owner (of the ox), they are stoned and have to pay the value of the ox to the owner thereof. This applies also to similar cases.

CHAPTER XXII

1. If two sets of witnesses contradict each other and later one of the first set and one of the second come to testify in another case, their evidence is not accepted, because it is certain that one of them—though we do not know who—is a false witness. But if the first set comes by itself to give evidence and the second comes by itself to give evidence in another case, each is accepted.

2. If A produces two notes against B, one for a maneh and the other for two maneh, and the witnesses signed on one of the notes are those of one of the two sets who contradicted each other and the witnesses on the other are the other set, and B denies both claims, B pays only one maneh. For in this case, the holder of the

note is at a disadvantage. B takes an oath that he does not owe the other note.

It seems to me that the oath is to be taken by the defendant while holding a sacred object, as is required in the case of one who admits part of a claim against him, because there are two witnesses testifying that he owes part of the claim, though he denies the whole of it. Certainly his own admission is no more effective than the evidence given by witnesses, as was stated before.

3. If A produces a note against C, the note bearing the signatures of one of the two sets, and B produces a note against C, the note bearing the signatures of the other set, and C denies both claims, A swears (that C owes him the amount named in the note) and collects his claim, and B swears (that C owes him the amount named in his note) and collects, because it is certain that one of the claims is a legitimate one. The oath thus imposed upon the claimants is a rabbinical oath, as is the case with a shopkeeper with his account book.

4. If A produces one note against B, the note having the signatures of one of the two sets, and another against C, the note having the signature of the other set, and each defendant denies the claim against him, the burden of proof rests upon the plaintiff. Since A cannot establish the validity of either note, both are worthless. The two defendants take the consuetudinal oath and do not have to pay. This rule holds only if both sets come to testify at the same time. But if only one note bearing the signatures of the witnesses of either set is produced at one time, the lender collects his due; if later another note bearing the signatures of the witnesses of the other set is produced either by the same lender or another, the lender recovers his due, whether the second note is against the same borrower or against a different one, because each set comes by itself to give evidence.

5. If a man produces witnesses whose evidence is examined and refuted, and then brings other witnesses who testify to the same effect and their evidence is refuted—even if this happens to a hundred sets—and subsequently he produces witnesses who give

the same evidence which is found to be correct, the case is decided on their evidence. For though the man is presumed to procure false witnesses, we are not warranted in assuming that the last witnesses have given false evidence. But if a note has been contested, as when two witnesses come and say, "He requested us to forge this note," no claim can ever be collected on such a note, even if the signatures thereon have been attested. It seems to me, however, that if the signatories themselves testify to their handwriting, the note is collectible.

TREATISE III

LAWS CONCERNING REBELS

Involving Nine Commandments

Three Positive and Six Negative

To Wit

1. To act in accordance with the law of Scripture, as the Supreme Court interprets it;
2. Not to turn aside from the directions of the Supreme Court;
3. Not to add to Scripture either with respect to the commandments in the Written Law or with respect to their traditional interpretation;
4. Not to subtract anything from the commandments;
5. Not to curse one's father or one's mother;
6. Not to smite either of them;
7. To honor them;
8. To revere them;
9. That a son shall not rebel against the authority of his father or his mother.

An exposition of these commandments
is contained in the following chapters.

CHAPTER I

1. The Great Sanhedrin of Jerusalem is the root of the Oral Law. The members thereof are the pillars of instruction; out of them go forth statutes and judgments to all Israel. Scripture bids us repose confidence in them, as it is said *according to the law which they shall teach thee* (Deut. 17:11). This is a positive command. Whoever believes in Moses, our teacher, and his Law is bound to follow their guidance in the practice of religion and to lean upon them.

2. Whoever does not act in accordance with their instruction transgresses a negative command, as it is said: *Thou shalt not turn aside from the sentence which they shall declare unto thee, to the right hand, nor to the left* (*ibid.*). The infraction of this negative command does not entail the penalty of flagellation, because this negative command was intended as a warning that the breach thereof involves a death sentence by the court; for any sage who defies their rulings is liable to death by strangulation, as it is said: *And the man that doeth presumptuously, in not hearkening . . . even that man shall die* (Deut. 17:12). Whether the direction given by them is with regard to matters that they learned by tradition—matters that form the contents of the Oral Law—or with regard to rulings deduced by any of the hermeneutical rules by which the Torah is interpreted—rulings which they approved—or with regard to measures devised by them to serve as a fence about the Law—measures designed to meet the needs of the times, comprising decrees, ordinances, and customs: with regard to any of these three categories, obedience to the direction given by them is a positive command. Whoever disregards any of these transgresses a negative command. For Scripture says: *according to the law which they shall teach thee* (Deut. 17:11); this refers to the ordinances, decrees and customs, which they promulgate in public, in order to strengthen religion and stabilize the social order. *And according to the judgment which they shall tell thee* (*ibid.*); this refers to the rulings derived by means of any of the exegetical

principles by which the Scripture is expounded. *From the sentence which they shall declare unto thee* (*ibid.*); this refers to traditional matters, transmitted to them by preceding generations in unbroken succession.

3. So far as traditional laws are concerned, there never was any controversy. If there was any, we may be sure that the tradition does not date back to Moses, our teacher. As for rules derived by means of hermeneutical principles, if they received the sanction of all the members of the Supreme Court, they were binding. If there was a difference of opinion among them, the Supreme Court followed the majority, and decided the law in accordance with their opinion. This principle obtained also with respect to decrees, ordinances, and customs. If some felt that there was need for instituting a decree, for enacting an ordinance, or for discontinuing a practice, and others were of the opinion that there was no reason for the (new) decree or ordinance, or for the abandonment of the practice, they discussed the matter, followed the majority opinion and acted accordingly.

4. So long as the Supreme Court was in existence, there were no controversies in Israel. Whoever was in doubt with regard to a point of law consulted the local court. If the members thereof knew the law, they stated it; otherwise, the questioner together with the members of that court or their deputies went up to Jerusalem and submitted the question to the court that sat at the entrance of the Temple Mount. If the members thereof knew the answer, they stated it; otherwise, they all went to the court meeting at the entrance of the Court. If the members thereof knew the law, they stated it; otherwise, they all proceeded to the Hall of Hewn Stones, the seat of the Supreme Court, and put the question to that body. If the law concerning which they were all in doubt, was known to the Supreme Court, either from tradition or from the application of one of the principles by which Scripture is expounded, they stated it forthwith. If they were not certain of the law, they considered the question at the time when it was submitted to them, discussed it until they either reached a unanimous decision or put it to a vote and decided in accordance with

the majority opinion, saying to the questioners, "This is the law," and the latter departed.

After the Supreme Court ceased to exist, disputes multiplied in Israel: one declaring "unclean," giving a reason for his ruling; another declaring it "clean," giving a reason for his ruling; one forbidding, the other permitting.

5. In case there is a difference of opinion between two scholars or two courts, one pronouncing "clean" what the other pronounces "unclean," one declaring "forbidden" what the other declares "permitted," and it is impossible to determine the correct decision, if the controversy is with regard to a scriptural law, the more stringent view is followed; if it is with regard to a rabbinical law, the more lenient view is followed. This principle obtains in post-Sanhedric times, and obtained even at the time of the Sanhedrin if the case had not yet reached that tribunal. It obtains whether those who hold different views are contemporaries or live at different times.

CHAPTER II

1. If the Great Sanhedrin, by employing one of the hermeneutical principles, deduced a ruling which in its judgment was in consonance with the Law and rendered a decision to that effect, and a later Supreme Court finds a reason for setting aside the ruling, it may do so and act in accordance with its own opinion, as it is said: *and unto the judge that shall be in those days* (Deut. 17:9), that is, we are bound to follow the directions of the court of our own generation.

2. If the Supreme Court instituted a decree, enacted an ordinance, or introduced a custom, which was universally accepted in Israel, and a later Supreme Court wishes to rescind the measure, to abolish the ordinance, decree, or custom, it is not empowered to do so, unless it is superior to the former both in point of wisdom and in point of number. If it is superior in wisdom but not in number, or in number but not in wisdom, it is denied the right to abrogate the measure adopted by its predecessor, even if the reason

which prompted the latter to enact the decree or ordinance has lost all force.

But how is it possible for any Supreme Court to exceed another in number, seeing that each Supreme Court consists of seventy-one members? We include in the number the wise men of the age, who agree to and accept without demur the decision of the (contemporaneous) Supreme Court.

3. The last ruling applies only to prohibitive measures, which, like many other measures, do not have as their purpose the safeguarding of the Torah. But decrees and prohibitions designed by the court to serve as a protective fence to the Law, if they have been universally accepted in Israel, no later Supreme Court, even if it be superior to the former, is empowered to abrogate or permit.

4. However, the court, even if it be inferior (to the former) is authorized to dispense for a time even with these measures. For these decrees are not to be invested with greater stringency than the commands of the Torah itself, which any court has the right to suspend as an emergency measure. Thus the court may inflict flagellation and other punishments, even in cases where such penalties are not warranted by the law if, in its opinion, religion will thereby be strengthened and safeguarded and the people will be restrained from disregarding the words of the Torah. It must not, however, establish the measure to which it resorts as a law binding upon succeeding generations, declaring, "This is the law."

So too, if, in order to bring back the multitudes to religion and save them from general religious laxity, the court deems it necessary to set aside temporarily a positive or a negative command, it may do so, taking into account the need of the hour. Even as a physician will amputate the hand or the foot of a patient in order to save his life, so the court may advocate, when an emergency arises, the temporary disregard of some of the commandments, that the commandments as a whole may be preserved. This is in keeping with what the early Sages said: *Desecrate on his account one Sabbath that he be able to observe many Sabbaths* (B. Yo 85b).

5. Before instituting a decree or enacting an ordinance or in-

troducing a custom which it deems necessary, the court should calmly deliberate (the matter) and make sure that the majority of the community can live up to it. At no time is a decree to be imposed upon the public which the majority thereof cannot endure.

6. If the court has issued a decree in the belief that the majority of the community could endure it, and after the enactment thereof the people made light of it and it was not accepted by the majority, the decree is void and the court is denied the right to coerce the people to abide by it.

7. If after a decree had been promulgated, the court was of opinion that it was universally accepted by Israel and nothing was done about it for years, and after the lapse of a long period a later court investigates the doings of Israel and finds that the decree is not generally accepted, the latter court, even if it be inferior to the former in wisdom and number, is authorized to abrogate it.

8. Any court that permits two things that have been declared forbidden should hesitate about permitting a third thing.

9. Since the court is authorized to issue decrees prohibiting what is permitted and the prohibition is binding upon succeeding generations; and since it is empowered to permit provisionally what is forbidden in Scripture, how are we to understand the scriptural injunction *Thou shalt not add thereto, nor diminish from it* (Deut. 13:1)? (It is to be understood as an admonition) not to add to the *precepts* of the Torah, nor to take any *precept* away from it; that is, not to impart to any regulation (evolved in the course of time) the character of an old, established law, as though it were a command embodied in the Written or the Oral Law. To elucidate this point: The Bible says: *Thou shalt not seethe a kid in its mother's milk* (Exod. 23:19). We have it on tradition that this verse prohibits the cooking or eating of flesh with milk, be it the flesh of a domestic animal or of a beast of chase; that the flesh of fowl with milk is permitted by biblical law. Should the court permit the flesh of a beast of chase with milk, it would be taking away (from the commands of the Torah). On the other hand, should it forbid the flesh of fowl (with milk) on the ground that the prohi-

bition in the text extends to (the cooking or eating of the flesh of) fowl with milk, it would add (to the commands of the Torah).

What the court should say, is: "By the law of Scripture, flesh of fowl (with milk) is permitted, but we forbid it." It is imperative that we inform the people that the prohibition has been decreed in order to obviate harmful results that might otherwise ensue. For some people would argue thus: flesh of fowl (with milk) is permitted because it is not expressly forbidden in the text; it follows therefore that the flesh of a beast of chase (with milk) is likewise permitted, since it is not expressly stated in the text. Others would contend that even the flesh of a domestic animal is permitted (with milk) except that of a goat; still others might assert that even the flesh of a goat may be eaten with the milk of a cow or of a sheep, because the text states "its mother's milk," that is, milk of its own kind; still others might (go so far as to) say that the flesh of a goat may be eaten even with the milk of a goat, provided that the milk is not that of its own mother, because the text reads "*its* mother's." Therefore, we forbid all flesh with milk, even the flesh of fowl. In this way, the court does not make any addition (to the precepts), but is only making a fence to the Torah. This applies to similar regulations.

CHAPTER III

1. He who repudiates the Oral Law is not to be identified with the rebellious elder spoken of in Scripture but is classed with the epicureans [whom any person has a right to put to death].

2. As soon as it is made public that he has repudiated the Oral Law, [he is cast into the pit and is not rescued from it]. He is placed on a par with heretics, epicureans, those who deny the divine origin of Scripture, informers, and apostates—all of whom are ruled out of the community of Israel. No witnesses or previous warning or judges are required. [Whoever puts any of them to death fulfills a great precept, for he removes a stumbling block.]

3. This applies only to one who repudiates the Oral Law as a result of his reasoned opinion and conclusion, who walks light-

mindedly in the stubbornness of his heart, denying first the Oral Law, as did Zadok and Boethus and all who went astray. But their children and grandchildren, who, misguided by their parents, were raised among the Karaites and trained in their views, are like a child taken captive by them and raised in their religion, whose status is that of an *'anus* (one who abjures the Jewish religion under duress), who, although he later learns that he is a Jew, meets Jews, observes them practice their religion, is nevertheless to be regarded as an 'anus, since he was reared in the erroneous ways of his fathers. Thus it is with those who adhere to the practices of their Karaite parents. Therefore efforts should be made to bring them back in repentance, to draw them near by friendly relations, so that they may return to the strength-giving source, i.e., the Torah.

4. The rebellious elder of whom the Bible speaks is one of the wise men of Israel who is at home in traditional lore, functions as judge, imparts instruction in the Torah as do all the wise men of Israel, but is in disagreement with the Supreme Court with regard to a question of law, refuses to change his view, persists in differing with them, gives a practical ruling which runs counter to that given by them. The Torah condemns him to death, and if he confesses before his execution he has a portion in the world to come. Though both he and the members of the Supreme Court base their respective decisions either on reason or on tradition, the Torah pays regard to their view. Even if they are willing to forego the honor due to them and let him go unpunished, it is not within their competence to do so, in order that strife may not increase in Israel.

5. A rebellious elder is not liable to death unless he is qualified to render decisions, that is, has been ordained by the Sanhedrin, takes issue with the latter either on a matter the wanton transgression of which involves the penalty of excision and the unwitting transgression a sin offering, or on a question bearing on the phylacteries, communicates his ruling to others who act upon it or acts upon it himself, and dissents from the ruling of the Supreme Court while that tribunal is meeting in the Hall of Hewn Stones. But if a disciple who is not qualified to render de-

cisions gives a practical ruling, he is not liable, for it is written: *If there arise a matter too hard for thee in judgment* (Deut. 17:8). This refers to one who finds difficulty only in deciding a hard matter.

6. If the elder is the outstanding member of a court and he dissents from a decision by the Supreme Court, persists in communicating his opinion to others, but does not give it in the form of a practical ruling, he is not liable, for it is said: *and the man that doeth presumptuously* (Deut. 17:12), that is, not who *sayeth* presumptuously but who instructs others to act upon his opinion or acts upon it himself.

7. If he meets the members of the Supreme Court outside the place assigned for their sessions and defies their ruling, he is not culpable, for it is said: *Then shalt thou arise and get thee up unto the place* (Deut. 17:8). This shows that the place conditions the death of the defiant elder. With regard to this offender and others, who are exempt from the death penalty, the Supreme Court is invested with authority to ban them, or segregate them, or flog them, or forbid them to impart instruction—to employ any of these measures it may deem necessary to meet the situation.

8. What is the procedure in the case of a rebellious elder? When a difficult question arises and the scholar who is qualified to render decisions has given his ruling, basing it either on reason or tradition, (and his colleagues take issue with him), he and they who dissent from his decision proceed to Jerusalem. They come first to the court which is at the entrance of the Temple Mount. The court states the law. If he accepts the ruling he heard, well and good; if not, they all go to the court which is at the entrance of the Court. The latter states the law; if he accepts the ruling, they all depart (for home); if not, they all appear before the Supreme Court, which meets in the Hall of Hewn Stones, whence Torah goes forth to all Israel, as it is written: *unto the place which the Lord thy God will choose* (Deut. 17:8); the Supreme Court states the law, and they all depart.

If after returning to his own city, he continues to impart to others the view held by him before, he is not culpable. If, however, he gives his opinion in the form of a practical ruling to be acted upon by others or acts upon it himself, he is liable to death without previous warning. Even if he offers a reason for his decision, no attention is paid to him. As soon as witnesses see that he acts upon his decision or tells others to act upon it, the local court passes the death sentence upon him. He is thereupon seized and taken to Jerusalem. He is executed neither by the local court nor even by the Supreme Court while it is away from Jerusalem, but is brought before the latter tribunal when it is in its assigned place, and kept in prison until the following festival when he is executed by strangulation, for it is said: *And all the people shall hear, and fear* (Deut. 17:13). From this we infer that it (the execution of the rebellious elder) requires public announcement. For public announcement must be made of (the execution of) four classes of offenders: a rebellious elder, plotting witnesses, an enticer, and a stubborn and rebellious son. Concerning each of these it is said: *And all the people shall hear, and fear.*

CHAPTER IV

1. If the elder dissents from a decision by the Supreme Court with regard to a law, the wanton transgression of which entails the penalty of excision and the unwitting transgression a sin offering, he is liable to death, whether the ruling of that tribunal forbids the matter (in question) and he permits it, or their ruling permits it and he forbids it. Even if he bases his ruling upon tradition, saying: "This is a tradition which I received from my teachers," while the members of the Supreme Court say: "Thus it appears to us," basing their conclusion upon a logical argument, he is culpable, because he opposes their decision and acts or instructs others to act upon his decision. This is all the more so if they base their decision upon tradition.

Likewise, if he differs with them in regard to any decree issued by them touching a matter the unwitting violation of which entails a sin offering and the wanton violation the penalty of excision, for instance, if he permits leaven to be eaten in the sixth hour on the fourteenth of Nisan, or prohibits the use of it in the fifth hour, he incurs the penalty of death. This applies also to similar cases.

2. The foregoing rule obtains whether the point at issue between them concerns a matter the wanton transgression of which carries with it the penalty of excision and the unwitting transgression a sin offering, or concerns a matter which may *lead* to a transgression the wanton commission of which carries with it the penalty of excision and the unwitting commission a sin offering. To cite concrete examples:

If the controversy between them centers around such questions as to whether a certain woman is included in the category of forbidden marriages; whether the discharge of a certain color of blood renders a woman unclean; whether (the discharge of blood after) childbirth renders the mother unclean, whether a woman's discharge of blood (during a certain period) is symptomatic of a running issue; or whether a particular kind of fat is forbidden or permitted—these and similar questions are instances of controversies with regard to matters the wanton transgression of which involves the penalty of excision and the unwitting transgression a sin offering.

The following are instances of issues which may lead to offenses the wanton commission of which involves the penalty of excision and the unwitting commission a sin offering. If the disagreement between them bears upon the question of the intercalation of the year, that is, whether a leap year must be proclaimed before Purim or may be proclaimed during the entire month of Adar, the rebellious elder is liable to death, because his ruling (if acted upon) would lead to the eating of leaven during Passover.

Likewise, if the dispute between them is with regard to a monetary case, or with regard to the number of judges required to adjudicate a civil suit, the rebellious elder is culpable. For on the view that the defendant is in debt to the claimant, the latter obtained what rightfully belongs to him, the court ruling in his favor; whereas on the view that the defendant is exempt (from paying the plaintiff), or that those who tried the case had no authority to adjudicate it, what the claimant obtained is sheer robbery. If therefore, he betroths a woman with the money, the betrothal is void; whereas, according to the first opinion that he got what he was entitled to, one who has relations with that woman is liable to the penalty of excision if he commits the offense wittingly and to a sin offering if he commits it unwittingly. Such a controversy thus leads to a transgression the deliberate commission whereof is punished by excision and the unwitting commission involves a sin offering.

So too, if the conflicting rulings relate to a question of flagellation, i.e., whether the accused has incurred this penalty, or relates to the number of judges required to decide cases of flagellation, the rebellious elder is culpable. For on the view that the accused is not liable to flogging, he is entitled to compensation for the injury inflicted upon him and whatever amount he will be awarded in compensation will be due to him; whereas on the view that he was deserving of flogging, whatever he will obtain in compensation is robbery and, if he betroths a woman with the money, the betrothal is void.

So too, if they disagree on the question concerning the valuation of a human being, whether he (who made the vow) is bound to pay it; or on a question concerning undesignated devotions (whether they are to be given to the priest or be applied to the needs of the Temple), the rebellious elder is culpable. For if we follow the opinion that he (who made the vow) is under no obligation to pay the valuation, the money exacted from him is sheer robbery, and if any one betroths a woman with it, the betrothal is void. So too, if the divergence of opinion relates to the number of men required to assess dedicated objects for redemption purposes, whether redemption effected by less than a certain number of assessors is valid, the rebellious elder is culpable; for on the view that the redemption is invalid, if the one who has redeemed it betroths a woman with the (dedicated) object, the betrothal is null.

In like manner, if the dispute between them is one with respect to the question as to which town is to furnish the heifer to be beheaded, the rebellious elder is liable. For, if (in determining the town nearest to the scene of slaying) one of the differing views is acted upon, the heifer supplied by that town cannot be used for other purposes; therefore, if a woman is betrothed with it, the betrothal is null. Similarly, if the disagreement is one touching a question of *'orlah;* or if they are at variance in their rulings on the question of the application of the laws regarding the gleanings of the harvest, forgotten sheaves, or the corner of the field, whether (in specific instances) these are to be left for the poor or belong to the owner, the rebellious elder is liable. For if the opinion that they belong to the owner be accepted, the poor man has taken them unlawfully and if he betroths a woman with them, the bethrothal is void.

So too, if the controversy is with respect to one of the original sources of defilement, such as (certain symptoms of) leprosy in man, in houses, or in garments, the rebellious elder is culpable. For, according to the opinion that the person is clean, he is permitted to enter the sanctuary or eat of holy things. But according to the opinion that he is unclean, if he enters the sanctuary or eats of holy things wittingly, he incurs the penalty of excision, if unwittingly, he is liable to a sin offering. Similarly, if they offer contrary opinions on the question of whether a leper (with certain physical defects) can meet the requirements of purification, the rebellious elder is liable. So too, if the dispute arises from a difference of opinion bearing upon the ordeal (prescribed) for a *soṭah,* whether the suspected woman has to undergo the ordeal, the rebellious elder is liable. For on the view that she is subject to the ordeal, if the husband dies before she has been made to drink (of the bitter waters), she is forbidden to her brother-in-law, but on the view that she is exempt from the ordeal, she is bound to her brother-in-law. So too, in all similar cases, it is of vital importance to consider carefully the immediate effect which will emerge from the controversy and also the chain of consequences it will set in motion, culminating in an offense the wanton commission whereof renders the transgressor liable to the penalty of excision and the unwitting commission to a sin offering. The defiant elder is liable, whether he adopts the more lenient opinion and the Supreme Court the more stringent opinion, or he adopts the more stringent view and the Supreme Court the more lenient view.

3. But if the difference of opinion between them is one that does not lead to so grave a consequence, the elder is not culpable, the sole exception being a controversy with regard to the *tĕfillin* (phylacteries). If the elder rules that a fifth compartment be added to the (head) tĕfillin and acts upon his ruling, he is liable, provided that he first makes four compartments according to the law and then makes a fifth and attaches it to the outer one, for if the outer compartment is not exposed to the open space, the tĕfillin are unfit. The liability of the rebellious elder in the matter of tĕfillin is a law which has come down to us by tradition. But if they disagree with respect to other precepts, for instance, as to the rules relating to the palm branch, the fringes, or the shophar, one holding the view that unless any of these objects follows certain regulations it is unfit, the other that it is fit; one maintaining that he who fulfills a precept in a certain manner has discharged his duty, the other that he has not discharged his duty; one declaring a person clean, the other that he is a secondary source of defilement—in all such instances, the defiant elder is not liable to death. This obtains also in similar cases.

CHAPTER V

1. Whoever curses his father or his mother is stoned, as it is said: *He hath cursed his father or his mother; his blood shall be upon him* (Lev. 20:9). Whether he curses them when they are alive or after their death, he is stoned, provided that he does it in the presence of witnesses after he has been given due warning, as is required in the case of all who are liable to death by the court. This punishment is meted out alike to man, woman, ṭumṭum, and hermaphrodite, if they have attained the age when they are subject to punishment.

2. The offender does not incur the penalty of death by stoning

unless he curses them by one of the special Names (of God). If however, he curses them by an attribute (of God), he is exempt from the penalty of stoning, but he is liable to flogging, as he would be if he cursed any worthy Israelite.

3. So too, he who curses his father's father, or his mother's father is as though he cursed any other member of the community.

4. Whence do we derive the prohibition of cursing a father or a mother? The punishment is explicitly stated. The prohibition is included in the negative command *Thou shalt not curse the deaf* (Lev. 19:14). Since one is forbidden to curse any Israelite, one's father is included.

5. Whoever strikes his father or his mother is executed by strangulation, as it is said: *And he that smiteth his father, or his mother, shall be surely put to death* (Exod. 21:15), provided that he does it in the presence of witnesses after receiving due warning, as is required in the case of all who are liable to death by the court. This applies alike to man, woman, ṭumṭum, and hermaphrodite, if they have reached the age when they are subject to punishment.

The offender does not incur the penalty of strangulation unless he has inflicted a wound upon the parent; otherwise, it is as though he struck any (other) Israelite. If he smites them after their death, he is not culpable.

6. He who strikes his father over the ear so that deafness ensues is culpable and is put to death, because it is impossible to cause deafness without first inflicting a wound. What happened was that a clot of blood got into his ear, as a result of which he became deaf.

7. If he let blood for his father, or if being a physician, he removed flesh or a limb from his father's body, he is not culpable. But although he is not culpable (if he has done it), he has no direct permission to do it; he should not even remove a thorn from the flesh of his father or his mother, lest he inflict a wound, provided, however, that someone else is capable of performing this service for them. But if he is the only one capable of doing it and his

parents are in pain, he may let blood for them and operate on them, if they permit him to do it.

8. Whence do we derive the prohibition of striking a father (or a mother)? The punishment is explicitly stated, the prohibition is not. But since one is forbidden to strike any Israelite, one's father and mother are included.

9. A *šĕṯuḳi* is culpable if he curses or strikes his mother, but is not culpable if he curses or strikes his (alleged) father. Even if his mother, on being questioned, declares, "He is the son of So-and-so," he is not stoned, or strangled, on the strength of her assertion.

But the son of a handwoman or of a heathen woman is not liable for either offense against his father or his mother. Likewise, a proselyte who was conceived in an unhallowed condition, although he was born in a hallowed condition, is not culpable if he strikes or curses his father.

10. Just as the last three are not liable for either offense against their father, so they are not liable for either offense against their mother, for it is said: *and he that curseth his father or his mother* (Exod. 21:17). Whoever is liable for cursing his father is liable also for cursing his mother, but whoever is not liable for cursing his father is not liable for cursing his mother.

11. A proselyte is forbidden to curse or strike his heathen father, nor is he to treat him disrespectfully, lest it be said that (in embracing the Jewish religion) he descended from a higher degree of holiness to a lower degree, seeing that he slights his father. It is his duty to show him some respect. A slave, however, is without pedigree. To all intents and purposes, his father has not the (legal) status of a father, even if they were manumitted.

12. One is forbidden to strike or curse one's father and mother who are thoroughly wicked, habitual transgressors, aye, even if they have been condemned to death and are going forth to be executed. If, however, he does curse or strike them, he is not culpable. But if they have repented, he is culpable and put to death, though they are being led forth to execution. This applies only to a son, but if a stranger comes and strikes or curses them after the

death sentence has been pronounced upon them, he is exempt, even if they have repented, since they are being led forth to execution. But if he insults them, he is liable to the payment of a fine which is imposed on any man who flings an insult at a fellow Jew.

13. If his father or his mother commits a transgression punishable by flogging and he is the attendant of the court, he must not administer the flogging. Likewise, if either parent incurs the penalty of the ban, he must not be the agent to pronounce the ban. He must not drive them (to the place of execution), or treat them with disrespect in his capacity as agent of the court, though they deserve such treatment seeing that they have not repented.

14. For no offense is the son to act as agent to smite or curse a parent, save if the latter is an enticer, for the Bible says: *Neither shalt thou spare, nor conceal him* (Deut. 13:9).

15. In case the father is required to swear an oath to his son, the practice in vogue is to administer one not accompanied by an imprecation, in order that the son curse not his father. The oath administered should be deleted of any execration.

We have already stated that if a father kills his son (accidentally), none of the brothers of the slain becomes a blood redeemer.

The Torah is rigorous not only with him who strikes or curses his parents, but also with him who treats them with contempt. For he who treats them with contempt, even by using harsh words against them, aye, even by a discourteous gesture, is cursed out of the mouth of God, as it is said: *Cursed be he that dishonoreth his father or his mother* (Deut. 27:16). It is written, moreover: *The eye that mocketh at his father and despiseth to obey his mother, the ravens of the valley shall pick it out* (Prov. 30:17). The court is empowered to beat him for disobedience, inflicting upon him as many strokes as it sees fit.

CHAPTER VI

1. The honoring of father and mother is a weighty positive command; so too, is reverence for them. The Bible attaches to the duty of honoring and revering parents an importance equal to that which it attaches to the duty of honoring and revering God. It is said: *Honor thy father and thy mother* (Exod. 20:12); and it is also written: *Honor the Lord with thy substance* (Prov. 3:9). Concerning the duty due to parents, it is said: *Ye shall fear every man his mother and his father* (Lev. 19:3); and concerning duty to God, it is said: *Thou shalt fear the Lord thy God* (Deut. 6:13). We are enjoined to honor and revere them in the manner that we are enjoined to honor and revere His great Name.

2. Whoever curses his father or his mother suffers death by stoning, and whoever blasphemes God suffers death by stoning. The penalty prescribed in both instances is the same.

In the matter of honor due to parents, the father is mentioned first, in the matter of reverence due to them, the mother is mentioned first. From this we infer that both are to be equally honored and revered.

3. What does reverence imply? What does honor imply? Reverence requires that the son should not stand in the place in which his father usually stands, or sit in his place, or contradict his words, or decide against his opinion, or call him, living or dead, by his name. When referring to his father, he should say, "My father, my teacher." If others bear the same name as his father or his teacher, he should designate them by another name. It appears to me, however, that this stricture applies only to a name that is not common. But in case of names that are in use in all languages and at all times, such as Abraham, Isaac, Jacob, Moses, and the like, he may in the absence of his father call those who bear them by their names and have no scruples about it.

What does honoring parents imply? It means providing them with food and drink, clothing and covering, the expense to be borne by the father. If the father is poor and the son is in a position to take care of his parents, he is compelled to do so. He must support his parents in accordance with his means, conduct his father in and out, and perform for him such personal services as disciples perform for their teacher. He rises before him, as he rises before his teacher.

4. If his father is his disciple, the father does not rise before him, but he is bound to rise before his father. It is his duty to honor him in other ways too, as when he is attending to business or personal matters. Thus if courtesy is shown to him in any place on account of his father, he should not say, "Speed me, for my own sake," or "Let me depart for my own sake," but he should say, "Speed me, for my father's sake," or "Let me depart for my father's sake," or use a similar expression. He should make it clear, in his dealings with others, that he is zealous for the honor of his father and that his attitude toward him is one of reverence.

5. It is the duty of the son to honor his father, even after the latter's death. Thus if he reports a law he heard from his father, he should not say, "Thus said my father." He should say, "Thus said my father, my teacher, may I be an atonement for his resting place." He should refer to him in these reverential terms only within twelve months of his death; but after twelve months, he should say, "May his memory be [for a blessing] for the life of the world to come."

6. Both man and woman are enjoined to revere and honor parents. A man, however, is in a position to supply them with their needs, while a woman is not, inasmuch as she is dependent on others. Therefore, if she has been divorced or widowed, she and the son share the duty equally.

7. To what lengths should the duty of honoring parents go? Even were they to take a purse of his, full of gold, and cast it in his presence into the sea, he must not shame them, manifest grief in their presence, or display any anger, but accept the divine decree without demur.

To what lengths should the duty of revering them go? Even if he is attired in costly garments, presiding over the congregation, and his parents come and rend his garments, strike him on the head, and spit in his face, he must not shame them. It behooves him to remain silent, to fear and revere the King, King of kings, who has thus decreed. For if a mortal king were to issue against him a decree, even more exasperating in character, he would be powerless to rebel against it, all the more so if the author of the decree is He who spoke and the world came into being in accordance with His will.

8. Although children are commanded to go the abovementioned lengths, the father is forbidden to impose too heavy a yoke upon them, to be too exacting with them in matters pertaining to his honor, lest he cause them to stumble. He should forgive them and shut his eyes; for a father has the right to forego the honor due him.

9. If a man beats a grown-up son, he is placed under the ban, because he transgresses the negative command *Nor put a stumbling block before the blind* (Lev. 19: 14).

10. If the mind of his father or his mother is affected, the son should make every effort to indulge the vagaries of the stricken parent until God will have mercy on the afflicted. But if the condition of the parent has grown worse, and the son is no longer able to endure the strain, he may leave the father or the mother, go elsewhere and delegate others to give the parent proper care.

11. A bastard is bound to honor and reverence his father, although he is not culpable if he strikes or curses him, unless the latter has repented. Even if one's father is a wicked man, a habitual transgressor, it is the duty of the son to honor and reverence him.

If the son sees his father violate a commandment, he should not say to him, "Father, you have disregarded a precept of the Torah." He should say to him, "Thus and thus is written in the Torah," speaking to him as though he were consulting him, instead of admonishing him.

12. If his father orders him to transgress a positive or a negative command set forth in the Bible or even a command which is of rabbinical origin, the son must disregard the order, for it is said: *Ye shall fear every man his mother, and his father; and ye shall keep my Sabbaths* (Lev. 19: 3), that is, all of you are bound to honor Me.

13. In the event the father says to his son, "Give me a drink of water," while the son has a commandment to perform, if the commandment can be performed by others, let him delegate it to others and attend to the duty of honoring his father, for one commandment is not to be neglected in order to fulfill another. But if there are no others to perform the commandment, he must perform it himself, and disregard the honor due to his father, because both he and his father are in duty bound to fulfill the commandment.

The duty of studying the Torah is greater than that of honoring parents.

14. If both his father and his mother ask him (at the same time) for a drink of water, he disregards the duty of honoring his mother and attends to the duty of honoring his father, for both he and his mother are bound to honor the father.

15. It is the duty of a man to honor his stepmother as long as his father is living. This is included in the command to honor one's father. Likewise, a man is bound to honor his stepfather as long as the mother is living. But after her death he is released from the obligation. By an ordinance of the Scribes one is bound to honor one's older brother, even as one is bound to honor one's father.

CHAPTER VII

1. The penalty incurred by the stubborn and rebellious son spoken of in Scripture, is stated to be death by stoning. But the Bible does not pronounce punishment without having expressed a warning. Where does the warning occur? It is said: *Ye shall not eat with the blood* (Lev. 19:26); i.e., do not indulge in eating which will eventuate in bloodshed. It refers to the way in which the stubborn and rebellious son gorges. He is executed for the loathsome manner in which he gratifies his appetite, as it is said: *He is a glutton and a drunkard* (Deut. 21:20). The traditional definition of these words is: a glutton is one who eats meat voraciously; a drunkard is one who drinks wine immoderately.

2. The death penalty for the self-indulgence of the stubborn

and rebellious son is hedged about with many limitations—all of which have been transmitted to us by tradition. He is not condemned to be stoned, unless he steals (money) from his father, buys meat and wine cheaply, consumes them outside his father's premises, in a company consisting wholly of worthless men, eats the meat partially raw and partially cooked, the way thieves eat their meat, and drinks the wine [partially] diluted, in the manner of drunkards. He is not liable, moreover, unless he gobbles down fifty denar weight of meat in one mouthful and gulps down half a *log̅* of wine in one draught. But if he steals (money) from his father and consumes the food in his father's premises, or if he steals it from others and stuffs himself in the above-described loathsome fashion, either in the premises of his father or those of others, he is not liable.

So too, if he steals from his father and indulges his voraciousness in the premises of others on an occasion when partaking of food involves the infraction of a command, even if the command be only of rabbinical origin, he is not liable. For it is said: *He doth not hearken to our voice* (Deut. 21:20); that is to say, only he is culpable who by his gluttony disobeys his parents, excluding one who thereby transgresses the words of the Torah.

Likewise, if he indulges in gluttony in connection with a religious command, he is not liable. Thus if he gratifies his craving in bad company gathered to celebrate a religious festivity or to eat the second tithe in Jerusalem or even to partake of the meal of comfort for mourners—which is based only on a rabbinical command—he is not liable. So too, if he eats flesh of an animal not slaughtered correctly or of an animal suffering from an incurable disease or eats abominable or creeping things, or even if he gormandizes on a fast day ordained by the Rabbis, he is not condemned to death.

3. If he consumes any food but the flesh of cattle, even if he eats the flesh of fowl, he is not liable. But if he eats the flesh of cattle (less than fifty denar weight) and completes the necessary amount by eating the flesh of fowl, he is culpable. If he drinks any beverage but wine, he is exempt.

4. If he eats raw meat or drinks undiluted wine, he is exempt. Since this is an abnormal way of appeasing one's appetite, it will have no attraction for him. Likewise, if he eats pickled meat from the third day it was salted or drinks wine from the vat, he is exempt, because it will have no attraction for him.

5. The Bible does not prescribe punishment for a minor, that is, one who has not come yet within the scope of the commandments. Likewise, a son who is grown up and is independent is not stoned if he steals, eats, and drinks voluptuously. Within what age limits does this law hold? It has been learned by tradition that it applies to one who has attained the age of thirteen years and one day, when he has produced two hairs, until the hair surrounds the entire membrum. Once the hair has surrounded the entire membrum, he is independent and is not stoned.

6. The maximum duration of a stubborn and rebellious son is three months from the time that he has produced two hairs. For it is possible that his wife will conceive and the embryo be felt at the end of three months. Scripture, however, says: *if a man have a stubborn and rebellious son* (Deut. 21:18), that is, not when the stubborn and rebellious is already a father. If therefore the hair has surrounded the membrum before the lapse of three months, he is exempt from punishment.

7. What procedure is followed in the trial of a stubborn and rebellious son? First his father and mother bring him before a court-of-three, declaring, "This our son is stubborn and rebellious." They produce two witnesses who testify that he has stolen (money) from his father, bought therewith meat and wine and consumed them after due warning had been given him. This is the "first testimony" against him. He is flogged, in the manner that all who have incurred this penalty are flogged, as it is said: *and though they flog him, will not hearken unto them* (Deut. 21:18). If he steals again from his father and indulges in gluttony, his father and mother take him to a court of twenty-three. They produce two witnesses who testify that he has stolen and yielded to his voluptuous cravings after receiving due admonition. This is the "second testimony." Even if the witnesses who give evidence

against him in this trial are the witnesses who gave evidence against him in the first trial, their evidence is accepted. After testimony has been taken, the stubborn and rebellious son is examined in order to ascertain that the hair has not surrounded the entire membrum. If it has not, and the three months are not yet over, he is sentenced to death and executed by stoning, as are all who have incurred this death sentence, but he is not stoned unless the first three are present, for it is said *this our son,* this one who was flogged in your presence.

8. If his father and mother pardon him before the death sentence has been passed on him, he is exempt.

9. If he ran away before sentence was passed on him and in the meantime his nether hair grew, he is exempt. But if he ran away after sentence had been passed on him, he is executed by stoning whenever he is located, even if he is beyond the age limit, because once the death sentence has been passed on him, he is accounted as dead, and one who slays him is not liable.

10. If his father is willing to bring accusations against him but the mother is not, or if the mother is willing but the father is not, he is not condemned as a stubborn and rebellious son, for it is said: *Then shall his father and his mother lay hold on him* (Deut. 21:19). If either parent is maimed in the hand, or lame, dumb, blind, or deaf, he is not condemned as a stubborn and rebellious son, for it is said: *Then shall his father and his mother lay hold on him;* this excludes (a parent) who is maimed in the hand. *And bring him out* (*ibid.*); this excludes (a parent) who is lame. *And they shall say* (Deut. 21:20); this excludes (a parent) who is dumb. *This our son* (*ibid.*); this excludes (a parent) who is blind. *He doth not hearken to our voice* (*ibid.*); this excludes (a parent) who is deaf.

11. The stoning of a stubborn and rebellious son is a scriptural decree and therefore does not apply to a daughter, who is not likely to be led to intemperance in the matter of eating and drinking, as a man is, as it is said: *a son* (Deut. 21:18), not a daughter, nor a ṭumṭum, nor a hermaphrodite.

12. A ṭumṭum, who undergoes an operation and is found to

be a male is not treated as a stubborn and rebellious son, for it is said: *if a man have a stubborn and rebellious son* (*ibid.*), implying that his status as a son was known at the time of his birth.

13. Public announcement must be made of the execution of a stubborn and rebellious son. How is it done? A communication is dispatched to all Israel to the following effect: "We, of such-and-such a court, have condemned So-and-so to death by stoning because he was proved a stubborn and rebellious son."

14. The law that the possessions of those who are executed by the courts passes to their heirs applies also in the case of a stubborn and rebellious son. Although his father caused his death, he inherits all his possessions.

TREATISE IV

LAWS CONCERNING MOURNING

Involving Four Commandments

One Positive and Three Negative

To Wit

1. That one should mourn for deceased relatives, and that even a priest should defile himself and mourn for deceased relatives; but no mourning is to be observed for those who have been condemned to death by the court;

   —I have nevertheless included this treatise in this Book because it embodies the duty of burying the deceased on the day of death, which (as in the case of one who is executed by order of the court) is a positive commandment *—

2. That the High Priest shall not defile himself for deceased relatives;
3. That he shall not enter a place where there is a dead body;
4. That an ordinary priest shall not defile himself for anyone save relatives.

An exposition of these commandments is contained in the following chapters.

* See above, I, xv, 8; and below, iv, 8; cf. SM, "Positive Commandments," No. 231.

CHAPTER I

1. It is a positive command to mourn for deceased relatives, as it is said: *And if I had eaten the sin offering today, would it have been well pleasing in the sight of the Lord?* (Lev. 10:19). According to scriptural law, mourning is observed only on the first day, that is, the day of death, which is also the day of burial. Mourning on the other of the seven days is not of biblical origin. For although we are told in the Bible: *And he (Joseph) made a mourning for his father seven days* (Gen. 50:10), when the Torah was given, the law was reinterpreted. It was Moses, our teacher, who instituted seven days of mourning and seven days of feasting.

2. When does the observance of mourning begin? From the time that the top stone closes the grave. But before the body is buried, the near of kin is not prohibited from doing any of the things a mourner is forbidden. For this reason, David washed and anointed himself before his deceased child was buried.

3. In the case of those who suffered martrydom and whose bodies the government would not release for interment, the observance of mourning rites and the counting of the seven and the thirty days commence from the time that the relatives have ceased petitioning the government for permission to bury the bodies, even if they have not yet given up hope of stealing them.

4. If one was drowned in a river or was devoured by a wild beast, (mourning commences) from the time that all further search for the body has been abandoned. If separate parts of the body have been found, the days of mourning are counted either from the time that the head and the greater part of the body are located, or from the time that all further search has been abandoned.

5. Those who convey the body of a deceased relative to another city and do not know when interment will take place commence to count the seven and the thirty days and to observe mourning from the time that they turn their faces away from the funeral cortege.

6. No mourning is observed for an abortive child. A newborn infant that does not survive thirty days is accounted abortive. Even if it dies on the thirtieth day, no mourning is observed.

7. If, however, it is certain that the birth occurred after the completion of nine months, mourning is observed, even if it dies on the first day of its birth.

8. A stillborn child after the ninth month, or one born after the eighth month that dies even after thirty days, or one that comes out of the mother's womb by pieces or crushed even after the completion of the nine months, is considered an abortion. No mourning is observed for these, nor are the last rites performed for them.

9. In the case of those who are executed by the State, although they are put to death by order of the king, who is empowered by Scripture to do so, their relatives observe mourning for them and do not deny them any of the rites (performed for the dead); their property goes to the king, and they are buried in their ancestral tombs. For those, however, who are executed by order of the court, no mourning rites are observed; but the relatives grieve for them, for grief is a matter of the heart; they are not buried with their ancestors until their flesh has wasted away; and their property passes to their heirs.

10. As for those who deviated from the practices of the congregation—that is, men who cast off the restraint of the commandments, did not join their fellow Jews in the performance of the precepts, observance of festivals, attendance at Synogague and House of Study, but felt free to do as they pleased, as well as for epicureans, apostates, and delators—for these no mourning is observed. In the event of their death, their brethren and other relatives don white garments, and wrap themselves in white garments, eat, drink, and rejoice, because the enemies of the Lord have perished. Concerning them, Scripture says: *Do not I hate them, O Lord, that hate Thee?* (Ps. 139:21).

11. For one who has committed suicide, no funeral rites are performed, no mourning is observed, no lamentation is made; but the relatives stand in line (to be comforted), the Mourner's Bene-

diction is recited, and all that is intended as a matter of honor for the living is done.

Who is to be regarded as a suicide? Not he who climbing up to the roof fell and died, but one who said: "Look! I am climbing to the top of the roof." If he was seen ascending it, agitated by anger or fear, and then fell and died, the presumption is that he committed suicide. But if he is found strangled or hanging from a tree, or slain, or fallen upon his sword, his status is that of any other person who died. His obsequies are attended to, and none of the last rites is denied him.

CHAPTER II

1. The following are those for whom the Torah prescribes mourning: a mother, father, son, daughter, and brother and sister by the same father. By the authority of the Rabbis, the husband is to observe mourning for the wife whom he has already married, the wife for her husband, a brother or sister for a brother or sister by the same mother.

2. Even a priest, who is forbidden to defile himself for a brother and an unmarried sister by the same mother, or for a married sister even if she is by the same father, is bound to observe mourning for them. If the married sister is by the same father, he is bound by biblical law to observe mourning for her.

3. If his son or his brother is the son of a bondwoman, or of a heathen woman, he does not observe any of the mourning rites for him. So too, if he and his children are converts to the Jewish religion, or he and his mother have been set free (from slavery), they do not observe mourning for one another.

Likewise in the case of a betrothed wife, the husband does not observe either the rites of mourning or those of *'ăninuṯ* for her, nor does the wife observe either the rites of mourning or those of 'ăninuṯ for him.

4. Whomever one is bound to mourn for, one is also bound, on the authority of the Scribes, to mourn with, in their presence. Thus if his son's son, or his son's brother, or his son's mother dies,

it is his duty to rend his garments and to observe mourning in the son's presence, but away from his presence, he is not bound to do it. This holds good also in the case of other relatives.

5. In the case of his married wife, although he observes mourning for her, he is not required to observe mourning with her for any of her relatives other than her father or mother, for whom he observes mourning in his wife's presence out of respect for her. Thus if his father-in-law or his mother-in-law dies, he overturns his couch and observes mourning in his wife's presence, but when he is away from her presence he does not observe mourning. So too, the wife is to observe mourning in the presence of her husband if her father-in-law or mother-in-law dies. But in case of the death of other relatives such as his wife's brother or her son, or the husband's brother or his son, they do not mourn one with the other.

Similarly, it appears to me, in the event of the death of the wife of his near of kin or the husband of his near of kin, such as his son's wife or his daughter's husband, he is not bound to observe mourning for the deceased. This applies also to similar cases.

6. How weighty is the command to observe mourning! The law forbidding a priest to contract uncleanness is set aside in the case of a near of kin, so that he may attend to the obsequies and observe mourning, as it is said: *Except for the kin that is near unto him, for his mother, and for his father . . . for her he may defile himself* (Lev. 21:2–3). This is a positive command. If he refuses to defile himself, he is compelled to do it. This applies only to priests, who are prohibited from contracting defilement, but women of priestly stock, who are not prohibited from contracting uncleanness, are not enjoined to defile themselves for a near of kin. It is left to them whether or not they should defile themselves.

7. If the wife of a priest dies, he is bound by the authority of the Scribes to defile himself for her. Her status, according to the Scribes, is that of a corpse the burial whereof is a religious duty; since he is her sole heir, there may be no one to attend to her obsequies. This applies only to his married wife. He is not permitted, however, to defile himself for his betrothed wife.

8. Nor must the priest defile himself for any relative for whom according to the Rabbis no mourning is to be observed, such as those who are put to death by order of the court, those who dissociated themselves from the community, abortives, and suicides.

How long is he bound to defile himself for his near of kin? Until the top stone closes the grave. After the grave is closed, their bodies are like those of others (not related to him), and if he defiles himself for them, he incurs the penalty of flagellation.

9. Nor must the priest defile himself for his unlawful wife. Therefore if the wife of a priest, on the strength of a report that her husband had died, married again (a priest) and subsequently her first husband returned, neither of them may defile himself for her, because she was forbidden to both. He may, however, defile himself for his mother, even if she was profaned. So too, he may defile himself for his son, daughter, brother, and sister, even if they were disqualified priests, aye, even if they were bastards.

10. He is forbidden to defile himself for his married sister even if her husband is a priest, as it is said *and for his sister a virgin, that is near unto him, that hath had no husband* (Lev. 21:3). *A virgin*—this excludes one that was violated or seduced. Lest one conclude that a sister who is of age, or who has lost her virginity through an accident, be also excluded, Scripture adds *that hath had no husband,* that is, whose changed condition was caused by a man; *that hath had no husband*—this excludes a betrothed sister, for whom he may not defile himself, even if the man to whom she is betrothed is a priest.

11. If his sister was divorced during the period of her betrothal, he may defile himself for her, for it is said *for his sister . . . that is near unto him*. This includes a sister that was divorced after her betrothal.

12. He must not defile himself for a brother or a sister by the same mother, for it is said: *There shall none defile himself . . . except . . . for his son, and for his daughter, and for his brother, and for his sister* (Lev. 21:1–3). (From the juxtaposition of the four, we infer that) even as the son (or daughter) is entitled to be

his heir, so the brother and sister (for whom he may defile himself) must be those that are entitled to be his heirs.

13. He must not defile himself in any doubtful case, for it is said: *For her he may defile himself* (Lev. 21:3), implying that he may contract defilement only when it is certain (that defilement is obligatory), not when there is doubt about it. Therefore, if children were mixed up, or it is doubtful whether the child is the offspring of the second husband, born at the completion of seven months, or the child of the first husband, born at the completion of nine months, and in all like instances of doubt, he may not defile himself. So too, if the divorce the wife has been granted (by him) is of doubtful validity or the bill of divorce she has procured is defective, he may not defile himself for her.

14. A priest must not defile himself for any limb severed from his living father or for any of his bones (after his death). So too, if the bones of his father are gathered, even though the spine is intact, he may not defile himself.

15. If his father's head was cut off, he must not defile himself for him, for it is said *for his father* (Lev. 21:2), implying that he (must defile himself for him) as long as his father is whole, not when a part is missing. This applies also to other relatives.

The law bearing upon levitical purity is only suspended in the case of the near of kin, but is not set aside to permit the priest to contract uncleanness from others. Therefore he is forbidden to defile himself for one who is not related to him, even at the time when he defiles himself for his near of kin, for it is said: *For her he may defile himself* (Lev. 21:3), implying that he must not simultaneously defile himself for others. He should not say: "Since I have defiled myself for my father, I may as well proceed to gather the bones of So-and-so," or "touch the grave of So-and-so." Hence a priest who has a death in his family should be careful to bury the body at the outer boundary of the cemetery, making it unnecessary for him to enter the cemetery and contract uncleanness from other graves, while burying his dead.

CHAPTER III

1. If a priest defiles himself for a dead body other than that of any of the six relatives expressly stated in the Bible or that of his wife, and there are witnesses to testify to this effect and due warning has been given him, he is subject to the penalty of flagellation, as it is written: *There shall none defile himself for the dead among his people* (Lev. 21:1). This holds good whether he touches the body, overshadows it, or carries it; whether the defilement is caused by a corpse or by any substance which exudes from it, as it is said: *There shall none defile himself for the dead among his people.* In the Treatise on Corpse Uncleanness, we have already enumerated what uncleanness contracted from a corpse defiles by biblical authority and what uncleanness defiles by rabbinical authority.

2. So too, if a priest touches a grave, he is flogged. He may, however, touch a garment that touched a corpse, even though he contracts thereby seven days uncleanness.

3. In like manner, if he enters a house where uncleanness penetrated, although the object of uncleanness is in another house, he is subject to flogging.

In the Treatise on Corpse Uncleanness, we set forth the kinds of houses that cause uncleanness to enter or to go out, the rules bearing upon interlaced foliage and protruding stones, the things that transmit pollution and those that serve as a screen against it, what is unclean by biblical law and what is unclean by rabbinical authority. We also stated in that treatise that the corpses of heathen do not defile by overshadowing, that their graves are not subject to levitical impurity, that a priest may therefore enter a heathen cemetery and tread upon the graves, that he is only forbidden to touch or carry the object of uncleanness.

4. In case a priest unknowingly enters a house where there is a dead body or enters a cemetery and after becoming aware of it is given warning, if he leaves forthwith, he is exempt; but if he stays there long enough for one to prostrate oneself, he is flogged, as was stated in connection with the subject of the defilement of

the sanctuary. In case he goes in and out repeatedly, if warning is given him each time he is about to enter, he is flogged for each entry.

So too, if he touches a corpse and on being warned desists, then touches it again and is warned again, even if this process is repeated a hundred times, he is flogged for each warning. But if he persists in touching the corpse and does not desist, or if, tarrying in the cemetery, he touches bodies of those not related to him, he is flogged only once even if many warnings have been given him, because as long as he does not desist, his status is that of one who is actually defiled already.

5. In case one defiles a priest, if the defilement is intentional on the part of both of them, the priest is flogged and the one who defiles him transgresses the negative command *Nor put a stumbling block before the blind* (Lev. 19:14). But if it is unintentional on the part of the priest and intentional on the part of the other, the latter is flogged.

6. The High Priest is forbidden to defile himself for his near of kin, as it is said: *Nor (shall he) defile himself for his father, or for his mother* (Lev. 21:11). Nor must he enter a house where there is a dead body, even if it be the body of a near of kin, as it is said: *Neither shall he go in to any dead body* (*ibid.*). We infer therefrom that in some instances he is liable for the transgression of the negative commands *He shall not go in* and *He shall not defile himself*. Thus if he touches or carries a corpse, he is flogged once. But if he enters a house (where a dying person is lying) and while sitting there the patient dies, or if he enters a box, chest, or turret and someone tears open the top of the box (or chest or turret), in which case the uncleanness and his entry occur simultaneously, he is flogged on two counts, because he has transgressed the negative commands *He shall not go in* and *He shall not defile himself*.

7. In case the High Priest has defiled himself and then enters a house (where there is a corpse), if previous warning has been given him, he is also flogged for entering (the house).

8. If a priest finds a *meṯ miṣwah* on the road, he must defile

himself for him. Even the High Priest is bound to defile himself for him and bury the body.

What is meant by a meṯ miṣwah? It is a body lying in the road with no one to bury it. The aforementioned rule has been transmitted to us by tradition. It obtains only if the priest is all alone, and no one accompanies him, so that even if he should call others (to tend the dead) there would be none to answer the call. But if there are others who would respond, it is not deemed a meṯ miṣwah. He should call others to attend to the body.

9. If a priest and a nazarite are on a journey and find an unburied dead, the nazarite should attend to it, because his sanctity is not a lifelong sanctity, but the priest should not defile himself, even though he is only an ordinary priest. If the two who find the body are a High Priest and an ordinary priest, the latter should defile himself. The higher the degree of sanctity, the greater the duty to delay defilement. If the Deputy High Priest and the "priest anointed for war" find an unburied body, the "priest anointed for war," rather than the Deputy High Priest, should attend to the body.

10. If a Naśi dies, all, even the priests, must defile themselves for him. The Rabbis enjoin upon us to regard him as a meṯ miṣwah, because it is the bounden duty of all to pay him respect. All, moreover, must observe for him the rites mandatory upon an *'onen*.

11. Women of priestly stock are not prohibited from defiling themselves for the dead, for it is said: *Speak unto the priests, the sons of Aaron* (Lev. 21:1), that is, not the daughters of Aaron. Likewise, profaned priests are permitted to defile themselves, for it is said *the sons of Aaron,* that is, those who have retained their priestly status.

12. As to a priest who is still a minor, his elders are forbidden to defile him. But if he is about to defile himself of his own accord, the court is under no obligation to keep him away (from the object of defilement). It is his father's duty, however, to initiate him into the rules of "levitical holiness."

13. A corpse communicates defilement to an area of four cubits.

Any priest who comes within four cubits thereof is administered a disciplinary flogging. If he enters a grave area, or goes outside Palestine, or defiles himself by blood oozing from a dying body, or by the top stone covering a grave, or by the buttressing stone, or the like, he is administered a disciplinary flogging, because, on rabbinical authority, these constitute chief sources of defilement, as was set forth in the Treatise on Corpse Uncleanness. But if he enters a cemetery, he is liable to flogging by biblical authority.

14. A priest may defile himself by passing through a grave area, or by going abroad, if he goes there for a religious purpose, such as marrying a wife or studying the Law, and he has no other way of getting there (except through the grave area). (He is permitted to go abroad for the purpose of studying the Law) even if there is a teacher in Palestine capable of imparting instructions to him, because it is not given to (every) one to acquire knowledge from all teachers. So too, he may defile himself by contact with what is unclean by rabbinical authority, for the sake of showing respect to his fellow men. Thus if a mourner walks through a grave area, all may follow him to offer condolence. Likewise, he is permitted to leap over coffins containing corpses in order to welcome the king of Israel, or even a heathen king, so that he be able to distinguish between the kings of the heathens and the kings of Israel, when the ancient glory of the latter will be restored. This obtains also in similar instances. He may also defile himself by contact with what is unclean by rabbinical authority in order to bring suit against a heathen who contests his claim, and thus recover what is due to him. This applies also to like cases.

CHAPTER IV

1. The Jewish practice with respect to the dead and their interment is as follows: they (who perform the last sacred offices) close his eyes; if his mouth is open, they bind up the jaws; after the body is washed, they stop up the organs of the lower extremities, rub him with divers spices, cut his hair, and dress him in an inex-

pensive shroud sewed with white linen thread. The Rabbis introduced the custom of using as a shroud a rough cloth worth a zuz, in order not to shame the poor. They cover the face of the dead in order not to shame the poor whose faces have turned livid as a result of undernourishment.

2. It is forbidden to bury even the Naśi in a silk shroud or gold-embroidered garments, for this is arrogance, extravagance, and a heathen practice. The body is carried to the cemetery on the shoulder.

3. The pallbearers are forbidden to have their shoes on, lest the shoestring of one of the bearers break and he be prevented from performing the religious act.

4. A grave is dug in the sand of a cave. On the side thereof, a niche is opened, where the body is buried face upward; then the grave is covered with dust and stones. It is permissible to bury the dead in a wooden casket. The escorts say to the deceased: "Go in peace," as it is said: *But thou shalt go to thy fathers in peace* (Gen. 15:15). All the graves in the cemetery are marked, and a monument is erected over each. For the righteous, however, no monument need be reared; their deeds are their (abiding) memorial; one need not therefore visit their graves too frequently.

5. One who is in a dying condition is regarded as a living person in all respects. It is not permitted to bind his jaws, to stop up the organs of the lower extremities, or to place metallic or cooling vessels upon his navel in order to prevent swelling. He is not to be rubbed, washed, or put on sand or salt until he expires. He who touches him is guilty of shedding blood. To what may he be compared? To a flickering flame, which is extinguished as soon as one touches it. Whoever closes the eyes of the dying while the soul is about to depart is shedding blood. One should wait a while; perhaps he is only in a swoon.

Likewise, there is to be no rending of garments, no baring of the shoulder, no lamentation for him, nor are a casket and shroud to be brought into the house, till he expires.

6. He whose dead lies before him eats his meal in another room; if he has no other room, he makes a partition and takes his

meal. If he has not the wherewithal to make a partition, he turns away his face and takes his meal. Under no circumstances, however, is he to recline while eating. He eats no meat, drinks no wine, nor does he recite the blessing (over bread), nor does he invite others to join him in saying grace (after the meal), nor do others say the blessing (over bread) for him, or invite him to join them in saying grace; he is exempt from reciting the *Shema,* from saying the *'Ămiḏah,* from putting on phylacteries, and from performing any of the religious duties prescribed in the Law. On Sabbath, however, he reclines (while eating), eats meat and drinks wine, recites the blessing (over bread), invites others to join him in saying grace, while others may recite the blessing for him and invite him to join them in saying grace, and he is bound to perform all the religious duties commanded in the Law, with the exception of marital intercourse.

After burial, he may eat meat and drink a little wine to help moisten the food in his bowels, but not to the point of intoxication.

7. It is forbidden to delay the burial of the dead; the bier should be removed forthwith. Whoever hastens the removal of the bier is praiseworthy; but in the case of a father or a mother, the son (who hastens the removal of the bier) is blameworthy.

8. If the death of a parent occurs on Friday or on the eve of a festival, or if rain is dripping on the bier, the son is permitted to expedite the interment, since he does it out of deference to his father or mother. Whoever keeps his dead overnight transgresses a negative command, unless he does it in honor of the dead, i.e., to supply what is needed (for the funeral).

9. Only on the first day is a mourner forbidden to put on phylacteries, and to eat of his own food, and is bound to sit on an overturned couch. But during the other (six) days of mourning, he is permitted to eat of his own, and to sit on a matting or on the ground, and is bound to put on phylacteries.

Whence do we derive that a mourner is forbidden to put on phylacteries the first day? It is written: *Bind thy headtire upon thee* (Ezek. 24:17). This implies that all others are forbidden (to put on phylacteries). And he (Ezekiel) was told, moreover: *Nor eat the bread of men* (Ezek. 24:22). This implies that all others must eat on the first day (of mourning) of the food of others and are forbidden to eat of their own.

CHAPTER V

1. The following things are forbidden to a mourner—on the first day by biblical law and on the other days by rabbinical authority. He is forbidden to cut his hair, to wash his clothes, to bathe, to anoint himself, to have conjugal relations, to put on shoes, to do work, to read the words of the Torah, to put up his couch, to remove the mourner's headdress, and to extend greetings—the total number of prohibitions is eleven.

2. Whence do we learn that a mourner is forbidden to cut his hair? The sons of Aaron were charged: *Let not the hair of your heads grow loose* (Lev. 10:6). We infer therefrom that any other mourner is forbidden to cut his hair, but must let it grow. Just as he is forbidden to cut the hair of his head, so he is forbidden to cut the hair of his beard or of any part of the body. This prohibition obtains whether the mourner cuts the hair of others or others cut his hair. If, while trimming the hair of another man or while another trims his hair, he learns of the death of his father, the trimming may be finished. The mourner is also forbidden to trim his upper lip or to pare his fingernails with an instrument, but he is permitted to bite them off or to remove one nail with another.

3. Whence do we derive that a mourner is forbidden to wash his clothes, to bathe, and to anoint himself? It is written: *Feign thyself to be a mourner, and put on mourning apparel, I pray thee, anoint not thyself with oil* (II Sam. 14:2). Anointing implies bathing, for the former is preceded by the latter, as it is written: *Wash thyself therefore, and anoint thee* (Ruth 3:3). Just as the mourner is forbidden to wash his clothes, so he is forbidden to put on new white clothes that have been ironed.

4. A mourner is forbidden to anoint even part of his body. If, however, it is his purpose to remove filth, he is permitted to do it.

He is also forbidden to wash even part of his body with warm water, but he may wash his face, hands, and feet, though not the entire body, with cold water.

5. Whence de we learn that a mourner is forbidden conjugal relations? It is written: *And David comforted Bath-Sheba his wife, and went in unto her, and lay with her* (II Sam. 12:24), which implies that before that time he was forbidden to do it. So too, a mourner is not permitted to take a wife, nor is a woman (in mourning) permitted to be married, even if marital relations are not contemplated. A mourner is permitted, however, to be alone with his wife, although conjugal relations are forbidden to him.

6. Whence do we learn that a mourner is forbidden to put on shoes? Ezekiel was told: *And put thy shoes upon thy feet* (Ezek. 24:17), which implies that all other mourners are forbidden to do it. If he is on the road, he walks with his shoes on; when he enters the city he removes them.

7. Where is it intimated that a mourner is forbidden to engage in work? It is written: *And I will turn your feasts into mourning* (Amos 8:10). Just as all are forbidden to do work during a festival, so is a mourner forbidden to engage in work. And just as he is forbidden to engage in work, so is he forbidden to buy and sell merchandise, to go on business from city to city.

8. During the first three days, he is forbidden to do work even if he is a poor man, a recipient of charity; thereafter, if he is poor he may do his work privately in his house, and a woman (in mourning) may ply the spindle in her house.

9. If two brothers or two other men own a shop in partnership and one of them suffers bereavement, the shop must be closed during the seven days of mourning.

10. Even those things which one is permitted to do during the intermediate days of a festival, a mourner is forbidden to do during the seven days; others, however, may attend to them. For instance, if it is necessary to turn over his olives, or to cork his jugs, or to take out his flax from its steeping, or his wool from the dyer's caldron, (he is forbidden to do it,) but he may engage

others to do it, lest they spoil. Others may sprinkle his field for him when [his] turn for water right comes.

11. (If the owner of a field suffers bereavement,) his tenant farmers, whether their tenancy is on the basis of *'ărisuṯ* or on the basis of *ḥăḵiruṯ* or on the basis of *ḳabbĕlanuṯ* may do their work as usual. But those who hire from him asses, camels, or boats are not permitted to use these means of transportation, unless they had hired them—either on a percentage basis or for a fixed sum—for a definite period of time before the bereavement occurred.

12. One who is hired by day may not work, even in another town.

13. If the mourner has the work of others on hand, whether he has contracted to be paid for the work by the piece or is to be paid for it by the day, he may not do it. If he has given out work, they may not do it in his house, but they may do it elsewhere.

14. If the mourner has a lawsuit against another man, he may not institute proceedings against him during the seven days of mourning. But if the delay will involve a heavy loss, he may delegate another man (to enter suit against his opponent). This is the ruling of the Geonim.

15. Whence do we infer that a mourner is forbidden to engage in the study of the Torah? Because Ezekiel was told: *Sigh in silence* (Ezek. 24:17).

16. He is forbidden to read the Pentateuch, Prophets, and Hagiographa, or to recite the Mishnah, Midrash, and Halakhah. If he is indispensable to the public, he may impart instruction, provided that he does not place an interpreter at his side. He whispers (the instruction) to another scholar at his side, who in turn whispers it to the interpreter, and the latter speaks aloud to the public.

17. Whence do we learn that a mourner should not sit on a bed? Because it is said: *Then the king arose, and rent his garments, and lay on the earth* (II Sam. 13:31).

18. He is bound to keep his bed overturned during the seven days of mourning. It is his duty to overturn not only his own bed

but all the beds in his house. Even if he has ten beds in ten houses in ten different cities, it is his duty to overturn them all. Even if there were five brothers and one of them died, they all overturn their beds. But a couch used exclusively for clothes or for keeping money therein need not be overturned. A couch of leather need not be overturned; the inner bolster frame is loosened and it collapses of itself. In the case of a bed, the two poles whereof protrude downward, all he has to do is to tilt it up, since it cannot be overturned.

If he overturns all his beds but sleeps in someone else's bed or in a chair, or on a chest or on the floor, he has not fulfilled his duty. He must sleep on the overturned bed.

19. Whence do we infer that a mourner is forbidden to remove the mourner's headdress? Ezekiel was commanded: *And cover not thy upper lip* (Ezek. 24:17). We conclude therefrom that all other mourners are bound to have the headdress on.

The cloth with which he wraps himself shall cover part of his mouth, as it is said: *And he shall cover his upper lip* (Lev. 13:45). This sentence is rendered by Onkelos, "He shall wrap himself up like a mourner."

20. Whence do we infer that a mourner is forbidden to extend greetings to others? Ezekiel was told: *Sigh in silence* (Ezek. 24:17). During the first three days he should not respond to greetings extended to him, but inform (the one who salutes him) that he is in mourning; after the third day and through the seventh, he may respond to the greetings of others; after the seventh and through the thirtieth, he may greet others, but others should not greet him. If he is in mourning for his father or his mother, others should not greet him until the expiration of twelve months.

If a mourner is forbidden to greet others, is it not an argument from the less to the greater that he is forbidden to talk much or to indulge in laughter, as it is said *in silence?* He should not hold a child in his arms, lest it lead him to levity. He should not enter a place where there is rejoicing, such as a house of feasting, or the like.

CHAPTER VI

1. On the authority of the Scribes some of the mourning rites are to be observed thirty days. What scriptural support have the Rabbis for this enactment? It is said: *And she shall bewail her father and her mother for a full month* (Deut. 21:13). From this we infer that a mourner should manifest sorrow for thirty days.

2. The following things are forbidden to a mourner during the thirty days: cutting the hair, putting on pressed clothes, taking a wife, attending social festivities, traveling on business—in all, five prohibitions.

3. What is the rule concerning the cutting of hair? Just as the mourner is forbidden to cut the hair of any part of his body, to trim his upper lip, or to pare his nails with an instrument, during the seven days, so he is forbidden to do any of these things during the thirty days. The restriction with regard to hair cutting applies to a man only, but a woman may have her hair trimmed after the seven days. A man, however, is forbidden to have it done before the thirty days are over; in case of mourning for a father or a mother, he is bound to let his hair grow long until it hangs loose, or until his companions chide him.

4. So too, he is forbidden during the thirty days to put on pressed clothes, if they are new and white. This prohibition applies to both man and woman. One may, however, put on pressed clothes that are colored. So too, one is permitted to put on pressed white clothes, if they are not new. The prohibition predicated of pressed clothes does not apply to clothes made of linen. After the thirty days, one is permitted to put on pressed clothes, even if one is in mourning for one's father or one's mother.

5. What is the rule concerning marriage (in case one suffers bereavement)? A mourner is forbidden to take a wife during the thirty days. He is permitted, however, to betroth a woman even on the day when the bereavement occurs. In the case of the death of his wife, if he has already fulfilled the duty of procreation and has someone to look after him and has no little children, he is forbidden to marry again until three festivals have passed. But if he has not

yet fulfilled the duty of procreation, or even if he did fulfill it but his children are little, or he has no one to look after him, he is permitted to betroth a woman and marry her forthwith; he is forbidden, however, to have connubial relations with her till the termination of the thirty days. So too, a woman who is in mourning is not to be cohabited with till the termination of the thirty days.

6. If it is his turn to entertain friends, he may do so immediately after the seven days; but if it is not his turn, he is forbidden to attend such entertainment till the termination of the thirty days.

7. This rule holds good in case of mourning for all relatives other than a father or a mother. In the latter case, he may under no circumstances participate in social festivities till the termination of twelve months.

8. In case of the death of (other) relatives, the mourner may go on a (long) business trip after the thirty days; but in case of the death of his father or his mother, he may not go until his friends chide him and say to him, "Come with us."

9. If he mourns for (other) relatives, it rests with him as to whether he should give less attention to his business or the same attention as usual; but if he lost his father or his mother he is bound to give less attention to it.

10. One who goes from place to place (on business, and learns of the death of a near of kin), if he can avoid all business affairs, should do so; if he cannot, he may procure what he needs for the road and the barest necessities of life.

11. One whose husband, wife, father, or mother was hanged is forbidden to reside in the city where the execution occurred until the flesh (of the executed) has been completely decomposed. But if the city is as large as Antioch, the surviving spouse, or son, may live in a section opposite the one where the hanging took place.

12. Part of the seventh day is reckoned as a full day; the seventh day enters into the count of both periods. Therefore the mourner is permitted on the seventh day to wash (his clothes), to bathe,

and to do the other things (forbidden during the seven-day period). Likewise, part of the thirtieth day is reckoned as a full day, and the mourner is permitted thereon to cut his hair and iron his clothes.

13. If a person suffers bereavements in immediate succession and his hair is too heavy on him, he may make it lighter with a razor, but not with scissors; he may wash his clothes with water, but not with natron or lye; he may, moreover, wash his entire body with cold but not warm water.

If a person suffers bereavements in immediate succession after he has returned from abroad, or from captivity, or from prison; or after he has been released from a ban, or absolved from a vow on application to a sage; or after he has emerged from a state of uncleanness to cleanness—under any of these circumstances he may cut his hair during the period of mourning, since he has suffered one bereavement after another and has had no earlier opportunity (to do it).

CHAPTER VII

1. If one is advised of the passing of a relative within thirty days of the latter's death, even if the news is conveyed to him on the thirtieth day, the information is deemed "recent" information, and he is bound to observe the seven days from the day on which the news reaches him. He rends his garments and counts (from that day) the thirty-day period during which hair cutting and other matters are forbidden. The general principle is: the day when "recent" information reaches the mourner is regarded as the day of burial. But if the news reaches him after thirty days, it is deemed "deferred" information; he observes only one day of mourning and does not rend his garment. In the latter case, the day when the information is received is treated as the seventh and the thirtieth day, and part of the day is reckoned as a full day.

2. What is meant by the statement that part of the day is reckoned as a full day? If one observes mourning even one hour, it is as though he has observed it all day. Therefore, during the remainder of the day, he is permitted to put on his shoes, to anoint

himself, to cut his hair and to do all other things one is forbidden (during the thirty days of mourning).

3. If one receives "recent" information on a festival or on a Sabbath, and by the time the Sabbath or the festival is over, it becomes "deferred" information, the Sabbath or the festival enters into the counting, and he observes only one day of mourning after the festival or the Sabbath, and part of the day is reckoned as a full day, as was stated before.

4. In case one sustains the loss of a near of kin and is unaware of it until he arrives home, if (at the time of the burial) he was in the vicinity—that is, within a distance of ten Persian miles and would have been able to return in one day—the days observed (by the other members of the family) enter into his counting, and he counts with them till the thirty days are terminated. This rule obtains even if he returns on the seventh day, provided, however, there are still comforters at the house of the most prominent person of the household, even if the comforters have made ready to leave. But if there are no longer any comforters in the house, he counts by himself. So too, if at the time of the burial he was in a distant place, though he returns on the second day, he counts the seven and the thirty days from the day of his return.

5. During the first three days, a mourner should not go even to the house of another mourner. Thereafter he may go; he takes a seat, however, not among the comforters but among those who are to be comforted. During the entire first week, he does not leave the house; the second week he goes out but does not occupy his (usual) seat (in the Synagogue); the third week he takes his (usual) seat (in the Synagogue) but does not converse (with people) as is his wont to do; the fourth week he is like any other person.

6. The High Priest is bound to observe all the laws of mourning. He is forbidden, however, to rend the upper part of his garment, to let his hair grow loose, and to follow the bier. The people come to his house to comfort him, and when he is served the meal of comfort all are seated on the floor and he sits on a stool. When others comfort him, they say, "May we be thy atonement," and he

replies, "May ye be blessed of Heaven"; when he desires to comfort others his deputy places him between [himself] and the people and the High Priest says (to the mourners), "Be ye comforted."

7. So too, the king is bound to observe all the laws of mourning. But he must not go out of the door of his palace to follow the bier of a deceased relative; it is needless to state that he must not follow the bier of a nonrelative. He does not comfort mourners. It is true that David followed the bier of Abner; but that was done by him to make it known to the people that the slaying of Abner was not with his consent.

8. None may enter the king's palace to comfort him save his servants and those who receive permission to do it. They have no right to offer him condolence, unless they obtain his permission to do so. When the meal of comfort is served him, all the people are seated on the floor, and he sits on a leather couch.

CHAPTER VIII

1. A mourner is bound to rend his garment, as it is said: *Neither rend your clothes, that ye die not* (Lev. 10:6), which implies that any other mourner is bound to rend his clothes. It must be done while he is standing, as it is written: *Then the king arose and rent his garments* (II Sam. 13:31). What part of the garment should be rent? The front part. If he rends the back part or the sides thereof or the lower part, he has not discharged his duty. The High Priest, however, rends the lower part.

2. What is to be the size of the tear? A handbreadth. It is not required that the mourner sever the stiff border around the neck. He may rend his garment with an instrument. The tear should be made on the inside, and not in the presence of the people. Therefore he puts his hand inside and rends the garment away from the bystanders. He is bound to rend only his uppermost garment.

3. During the seven days of mourning, the tear is to be in the front part. If he wishes to change his garment, he may do it, and does not have to rend the garment (he puts on), for any rent which is not made in the poignancy of grief is not a proper rending.

These rules apply only in the case of relatives other than a father or a mother. In the case of a father or a mother, he tears his garments until he bares his chest. He must sever the stiff border around the neck, and rend it with the hands on the outside in the sight of all the people and must tear all his garments, but the rending of the undershirt, that is, the shirt close to his body, is not indispensable; and if he puts on another garment during the seven days, he is bound to rend it. Furthermore, in case of the death of a father or a mother, he must bare his shoulder, removing his arm from the shirt so that his shoulder and arm are exposed. In this wise he walks before the bier. But after the burial of the parent, it is unnecessary for him to bare the shoulder.

4. A minor (who suffers bereavement) is made to rend his clothes in order to arouse grief. If one who is ill sustains bereavement, he is not made to rend his clothes; nor should he be informed of the death, lest he become distracted in mind, and the women are directed to keep silent on his account.

5. The garment is rent for a father-in-law or a mother-in-law, out of respect for one's wife. Likewise a woman rends her garment for her father-in-law or her mother-in-law, out of respect for her husband.

6. If one has no cloak to rend (at the time when a near of kin dies) and obtains one during the seven days, he must rend it; but if (he obtains it) after the seven days, he does not have to rend it. For his father or mother, however, he must rend it during the thirty days.

If one goes forth before the bier with a garment already rent, making others believe that he has just rent it, he deceives the people and is guilty of disrespect for the living and the dead.

7. If one says to another man, "Lend me your cloak that I may visit my father who is ill," and he goes and finds him dead, he rends it, mends the rent, returns the cloak and compensates the lender for the damage done by the rent. But if he does not advise the lender that he is going to visit his sick father, he must not touch it.

8. In case a sick person falls into a swoon and the near of kin,

deeming him dead, tears his garment, and subsequently the patient dies, if the death occurs within the space of time of an utterance, he need not tear his garment again; but if it occurs after the interval of an utterance, he is bound to make another rent. So too, in the event he is told that his father died, and he rends his clothes and then discovers that it is his son who died; or he is advised that someone (in his family) died and he thinks that it is his father and rends his clothes, but soon finds that the dead is his son, if he ascertains the truth within the interval of an utterance, he has discharged the duty of rending his clothes; if he ascertains it after the interval of an utterance, he has not fulfilled his duty and is bound to make another tear.

9. If one sustains several bereavements at the same time, he makes one rent for all of them. But if among the deceased is his father or his mother, he makes one rent for the others, and another one for his father or his mother.

10. In case one suffers a bereavement and rends his garment and soon suffers another bereavement, if the second death occurs during the seven days (of the first), he makes another rent; if it occurs after the seven days, he extends somewhat the first rent. If he suffers a third loss after the termination of the seven days for the second, he extends the rent somewhat and continues extending it until the rent reaches (the region of the) navel. Having reached the region of the navel, he leaves a space of three fingers (from the last rent) and rends anew. If the front part has become full of rents, he turns the garment front to back (and rends again). If the upper part has become full of rents, he turns it (upside) down (and rends again).

If he is informed of the death of his father and rends his garments and after the seven days his son dies and he extends the rent, the lower one may be sewed up but not the upper one, as will be stated later. If he is advised of the death of his son and he rends his garment and after the seven days his father dies, he may not extend the rent but rends anew, because the rule that a rent may be extended does not obtain in case of (the death) of a father or mother.

CHAPTER IX

1. A rent made for all other deceased relatives may be basted after the seven days and sewed up after the thirty days, but one made for a father or a mother may be basted only after thirty days but is never to be sewed up. A woman, however, out of regard for her dignity, may baste immediately the rent made by her for her father or mother.

2. Just as a mourner is bound to rend his clothes for his father or mother, so one is bound to rend his clothes for his teacher who taught him Torah, for a Naśi, for an 'Aḇ beṯ din, (on learning) of a slaying (that affected) the larger part of the community, (on hearing) God's name blasphemed, on witnessing the burning of a scroll of the Law, (on seeing the ruins) of the cities of Judea, of Jerusalem, or of the sanctuary.

3. In all these instances, he rends his clothes till he bares his chest. These rents he may never sew up, but he may baste them, hem them, or pick up (the frayed edges) with a cross-stitch, or mend them in the form of a ladder stitch. The only mending which is forbidden is the Alexandrian mending. Whoever rends his garment in a place that has been basted, hemmed, or picked up has not discharged his duty; but one may rend in the part where an Alexandrian mending has been done. Even if he turns the garment upside down, so that the border (around the neck) is now the lower part, he may not sew it up.

4. Just as the seller is forbidden to sew it up, so is the buyer forbidden. Therefore the seller must inform the buyer thereof that it cannot be sewed up.

5. Whence do we derive that a disciple must tear his clothes for his teacher? It is written: *And he (Elisha) cried: My father, my father, the chariots of Israel and the horsemen thereof. And he saw him no more; and he took hold of his own clothes and rent them in two pieces* (II Kings 2: 12). We conclude therefrom that a disciple is bound to sever the stiff border (around his neck).

6. Whence do we derive that one must rend one's clothes for a

Naśi, an 'Ab̲ bet̲ din, or on receipt of tidings of a slaying (which affected) the larger part of the community? It is written: *Then David took hold on his clothes, and rent them; and likewise all the men that were with him. And they wailed and wept and fasted until even, for Saul, and for Jonathan his son, and for the people of the Lord, and for the house of Israel; because they were fallen by the sword* (II Sam. 1: 11–12). For *Saul,* that is, the Naśi; for *Jonathan,* that is, the 'Ab̲ bet̲ din, *and for the people of the Lord, and for the house of Israel; because they were fallen by the sword,* that is, they rent their clothes on hearing sad tidings.

7. Whence do we derive that one must rend one's clothes on hearing God's name blasphemed? It is written: *Then came Eliakim the son of Hilkiah, who was over the household, and Shebna the scribe, and Joah the son of Asaph the recorder, to Hezekiah with their clothes rent* (II Kings 18: 37). Whether one hears (the blasphemy) himself or hears it from him who reports it, one is bound to rend one's clothes.

8. The witnesses, however, are not bound to rend again when they testify in court, as they have already done so at the time they heard it.

9. Whence do we derive that those who witness the burning of a scroll of the Law are in duty bound to rend their clothes? It is written: *And it came to pass, when Jehudi had read three or four columns, that . . . he cast it into the fire . . . until all the roll was consumed in the fire that was in the brazier. Yet they were not afraid, nor rent their garments, neither the king, nor any of his servants* (Jer. 36: 23–24). From this we gather that those who witness the burning of a scroll must rend their clothes, provided that the burning thereof is an act of violence, as in the (above cited) instance. Moreover, (on seeing a scroll burned) one is bound to make two rents: one for the parchment and one for the writing, as it is said *after that the king had burned the roll and the words* (Jer. 36: 27).

10. Whence do we derive that one who sees the ruins of the cities of Judea or of Jerusalem or of the sanctuary should rend his clothes? It is written: *There came certain men from Shechem,*

from Shiloh, and from Samaria, even fourscore men, having their beards shaven and their clothes rent (Jer. 41:5).

11. Whoever is with a dying person at the time when the latter breathes his last is bound to rend his garment, even if he is not related to the deceased. So too, if a worthy person dies, all are in duty bound to rend their garment, even if he was not a scholar; the rent to be made is to be a handbreadth (in extent), as is required in the case of the death of a near of kin.

But if a sage dies, all are (like) his near of kin; all rend their clothes for him till their chests are exposed; they bare their shoulders on the right; and his school is closed for seven days. It has long been the practice of scholars everywhere to rend their garment for one another to the extent of a handbreadth, even if they were on the same level of knowledge, none imparting instruction to the other.

12. All who rend their garments for a deceased sage may baste the rent as soon as they have turned away their faces from the rear of the bier. It seems to me that he who rends his clothes for a sage may sew it up the following day; for even if his master dies, he observes mourning for him only one day, either the day of death or the day when the news of the death reaches him. So too, it appears to me that one who rends his clothes for the Naśi or for a similar grievous misfortune may baste the rent the following day, although he may never sew it up.

13. If news of the passing of a sage is received, the rending of clothes takes place at the memorial service held for him, for that is the occasion on which he is honored. The rent may be basted on the same day and sewed up the following day.

14. If the 'Aḇ beṯ din dies, all rend their clothes for him and bare their shoulders on the left; all the Houses of Study in his city are closed. The (steady) attendants at the Synagogue come to Synagogue but change their (usual) places; those that usually sit on the north side take their seats on the south side and those that usually sit on the south side take their seats on the north side.

15. When a Naśi dies, all rend their clothes for him and bare both arms and shoulders; all Houses of Study are closed. The

(steady) attendants at the Synagogue come to Synagogue only on the Sabbath, and seven persons read (the weekly portion). They do not walk about in the street, but each family stays all day at home in a state of anguish.

CHAPTER X

1. The Sabbath counts as one of the seven days of mourning. But no mourning is observed thereon save in matters relating to domestic privacy, such as wrapping oneself up with a mourner's hood, conjugal relations, and washing (the hands and feet) with warm water. But no mourning is to be observed in public. The bereaved puts on his shoes, places his couch in an erect position, and extends greetings to others. If he has another garment he changes; he should not put on a rent garment on the Sabbath even if he is mourning for his father or his mother. If he has no other garment, he turns the part that is rent to the back.

2. From what time on the eve of the Sabbath is the mourner's couch put up again? From the time of the Afternoon Service and onward. Nevertheless, the mourner must not sit down on the couch until it gets dark; and when the Sabbath is over, he overturns it (again), although he may have but one day more (to complete the seven days).

3. None of the mourning rites are observed either on the (Pilgrim) Festivals or on the New Year or on the Day of Atonement. If one buries his dead even an hour before a festival or before the New Year or before the Day of Atonement, the restrictions prescribed for the seven days are annulled. Hence (if the burial takes place before the New Year or before the Day of Atonement) he counts after the termination of the New Year or of the Day of Atonement twenty-three days. If the burial takes place before Passover, he counts after the conclusion of the festival sixteen days, because (the seven days of mourning) the restrictions whereof have been annulled (by the observance of one hour before the festival), together with the seven days of Passover, account for fourteen days.

So too, if he buries his dead before Pentecost, he counts after the festival sixteen days, for though Pentecost lasts only one day, it counts as seven days, as do the other festivals.

4. If one buries his dead before Tabernacles, he counts only nine days after the festival. For the Eighth Day of Solemn Assembly is a distinct festival. Hence the first festival, (the advent of) which interrupts the seven days, together with the seven days of the festival and the Eighth Day of Solemn Assembly, which is a distinct festival, account for twenty-one days.

5. If one buries his dead seven days before any of the Pilgrim Festivals or before the New Year or before the Day of Atonement, all the mourning rites prescribed for the thirty days are annulled. He may cut his hair and wash his clothes on the eve of the festival or of the New Year or of the Day of Atonement, for part of the day is reckoned as a full day, and the thirty days are regarded as terminated. But if he is mourning for his father or his mother, even if the parent was buried thirty days prior to the festival, he is not permitted to cut his hair till it hangs loose or till his friends chide him. The festivals do not remove this restriction.

6. If the sixth day (of mourning) occurs on the day before a festival, all the more so if (the day before the festival) is the fifth or the third day (of mourning), he is not permitted to cut his hair. Only the restrictions prescribed for the seven days are annulled. He is not permitted to wash his body or anoint himself or do any of the things (forbidden to a mourner) until the festival sets in. The festival cancels the remainder of the seven days. After its conclusion, he completes the thirty days, (counting) from the day of death, and during this period all the five things are forbidden to him.

7. If the seventh day occurs on a Sabbath coinciding with the eve of Passover or Tabernacles, all restrictions prescribed for the thirty days are annulled and he may cut his hair during the festival, because he was unavoidably prevented (from doing it before), since he could not cut his hair on a Sabbath. Likewise, if the seventh day occurs on a Sabbath coinciding with the day before Pentecost or the New Year or the Day of Atonement, he may cut his hair after

these sacred days, because the restrictions relating to the thirty days have been annulled. He may therefore cut his hair anytime he desires to do it.

8. If he buries his dead during a festival, the laws of mourning are not binding upon him. He does not observe mourning rites during the festival, but at the termination thereof he begins to count the seven days and observes all mourning rites, and he counts the thirty days from the day of the burial, observing during the remaining of the thirty days all the restrictions relating to that period.

9. In places where festivals are kept two days, if a funeral occurs during a festival the mourner counts the seven days from the day which brings the festival to a close, although no mourning is observed thereon. For since the second day is only of rabbinical derivation, it is included (in the seven days). He counts thereafter only six days, and counts the thirty days from the day of the burial, as was stated before.

10. If one buries his dead on the second day of a festival which is also the last day thereof or on the second day of Pentecost, he observes mourning thereon, because the observance of the second day of a festival is on the authority of the Rabbis, while the observance of mourning on the first day is on the authority of Scripture. Therefore, the rabbinical positive command is superseded by the biblical positive command. If, however, the burial occurs on the second day of the New Year, he does not observe mourning thereon, for the two days of New Year are regarded as one long day, as was stated in the Treatise on the Sanctification of the New Moon.

CHAPTER XI

1. Although there is no mourning observed on a festival, the mourner rends his garment thereon and bares the shoulder and is served the meal of comfort. This is done only during the intermediate days of a festival; on the festival itself, even on the second day thereof, there is no rending of clothes, no baring of the shoulder, and no serving of the meal of comfort.

2. Only the near of kin, who are in duty bound to observe mourning, rend their garment and bare the shoulder during the intermediate days of a festival. These rites are also performed (during the intermediate days of a festival) for a sage; so too, is the rite of rending performed (by all, on the intermediate days of a festival) for a worthy person, and (for any person) by those who are present at the time when he breathes his last. In the case of a sage, the meal of comfort is provided for all, even during the intermediate days of a festival, in the open space in the manner that mourners are served, because all mourn for him.

3. During the intermediate days of a festival the meal of comfort is taken by the mourners (while seated) on an upright couch. The Mourner's Benediction is not said; but the comforters stand in a row and tender condolence (to the mourners), and the latter give them leave to depart. The bier is not set down in the public square, so as not to invite lamentation, since lamentation and fasting are forbidden on a festival. Nor are the bones of a father or mother to be gathered during the festival week, because this is an occasion of mourning for the son. Needless to say, (the gathering of the bones of) other relatives (is forbidden).

Nor is lamentation to be made on Ḥanukkah or Purim or the New Moon, but all laws pertaining to mourning are observed on these days. It is permitted, however, to make lamentation on the day before and the day after Ḥanukkah and Purim.

4. Women may raise a wailing during the intermediate days of a festival, but they may not clap their hands. On the New Moon, Ḥanukkah, and Purim they may wail and clap hands; but on none of these occasions may they raise lamentation. Once the dead has been interred, they may neither raise a wailing nor clap hands.

5. What is meant by "raising a wailing" (*'innuy*)? When all chant in unison; "raising a lamentation" (*ḳinah*) means that one leads and all respond after her (in chorus), as it is written: *And teach your daughters wailing, and everyone her neighbor lamentation* (Jer. 9:19). This prohibition (of lamentation) obtains only in case of death of an ordinary man. But if a scholar dies, lamentation

is made for him during the intermediate days of a festival, and, needless to say, it is made for him on the New Moon, Ḥanukkah, and Purim, but not on the second day of a festival. Lamentation is made for him only in his presence. Once he is buried, no lamentation is made for him.

The day when news of the death of a scholar is received is regarded as though one were in his presence, and lamentation is made for him, though the place of burial is distant.

6. For thirty days before a festival, a woman should not (avail herself of the services of a professional wailer to) stir up grief for her dead, so that the festival should not find the family in a depressed mood, because the dead are not dismissed from the mind (at least) thirty days. This stricture obtains only if the death occurred some time before (the thirty days). But if the death occurred within thirty days of the festival, she may use the services of a professional wailer.

7. The wedding week is accounted a festival. Therefore if the death of a near of kin occurs during the week of feasting, even if it be the death of the groom's father or mother, he completes the seven days of feasting and then observes the seven days of mourning and counts the thirty days from the termination of the days of rejoicing.

8. In case one has prepared everything needed for the wedding feast, has baked bread and dressed meat in readiness for the feast, when a near of kin dies, if the death occurs before he has poured water over the meat, he sells the meat and the bread, observes the seven days of mourning and then the seven days of feasting. But if the death occurs after he has poured water over the meat, so that he can no longer sell the meat, the dead body is taken to another room, the groom and the bride are led under the canopy, he performs his marital duty and abstains, observes the seven days of feasting, and after that the bereaved keeps the seven days of mourning. During the days of feasting he observes all the mourning rites included in the category of domestic privacy—the rites which are observed on the Sabbath. Therefore he sleeps among the men and his wife among the women, so that they have no

conjugal relations. But she is not denied ornaments even during the thirty days.

If they reside in a place where meat upon which water has been poured can be sold, he sells it, and observes first the seven days of mourning. If it is a place where meat cannot be sold, even though no water has been poured over it, he observes first the seven days of feasting.

The foregoing holds good only if the father of the groom or the mother of the bride dies, in which case if the meal (already prepared) goes to waste, there will be no one to prepare another for them. But if the father of the bride or the mother of the groom or any other member of either family dies, the seven days of mourning are observed first, then the marriage takes place and the seven days of feasting are kept.

CHAPTER XII

1. Funeral services are held in honor of the dead. Therefore the heirs are compelled to pay the cost of professional wailers, male as well as female, and a funeral address is delivered. If the deceased left word that no lamentation be made for him, his wish is complied with. But if he left word that he should not be buried, no heed is paid to his wish, for burial is a commandment, as it is said: *But thou shalt surely bury him* (Deut. 21:23).

2. Whoever fails to mourn for a sage will not live long, and whoever fails to mourn for a worthy person deserves to be buried alive. Whoever sheds tears for a worthy person, the Holy One, blessed be He, has a reward in store for him.

3. No scroll of the Law may be placed on the bier of a sage. He is not to be transferred from bier to bier, nor is the bier to be taken out save through the doorway; it is not to be let down from the roof—all of which is permitted in the case of other men.

4. No less than seven halts are made for the dead, provided that no less than ten members of the family are present. They are made only the first day in the cemetery and in those places where it is the custom to do so.

What is the procedure in the matter of halts in places where it is customary to make them? All relatives and members of the family who are not bound to observe mourning rites are made to rise. Thereupon selections from the Book of Lamentations and passages of similar import are read to them. He who conducts the service then says to them, "Sit down, friends, sit." While they are seated, he addresses additional words to them; then he says to them, "Rise, friends, rise." He reads to them again. This process is repeated seven times.

5. Wherever it is the custom to make halts for men, they are also made for women. Funeral addresses are given on them as they are on men. But the bier of a woman is never set down in the public square, for that would be an act of disrespect for her; her burial should immediately follow her death.

6. When the bones of a near of kin are gathered, no words of lamentation and wailing are recited, neither is the Mourner's Benediction or the Mourner's Consolation said; but words of praise to the Holy One, blessed be He, and words of admonition (to the living) are spoken.

7. In case a coffin containing the remains of a near of kin is transferred from (a temporary) place to (a permanent) place, if the spinal column is intact the comforters stand in a row, say the Mourner's Benediction and the Mourner's Consolation, and a memorial address is delivered, though the transfer takes place twelve months after the death. But if the spinal column is no longer intact, no address is delivered, comforters do not stand in a row, neither is the Mourner's Benediction nor the Mourner's Consolation recited.

The Mourner's Benediction is the blessing recited in the mourner's house; the Mourner's Consolation is the condolence tendered by those who stand in a row.

8. If a son gathers the bones of his father or mother, he mourns for the departed parent all day; but in the evening he does not mourn, though he has the bones with him wrapped up in a sheet, and no selections from the Book of Lamentations are read.

9. No funeral service is held for very young children. At what

age is a service held for them? In the case of poor or elderly parents for children of five; in the case of rich parents for children of six. This applies to both male and female children.

10. If an infant up to thirty days old dies, it is carried (to the grave) in arms and buried by one woman and two men, but not by one man and two women on account of the prohibition of privacy. The people do not stand in a row, do not recite the Mourner's Benediction or the Mourner's Consolation. An infant that is past thirty days is taken out on a board carried in the arms; the people stand in a row, the Mourner's Benediction is recited, the Mourner's Consolation is said. A child twelve months old is taken in a bier.

11. For any child that is carried out in a bier, the public manifest grief; for one that is not carried out in a bier, the public need not manifest grief. In the case of a child that is known to the public at large, the public should take part in the funeral proceedings. If it is not known to the public at large, the public need not take part in the funeral proceedings. In places where it is customary for women to precede the bier, they precede it; where it is customary for them to follow the bier, they follow it.

12. No funeral services are held for menservants or maidservants. The people do not stand in a row for them, neither is the Mourner's Benediction recited, nor is the Mourner's Consolation said, but they say to him (the master), as they would say to him in the case of a loss of an ox or an ass: "The Lord replace your loss."

CHAPTER XIII

1. What procedure is followed in consoling mourners? After the body is buried, the mourners assemble and station themselves at the border of the cemetery. All who have escorted the dead stand around them, forming themselves into rows, row after row, each consisting of no less than ten people, excluding the mourners.

2. The mourners stand on the left of the comforters, and all the comforters, one by one, pass by, saying to them, "Be ye com-

forted of Heaven." Then the mourners go home. On each of the seven days of mourning, condolence is tendered them, whether by the same visitors or new ones.

3. The mourner reclines in the most prominent place (when the meal of comfort is served). The comforters are permitted to sit only on the ground, as it is written: *So they sat down with him upon the ground* (Job 2:13), and they are not to say anything to him until he speaks first, as it is written: *And none spake a word to him* (*ibid.*); Scripture continues: *After this opened Job his mouth* (Job 3:1) . . . *Then answered Eliphaz* (Job 4:1). As soon as he nods his head, the comforters are not permitted to stay any longer so that they fatigue him not.

4. If the deceased has left no near of kin to be comforted, ten worthy people come and sit in his place all the seven days of mourning and others come (to comfort them). If ten steady attendants are unavailable, the requisite number is supplied daily by those who volunteer their services. They come and sit in his place.

5. It is the duty of all to rise before the Naśi, except a mourner and a sick person. To all who rise before him, he may say, "Be seated," except to a mourner and a sick person, because it might be construed to mean that the person thus addressed should continue in a "state of mourning" or "in a state of illness."

6. It is permitted to sweep or sprinkle water (on the floors) in a house of mourning, to wash dishes, cups, jugs, and flasks, and to kindle the lights. It is forbidden, however, to bring there perfumes and spices.

7. The victuals for the meal of comfort should not be taken to the mourner's house in vessels of silver or of bamboo, or the like, but in wicker vessels of peeled willow twigs, or the like, in order that the poor be not put to shame; nor are drinks to be served in white glass vessels, but in colored glass, in order not to put to shame the poor, whose wine is not of good quality.

8. None (of the consolers who partake of the meal of comfort) should drink more than ten cups of wine: three before the meal, three during the meal, and four after the meal. None should exceed this number lest he become inebriated.

9. Neither a halakhic nor an aggadic theme should be discussed in the house of mourning, but all should sit in a depressed mood. In the presence of the dead, nothing but things pertaining to the dead should be the topic of conversation. It is forbidden to engage in words of Torah in his presence or in the cemetery.

10. One should not weep for the dead more than three days nor lament for him more than seven days. This obtains only in the case of the death of ordinary people, but in the case of scholars, the length of the period of weeping and lamentation is in proportion to their wisdom. But the weeping should not last longer than thirty days. For none is greater than was Moses, our teacher, yet it is said: *And the children of Israel wept for Moses . . . thirty days; so the days of weeping in the mourning for Moses were ended* (Deut. 34:8); nor are memorial services to be held after twelve months. For none is greater in wisdom than was our Teacher, the Saint, yet memorial services for him were held only (for a period) of twelve months. So too, if the news of the demise of a sage is received after twelve months (of his death), no lamentation is made for him.

11. One should not indulge in excessive grief over one's dead, for it is said: *Weep ye not for the dead, neither bemoan him* (Jer. 22:10), that is to say, (weep not for him) too much, for that is the way of the world, and he who frets over the way of the world is a fool. What rule should one follow in case of bereavement? (The rule is:) three days for weeping, seven days for lamenting, and thirty days for (abstaining) from cutting the hair and the other four things (forbidden to a mourner).

12. Whoever does not mourn the dead in the manner enjoined by the Rabbis is cruel. (If one suffers bereavement,) one should be apprehensive, troubled, investigate his conduct, and return in repentance. If one of a company dies, all the members thereof should be troubled. During the first three days the mourner should think of himself as if a sword is resting upon his neck, from the third to the seventh day as if it is lying in the corner, thereafter as if it is moving toward him in the street.

Reflections of this nature will put him on his mettle, he will bestir himself and repent, for it is written: *Thou hast stricken them, but they were not affected* (Jer. 5:3). He should therefore be wide awake and deeply moved.

CHAPTER XIV

1. The following positive commands were ordained by the Rabbis: visiting the sick; comforting the mourners; joining a funeral procession; dowering a bride; escorting departing guests; performing for the dead the last tender offices; acting as pall-bearer; going before the bier; making lamentation (for the dead); digging a grave and burying the body; causing the bride and the bridegroom to rejoice; providing them with all their needs (for the wedding). These constitute deeds of loving kindness performed in person and for which no fixed measure is prescribed. Although all these commands are only on rabbinical authority, they are implied in the precept: *And thou shalt love thy neighbor as thyself* (Lev. 19:18), that is: what you would have others do unto you, do unto him who is your brother in the Law and in the performance of the commandments.

2. The reward for escorting strangers is greater than the reward for all the other commandments. It is a practice which Abraham, our father, instituted, and the act of kindness which he exercised. He gave wayfarers food to eat and water to drink and escorted them. Hospitality to wayfarers is greater than receiving the Divine Presence, as it is said: *And he looked, and, lo, three men stood over against him, and when he saw them, he ran to meet them* (Gen. 18:2). But escorting guests is even greater than according them hospitality. Said the Rabbis: *Whoever does not accompany guests is as though he would shed blood* (So 46b).

3. A person may be compelled to escort a visitor, just as he is compelled to contribute to charity. The court used to provide escorts for itinerants. If it neglected to do so, it was accounted as if it had shed blood. Even if a person accompanies another the distance of four cubits a great reward is in store for him.

How far is one bound to escort another? A teacher accompanies his pupil as far as the outskirts of the city; one accompanies one's equal up to the Sabbath limit; a pupil escorts his master a distance of a Persian mile; in the case of one's chief teacher, one is to escort him a distance of three Persian miles.

4. All are in duty bound to visit the sick. Even a man of prominence must visit a less important person. The ill should be visited many times a day. The more often a person calls on the sick, the more praiseworthy he is, provided that he does not inconvenience the patient. He who visits the sick is as though he would take away part of his sickness and lighten his pain. Whoever does not call to see the sick is as though he would shed blood.

5. A sick person should not be visited before the third day. If his illness came on suddenly and his condition is growing worse, he may be called on forthwith. He should not be visited either during the first three hours or during the last three hours of the day, because (during those hours), they who look after him are busy attending to his needs. Those who suffer from intestinal trouble or have eye trouble or headaches should not be visited, because it is hard for them to see callers.

6. One who visits a sick person shall not sit upon the bed, or in a chair or on a bench or any elevated place, or above the head side of the patient, but should wrap himself up and sit below the head side, pray for his recovery, and depart.

7. It seems to me that the duty of comforting mourners takes precedence over the duty of visiting the sick, because comforting mourners is an act of benevolence toward the living and the dead.

8. If one has a dead body to look after and a wedding to attend, he should let the wedding go by and tend the dead. For thus it is written: *The heart of the wise is in the house of mourning* . . . (Eccles. 7:4). If a funeral and a bridal procession meet, the funeral procession must make way for the bridal procession, and both of these make way for the king.

9. The study of the Law is suspended for the duty of joining a funeral procession or a procession conducting a bride to the canopy. This rule obtains only if there is not a sufficient number

present (to pay the deceased their last respects), but if there is a sufficient number present, the study of Torah is not to be interrupted. However, those who are not engaged in study are in duty bound to attend to the dead.

10. If a person dies, all the townspeople are forbidden to do work until the burial has taken place. But if there are others who will attend to the obsequies, they may carry on their work.

11. If a scholar dies, even if close to sixty myriads are present (to pay him the honor due him), study is interrupted for the duty of escorting the body; if, however, sixty myriads are present, study is not interrupted. But if the deceased was imparting instruction to others, there is no maximum limit. All must suspend their studies in order to escort the body.

12. We bury the dead of the heathens, comfort their mourners, and visit their sick, in the interest of peace.

13. It is forbidden to use cemeteries for profane purposes. Thus one must not eat or drink in them, do any work there, or read the Scriptures or study the Mishnah there. The general rule is: it is forbidden to make use of them. They must not be treated disrespectfully. One must not walk within four cubits of a grave with phylacteries in his hand or a scroll of the Law in his arm, or pray there. It is permitted, however, to do these things at a distance of four cubits from a grave.

14. One who carries bones from one place to another for burial must not put them in a saddlebag and place them across the back of an ass and ride (sitting on them), because this is a disgraceful treatment of the remains (of the dead). But if he is afraid of thieves or robbers, he is permitted to do it.

15. It is forbidden to remove a corpse from one grave to another, even from a poorer grave to a better one. But if the grave (to which it is transferred) is on his own ground, it is permitted to remove the body even from a better grave to a poorer one.

16. It is forbidden to bury one body upon another or to bury two bodies in the same grave. It is disrespectful to do so. But a very young child that still sleeps with its mother may be buried with her.

17. The earth of a grave is not forbidden for use, for no prohibition attaches to natural soil, but a built grave is forbidden for use.

18. A grave erected for a dead person is not forbidden for use until the body has been buried there; but even if an abortion had been laid therein, it is forbidden for use.

19. A tomb, erected for a person while he was alive, to which a row of stones was added after the remains of that person had been laid therein, is forbidden for use, even if the remains were transferred. But if the additional row can be recognized, it may be removed and the remainder is permitted for use. If the tomb was built for a dead person as soon as the remains are laid therein, the tomb may not be used (for other purposes), even if the remains have been subsequently removed.

20. If one hews a grave for his father and then goes and buries him elsewhere, no other person may ever be buried therein. The grave may never be used, out of deference to his father.

21. It is forbidden to make use of any part of a corpse save the hair which is not an integral part of the body. So too, the coffin and shroud are forbidden for use. But material held ready for making a shroud is not forbidden for use. Even if a shroud was woven for a dead person, it is not forbidden until it has actually touched the bier which is buried with the body, for mere designation does not impose the prohibition thereof (for any other purpose).

22. All garments thrown upon the dead in the bier which is buried with him are forbidden for use, lest confusion arise with regard to the shroud.

23. If the father and mother in their grief are throwing garments upon their deceased son, it is the duty of others to save those garments. But once they have reached the bier which is buried with the dead, no effort should be made to save them.

24. One should be trained not to be wasteful, not to damage or destroy garments. It is better that they be given to the poor than that they be cast to the maggots and worms. Whoever throws many garments upon the dead transgresses the negative command *Thou shalt not destroy* (Deut. 20:19).

25. If a king dies, the horse which he used to ride is mutilated; the tendons of the hoofs of the calf which drew the carriage in which he sat are cut from the ankle downward, so that its vitality is not affected. Scholars' meetings are held at his grave for seven days, as it is written: *And all Judah and the inhabitants of Jerusalem did him honor at his death* (II Chron. 32:33) that is, they set up an academy near his grave. If a Naśi dies, his academy is closed for not more than thirty days.

26. When a king or Naśi dies, his bed and all his implements are burned. This is not regarded as "the way of the Amorites," nor is it to be deemed "wanton destruction," for it is written: *Thou shalt die in peace; and with the burnings of thy fathers, the former kings that were before thee, so shall they make a burning for thee* (Jer. 34:5).

TREATISE V

LAWS CONCERNING KINGS AND WARS

Involving Twenty-three Commandments

Ten Positive and Thirteen Negative

To Wit

1. To appoint a king over Israel *;
2. Not to choose him from a community of proselytes;
3. That he shall not have many wives;
4. That he shall not acquire many horses;
5. That he shall not accumulate much silver and gold;
6. To destroy the seven (Canaanite) nations;
7. Not to spare the life of any of them;
8. To blot out the seed of Amalek;
9. To remember what Amalek did;
10. Not to forget his evil deeds, his lying in wait on the road;
11. Not to reside (permanently) in the land of Egypt;
12. To offer terms of peace to the inhabitants of a city which is to be besieged, and to deal with it in the manner set forth in Scripture, whether it accepts or rejects the terms of peace;
13. That only in the case of Ammon and Moab no peace is to be offered when siege is to be laid to their cities;
14. Not to destroy a fruit-bearing tree while besieging a city;

* Literally: "in Israel." The first rule in this treatise, as in the preceding treatises, sets forth the first command, which is amplified in i, 1.

15. To provide a latrine whither the men of the camp shall go to relieve themselves;
16. To have a paddle to dig therewith;
17. To anoint a priest to speak to the men of the army in wartime;
18. That one who has betrothed a wife, built a house,† or planted a vineyard ‡ shall be sent back home from the war, that he may rejoice in his acquisition a full year §;
19. That no service, municipal, military, or the like, is to be exacted from those who are exempt from joining the army;
20. Not to be afraid or retreat while a battle is waged;
21. The law relating to a woman taken captive in war;
22. Not to sell her;
23. Not to reduce her to the level of a bondwoman after cohabitation with her.

An exposition of these commandments
is contained in the following chapters.

† And has not dedicated it; see below, vii, 3, 9.

‡ And has not used the fruit thereof; *ibid.*

§ See Deut. 24: 5. Maimonides offers it as a reason why the above-mentioned recruits should be discharged from the army, although that verse refers to those who are exempt from joining the army; see below, vii, 10.

CHAPTER I

1. Three commandments—to be carried out on entering Palestine—were enjoined upon Israel: to appoint a king, as it is said: *Thou shalt in anywise set him king over thee* (Deut. 17:15); to destroy the seed of Amalek, as it is said: *Thou shalt blot out the remembrance of Amalek* (Deut. 25:19); and to build the sanctuary, as it is said: *Even unto His habitation shall ye seek, and thither thou shalt come* (Deut. 12:5).

2. The appointment of a king was to precede the war with Amalek, as it is written: *The Lord sent me to anoint thee to be king over His people. . . . Now go and smite Amalek* (I Sam. 15:1, 3). The destruction of the seed of Amalek was to precede the erection of the sanctuary, as it is written: *And it came to pass, when the king dwelt in his house, and the Lord had given him rest from all his enemies round about, that the king said unto Nathan the prophet: . . . I dwell in a house of cedar but the ark of God dwelleth within curtains* (II Sam. 7:1–2).

Seeing that the setting up of a king was a commandment, why did the Holy One, blessed be He, look with disfavor upon the request (made by the people) of Samuel for a king? Because they asked it in a querulous spirit. Their request was prompted not by a desire to fulfill the commandment but by a desire to rid themselves of Samuel the prophet, as it is written: *For they have not rejected thee, but they have rejected Me* (I Sam. 8:7).

3. The first king of a dynasty cannot be set up save by the court of seventy (-one) elders and a prophet, as was the case with Joshua, who was appointed by Moses, our teacher, and his court; and as was the case with Saul and David, who were appointed by Samuel the Ramathite and his court.

4. No king is appointed from a congregation of proselytes, even after the lapse of many generations, unless his mother is a Jewess by descent, as it is said: *Thou mayest not put a foreigner over thee, who is not thy brother* (Deut. 17:15). This rule applies not only to the office of king but also to any other office. One cannot

serve as captain of a host, or even of fifty or even of ten, or as superintendent of the distribution of water from the water channel, not to say as judge or Naśi, unless one is an Israelite by descent, as it is said: *One from among thy brethren shalt thou appoint king* (*ibid.*), that is, whatever appointments you make shall be from among your brethren.

5. No woman is eligible to head the State, for it is said *king* (*ibid.*), that is, not a queen. So too, whatever the office to which appointment is made, only a man is qualified to hold it.

6. The following may not be set up as king or High Priest: a butcher, a barber, a bathhouse keeper, or a tanner, not because these are legally disqualified but because their occupations are despised and the people will always have a low opinion of (those who were engaged in) them. Therefore one who was engaged even one day in any of these occupations is ineligible.

7. When a king is installed, he is anointed with anointing oil, as it is written: *Then Samuel took the vial of oil, and poured it upon his* (Saul's) *head* (I Sam. 10:1). As soon as he is anointed, he acquires the office for himself and his children forever. The right thereto is transmitted as a legacy, as it is said *to the end that he may prolong his days in his kingdom, he and his children, in the midst of Israel* (Deut. 17:20). If he left a son who is a minor, the kingdom is held for him until he grows up, as Jehoiada acted in the case of Joash. Whoever is first in the order of inheritance is first in the order of succession to the kingship. The older son takes precedence of the younger one.

But not only the office of king but every position or appointive office held by the father descends to his son and son's son in perpetuity, provided that the son is entitled to fill the vacancy by reason of wisdom and piety. If he is qualified to take his father's place by reason of piety, but is not his father's equal in wisdom, he is appointed and given additional instruction. But if he is wanting in piety, he is not appointed to any office, be his knowledge ever so great.

As soon as David was anointed king he acquired the crown of royalty, which became hereditary in his male line forever, as it is written: *Thy throne shall be established forever* (II Sam. 7:16). But he acquired it only for the deserving ones (among his descendants), as it is written *if thy children keep My covenant* (Ps. 132:12). But although he acquired it only for the deserving (among his children), the kingdom will not be cut off from the seed of David forever. The Holy One, blessed be He, made him this promise, as it is written: *If his children forsake My law, and walk not in Mine ordinances . . . then will I visit their transgression with the rod, and their iniquity with strokes. But My Mercy will I not break off from him* (Ps. 89:31, 33).

8. If the prophet appoints a king from any tribe of Israel (other than that of Judah) and that king walks in the way of the Law and the commandments and fights the battles of the Lord, he is deemed a legitimate king, and all the rules set forth with regard to the king apply to him, even though the kingship belongs primarily to David and therefore one of his descendants should be the ruling monarch. For Ahijah the Shilonite appointed Jeroboam king and said to him: *And it shall be, if thou wilt hearken unto all that I command thee . . . I will build thee a sure house, as I built for David* (I Kings 11:38). He said, moreover: *And unto his son will I give one tribe, that David My servant may have a lamp always before Me in Jerusalem* (I Kings 11:36).

9. The kings of the House of David will endure forever, as it is written: *And thy throne shall be established forever* (II Sam. 7:16). But in case of a king selected from any other tribe of Israel, the kingship will be wrested from his house, as it was said to Jeroboam: *And I will . . . afflict the seed of David, but not forever* (I Kings 11:39).

10. Kings of Israel are anointed not with anointment oil but with balsam oil. Only the descendants of David are anointed with anointment oil. In Jerusalem, none but a descendant of David is ever appointed king.

11. Kings of the dynasty of David are anointed at a spring.

12. A king succeeding his father is not anointed unless his right to succession is contested or violently resisted, in which case he is anointed to put an end to the opposition. Thus Solomon was

anointed because of the pretensions of Adonijah, Joash because of the machinations of Athaliah, and Jehoahaz because of the claim of Jehoiakim, his brother.

CHAPTER II

1. The king is to be accorded great honor. The attitude of his subjects toward him should be one of awe and reverence, as it is said: *Thou shalt in anywise set him king over thee* (Deut. 17:15), implying that his awe should be over you. No commoner may ride on his horse, sit on his throne, make use of his scepter or crown, or any of his general utensils. At his death, these objects are burned in his honor. Nor is anyone but a king to make use of his menservants, maidservants, or attendants. Therefore Abishag would have been permitted to Solomon but was forbidden to Adonijah.

2. A commoner is never permitted to have relations with a king's wife. Not even a king may marry the widow or the divorced wife of another king.

3. It is forbidden to see the king when he is naked, or when his hair is being cut, or when he is taking a bath, or when he dries himself (after his bath). He may not perform ḥăliṣah, for it is said: *And she shall spit in his face* (Deut. 25:9). This is an act of humiliation. Even if he is willing to submit to the humiliation, no heed is paid to him, for in the case of a king, if he foregoes the honor due him, it is not remitted. Since he cannot perform ḥăliṣah he cannot contract a levirate marriage.

So too, if a king dies, none of the brothers may release his wife, since none of them may contract levirate marriage with her. She therefore remains forever bound to her husband's brothers.

4. If any of his near of kin dies, the king may not go out of the door of his palace. When he is served the meal of comfort, all the people sit on the ground and he sits on a leather couch. If he is of the Davidic dynasty and enters the Temple Court, he may sit there, for none but the kings of the House of David may sit in the Temple Court, as it is said: *Then David the king went in, and sat before the Lord* (II Sam. 7:18).

5. The king has his hair trimmed every day, pays due regard to his personal appearance, adorns himself with beautiful clothes—as it is written: *Thine eyes shall see the king in his beauty* (Isa. 33:17)—sits on his throne in his palace, sets his crown on his head. All the people come before him when he is disposed to see them, they stand in his presence, and bow down to the ground. Even the prophet stands in the presence of the king and bows down to the ground, as it is written: *"Behold Nathan the prophet." And when he was come in before the king, he bowed down before the king with his face to the ground* (I Kings 1:23).

The High Priest, however, comes before the king only when he is disposed to do it; he does not stand in his presence, but the king stands before him, as it is said: *And he shall stand before Eleazar the priest* (Num. 27:21). Nevertheless, it is the duty of the High Priest to give honor to the king, to ask him to be seated, to rise before him when the latter comes to see him. The king therefore shall not stand in his presence save when he asks him for directions given by means of the Urim.

So too, it is incumbent upon the king to give honor to students of the Torah. When the members of the Sanhedrin and Sages of Israel visit him, he shall rise before them and seat them at his side. This is the way Jehoshaphat the King of Judah acted. When he saw even the disciple of a scholar, he rose from his throne, kissed him, called him, "my teacher, my master." This humble attitude becomes the king in the privacy of his home only, when none but he and his servants are there. He may not act thus in public, he may not rise before any man, nor be soft of speech, nor call anyone but by his name, so that his fear be in the hearts of all.

6. Just as Scripture accords great honor to the king and bids all pay him honor, so it bids him cultivate a humble and lowly spirit, as it is written: *And my heart is humbled within me* (Ps. 109:22). He must not exercise his authority in a supercilious manner, as it is said: *that his heart be not lifted up above his brethren* (Deut. 17:20). He should deal graciously and compassionately with the small and the great, conduct their affairs in their best interests, be wary of the honor of even the lowliest. When he addresses the

public collectively, he shall use gentle language, as did David when he said: *Hear me, my brethren, and my people* (I Chron. 28:2). It is also written *if thou wilt be a servant unto this people this day . . . then they will be thy servants forever* (I Kings 12:7). At all times, his conduct should be marked by a spirit of great humility. None was greater than Moses, our teacher; yet he said: *And what are we? Your murmurings are not against us* (Exod. 16:8). He should put up with the cumbrances, burdens, grumblings, and anger of the people as a nursing father puts up with a sucking child. The Bible styles the king "shepherd," [as it is written] *to be shepherd over Jacob His People* (Ps. 78:71). The way in which a shepherd acts is explicitly stated in the prophetic text: *Even as a shepherd that feedeth his flock, that gathereth the lambs in his arms, and carrieth them in his bosom and gently leadeth those that give suck* (Isa. 40:11).

CHAPTER III

1. As soon as the king ascends the throne, he must write a scroll of the Law for himself, in addition to the one which his ancestors have left him. He is to have it corrected by the court of seventy-one from the scroll in the Temple Court. If his father left him no scroll or it was lost, he must write two copies; one, the writing of which is obligatory upon every Jew, he shall place in his treasure-house, and the other is to be with him all the time, except when he enters the privy or bathhouse or any other place where it is improper to read it. When he goes forth to war, it shall be with him; when he returns (from war), it shall be with him; when he sits in judgment, it shall be with him; when he sits down to eat, it shall be before him, as it is said: *And it shall be with him, and he shall read therein all the days of his life* (Deut. 17:19).

2. *He shall not multiply wives to himself* (Deut. 17:17). It has been learned by tradition that he may not have more than eighteen wives, including concubines. If he adds a single one to this number and has relations with her, he is flogged. But he may divorce one and marry another in her place.

3. *He shall not multiply horses to himself—only as many as are required for his chariot* (San. 2:4). He is forbidden to add even one idle horse to run before him, as other kings do. If he adds, he is flogged.

4. Nor shall he multiply to himself silver and gold to store them away in his treasury in order to satisfy his pride and vainglory, but only enough to pay the army, servants, and attendants. It is commendable, however, to store silver and gold in the treasury of the House of the Lord, in order to provide for the needs of the community and for war purposes. He is forbidden only to fill his own coffers, as it is said: *And he shall not multiply to himself* (Deut. 17:17). If he does, he is flogged.

5. The king is forbidden to drink to the point of intoxication, as it is written: *It is not for kings to drink wine* (Prov. 31:4). He shall be occupied day and night with the study of the Law and the needs of Israel, as it is said: *And it shall be with him, and he shall read therein all the days of his life* (Deut. 17:19).

6. So too, he must not indulge in sexual excess. Even if he has only one wife, he shall not have frequent relations with her, as fools do, for it is written: *Give not thy strength unto women* (Prov. 31:3). Scripture lays particular stress on (the danger) of his heart being turned away from God, as it is said *that his heart turn not away* (Deut. 17:17); for his heart is the heart of the whole congregation of Israel. Therefore Scripture exhorts him more than any other Israelite to cleave to the Law, as it is said *all the days of his life* (Deut. 17:19).

7. We have already stated that the kings of the House of David may be judged and testified against. But with respect to the kings of Israel, the Rabbis enacted that they neither judge nor be judged, neither testify nor be testified against, because they are arrogant, and (if they be treated as commoners) the cause of religion would suffer.

8. The king is empowered to put to death anyone who rebels against him. Even if any of his subjects is ordered by him to go to a certain place and he does not go, or is ordered to stay home and fails to do so, he is culpable, and the king may, if he so decides, put

him to death, as it is written: *Whosoever he be that shall rebel against thy commandment . . . shall be put to death* (Josh. 1:18).

So too, if one reviles him, or taunts him, as did Shimei, the son of Gera, the king is empowered to condemn him to death. But the only mode of execution within his jurisdiction is decapitation with the sword. To uphold his honor, the king is permitted to inflict the penalties of imprisonment and chastisement with whips. He may not, however, expropriate the property of an offender. If he does, he is guilty of robbery.

9. Whoever disobeys a royal decree because he is engaged in the performance of a religious command, even if it be a light command, is not liable, because (when there is a conflict) between the edict of the Master (God) and the edict of the servant (the king), the former takes precedence of the latter. It goes without saying that if the king issues an order annulling a religious precept, no heed is paid to it.

10. If a person kills another and there is no clear evidence, or if no warning has been given him, or there is only one witness, or if one kills accidentally a person whom he hated, the king may, if the exigency of the hour demands it, put him to death in order to insure the stability of the social order. He may put to death many offenders in one day, hang them, and suffer them to be hanging for a long time so as to put fear in the hearts of others and break the power of the wicked.

CHAPTER IV

1. It is within the province of the king to levy taxes upon the people for his own needs or for war purposes. He fixes the customs duties, and it is forbidden to evade them. He may issue a decree that whoever dodges them shall be punished either by confiscation of his property or by death, as it is written: *And ye shall be his servants* (I Sam. 8:17). Elsewhere it is said: *All the people found therein shall be tributary unto thee, and shall serve thee* (Deut. 20:11). From these verses we infer that the king imposes taxes and fixes customs duties and that all the laws enacted by him with re-

gard to these and like matters are valid, for it is his prerogative to exercise all the authority set forth in the section relating to the king.

2. He may send (messengers) throughout all the borders of Israel, take from the people the strong and valiant men, place some of them in his chariots and among his horsemen, appoint others to attend to him, and still others to run before him, as it is written: *And he will appoint them unto him, for his chariots, and to be his horsemen, and they shall run before his chariots* (I Sam. 8:11). He may take of the handsomest among them to minister to and wait on him, as it is written: *And he will take your goodliest young men . . . and put them to his work* (I Sam. 8:16).

3. So too, he may take all the craftsmen that he requires, put them to his work and pay them their wages; he may take all the animals (of the people), their menservants and maidservants for his work, paying (the owners) for their use or their price, as it is written: *And to plow his ground, and to reap his harvest, and to make his instruments of war, and the instruments of his chariots. . . . And he will take your menservants and your maidservants, and your goodliest young men, and your asses, and put them to his work* (I Sam. 8:12, 16).

4. So too, he may take from the confines of Israel wives and concubines. Wives are those who have a marriage contract and are acquired by an act of legal betrothal; concubines are those who have no marriage contract and are acquired not by an act of legal betrothal but by one of intimacy. The latter are permitted to the king, but forbidden to a commoner, who may, however, acquire his maidservant after he has designated her for himself.

The king may employ the concubines in his palace as cooks, bakers, and perfumers, as it is written: *And he will take your daughters to be perfumers, and to be cooks, and to be bakers* (I Sam. 8:13).

5. Similarly, he may draft those capable of holding office, appoint them heads of groups of thousands, and of groups of fifties, as it is written: *And he will appoint them unto him for captains of thousands, and captains of fifties* (I Sam. 8:12).

6. He may seize fields, oliveyards, and vineyards, and give them to his servants when they go forth to war and are encamped around those places and have no other supply of food, and he pays for what he seizes, as it is said: *And he will take your fields, and your vineyards, and your oliveyards, even the best of them, and give them to his servants* (I Sam. 8:14).

7. He may take the tenth of their seed, their trees, and their flocks, as it is written: *And he will take the tenth of your seed, and your vineyards. . . . He will take the tenth of your flocks* (I Sam. 8:15, 17).

8. King Messiah will receive one thirteenth of all the provinces to be conquered by Israel. This is the share that will be assigned to him and his descendants forever.

9. The property of those who are executed by the State belongs to the king. The royal treasures of the kingdoms he subdues belong to him. The plunder that the people take is brought to him and he first takes one half thereof. The other half is distributed equally among those who were in the thick of the fight and those who stayed behind, looking after the baggage, as it is written: *For as is the share of him that goeth down to the battle, so shall be the share of him that tarrieth by the baggage; they shall share alike* (I Sam. 30:24).

10. All the land he conquers belongs to him. He may give thereof to his servants and warriors as much as he wishes; he may keep thereof for himself as much as he wishes. In all these matters he is the final arbiter. But whatever he does should be done by him for the sake of Heaven. His sole aim and thought should be to uplift the true religion, to fill the world with righteousness, to break the arm of the wicked, and to fight the battles of the Lord. The prime reason for appointing a king was that he execute judgment and wage war, as it is written: *And that our king may judge us, and go out before us, and fight our battles* (I Sam. 8:20).

CHAPTER V

1. The primary war which the king wages is a war for a religious cause. Which may be denominated a war for a religious cause? It includes the war against the seven nations, that against Amalek, and a war to deliver Israel from the enemy attacking him. Thereafter he may engage in an optional war, that is, a war against neighboring nations to extend the borders of Israel and to enhance his greatness and prestige.

2. For a war waged for a religious cause, the king need not obtain the sanction of the court. He may at any time go forth of his own accord and compel the people to go with him. But in case of an optional war, he may not lead forth the people save by a decision of the court of seventy-one.

3. He may break through (private property) to make a road for himself, and none may protest against it. No limit can be prescribed for the king's road; he expropriates as much as is needed. He does not have to make detours because someone's vineyard or field (is in his way). He takes the straight route and attacks the enemy.

4. It is a positive command to destroy the seven nations, as it is said: *But thou shalt utterly destroy them* (Deut. 20:17). If one does not put to death any of them that falls into one's power, one transgresses a negative command, as it is said: *Thou shalt save alive nothing that breatheth* (Deut. 20:16). But their memory has long perished.

5. So too, it is a positive command to destroy the memory of Amalek, as it is said: *Thou shalt blot out the remembrance of Amalek* (Deut. 25:19). It is a positive command always to bear in mind his evil deeds, the waylaying (he resorted to), so that we keep fresh the memory of the hatred manifested by him, as it is said: *Remember what Amalek did unto thee* (Deut. 25:17). The traditional interpretation of this injunction is: *Remember,* by word of mouth; *do not forget,* out of mind.

6. All provinces conquered by the king at the decision of the court are deemed a national conquest and become in all respects

an integral part of the Land of Israel conquered by Joshua, provided that they are annexed after the whole of Palestine, the boundaries of which are specified in the Bible, has been reconquered.

7. It is permitted to settle everywhere except in Egypt from the Great Sea to the west thereof, an area of four hundred square Persian miles, opposite Ethiopia and the wilderness. In all this territory it is forbidden to settle.

Three times the Torah admonishes us not to return to Egypt, as it is said: *Ye shall henceforth return no more that way* (Deut. 17:16); *And thou shalt see it no more again* (Deut. 28:68); *Ye shall see them again no more forever* (Exod. 14:13). Alexandria is included in the forbidden area.

8. It is permitted to go to Egypt on business or for the purpose of conquering it. The interdiction applies only to settling there; but the infraction of the negative command does not subject (the offender) to the penalty of flogging, because he is permitted to enter the land and his decision to reside there permanently does not involve a tangible act.

It appears to me that were the king of Israel with the approval of the Supreme Court to conquer Egypt, it would be permitted to settle there. The prohibition is directed only at individuals or at those who would take up their abode there while it is in the hands of the heathens, because the practices of the Egyptians are more corrupt than those of the inhabitants of all other lands, as it is said: *After the doings of the land of Egypt . . . shall ye not do* (Lev. 18:3).

9. It is forbidden to emigrate from Palestine and go abroad, unless one goes to study the Law, or to marry a wife, or to rescue property from heathens, and then returns to Palestine. So too, one may leave on business. But one is forbidden to make one's home abroad, unless there is a famine in Palestine so severe that a *denar's* worth of wheat is selling at two *denar*. This holds good only if money is available and food is high. But if food is cheap and money scarce and one is unable to earn it and has no savings, one may go to any place where one can make a living. But though

one is permitted to emigrate, if one does, the act is not in conformity with the law of saintliness. Remember Mahlon and Chilion! They were the two great men of their generation. They left Palestine at a time of great distress; nevertheless, they incurred thereby the penalty of extinction.

10. The greatest of our Sages used to kiss (the rocks) on the borders of Palestine. They used to kiss the stones of the land and roll themselves in its dust, as it is written: *For thy servants take pleasure in her stones, and love her dust* (Ps. 102:15).

11. The Rabbis said that the sins of him who lives in Palestine are forgiven, as it is written: *And the inhabitant shall not say: "I am sick"; the people that dwell therein shall be forgiven their iniquity* (Isa. 33:24). Even if one walks four cubits in it, one is assured of life in the world to come. So too, one who is buried there will obtain atonement; it is as though the place (where one lies) were an altar which effects atonement, as it is said: *And the land doth make expiation for His people* (Deut. 32:43). In (forecasting) punishment, (the prophet) says: *And thou thyself shalt die in an unclean land* (Amos 7:17). There is no comparison between one whom Palestine receives while he is living and one whom it receives after his death; nevertheless the greatest among our wise men brought their dead there. Think of Jacob, our father, and of Joseph, the righteous!

12. At all times one should live in Palestine even in a place the majority of whose population is heathen, and not live outside Palestine even in a place the majority of whose population is Jewish; for he who leaves Palestine is as though he would serve idolatry, as it is written: *For they have driven me out this day that I should not cleave unto the inheritance of the Lord, saying: Go, serve other gods* (I Sam. 26:19). In (predicting) punishment, the prophet says: *Neither shall they enter into the land of Israel* (Ezek. 13:9).

Just as it is forbidden to emigrate from Palestine to other lands, so it is forbidden to emigrate from Babylon to other lands, as it is written: *They shall be carried to Babylon, and there shall they be* (Jer. 27:22).

CHAPTER VI

1. No war is declared against any nation before peace offers are made to it. This obtains both in an optional war and a war for a religious cause, as it is said: *When thou drawest nigh unto a city to fight against it, then proclaim peace unto it* (Deut. 20:10). If the inhabitants make peace and accept the seven commandments enjoined upon the descendants of Noah, none of them is slain, but they become tributary, as it is said: *They shall become tributary unto thee, and shall serve thee* (Deut. 20:11). If they agree to pay the tribute levied on them but refuse to submit to servitude, or if they yield to servitude but refuse to pay the tribute levied on them, their overtures are rejected—they must accept both terms of peace.

The servitude imposed on them is that they are given an inferior status, that they lift not up their heads in Israel but be subjected to them, that they be not appointed to any office that will put them in charge of Israel. The terms of the levy are that they be prepared to serve the king with their body and their money, such as building walls, fortifying strongholds, constructing the king's palace, and similar services, as it is written: *And this is the account of the levy which King Solomon raised; to build the house of the Lord, and his own house, and Millo, and the walls of Jerusalem . . . and all the store cities that Solomon had. . . . All the people that were left of the Amorites . . . of them did Solomon raise a levy of bond servants, unto this day. But of the children of Israel did Solomon make no bond servants, but they were the men of war, and his servants, and his princes, and his captains, and rulers of his chariots and of his horsemen* (I Kings 9:15, 19–22).

2. The king may lay down as a condition of peace that he take half their money or land and leave in their possession all chattel, or that he take all their chattel and leave the land in their possession.

3. Once they make peace and take upon themselves the seven commandments, it is forbidden to deceive them and prove false to the covenant made with them.

4. If they refuse to accept the offer of peace, or if they accept the offer of peace but not the seven commandments, war is made

with them; all adult males are put to death; all their money and little ones are taken as plunder, but no woman or minor is slain, as it is said: *But the women and the little ones . . . shalt thou take as a prey unto thyself* (Deut. 20:14); the phrase *the little ones* refers to male minors.

This applies only to an optional war, that is, a war against any other nation; but in war waged against the seven nations or against Amalek, if these refuse to accept the terms of peace, none of them is spared, as it is said: *Thus shalt thou do unto all the cities which are very far off from thee. . . . Howbeit of the cities of these peoples . . . thou shalt save alive nothing that breatheth* (Deut. 20:15, 16). So too, with respect to Amalek, it is said: *Thou shalt blot out the remembrance of Amalek* (Deut. 25:19).

Whence do we derive that the (above-cited) command refers only to those who refuse to accept terms of peace? Because it is written: *There was not a city that made peace with the children of Israel, save the Hivites the inhabitants of Gibeon; they took all in battle. For it was of the Lord to harden their hearts, to come against Israel in battle, that they might be utterly destroyed* (Josh. 11:19–20). We infer therefrom that the offer of peace had been made, but they did not accept it.

5. Three proclamations Joshua sent (to the inhabitants of Canaan) before he entered the land. The first read: "Whoever wishes to emigrate, let him emigrate"; this was followed by a second which read: "Whoever wishes to make peace, let him do so"; the third proclamation read: "Whoever wants war may have war."

Why then did the Gibeonites resort to stratagem? Because they had first ignored the proclamation (issued to the seven nations) in general, and, not knowing the law of Israel, they thought that the opportunity for making peace was gone. Why did the princes find the case of the Gibeonites difficult, arguing that but for the oath, the latter deserved to be smitten with the edge of the sword? Because the princes had made a covenant with them, which was contrary to the injunction *Thou shalt make no covenant with them* (Exod. 23:32); they should have made them servants, doing task work.

And since the oath was made in error, the Gibeonites, by right, should have been put to death for the deceit practiced by them, but the result of such a procedure would have been the desecration of the name of God.

6. No peace offer is made to Ammon and Moab, as it is said: *Thou shalt not seek their peace nor their prosperity all thy days* (Deut. 23:7). Say the Rabbis: "Because it is said: *When thou drawest nigh unto a city to fight against it, then proclaim peace unto it* (Deut. 20:10), one might think that this applies also to the cities of Ammon and Moab, therefore Scripture says: *Thou shalt not seek their peace nor their prosperity*. Because it is said: *He shall dwell with thee, in the midst of thee . . . where it liketh him best; thou shalt not wrong him* (Deut. 23:17), one might think that this applies also to an Ammonite and a Moabite, therefore Scripture says: *Thou shalt not seek . . . his prosperity*." (Sif Deut. 23:7, p. 92b [184]). But though no peace offer is made to them, if they of their own accord sue for peace, it is granted to them.

7. When siege is laid to a city for the purpose of capture, it may not be surrounded on all four sides but only on three in order to give an opportunity for escape to those who would flee to save their lives, as it is said: *And they warred against Midian, as the Lord commanded Moses* (Num. 31:7). It has been learned by tradition that that was the instruction given to Moses.

8. It is forbidden to cut down fruit-bearing trees outside a (besieged) city, nor may a water channel be deflected from them so that they wither, as it is said: *Thou shalt not destroy the trees thereof* (Deut. 20:19). Whoever cuts down a fruit-bearing tree is flogged. This penalty is imposed not only for cutting it down during a siege; whenever a fruit-yielding tree is cut down with destructive intent, flogging is incurred. It may be cut down, however, if it causes damage to other trees or to a field belonging to another man or if its value for other purposes is greater (than that of the fruit it produces). The Law forbids only wanton destruction.

9. One is permitted to cut down a non-fruit-bearing tree even if

one does not need it. So too, an old fruit tree which produces a quantity too small to trouble about may be cut down. How much is an olive tree to produce (and the owner be forbidden to cut it down)? A quarter of a *ḳaḇ;* and a palm tree yielding one ḳaḇ may not be cut down.

10. Not only one who cuts down (fruit-producing) trees, but also one who smashes household goods, tears clothes, demolishes a building, stops up a spring, or destroys articles of food with destructive intent, transgresses the command *Thou shalt not destroy*. He is not flogged, but is administered a disciplinary beating imposed by the Rabbis.

11. It is permitted to invest the towns of the heathen three days before the Sabbath, and to make war with them every day, even on the Sabbath, as it is said *until it fall* (Deut. 20:20), that is, even if (its fall) occurs on the Sabbath. What has been said, applies both to a war for a religious cause and to an optional war.

12. The men in the camp may encamp anywhere. Whoever is killed in battle is buried on the spot where he falls; he acquires the right to the place as does one who is found lying in the road.

13. Four things are permitted to men who are in camp. They may eat of "dubious" produce. They are exempt from the washing of hands (before eating). They may fetch wood from any place; even if the wood is already detached from the ground and is dry, the law is not particular in this matter with the men that are in camp. They are exempt from an *'eruḇ* of courtyards, and are permitted to carry objects from tent to tent and from hut to hut, provided that the whole camp is surrounded by a partition ten handbreadths high to mark it off as private ground, as was set forth in the Treatise on the Sabbath; but no partition is to be less than ten handbreadths high. Just as they are permitted these (four) things when they go forth to war, so they are permitted these things when they return (before they are mustered out).

14. It is forbidden to relieve oneself in the camp or in the field at large. It is a positive command to set aside a special place for this purpose, as it is said: *Thou shalt have a place also without thy camp* (Deut. 23:13).

15. It is a positive command for everyone in the army to have a paddle attached to his weapons, so that when he repair to the place of sanitation he dig a hole therewith, attend to the call of nature, and cover the hole, as it is said: *And thou shalt have a paddle among thy weapons* . . . (Deut. 23:14). This is to be done whether or not the Ark is in the camp, as it is said: *Therefore shall thy camp be holy* (Deut. 23:15). [What has been said applies both to a war for a religious cause and to an optional war.]

CHAPTER VII

1. A priest is appointed to address the troops in time of war. He is anointed with the oil of anointment and is designated as "the priest anointed for war."

2. Twice the priest anointed for war addresses the troops. Once he speaks to the men on the frontier when they are about to cross the border to give battle to the enemy. He says to them: *What man is there that hath built a new house and hath not dedicated it? . . . And what man is there that hath planted a vineyard, and hath not used the fruit thereof? . . . Let him go and return unto his house, etc.* (Deut. 20:5–7). Those who come under this category are to hold themselves ready for discharge when they hear the proclamation again. The second time he addresses them when they are arrayed for battle, saying to them: *Fear not, nor be alarmed, neither be ye affrighted at them* (Deut. 20:3).

3. When the battle lines are being drawn, getting ready to meet the enemy, the anointed priest mounts a platform and, facing the armed forces, says in Hebrew: *Hear, O Israel, ye draw nigh this day unto battle against your enemies, let not your heart faint; fear not, nor be alarmed, neither be ye affrighted at them. For the Lord your God is He that goeth with you, to fight for you against your enemies, to save you* (Deut. 20:3–4). Thus far the anointed priest speaks; another priest proclaims these words in a loud voice. The anointed priest then continues: *What man is there that hath built a new house . . . and what man is there that hath planted a vineyard . . . and what man is there that hath betrothed a wife* . . .

Let him go and return unto his house (Deut. 20:5–6). Thus far the anointed priest speaks; an officer proclaims these words in a loud voice. Then the officer, unprompted by the priest, continues: *What man is there that is fearful and faint-hearted?* . . . (Deut. 20:8) and another officer proclaims these words to the armed forces.

4. After those who come under these categories have been sent back home, the battle lines are set in order; officers are appointed to lead the forces; strong and brave guards are stationed behind each line, and if anyone seeks to retreat they are empowered to break his leg, for flight marks the beginning of defeat.

What has been said touching the discharge from the army applies only to an optional war, but in a war for a religious cause, all are in duty bound to go forth, even the bridegroom out of his chamber and the bride out of her pavilion.

5. It makes no difference whether one has built a house to live in or a stable for cattle or a shed for wood, or a storehouse [or a straw magazine], as long as any of these is fit for habitation, he is sent back home. He is sent back home whether he has built it, bought it, received it as a gift, or inherited it. But if he has built a gatehouse, portico, or balcony, or a house that is not four cubits square, or has unlawfully taken possession of a house, he is not sent back home.

6. Whether one has planted a vineyard, or five fruit trees, even if they are of different kinds, (he is sent back home). It makes no difference whether he has planted them, or sunk them into the ground, or grafted them, since the vines thus sunk or grafted are subject to the law of ʻorlah; whether he has planted them, bought them, inherited them, or received them as a gift—(in all of these instances he is sent back home). But if he has planted only four fruit-bearing trees, or five non-fruit-bearing trees, or if he has unlawfully seized a vineyard, he is not sent back home. So too, if the vineyard is owned by two partners, neither is sent back home.

7. Whether one has betrothed a virgin or a widow or is under the obligation of marrying the widow of his brother, he is discharged. Even if there were five brothers and one of them dies,

all the surviving brothers are sent back home. If one betrothed a woman, stipulating that the marriage should take place within a period following twelve months of betrothal, and he has served twelve months in the army, he is discharged.

8. One who remarried his divorced wife, or contracted a marriage that was forbidden to him, as when a High Priest married a widow, or an ordinary priest married a woman that was divorced or a woman that was released from levirate marriage by ḥăliṣah, or an Israelite who married a bastard or a Nethinah, or a bastard or a Nathin who married the daughter of an Israelite—these are not discharged.

9. All who are eligible for discharge from the army return home on hearing the proclamation of the priest, but provide water and food for their brethren in active service, and repair the roads.

10. The following are exempt from joining the army and are not requisitioned for any service whatsoever: he who built a house and dedicated it; he who married his betrothed wife or the wife of his deceased brother; he who planted a vineyard and used the fruit thereof—these do not go forth (to battle) till the completion of one year, as it is said: *He shall be free for his house one year, and shall cheer his wife whom he hath taken* (Deut. 24:5). It has been learned by tradition that he shall be free one year whether he acquired a house, or married a wife, or planted a vineyard the fruit whereof he has begun to use.

11. All year these are exempt from supplying water and food (to the army), repairing the roads, guarding the fortifications, and paying town taxes; no duties whatever shall be laid upon them, as it is said: *He shall not go out in the host, neither shall he be charged with any business* (*ibid.*), i.e., they are exempt from municipal and military duties. Drafting them into the army involves the transgression of two negative commands.

12. In case one built a house and rented it to others, if the rent was paid in advance, it is as though he has already dedicated it; if the rent was paid at the end of the twelve months, it is as though he has not dedicated it until the expiration of the twelve months.

13. In case one built a house, put his things there and locked it up, if he has to spend time to watch the things, it is as though he has dedicated the house and begun to occupy it; but if he does not have to sit and watch them, it is as though he has not dedicated it.

14. One who built a house or planted a vineyard outside Palestine is not discharged.

15. *What man is there that is fearful and fainthearted?* (Deut. 20:8). This is to be understood literally, that is, the man who is not physically fit to join the ranks in battle. Once, however, he has joined the ranks, he should put his reliance upon Him who is the hope of Israel, their Savior in time of trouble. He should know that he is fighting for the oneness of God, risk his life, and neither fear nor be affrighted. Nor should he think of his wife or children, but, forgetting them and all else, concentrate on the war. He who permits his attention to be diverted during a battle and becomes disturbed, transgresses a negative command, as it is said: *Let not your heart faint, fear not, nor be alarmed, neither be ye affrighted at them* (Deut. 20:3). Moreover, he is accountable for the lives of all Israel. If he does not conquer (because) he did not fight with all his heart and soul, it is as though he had shed the blood of all, as it is said: *Lest his brethren's heart melt as his heart* (Deut. 20:8). This truth is brought out with notable clearness in the injunction of the prophet: *Cursed be he that doth the work of the Lord with a slack hand, and cursed be he that keepeth back his sword from blood* (Jer. 48:10).

He who fights with all his heart, without fear, with the sole intention of sanctifying the Name, is assured that no harm will befall him and no evil will overtake him. He will build for himself a lasting house in Israel, acquiring it for himself and his children forever, and will prove worthy of life in the world to come, as it is written: *For the Lord will certainly make my lord a sure house, because my lord fighteth the battles of the Lord; and evil is not found in thee. . . . Yet the soul of my lord shall be bound in the bundle of life with the Lord thy God* (I Sam. 25:28, 29).

CHAPTER VIII

1. The armed men who invade heathen territory, conquer the (enemy) forces, and take captives are permitted to eat nĕḇelah, ṭĕrefah, pork, and the like, if no other articles of food are available to them. So too, they may drink forbidden wine. It has been learned by tradition that the phrase *houses full of good things* (Deut. 6:11) refers to chines of pork and similar things.

2. A soldier in the invading army may also, if overpowered by passion, cohabit with a captive woman. He may not, however, leave her after cohabiting with her. He must take her into his house, as it is said: *And thou seest among the captives a woman of goodly form . . . then thou shalt bring her home to thy house* (Deut. 21:11–12). He is forbidden to cohabit with her a second time before he marries her.

3. Coition with her is permitted only at the time when she is taken captive, as it is said *And thou seest among the captives.* It is all one whether she is still a virgin, or is no longer a virgin, or is a married woman. For the marriage of a heathen does not give the woman a legal marital status.

And thou hast a desire (*ibid.*), even if she is not beautiful; *unto her* (*ibid.*), and not unto her companion (too), that is, he shall not have relations with two; *and wouldst take her to thee to wife* (*ibid.*), that is, he shall not choose two, have relations with one, and designate the other for his father or his brother.

How do we know that he must not force her (to yield to him) in the open field of battle? Because it is said: *Then thou shalt bring her home to thy house,* that is, he shall take her to a private place and cohabit with her.

4. A priest (too), is permitted to have relations with a captive woman once, for permission to have relations with a captive woman is a concession to man's evil impulse; but he is not permitted to marry her, because she is a proselyte.

5. What is the law with regard to a captive woman? If after the first coition, while she is still a heathen, she expresses her willingness to accept Judaism, arrangements are forthwith made for

her ablution for the purpose of conversion. If she is unwilling to accept the Jewish religion, she remains in his house thirty days, as it is said: *She shall bewail her father and her mother a full month* (Deut. 21:13). She weeps also for her religion and he may not stop her. She lets her nails grow, shaves her head, in order to become repulsive to him; she remains with him in the house, he comes in and looks at her, goes out and looks at her, so that he comes to loathe her. He puts up with her, in the hope that she might accept Judaism. If she does, and he desires to marry her, she is converted and takes a ritual bath as all proselytes do.

6. She then waits three months, one month for weeping and two months thereafter, and he marries her by a kĕṯubbah and a legal betrothal. If (after the marriage) he no longer cares for her, he lets her go where she pleases. But if he sells her, he transgresses a negative command, as it is said: *But thou shalt not sell her at all for money* (Deut. 21:14); the sale therefore is not valid and the money is returned. So too, if after cohabiting with her he impresses her into his service as a bondwoman, he transgresses a negative command, as it is said: *Do not deal with her as a slave* (*ibid.*).

7. If she refuses to be converted, she is put up with for twelve months. If (at the end of that period) she still refuses, she accepts the seven commandments enjoined upon the descendants of Noah and he lets her go where she pleases. Her status then is that of a resident alien. He is not permitted to marry her, since it is forbidden to marry a (heathen) woman who has not been converted.

8. If she conceived on her first intercourse, the child is a proselyte, and is in no respect to be regarded as his son, because his mother is a heathen. But the court on its authority arranges for his ablution. Tamar, the daughter of a captive woman, was conceived on her mother's first intercourse, but Absalom was born after his mother's marriage. Hence Tamar was Absalom's sister by the same mother, but she was permitted to be married to Amnon, as it is written: *Now therefore, I pray thee, speak unto the king; for he will not withhold me from thee* (II Sam. 13:13).

9. A captive woman who refuses, after the lapse of twelve months, to renounce idolatry, is put to death. Likewise, if a city sues for peace, no covenant is made with it, unless the inhabitants repudiate idolatry, destroy all places of idol worship and accept the other commandments mandatory upon the descendants of Noah, for any heathen who refuses to accept those seven commandments is put to death if he is under our control.

10. Moses, our teacher, bequeathed the Law and commandments to Israel, as it is said *an inheritance of the congregation of Jacob* (Deut. 33:4), and to those of other nations who are willing to be converted (to Judaism), as it is said: *One law and one ordinance shall be both for you, and for the resident alien* (Num. 15:16). But no coercion to accept the Law and commandments is practiced on those who are unwilling to do so. Moreover, Moses, our teacher, was commanded by God to compel all human beings to accept the commandments enjoined upon the descendants of Noah. Anyone who does not accept them is put to death. He who does accept them is invariably styled a resident alien. He must declare his acceptance in the presence of three associates. Anyone who has declared his intention to be circumcised and fails to do so within twelve months is treated like a heathen infidel.

11. A heathen who accepts the seven commandments and observes them scrupulously is a "righteous heathen," and will have a portion in the world to come, provided that he accepts them and performs them because the Holy One, blessed be He, commanded them in the Law and made known through Moses, our teacher, that the observance thereof had been enjoined upon the descendants of Noah even before the Law was given. But if his observance thereof is based upon a reasoned conclusion he is not deemed a resident alien, or one of the pious of the Gentiles, but one of their wise men.

CHAPTER IX

1. Six precepts were given to Adam: prohibition of idolatry, of blasphemy, of murder, of adultery, of robbery, and the command

to establish courts of justice. Although there is a tradition to this effect—a tradition dating back to Moses, our teacher, and human reason approves of those precepts—it is evident from the general tenor of the Scriptures that he (Adam) was bidden to observe these commandments. An additional commandment was given to Noah: prohibition of (eating) a limb from a living animal, as it is said: *Only flesh with the life thereof, which is the blood thereof, shall ye not eat* (Gen. 9:4). Thus we have seven commandments. So it was until Abraham appeared who, in addition to the aforementioned commandments, was charged to practice circumcision. Moreover, Abraham instituted the Morning Service. Isaac set apart tithes and instituted the Afternoon Service. Jacob added to the preceding law (prohibiting) the sinew that shrank, and inaugurated the Evening Service. In Egypt Amram was charged to observe other precepts, until Moses came and the Law was completed through him.

2. A Noahide (descendant of Noah) who worships an idol is liable to death, provided that he worships it in the regular mode (in which it is worshiped). With regard to idolatry, any act for which a Jewish court imposes the death penalty (upon a Jew) carries with it the death penalty if the culprit is a Noahide; and any act for which the Jewish court does not impose the death penalty (upon a Jew) does not carry with it the death penalty if the culprit is a Noahide. But though he is not liable to death, he is forbidden to worship an idol in any manner. He is not permitted to set up a pillar, to plan an asherah, or to make an image, or the like for ornament.

3. A Noahide who blasphemes the Name (of God) is liable to death, whether he employs the ineffable Name or any attribute (of God) in any language. It is different, however, if the blasphemer is a Jew.

4. A Noahide who kills a person, even if he kills an embryo in the mother's womb, is put to death. So too, if he kills one suffering from a fatal disease, or ties a man with a rope and puts him before a lion, or leaves him in a famished condition in consequence of which the man dies of starvation, he is executed, for in the last

analysis he caused the death of the victim. Likewise, if he kills one who is pursuing him (with the intention of slaying him) while he can save himself by maiming a limb of the pursuer, he is put to death. In none of these cases is an Israelite put to death.

5. A Noahide is forbidden to have intercourse with any of the following six prohibited degrees: his mother, his father's wife, a married woman, his sister by the same mother, a male, and a beast. For it is said: *Therefore shall a man leave his father and his mother* (Gen. 2:24); *his father* means his father's wife, *his mother* is to be understood literally. *And he shall cleave unto his wife* (*ibid.*); to *his* wife, not to his neighbor's wife; to his *wife,* not to a male. *And they shall be one flesh* (*ibid.*); this excludes cattle, beasts of chase, and fowl, because he and any of these cannot become one flesh. (He is forbidden to have intercourse with his sister by the same mother), as it is said: *She is indeed my sister, the daughter of my father, but not the daughter of my mother; and so she became my wife* (Gen. 20:12).

6. In case a Noahide has seduced or violated a woman, their son is liable if he has relations with his mother, because she is his mother. A Noahide is culpable if he has relations with his father's wife even after the father's death. He is liable if he has connections with a male, whether the latter be a minor or an adult. He is liable if he has connections with a beast, be it small or large; but only he is executed, not the beast, for the command to kill a beast obtains only if an Israelite commits bestiality.

7. A Noahide who commits adultery is not liable unless he has a natural connection with the woman after her marriage has been consummated. If, however, she is only betrothed to her husband, or even if she has already been married but the union has not been consummated, he is not liable, as it is said: *For she is a man's wife* (Gen. 20:3). This applies only to a Noahide who has relations with a Noahide woman; but if he has connection with a Jewess, he is liable, whether the connection is a natural or unnatural one. If she is a betrothed maiden, he is executed by stoning—the sentence imposed by the Jewish law. If he has relations with her after her wedding ceremony has taken place but before

the marriage has been consummated, he is executed by strangulation—the punishment imposed by the Jewish law. But if he has relations with her after her marriage has been consummated, it is as though he has had relations with a married heathen woman, and he is put to death by decapitation.

8. If a Noahide has designated a handmaid (as wife) for his slave and then has connection with her, he is put to death for adultery. He is not culpable, however, unless her relation to the slave has become a matter of common knowledge, when people refer to her as the wife of So-and-so. When is she again considered free? From the time that he (the master) separates her from his slave and she goes bareheaded in the street.

When does a married heathen woman acquire a status corresponding to that of a divorced woman in the Jewish law? From the time that her husband turns her out of his house and lets her go where she pleases, or from the time that she leaves his house and goes away. For divorce by a written document is a practice which does not exist among heathens and the severance of the marital tie does not depend upon the husband only; they separate whenever he or she wishes to do so.

9. A Noahide incurs the death penalty for robbery, whether he robs a heathen or an Israelite, whether he steals money or takes it by force, or kidnaps a person, or withholds a laborer's wage, or is guilty of a similar act. It applies even to a hired laborer who eats of the produce while he is not engaged in gathering it—for any of these things a Noahide is culpable and is deemed a robber, which is not the law in the event the offender is an Israelite.

He is culpable if he takes by force an article worth less than a pĕruṭah. If he takes an article worth less than a pĕruṭah and another Noahide robs him of it, both are liable to death.

10. So too, he is culpable if he eats a limb from a living animal, or flesh removed from a living animal—however small the quantity of the flesh be—for fixed measures are prescribed only for Israelites. A Noahide is permitted, however, to eat blood drawn from a living animal.

11. It makes no difference whether the limb or flesh is from a

cattle or a beast of chase. It appears to me, however, that a Noahide is not liable to death if he eats a limb from a living fowl.

12. If one slaughters cattle, even if he cuts both organs, as long as the animal is still jerking, a limb or flesh removed from it is forbidden to a Noahide on account of the prohibition of "a limb from a living animal."

13. Whatever is forbidden to an Israelite on account of the prohibition of a limb cut from a living animal is also forbidden to a Noahide. There are, however, cases with respect to which a Noahide is culpable and an Israelite is not. The former is culpable on account of the prohibition of a limb or flesh removed from a living animal, whether the limb or flesh he eats is of a clean or an unclean animal or beast of chase. Moreover, a limb or flesh separated from an animal, both organs of which have been properly cut by an Israelite, is forbidden to a Noahide on account of the prohibition of a limb of a living animal, as long as the animal is still jerking.

14. As regards the commandment laid upon Noahides to establish courts of justice, the duty is enjoined upon them to set up judges in each district to deal with these six commandments and to caution the people. A Noahide who violates any of the seven commandments is executed by decapitation with the sword. Therefore all the inhabitants of Shechem were condemned to death by beheading because Shechem had been guilty of robbery. They saw it, knew it, and failed to impose sentence upon him.

A Noahide is slain on the evidence of one witness, on the ruling of one judge, and without previous warning. He is condemned even (on the evidence of) a relation, but not on that of a woman; nor may a woman act as judge in his case.

CHAPTER X

1. A Noahide who inadvertently violates any of the commandments binding upon him is exempt from all punishment. If, however, he killed another Noahide accidentally and the avenger of the blood slays him, the latter is not put to death on his account.

(Otherwise, in case of unintentional homicide), while the cities of refuge do not offer him an asylum, the Noahide court does not condemn him to death. This leniency obtains only if the act which involves a transgression is committed by him in error, as when he cohabits with another man's wife thinking that she is his own wife or an unmarried woman. But if he knows that she is a married woman but does not know that he is forbidden to have relations with a married woman, or if he kills a person and does not know that slaying a human being is prohibited, he is akin to a deliberate offender and is put to death. It is not accounted an error on his part, because it was his duty to familiarize himself with these things and he failed to do so.

2. A Noahide who is coerced by a man of violence to transgress any of the commandments mandatory upon him, may transgress it. Even if he is forced to worship idolatry he may do it, because Noahides are not commanded to sanctify the Name (of God). Neither a minor nor a deaf-mute, nor an imbecile among them is ever punished, because he is not bound to observe the commandments.

3. If a Noahide has embraced Judaism and submitted to the rites of circumcision and ablution, and subsequently decides to renounce the Jewish religion, wishing to be only a resident alien as he had been before his conversion, his wish is disregarded. He must either remain an Israelite in every respect or else he is put to death. But if at the time when the court arranged for his ablution he was a minor, he may on reaching maturity protest (against the action of the court) and be only a resident alien. If, however, he did not protest at that time, he can no longer object and is accounted a full proselyte. Therefore, if an Israelite cohabited with a (heathen) minor, whose immersion had been arranged for by the court, the amount stipulated in her kĕṯubbah, or the fine paid for violating or seducing her, is deposited with the court (to be kept) until she comes of age and does not protest against her conversion. For should the money be given to her and she on coming of age protests against her conversion, she, a heathen, will have used money to which she was entitled only according to Jewish law.

4. A Noahide who blasphemed the Name (of God), or worshiped an idol, or had relations with a married heathen woman, or killed a Noahide, and later embraces Judaism, is exempt from punishment. But if he killed a Jew or committed adultery with a Jewish woman and later embraces Judaism, he is liable; he is decapitated for slaying a Jew, but for adultery with a Jewish woman he is strangled, because his status has changed.

5. We have already stated that whenever a Noahide incurs the death penalty, he is executed by decapitation with the sword save if he has relations with a married Jewish woman before the marriage has been consummated, in which case he is strangled; or if he has relations with a betrothed Jewish maiden, in which case he is stoned.

6. It has been learned by tradition that Noahides are forbidden only to couple heterogeneous animals and to graft trees of different kinds; but they are not put to death for the violation of these commands.

If a heathen strikes a Jew—an offense for which he deserves death, no matter how slight the wound he inflicts—he is not put to death (by the court).

7. The practice of circumcision is a commandment given only to Abraham and his descendants, as it is said: *Thou shalt keep My covenant, thou and thy seed after thee* (Gen. 17:9). The descendants of Ishmael were excluded, for it is said: *For in Isaac shall seed be called to thee* (Gen. 21:12). Esau was excluded, because Isaac said to Jacob: *And (God) give thee the blessing of Abraham, to thee and to thy seed* (Gen. 28:4), implying that he only is of the seed of Abraham who adheres to his religion and follows in his way of righteousness. Jews therefore are bound to practice the rite of circumcision.

8. The Rabbis said that the sons of Keturah, who are of the seed of Abraham and who were born after Ishmael and Isaac, are bound to observe the precept of circumcision. Since today the descendants of Ishmael are intermingled with the descendants of Keturah, they are bound to observe the rite of circumcision on the eighth day, but they are not put to death if they neglect to do it.

9. A heathen who busies himself with the study of the Law deserves death. He should occupy himself with the (study) of the seven commandments only. So too, a heathen who keeps a day of rest, even if it be on a weekday, if he has set it apart as his Sabbath, is deserving of death. It is needless to state that he merits death if he makes a new festival for himself. The general principle is: none is permitted to introduce innovations into religion or devise new commandments. The heathen has the choice between becoming a true proselyte by accepting all the commandments, and adhering to his own religion, neither adding to it nor subtracting anything from it. If therefore he occupies himself with the study of the Law, or observes a day of rest, or makes any innovation, he is flogged, or otherwise punished and advised that he is deserving of death, but he is not put to death.

10. A Noahide who wishes to perform any other commandment of the Law with a view to receiving a reward, is not to be hindered from performing it properly. If he brings a burnt offering, it is accepted. If he contributes to charity, his contribution is accepted. It appears to me that the money thus contributed is to be given to the poor among the Jews, because the Noahide makes his living out of Jews and it is the duty of Jews to sustain him. But if a heathen makes a contribution, it is accepted and given to the poor among the heathens.

11. The Jewish court is in duty bound to provide the resident aliens with judges who should render decisions in consonance with the laws enjoined upon them, so that the moral order be not destroyed. It rests with the court whether to appoint heathen or Jewish judges.

12. If two heathens come before Jewish judges, both requesting that their case be adjudicated according to Jewish law, their request is granted. If one wishes that it be decided according to Jewish law and the other does not, no pressure is brought to bear upon the latter to submit to the Jewish law, but the case is adjudicated according to their law. In a suit involving a Jew and a heathen, if the Jew can be vindicated by the law of the heathens, judgment is rendered according to the heathen law, and the

(heathen) litigant is told: "This is your law." If the Jew can be vindicated by our law, the suit is decided according to the Jewish law and the (heathen) litigant is told: "This is our law."

It seems to me that this procedure is not to be followed if the other party to the suit is a resident alien; in that case the suit is always adjudicated according to their laws. So too, it seems to me that we should treat resident aliens with the consideration and kindness due to a Jew; for we are bidden to sustain them, as it is said: *Thou mayest give it unto the stranger that is within thy gates, that he may eat it* (Deut. 14:21). As to the statement of the Rabbis that we must not double the greetings when (saluting a heathen), that refers to a heathen, not to a resident alien. Even with respect to heathens, the Rabbis bid us visit their sick, bury their dead along with the dead of Israel, and maintain their poor with the poor of Israel in the interests of peace, as it is written: *The Lord is good to all; and His tender mercies are over all His works* (Ps. 145:9). And it is also written *Her ways are ways of pleasantness, and all her paths are peace* (Prov. 3:17).

CHAPTER XI

1. King Messiah will arise and restore the kingdom of David to its former state and original sovereignty. He will rebuild the sanctuary and gather the dispersed of Israel. All the ancient laws will be reinstituted in his days; sacrifices will again be offered; the Sabbatical and Jubilee years will again be observed in accordance with the commandments set forth in the Law.

He who does not believe in a restoration or does not look forward to the coming of the Messiah denies not only the teachings of the Prophets but also those of the Law and Moses, our teacher, for Scripture affirms the rehabilitation of Israel, as it is said: *Then the Lord thy God will turn thy captivity, and have compassion upon thee, and will return and gather thee . . . if any of thine that are dispersed be in the uttermost parts of heaven . . . and the Lord thy God will bring thee into the land which thy fathers possessed* (Deut. 30:3, 4, 5). These words stated in

Scripture include all that the Prophets said (on the subject). They recur in the section treating of Balaam. The prophecy in that section bears upon the two Messiahs: the first, namely, David, who saved Israel from the hand of their enemies; and the later Messiah, a descendant of David, who will achieve the final salvation of Israel. There it is said: *I see him, but not now* (Num. 24:17), this refers to David; *I behold him, but not nigh* (*ibid.*), this refers to King Messiah. *There shall step forth a star out of Jacob* (*ibid.*), this refers to David; *And a sceptre shall rise out of Israel* (*ibid.*), this refers to King Messiah. *And shall smite through the corners of Moab* (*ibid.*), this refers to David, for we are told: *And he smote Moab, and measured them with the line* (II Sam. 8:2); *and break down all the sons of Seth* (Num. 24:17), this refers to King Messiah, as it is written concerning him: *And his dominion shall be from sea to sea* (Zech. 9:10). *And Edom shall be a possession* (Num. 24:18), this refers to David, as it is written: *And all the Edomites became servants to David* (II Sam. 8:14); *And Seir shall be a possession* (Num. 24:18), this refers to (the days of) King Messiah, as it is written: *And saviours shall come up on Mount Zion to judge the mount of Esau* (Obad. 1:21).

2. So too, with reference to the cities of refuge, the Bible says: *And if the Lord thy God enlarge thy borders . . . then thou shalt add three cities more for thee* (Deut. 19:8, 9)—a precept which has never been carried out. Yet, not in vain did the Holy One, blessed be He, give us this commandment. As for the prophetic utterances on the subject (of the Messiah), no citations are necessary, as all their books are full of this theme.

3. Do not think that King Messiah will have to perform signs and wonders, bring anything new into being, revive the dead, or do similar things. It is not so. Rabbi Akiba was a great sage, a teacher of the Mishnah, yet he was also the armor-bearer of Ben Kozba. He affirmed that the latter was King Messiah; he and all the wise men of his generation shared this belief until Ben Kozba was slain in (his) iniquity, when it became known that he was not (the Messiah). Yet the Rabbis had not asked him for a sign or token. The general principle is: this Law of ours with its

statutes and ordinances [is not subject to change]. It is for ever and all eternity; it is not to be added to or to be taken away from. [Whoever adds aught to it, or takes away aught from it, or misinterprets it, and strips the commandments of their literal sense is an impostor, a wicked man, and a heretic.]

4. If there arise a king from the House of David who meditates on the Torah, occupies himself with the commandments, as did his ancestor David, observes the precepts prescribed in the Written and the Oral Law, prevails upon Israel to walk in the way of the Torah and to repair its breaches, and fights the battles of the Lord, it may be assumed that he is the Messiah. If he does these things and succeeds, rebuilds the sanctuary on its site, and gathers the dispersed of Israel, he is beyond all doubt the Messiah. He will prepare the whole world to serve the Lord with one accord, as it is written: *For then will I turn to the peoples a pure language, that they may all call upon the name of the Lord to serve Him with one consent* (Zeph. 3:9).

CHAPTER XII

1. Let no one think that in the days of the Messiah any of the laws of nature will be set aside, or any innovation be introduced into creation. The world will follow its normal course. The words of Isaiah: *And the wolf shall dwell with the lamb, and the leopard shall lie down with the kid* (Isa. 11:6) are to be understood figuratively, meaning that Israel will live securely among the wicked of the heathens who are likened to wolves and leopards, as it is written: *A wolf of the deserts doth spoil them, a leopard watcheth over their cities* (Jer. 5:6). They will all accept the true religion, and will neither plunder nor destroy, and together with Israel earn a comfortable living in a legitimate way, as it is written: *And the lion shall eat straw like the ox* (Isa. 11:7). All similar expressions used in connection with the Messianic age are metaphorical. In the days of King Messiah the full meaning of those metaphors and their allusions will become clear to all.

2. Said the Rabbis: *The sole difference between the present and*

the Messianic days is delivery from servitude to foreign powers (B. San 91b). Taking the words of the Prophets in their literal sense, it appears that the inauguration of the Messianic era will be marked by the war of Gog and Magog; that prior to that war, a prophet will arise to guide Israel and set their hearts aright, as it is written: *Behold, I will send you Elijah the prophet* (Mal. 3:23). He (Elijah) will come neither to declare the clean unclean, nor the unclean clean; neither to disqualify those who are presumed to be of legitimate descent, nor to pronounce qualified those who are presumed to be of illegitimate descent, but to bring peace in the world, as it is said: *And he shall turn the hearts of the fathers to the children* (Mal. 3:24).

Some of our Sages say that the coming of Elijah will precede the advent of the Messiah. But no one is in a position to know the details of this and similar things until they have come to pass. They are not explicitly stated by the Prophets. Nor have the Rabbis any tradition with regard to these matters. They are guided solely by what the scriptural texts seem to imply. Hence there is a divergence of opinion on the subject. But be that as it may, neither the exact sequence of those events nor the details thereof constitute religious dogmas. No one should ever occupy himself with the legendary themes or spend much time on midrashic statements bearing on this and like subjects. He should not deem them of prime importance, since they lead neither to the fear of God nor to the love of Him. Nor should one calculate the end. Said the Rabbis: *Blasted be those who reckon out the end* (B. San 97b). One should wait (for his coming) and accept in principle this article of faith, as we have stated before.

3. In the days of King Messiah, when his kingdom will be established and all Israel will gather around him, their pedigrees will be determined by him through the Holy Spirit which will rest upon him, as it is written: *And he shall sit as a refiner and purifier* . . . (Mal. 3:3). First he will purify the descendants of Levi, declaring: "This one, of good birth, is a priest; this one, of good birth, is a Levite." Those who are not of good birth will be demoted to the rank of (lay) Israelites, for it is written: *And the Tir-*

shatha said unto them that they should not eat of the most holy things, till there stood up a priest with Urim and Tummim (Ezra 2:63). It is inferred therefrom that the genealogy of those considered to be of good lineage will be traced by means of the Holy Spirit, and those found to be of good birth will be made known. The descent of the Israelites will be recorded according to their tribes. He will announce: "This one is of such-and-such a tribe, and this one of such-and-such a tribe." But he will not say concerning those who are presumed to be of pure descent: "This is a bastard; this is a slave." For the rule is: once a family has been intermingled with others, it retains its status.

4. The Sages and Prophets did not long for the days of the Messiah that Israel might exercise dominion over the world, or rule over the heathens, or be exalted by the nations, or that it might eat and drink and rejoice. Their aspiration was that Israel be free to devote itself to the Law and its wisdom, with no one to oppress or disturb it, and thus be worthy of life in the world to come.

5. In that era there will be neither famine nor war, neither jealousy nor strife. Blessings will be abundant, comforts within the reach of all. The one preoccupation of the whole world will be to know the Lord. Hence Israelites will be very wise, they will know the things that are now concealed and will attain an understanding of their Creator to the utmost capacity of the human mind, as it is written: *For the earth shall be full of the knowledge of the Lord, as the waters cover the sea* (Isa. 11:9).

The Treatise on Kings and the entire Code are completed. Blessed be He who spake and the world in its particularity and in its totality came into existence.

The fourteenth Book, namely, the Book of Judges, now completed, contains five Treatises, totaling eighty-one chapters. It comprises: the Treatise on Sanhedrin, twenty-six chapters; the Treatise on Evidence, twenty-two chapters; the Treatise on Rebels, seven chapters; the Treatise on Mourning, fourteen chapters; the Treatise on Kings and Wars, twelve chapters.

The total number of Treatises in the Code is eighty-three; the total number of chapters, nine hundred and eighty-two. Praise unto God, the Creator of the universe.

NOTES

References consisting of numbers only indicate passages found in the Code outside the present volume, the numbers referring, respectively, to the Book, the Treatise, the Chapter, and the Section where the passage in question occurs.

Treatise I: Sanhedrin

Chapter I

1. B. Mak 7a; see B. San 7b.
"the rod and the lash"—to punish offenders.
"before the judges"—ready to take orders and carry them into effect.
"squares"—omitted in some Mss.
"correcting abuses." A variant reading suggests: "beating lawbreakers."

2. Tos San 3: 5; B. Mak 7a; P. *ibid.,* 1: 8, p. 4b (8).
"[only] in every district"—i.e., courts are established in every district, not in every city. The word "only" is to be supplied; see LM *ad loc.;* but cf. Naḥmanides on Deut. 16: 18; L. Finkelstein, *JQR* (1934–35), p. 484.
"giveth thee." Only in Palestine, your own land, must provision be made for a tribunal in each city.

3. San 1: 6; 4: 3; 11: 2; Tos *ibid.,* 8: 1.
"regular tribunals." According to one Ms. the rendering should be: "How many tribunals are to be set up?"
"sanctuary"—in the Hall of Hewn Stones.
"always . . . as *Naśi.*" By reason of his preeminence, the Naśi is sometimes referred to as *Mufle* (the "outstanding" member of the Sanhedrin; see PhM, Hor 1: 4).
"*'Ab bet din*"—"vice-president," literally: "the father of the court."
"seated with them." According to the reading in the Venice edition and some Mss.: "both of them."
"with them"—literally: "before them."
"semicircular threshing floor"—i.e., they sat in semicircular rising tiers, as in an amphitheater.
"Temple Court"—at the entrance of the Court of the Israelites.
"Temple Mount"—on the east gate in front of the Women's Court.

4. "a court-of-three." Each town must have a tribunal. If it is not large enough to be the seat of a Small Sanhedrin, a court-of-three is set up there.

5. B. San 17b.
"the whole Torah"—written and oral.
"understands (the whole Torah)." The above translation is based on KM *ad loc.*

6. B. San 17b; cf. Tos *ibid.,* 8: 1.

7. San 4: 4.

"directly in front of"—literally: "close to."

8. San 4: 4.

"serve as judge"—literally: "to add to their number." This, however, would imply an increase in the membership of the Sanhedrin (see TYṬ San 5: 4; cf. note below, x, 8).

"ordained"—and seated on the judge's dais.

"the first in the second row"—each being moved up one place.

9. San 4: 3; 11: 2.

10. B. San 17b.

"ten men of leisure"—to ensure the requisite quorum of ten men for public worship; cf. B. Meg 3b.

"clerks." See the preceding section.

"court attendants"—to serve summonses and to execute sentences. These were some of the manifold duties with which the functionary known as *hazzan* was charged; cf. F. G. Moore, *Judaism,* I, 289 f.; S. M. Baron, *The Jewish Community,* I, 104.

"to refute." No evidence is admissible unless there is the possibility of refuting it.

"to rebut"—lest false witnesses be engaged to refute the evidence of witnesses.

"a scribe"—to write scrolls, etc.

Chapter II

1. San 4: 2; B. *ibid.,* 17a, 36b.

"wise men and understanding." This phrase occurs in Deut. 1: 13 (see below, Sec. 7). In what follows, Maimonides proceeds to explain the implications of the phrase.

"medicine"—to be able to distinguish, in case of an assault by one man on another, between injuries that are fatal and injuries that are not fatal (see San 9: 1; cf. XI, v, iv, 3); cf. also Juda Halevi, *Kuzari,* 2: 64.

"mathematics"—knowledge requisite for intercalation of months and years.

"(lay) Israelites"—i.e., who are neither priests nor levites.

2. Sif Deut. 17: 9, p. 81 (162).

3. Tos San 7: 3, and B. *ibid.,* 36b.

"any Sanhedrin"—i.e., the Great or a Small Sanhedrin.

4. San 2: 2, and B. *ibid.,* 18b, 19a.

"king of Israel"—i.e., one who is not of the House of David.

5. B. San 19a, b.

"untoward consequences." Hence they cannot be judged, and since they cannot be judged, they cannot judge; cf. B. San 19a.

6. B. San 17a, 36a; see B. Ḥag 13a, 14a.

"express . . . words." See Maimonides' interpretation (*Guide,* Part I, chap. XXXIV) of the two Hebrew words involved; cf. B. Ḥag 14a.

7. Deut. R 1: 11, p. 98a (195); see Sif Deut. 1: 15, p. 55a (109). Mek Exod. 18: 21, II, p. 183. Tanḥ Exod. 18: 1, p. 121a (241). Cf. Per ṬḤM 7: 15; see Prov. 28: 20, 22.

"beloved of your tribes"—usually translated: "and full of knowledge"; but the Hebrew verb involved means also "to love."

"is pleased"—i.e., one who is popular.

"A good eye"—i.e., who is free from envy; see Ab 2:9.

"gentleness in speech"—BY ṬḤM 7:15 quotes this section, but has "gentleness in their business dealings with others."

"Elsewhere"—literally: "there, below."

"hating gain"—usually translated: "hating unjust gain"; but the Hebrew word involved means also "any gain" (regardless of the means by which it is obtained); see Judg. 5:19.

8. Tos San 7:1; B. *ibid.,* 88b.

"Whoever was found." The text has an imperfect.

"promoted"—when a vacancy occurred in that tribunal.

"the court situated at the entrance of the Court." This was a higher court than the one at the entrance of the Temple Mount. Cf. Rashi on B. San 88b; see note below, III, i, 4.

9. B. Yeb 102a; B. San 36b, 34b; San 4:2.

"a Jewess by descent." So, too, if his father is a Jew by descent, he is competent. Cf. KM *ad loc.*

"competent." So is a court of three proselytes competent if their mothers are Jewesses.

"Sanhedrin." A member of the Sanhedrin must be one of good birth; see above, Sec. 2.

10. B. San 3a; P. *ibid.,* 1:1, p. 1b.

11. B. San 5a; see below, V, 18.

"well qualified"—literally: "a skilled or experienced judge." However, when Maimonides speaks of *mumḥe* he refers to one who is both erudite and resourceful, that is, one who possesses adequate knowledge of the law and knows how to apply his knowledge (PhM, San 3:1).

"obtained authorization"—but is also erudite and resourceful, though the public at large does not know that he possesses these qualifications. See KM *ad loc.*

"In some respects . . . court." See KM *ad loc.*

12. B. BḲ 27b.

13. B. San 7b.

14. B. San 23a.

Chapter III

1. B. Shab 10a; B. San 88b.

"During what hours"—literally: "until when."

"the end of the sixth hour"—about 12 M.

"evening tamiḏ"—about 2:30 P.M.

"in the House of Study"—not to give the impression that they are holding sessions on Sabbaths and festivals.

2. B. San 37a.

"in the sanctuary," i.e., in the Hall of Hewn Stones.

3. San 4:1 and B. *ibid.,* 34b.

"leprosy." In the Deuteronomy passage quoted in the text, the word is usually rendered: "stroke."

"controversy and leprosy." The two are placed in juxtaposition.

4. B. RH 25b; B. San 34b.

"In civil cases"—i.e., though no trial is to be begun at night (see the preceding section).

5. B. San 34b.

The reference in verse 11 is to the order of inheritance. Assignment of estates is thus spoken of as "judgment," i.e., it is regarded as a judicial procedure.

6. B. San 34b.

Two men can act as witnesses and therefore can record the bequest; they do not, however, constitute a court and cannot execute it.

7. B. San 7a.

8. Sif Deut. 1: 17, p. 55b (110). Deut. R 16: 18, p. 110a (219). B. San 7b.

"exilarch"—chief of the Babylonian Jews, a descendant of the Davidic dynasty in the male line.

"qualities." BY ṬḤM 8: 1, n. 1, quotes the first part of this section verbatim. In his quotation the word *middoṯ*, "qualities," is added.

"asherah"—a tree or grove devoted to idolatry.

"beside the altar." Scholars are likened to the altar because they urge sinners to abandon their evil ways and achieve atonement.

"gods"—'ĕlohim is a designation for "judges"; see Exod. 21: 6; 22: 7.

9. P. Bik 3: 3, p. 11b (22).

10. B. San 14a.

"the people." The text prefixes, erroneously, the nota acusativa (*'eṯ*).

Chapter IV

1. B. San 5a, 13b.

"No one." So according to the reading of TYṬ (San 1: 3) and two Mss.

2. B. San 13b.

"the laying of hands upon"—as was the case in the ordination of Joshua; see the preceding section.

" 'cases involving fines' "—which only an ordained judge can adjudicate.

3. "as was stated before"—Sec. 1.

4. *" 'Ĕlohim"*—B. BḲ 84b. See note above, iii, 8.

"They are the scholars." See above, ii, 8.

5. P. San 1: 2, p. 6a, b (11, 12). The text referred to implies that the Naśi ordained no one without authorization from the court. Cf. RaDbeZ *ad loc.;* see also L. Ginzberg, "Abbreviations in the Jerusalem Talmud," *Student's Manual,* Jewish Theological Seminary (1914), p. 145, n. 33.

6. B. San 14a, 5a.

"If both"—the ordainer and the ordained.

"those who came up from Egypt." The area occupied by them was larger than that occupied by those who at the time of the Second Restoration came up from Babylon.

7. P. San 10: 1, p. 52b (104). It is to be noted, however, that the number of candidates ordained by David is stated to have been 90,000.

8. B. San 5a, b; P. Ḥag 1: 8, p. 7a (13).

"questions of ritual"—what is permitted and what is forbidden.

"first-born animals." When the Temple was in existence, a firstling with a permanent blemish could not be offered as a sacrifice but became the property of the priest; after the destruction of the Temple, the owner was permitted to slaughter it and make use of it. It required, however, a well-qualified judge to certify that the blemish was a permanent one.

"absolution of vows." The person who made a vow applies to a sage for absolution thereof; the sage, finding that at the time when the vow was made special circumstances were not taken into consideration, pronounces the absolution.

"examination of stains"—in the case of a menstruous woman.

9. B. San 5b.

10. B. San 36b; see above, ii, 9.

11. B. San 14a.

"invite two others"—and thus constitute a court-of-three, one of whom is ordained; cf. above, Sec. 3.

"If what we have said"—that ordination can be revived.

"If, however, there were one ordained," etc. That is why they were anxious to perpetuate the institution of ordination.

"this matter"—the renewal of ordination.

"requires careful reflection." Cf. PhM, San 1:3, where Maimonides states definitely that, by common consent of the Sages in Palestine, the institution of ordination can be revived. See RaDbeZ *ad loc.*

12. Mak 1:10.

"without the Land of Israel." Hence those ordained in Palestine and empowered to decide cases entailing fines cannot be denied this authority.

13. B. San 5a.

"exilarchs." See note above, iii, 8.

14. B. San 5a.

"denied the right." The right to adjudicate cases involving fines is reserved for those who have been clothed with this authority by the Sanhedrin.

"on the border"—cities on the Babylonian border under the jurisdiction of Palestine.

15. B. San 7b.

Chapter V

1. San 1:5; Tos *ibid.*, 3:2; B. *ibid.*, 18b, 16a (see Deut. 17:12–13); So 1:4.

"each city"—if its population is large enough to make it the seat of a Small Sanhedrin. See above, i, 4.

"pronounced condemned"—if its inhabitants are seduced to idolatry (Deut. 13:13–18).

"an optional war"—in contradistinction to a war for a religious cause; see below, v, v, 1.

"a slain body"—found in the road, and the murderer is not known, and there is no one to attend to the body (Deut. 21:1–9).

"measured"—to ascertain which city is nearest to the spot where the slain was found. The decision to measure these cities must be made by the full court of seventy-one, but the actual measuring is done by five of them (So 9:1); see below, Sec. 5.

2. San 1:4; B. *ibid.*, 15b.

"owners"—i.e., the person who acquires legal title to them.

3. San 1: 1, 4, 6; B. *ibid.*, 8b.

"an evil report." He alleges that she was not a virgin at marriage but does not produce witnesses that she committed adultery, in which case she forfeits her marriage settlement.

"due to him"—the hundred pieces of silver representing compensation for libel (Deut. 22: 19).

"tried by three"—i.e., by three ordained judges.

"a majority that can be followed." In a capital case a majority of at least two is required to condemn the accused.

4. San 1: 2.

5. San 1: 3.

"heifer's neck"—in case a slain man is found lying in the road. Maimonides reproduces in this section the language of the Mishnah (San 1: 3). The law as stated in this section refers to the actual measuring of the cities close to the scene of the murder. The breaking of the heifer's neck is done in the presence of all the local elders. Cf. XI, v, ix, 1–3.

6. San 1: 2.

"intercalation of the month"—adding a day to the month.

7. San 1: 2; see III, VIII, iv, 10; see above, iv, 1.

"intercalation of the year"—adding a month to the year.

8. B. San 3a, 5a; B. BḲ 84b; see Exod. 22: 3; 21: 35; 22: 15–16; Lev. 24: 19; Deut. 22: 28–29.

"mayhem"—personal injury.

"not involve action in tort"—i.e., suits arising from commercial transactions.

"admission of indebtedness"—witnesses testifying that the defendant admitted his liability.

"transaction of loans"—witnesses testifying that the loan was made in their presence.

" 'Ĕlohim." See notes above, iii, 8, and iv, 4.

9. BḲ 8: 6 (cf. PhM); B. *ibid.*, 15b, 84b.

"loss of money"—caused by damage.

"half damage"—in case an animal was gored by another. The half damage to be paid is regarded as a fine (B. BḲ 15b).

"pebbles"—kicked from under an animal's foot and causing damage.

10. B. BḲ 84a.

"a slave"—to be sold in the market. The damage is determined by assessing how much he was worth as a slave before he suffered the injury and how much he is worth now.

"inflicts a wound upon another." He is liable on five counts: for inury, for pain, for medical expense, for loss of time, and for degradation (BḲ 8: 1).

11. B. BḲ 84a, b.

"always"—literally: "from the beginning," i.e., the owner is liable to pay full restitution even for damage done by the animal the first time.

"rubbing itself"—for the gratification which the act affords. Such injury is a derivative of "tooth" (B. BḲ 3a).

"causes similar injury"—included in the category of injury caused by the "tooth" (*ibid.*).

"injury of the kind"—included in the category of injury caused by the "foot" (*ibid.*).

"tam"—an animal that has not gored or done damage coming under the category of "horn" three times, in which case the owner pays only half the damage. The half damage thus paid is regarded as a fine and is therefore not collected outside Palestine.

"forewarned"—to keep it in. Failure on the part of the owner to keep the animal in after three gorings renders him liable to payment of full compensation, i.e., he stands "forewarned."

12. B. BḲ 84a, b.

"the law of 'forewarning' "—in the case of a goring animal.

13. B. BḲ 84a, b.

"additional amount"—the correct reading is *tosefet̲,* including twofold, fourfold, and fivefold restitution.

14. Ket 3: 9.

15. B. BḲ 98b.

"indirectly"—as when one destroys a creditor's note.

16. B. BḲ 117a.

"no overt action"—i.e., he did not turn over a fellow Jew's money to a heathen, but gave the latter information which made it possible for him to obtain the money.

17. B. BḲ 15b; Alf, *ibid.,* 84b.

18. B. BB 31a (see BhG ḤM 3: 2, n. 18); see above, ii, 11.

"as has already been stated"—XIII, iv, vi, 2.

Chapter VI

1. B. San 33a.

"a judge"—who is well qualified or the litigants accepted him as judge. See Sec. 4.

"in a noncapital case"—literally: "in a monetary case." This rendering, however, is impossible, as this section deals also with ritual matters.

"Mishnah"—body of traditional laws redacted by the Patriarch Judah, at the close of the second century (see Glossary).

"Gemara"—commentary on and discussion of the Mishnah (see Glossary).

2. B. San 33a; Alf, B. *ibid.;* see above, iv, 14.

"Tanna'im"—authorities, whose teachings are embodied in the Mishnah or in the Baraita̲ (see Glossary).

"Amora'im"—expounders of the Mishnah.

"the following distinctions are to be observed." The rest of this section, and Secs. 3–4, set forth the distinctions.

"since he is a well-qualified judge"—i.e., the case is reconsidered for the benefit of the litigant against whom judgment was given. The judge himself is exempt from making good the loss due to his wrong decision, even if he implemented it, because he is well qualified, and holds authorization from the exilarch or the court, or was accepted by the litigants.

3. B. San 5a.

4. "a man of violence." See above, iv, 15.

"[But if he did not . . .]." The bracketed sentence is inserted by KM *ad loc.* The correction is fully borne out by Alf, B. San 33a.

"[. . . what he has given him]"—at the instance of the judge.

"it was his intention." Since he is deficient in the knowledge requisite for the office of judge, it is as if he had intentionally caused the loss.

5. *Responsum* by Alf, cited in NY on Alf, B. San 5b, 6a, in the name of *'Iṭṭur.*

"*ḳinyan*"—literally: "acquisition." It has come to designate a symbolic delivery or transfer; also an agreement or pledge confirmed by a symbolic act; see also Glossary.

"to pay the claim"—if the *defendant* had been ordered to take the oath.

"to waive it"—if the *plaintiff* had been ordered to take the oath.

"every agreement . . . by a ḳinyan"—B. Giṭ 14a.

6. B. San 31b. The phrase used in the Talmud is: "Place of Assembly."

"If he (subsequently) says"—after the court has decided against him.

"payment is exacted." Recovery of claim is not put off till the Supreme Court gives its ruling.

7. B. San 31b.

"litigants appear as claimants"—i.e., their claims are equally balanced, as, e.g., a suit between partners; or one with regard to a find, each claiming to be the finder of an object; or one bearing on deposits, if both entrusted to the keeping of another person unequal amounts of money, and each claims to be the owner of the larger amount, cf. BḤ ṬḤM, 14:2, n. 2; SME ḤM 14:1, n. 6.

8. "unsupported"—literally: "empty."

"the defendant is not compelled." Otherwise anyone who wishes to extort money from another will trump up a charge against him, demanding that the suit be tried by the Supreme Court, and the defendant, to save time and money, will be compelled to settle the unfounded claim.

9. B. San 32b.

Chapter VII

1. San 3:1.

"by one of the parties." In the text the plural is erroneously used in lieu of the singular.

2. San 3:2; B. *ibid.,* 24b.

"ḳinyan"—see note above, vi, 5, and Glossary.

"ordered to pay." This is the correct reading. See RaDbeZ LhR, 82.

"ordered to pay the claim"—i.e., if the defendant obligated himself to abide by the evidence or the decision; in case the plaintiff obligated himself, the claim is remitted.

3. San 3:2; B. BB 128a.

" 'Swear . . . by the life,' " etc. This is a minor oath. A proper judicial oath is one in which the name of God is invoked.

"must pay the claim." See note above, Sec. 2 ("ordered to pay the claim").

4. B. BB 128a; B. San 24b.

"consuetudinal oath." According to scriptural law, if the defendant meets the plaintiff's claim with a complete denial, the case is dismissed. The Rabbis, however, as a matter of equity imposed an oath upon the defendant. The oath is designated as "consuetudinal." Cf. B. Shebu 40b.

"but transferred it." A rabbinical oath can be transferred from the defendant to the plaintiff. The former can say to the latter, "Substantiate your claim by an oath and I will make good the claim." (B. Shebu 41a).

5. B. BB 127b, 128a.

6. San 3:8.

7. B. San 31b.

"no attention is paid." Since he said that his arguments were closed, there is reason to suspect that the witnesses who are to testify for him are false witnesses, or that the documentary evidence he is about to adduce is forged.

8. B. San 31b.

9. B. San 31a.

"his father"—literally: "his testator."

10. B. Ned 27a, b. Cf. ShK ḤM 21, n. 3.

"forfeits his right"—i.e., if the plaintiff stipulated the condition; in case the defendant stipulated it, the claim is collected.

Chapter VIII

1. San 1:6.

"to side with a majority." The literal translation of the phrase is: "to turn aside after a multitude."

2. San 3:6; Tos *ibid.,* 6:5 (see MB *ad loc.*)

"has formed no opinion"—literally: "does not know."

"two more judges are added." Since the third is undecided, the court to all intents and purposes consists of two judges only.

"five judges." In civil suits, the judge who is undecided may, on further study, take a definite stand either for or against the defendant. Cf. P. San 5:5, p. 26b, 27a (52, 53).

"at the outset"—when the three tried the case.

"evenly divided"—that is, six against six.

3. B. San 17a. Cf. BhG ḤM 18:3, n. 15; LM *ad loc.*

Chapter IX

1. B. San 17a.

"is acquitted." Sentence is not passed upon the accused till the following day in the hope of finding a point in his favor. This possibility is precluded in a case where there is at the very outset a unanimous opinion for conviction.

2. San 5:5; see TYṬ *ad loc.*

"besides the one who is undecided." He may later argue in favor of the accused, therefore he is included among the judges.

" 'an impasse' "—literally: "the case has become old"; all arguments have been exhausted, and further discussion is futile. This is the interpretation R. Huna ben Manoah gives to the statement *nizdakan had-din* (B. San 42a). It is the interpretation which Maimonides favors.

3. B. San 42a.

"acquitted"—by a majority of one.

"convicted"—by a majority of at least two; i.e., a majority of one suffices to decide a monetary case or a question with regard to any of the rules of the Law, or to acquit one accused of a capital charge; but it requires a majority of two to convict a defendant in a capital case (see ḤMḤ *ad loc.*).

The reading of the last part is uncertain. The Oxford Codex adds the word meaning "before them." If that reading is correct, Sec. 3 should be rendered thus: "If a question concerning which there is a difference of opinion is submitted to the Supreme Court—whether the question is one bearing on a capital charge, or a monetary matter, or any of the rules of the Torah—the number of judges is not increased (in the event the court is divided); they argue the case one with the other and the decision of the majority is (invariably) followed. But if it is a capital charge in which the Supreme Court acts as trial court (see above, v: 1), the members thereof argue the case one with the other until the defendant is either acquitted (by a majority of one) or convicted (by a majority of two)." That is to say, in a capital charge that is within the jurisdiction of the lower courts (i.e., the Small Sanhedrin), the Great Sanhedrin, the court of highest instance, on being consulted, is empowered to declare for conviction by a bare majority; but in a capital charge over which the Great Sanhedrin has sole jurisdiction, it is denied the right to pronounce the death sentence unless there is a majority of two for conviction. Cf. RaDbeZ, *Responsa* (1836), III, 537.

Chapter X

1. MRSY Exod. 23: 2; see SM, "Negative Commandments," 283; see also MM, p. 122.

" 'If I follow So-and-so.' " The construction which tradition places upon the injunction is: Do not lean upon a great man (*raḇ*) to echo his opinion.

2. MRSY Exod. 23: 2; B. San 34a.

"stage of discussion"—when every effort should be made to find ground for the acquittal of the accused.

3. B. San 43a.

"he is regarded"—when the poll is taken.

4. B. San 43a.

"his declaration is disregarded"—literally: "he is regarded as nonexistent."

5. B. San 34a.

"counted as one only." No two biblical verses teach one and the same thing. Hence the interpretation of one of them is wrong. The above translation is based upon a correction of the text by ShK ḤM 25: 2, n. 19b.

6. San 4: 2.

7. San 4: 1; B. *ibid.*, 32b.

"the opening statement"—i.e., after the examination of the witnesses, and before the discussion of the case, the judges say a word of encouragement to the accused. See below, xii, 3.

8. San 5: 4.

"brought up." The judges sat on raised seats.

"[and is allowed to vote]." In the Hebrew text this statement refers to the accused, i.e., if he has a plea to make in his own behalf and there is substance in what he says, he is allowed to vote; this is contrary to the ruling in P. San. 5: 5, p. 26b (52), where it is expressly stated that even if, as a result of his plea, the accused is cleared of the charge against him, he cannot act as judge in the case. (See LM *ad loc.*) Rabbi S. Strashum on B. San 40a suggests that this statement is misplaced, that it belongs to the first part of the section.

"does not descend . . . any more." He does not become a regular member of the Sanhedrin, but is permitted to participate in the deliberations of that body. Cf. TYṬ San 5: 4; see L. Ginzberg, *A Commentary on the Palestinian Talmud,* III, 215, n. 241.

"does not descend . . . that day." If he were to descend after making his statement, he would be humiliated.

9. San 4: 1, B. *ibid.,* 33b.

"Sadducees"—a sect that denied the authority of the Oral Law.

"the verdict is reversed"—even the Sadducees agree that in this case the offender is liable to death.

"the decision is not reversed." The Sadducees do not admit that this is a capital offense.

Chapter XI

1. San 4: 1; see above, x, 7; x, 9; x, 2.

"at night"—if the discussion has been prolonged.

"the following day"—in the hope that in the meantime ground for acquittal will be found.

2. San 4: 1.

"are not tried." Execution must take place on the day when the verdict is announced. Were the trial to be held on Friday or on the eve of a festival and the accused be found guilty, execution could not be carried out on the Sabbath or on the festival.

3. P. San 4: 6, p. 22a (43).

"any day"—even on Friday or the eve of a festival.

4. B. San 33b, 36b.

"the rules"—stated in Sec. 1.

" 'an ox to be stoned' "—for killing a person (Exod. 21: 28).

5. San 7: 10; B. *ibid.,* 33b, 29a, 36b.

"enticer"—one who entices individuals to idolatry (Deut. 13: 7–12).

"in hiding"—to overhear what he says.

6. San 4: 2.

"is heard last"—that the others feel free to express their opinion.

7. Tos San 7: 2; B. San 36a.

"In monetary matters"—Maimonides' text of Tos San 7: 2 would appear to have differed from the text in our possession.

"count as two." Cases of uncleanness and cleanness can be decided by a single person. Likewise, monetary cases, according to scriptural law, can be adjudicated by one well-qualified judge. Hence, when a difference of opinion arises, father and son, teacher and disciple, are each given a separate vote.

"count as one." Each of these cases requires more than one judge.

8. "for or against the defendant"—i.e., in civil suits; in a capital case, the disciple is given a hearing only if his plea is in favor of the accused. See above, x, 8.

"the right to vote"—in the preliminary poll, i.e., while the discussion is still in progress. Cf. LM *ad loc.*

9. "as will be stated later"—see note on II, xvi, 5.

10. B. San 36a, b.

"pronounces judgment"—since the disciple will know how to apply the traditional law transmitted to him.

11. San 4: 2; B. Yeb 102a; see above, ii, 9.

Chapter XII

1. San 5: 1.

"(the accused)." See below, Sec. 3.

"If they say." In the text the singular is erroneously used.

2. B. San 8b; Tos *ibid.*, 11: 1 (see ḤMḤ *ad loc.*); B. *ibid.*, 81b; B. Ket 33a.

"the possibility . . . unwittingly." This applies also to a scholar. He may have been unaware that the fat he ate was forbidden fat, or that the day on which he did the work was the Sabbath.

"within an utterance"—the time it takes a disciple to greet his teacher, saying to him: "Peace be unto thee, my master and teacher" (B. BḲ 73b), to make sure that the warning has not escaped the culprit's memory.

"by himself"—i.e., by the accused himself.

3. San 4: 5; 5: 5; 6: 1; see above x, 5, 7 and below, II, i, 4 ff.

"'the blood of the man'"—wrongfully convicted.

"'a single man was created.'" Every human being should be fully conscious of the great responsibility resting upon him; his conduct may determine the fate of the whole human race.

"the oldest"—if there are more than two witnesses.

"to add to the judges"—in case the vote is tied or there is a majority of only one for conviction.

"the distance between the court of Moses." The whole encampment in the wilderness was twelve miles long. The Tent of Meeting, where the court was located, occupied the central portion thereof. Hence the distance between the court and the outer limit of the camp of the Israelites was six miles.

"[outer limit.]" The Hebrew word for "outer limit" is inserted by TYṬ San 6: 1, occurs also in Mss.

4. B. San 35a; Ar 1: 4; B. *ibid.*, 7a.

5. B. Ar 7a.

Chapter XIII

1. San 6: 1, 2; B. *ibid.*, 43a, 45b.

"flag"—literally: cloth.

"at such-and-such a time"—i.e., on such-and-such a day, at such-and-such an hour (B. San 43a).

"two scholars accompany him"—after he has been returned twice.

"this form of confession"—i.e., he must not say anything disparaging of the court or the witnesses.

2. B. San 43a.

3. B. San 43a.

"the sword"—depending upon the mode of execution prescribed for the culprit.

4. B. San 63a.

"does not involve . . . flagellation." The prohibition *Ye shall not eat with the blood* is a comprehensive negative command and therefore does not entail the penalty of flogging; see below, xviii, 2.

5. B. MḲ 14b.

6. San 6: 6.

"mourning rites"—the seven days, the thirty days, and the twelve months of mourning ordinarily observed.

7. Mak 1: 10; B. San 45b; see above, Sec. 1.

"before another court"—a court outside Palestine.

8. B. Mak 7a.

"under all circumstances"—even if the original witnesses appear and testify that he has been condemned to death.

Chapter XIV

1. San 7: 1; 9: 1; B. *ibid.*, 52b.

2. "It is a positive command." See SM, "Positive Commandments," Nos. 226–230; Tos San 9: 3.

"The State"—the Jewish State, literally: "the king."

3. MRSY Exod. 22: 17 (cf. MM, p. 124).

4. San 9: 4; B. *ibid.*, 49b, 50a, b, 81a.

"two death penalties"—e.g., if his widowed mother-in-law married again and he had intercourse with her, he is liable to two death penalties, i.e., for relations with a married woman—an offense punishable by strangulation—and for relations with his mother-in-law—an offense punishable by burning. Therefore the severer one, burning, is imposed upon him.

"a lighter mode"—for a lighter offense.

5. B. BḲ 15a; B. Ḳid 35a.

6. San 9: 3.

7. B. San 79b.

"mixed up with others"—i.e., with innocent people.

"except in his presence"—since the culprit cannot be identified, it is as though he were absent.

8. B. San 45b.

"were cut off"—after they testified.

9. San 6: 5; B. *ibid.*, 47a.

"This ordinance"—that only two burial places be provided and not four, one for each mode of execution.

"to procure . . . a coffin and a shroud"—after the flesh has been decomposed and the remains are to be burried in the ancestral tomb; see RaDeZ *ad loc.*

10. Mak 1: 10; San 6: 4; B. *ibid.*, 46a.
11. MRSY Exod. 21: 14 (see MM, p. 124); B. San 52b.
"before the Lord Thy God"—i.e., in the sanctuary.
"right place"—the Hall of Hewn Stones.
12. Mid 5: 4; B. San 101b.
13. MRSY Exod. 21: 14; B. San 41a.
14. Mak 1: 10.
"as was stated before"—iv: 12.

Chapter XV

1. San 6: 3, 4; B. *ibid.*, 45a.
"stripped"—to hasten death and lessen pain (PhM San 6: 3).
"twice a man's height"—i.e., six cubits. Normal man's height is three cubits.
"cast down." The usual translation of the Hebrew verb in the quotation from Exod. 19: 13 is: "shot through." But the verb means also: "cast"; see Exod. 15: 4.
"the stone falling." The text prefixes, erroneously, the nota acusativa (*'et*).
2. B. Ket 45b.
3. San 7: 2.
"placed in a soft one"—not to bruise his skin and thus intensify the pain.
4. San 7: 3.
"the government"—the Roman Government.
5. San 7: 3.
"soft one." See note on Sec. 3.
6. San 6: 4.
"a curse against God." The usual interpretation of the verse from Deuteronomy is: "for he that is hanged is a reproach to God."
"with reference to an idolater." His sin is described as blasphemy.
7. San 6: 4; 6: 5; B. *ibid.*, 46b.
8. San 6:5.
9. B. San 46b, 45b; see above, xiii, 3.
10. San 7: 4.
"Molech"—deity of heathen Semites, worshiped by child sacrifice.
"an enticer"—who entices individuals to idolatry. See note above, xi, 5.
"a seducer"—one who seduces a whole town to idolatry.
11. San 9: 1; B. *ibid.*, 76b.
"his wife's daughter"—by a previous marriage.
"excision" (*karet*, literally: "cutting off"). Opinions differ concerning the nature of this punishment. According to some, it means premature death, i.e., death at the age of fifty or between fifty and sixty (B. MK 28a); according to others it means dying childless (B. Yeb 55a); still others interpret it as the cutting off of the soul in the world to come (B. San 64b; see I, v, viii, 2).
12. San 9: 1.
13. San 11: 1.

Chapter XVI

1. San 1: 2, and B. *ibid.*, 10a.

"substitute for death." Many of the rules applying to capital punishment apply also to corporal punishment; see below Sec. 2, 4; cf. above xi, 4.

2. "in the presence"—i.e., cases involving the penalty of flogging are tried by, and the punishment is inflicted in the presence of, three ordained judges; see above, v, 4, 6.

3. " 'beating for disobedience' "—since there are no ordained judges at the present time.

4. B. Mak 15b.

"due warning"—before the commission of the offense.

"as . . . capital charges"—since flogging is a substitute for death.

"a prohibition transformed into a positive command"—i.e., a negative command, the infraction whereof can be repaired by obeying the positive command accompanying the prohibition. Thus the Bible says: *And ye shall let nothing remain of it* [the flesh of the Paschal lamb] *until the morning; but that which remaineth of it until the morning ye shall burn with fire* (Exod. 12: 10). The negative command: "let nothing remain of it until the morning" is followed by the positive command: "that which remaineth of it until the morning ye shall burn with fire"; the latter is intended to correct the violation of the negative command. Therefore, if the act urged in the positive command is carried out, the transgression of the negative command does not entail the penalty of flogging.

So, too, Scripture says *And when ye reap the harvest of your land, thou shalt not wholly reap the corner of thy field, neither shalt thou gather the gleaning of thy harvest; thou shalt leave them for the poor* (Lev. 23: 22). If, therefore, the owner left the corners he reaped or the gleanings he gathered for the poor, he has redressed the wrong done by him and is not liable to flogging.

"a qualified warning"—literally: "a dubious warning." At the time when the negative command was contravened, it was not known whether the offender would fulfill the attendant positive command. The warning given him was therefore only a qualified one.

5. B. Ḥul 81b.

"an animal and its young"—a transgression entailing the penalty of flogging.

"to an idol"—a capital offense.

6. B. Giṭ 2b, 54b; B. Ḳid 65b.

" 'fat of kidney' "—forbidden to be eaten.

"had connection"—the offender being a priest.

7. B. Ḳid 65b.

8. Mak 3: 12–13.

"ripped open"—at the seams.

"navel"—the edge of the abdomen.

9. Mak 3: 13, and B. *ibid.*, 23a.

"[on the chest]." This probably is a combination of two variant readings: (a) "in front between the nipples," (b) "on the chest between the nipples."

10. Mak 3: 13; Sif Deut. 25: 3, p. 96b (192).

"to stoop." The usual rendering of the Hebrew verb involved is: "to cause him to lie down."

11. P. Mak 3: 11; B. *ibid.*, 23a.

Maimonides follows the wording of the Mishnah in P. Mak 3: 11, which differs from that in B. Mak 3: 14.

12. Mak 3: 14; 1: 2; Sif Deut. 25: 3, p. 96b (192); Mek Exod. 21: 15, III, 44; BḲ 8: 3.

"the estimated number"—that the culprit can endure, see below, xvii, 1.

"[in excess of]." The word *yeṯer* ("more than") has been inadvertently omitted.

"pĕruṭah"—the smallest copper coin.

Chapter XVII

1. Mak 3: 10; Num. R 16: 1, p. 77a (153).

"How many stripes"—correct reading: "how many," not: "how."

"the number estimated." The usual translation of the Hebrew noun in Deut. 25: 2 is: "by number," i.e., in proportion to his crime.

2. Mak 3: 11.

3. B. Mak 22b.

4. Mak 3: 11.

"One prohibition . . . several floggings." When, e.g., he plows with an ox and an ass yoked together over two different kinds of seed in his vineyard, he transgresses the negative commandments *Thou shalt not sow thy vineyard with two kinds of seed* (Deut. 22: 9) and *Thou shalt not plow with an ox and an ass together* (Deut. 22: 10).

"but if not"—if the estimate was only for one flogging.

"for every offense"—if he is liable to more than two floggings.

5. Mak 3: 14; B. *ibid.*, 23a.

"has been dishonored"—has suffered humiliation.

"the night before"—after he was sentenced to be flogged.

6. B. Mak 23a.

"escapes." It shows cowardice on his part and he has thus been humiliated enough to warrant exemption from further degradation.

7. Sif Deut. 25: 3, p. 96b (192); Mak 3: 15.

"excision." See note above, xv, 11.

8. P. Hor 3: 1, p. 11b (22).

9. P. Hor 3: 1, p. 11b (22).

"the Head of the College"—the president of the Sanhedrin.

Chapter XVIII

1. Mak 3: 2; B. *ibid.*, 13a, b; 16a; Tos *ibid.*, 4: 5, 8.

"fat"—forbidden fat such as the fat of kidney.

"ṭeḇel"—produce from which the priestly and levitical dues have not been separated.

2. Mak 1: 2; 3: 4; Tos *ibid.*, 4: 5; B. *ibid.*, 13b, 16a; B. San 63a.

"by the Name"—invoking the name of God.

"as a warning." No transgression is punishable unless the prohibition "thou shalt not" is explicitly stated in the Bible.

"*(any manner of)*." The Hebrew word in Exod. 20: 10 usually rendered "any manner of" is omitted in the text.

"does not carry . . . flogging"—if the warning given the offender was only with regard to flogging.

"Nor shalt." So the text in Leviticus.

"transformed into a positive command." See note above, xiii, 4.

"with the young." This prohibition is followed by the positive command *Thou shalt in any wise let the dam go* (Deut. 22: 7).

"the corner of thy field." This is followed by the positive command *Thou shalt leave them for the poor* (Lev. 19: 10). In this instance and the preceding one the fulfillment of the positive command would correct the wrong done by transgressing the negative command.

"comprehensive negative command." See the next section.

3. B. Pes 41b; B. Ker 4b, 5a.

See SM, *Root Nine,* where Maimonides discusses at great length the law embodied in this section.

"Ye shall not eat with the blood." This negative command is interpreted to include the following prohibitions:

(a) eating of the flesh of sacrifices before the blood is sprinkled (B. San 63a);
(b) eating of the flesh of an animal before it expires (*ibid.*);
(c) eating of the meal of comfort (see below, IV, xi) for a culprit executed by the order of the court (*ibid.*);
(d) partaking of food by the members of the Sanhedrin on the day of the execution of a culprit they condemned to death (*ibid.*);
(e) eating before the Morning Prayers are said (B. Ber 10b);
(f) it also contains a warning to the stubborn and rebellious son (B. San 63a).

"no special injunction"—i.e., each of the separate acts is not preceded by "thou shalt not." In other words, the Bible does not say: "Do not this and (do not) that."

"single out"—thus indicating that the violation of each is punishable by flogging.

"the Bible says"—with reference to the Paschal lamb.

"raw *and* sodden . . . once." It goes without saying that he is flogged but once if he eats of it raw or even sodden.

"new produce"—not permitted to be eaten before the *'omer* (i.e., the first sheaf) is presented at the sanctuary (Lev. 23: 10).

"nor soothsaying." Just as divination or soothsaying constitutes an infraction punishable by flogging, so does any of the other acts mentioned in Deut. 18: 10.

4. San 9: 5.

"prison cell"—i.e., he is given lifelong imprisonment.

"bread of adversity," etc.—i.e., a meager diet.

5. San 9: 5, B. *ibid.*, 81b; see above, xii, 2.

"he did not . . . the warning." The offender does not suffer the punishment prescribed for him, unless he expressly states his readiness to commit the offense despite the warning (see above, xii, 2).

"not put to death"—if the offense carries with it the penalty of death by order of the court.

"nor is he flogged"—if the offense entails the penalty of excision.

6. San 9: 6; see Josh. 7: 25; II Sam. 1: 13–16; Job 3: 20–21; Judg. 3: 21. See V, 1, xii, 8.

"by an idol." Cf. PhM, San 9: 6.

"Zealots"—those zealous for the honor of God.

"deal with him"—literally: "meet him," i.e., attack him.

Chapter XIX

1. Mak 3: 1–2.

(4) "his wife's sister"—during his wife's lifetime.

(10) bread, or any matter containing the "five kinds of grain" in a fermented state.

(13) "what is left"—portion of sacrifice left over beyond the legal time for consumption (Exod. 29: 34; Lev. 7: 15–17).

(14) "loathsome." A sacrifice which at the time it was slaughtered, or the blood thereof was received, carried, or sprinkled, was unlawfully intended to be eaten beyond the legal time set for its consumption.

(19) "compounds oil"—for secular use.

(21) "compounds incense"—for secular use.

2. Most of the offenses enumerated in this section are mentioned in B. San 83a; others are culled from different parts of the Talmud. They are given fuller treatment by Maimonides in his SM in the part dealing with Negative Commandments. In the notes that follow, with the exception of (16), the reference is to that work.

(1)—133. (2)—133. (3)133. (4)—133. (5)—153. (6)—153. (7)—136.

(8)—68; cf. B. Men 27b. (9)—165. (10)—72. (11)—74. (12)—74. (13)—75. (14)—73. (15)—76. (16)—B. San 83a. (This contradicts the ruling given by Maimonides in VIII, iii, iv, 4; see KM *ad loc.*) (17)—163. (18)—164.

(1) "lay person"—one who is not a priest, nor the wife of a priest, nor the unmarried daughter of a priest.

"great heave offering"—the first levy on the annual produce which is the priest's due.

"defiled"—Tos Ter 6: 6; P. Bik 2: 1, p. 7a (13).

(2) "tithe of the tithe"—literally: "the heave offering of the tithe"—the priest's due from the Levite from the tithes which the latter receives (Num. 18: 26).

(4) *"ḥallah"*—the priest's share of the dough (Num. 15: 19–21).

(5) "before the heave offerings," etc.—i.e., *ṭeḇel.*

(8) "when he does not perform service." This refers to the High Priest. Only four times during the Day of Atonement was he to enter the Holy of Holies to perform service. If he entered a fifth time on the Day of Atonement, or if he entered on any other day of the year, he incurred the penalties of death by divine intervention and flogging.

(12) "as a nonpriest"—B. San 83b.

(15) Even after taking the ritual bath, he could not minister until after sunset.

(16) I.e., he has not yet brought the sacrifice prescribed as an atonement.

3. San 11: 5; B. *ibid.*, 83a; B. Pes 41b.

4. In the notes that follow, with the sole exception of (31), reference is to SM, the part dealing with Negative Commandments.

(1)—2, 3. (2)—4. (3)—10; see I, iv, ii, 2–3. (4)—11. (5)—13. (6)—12. (7)—14. (8)—14. (9)—25. (10)—23. (11)—24. (12)—30. (13)—31; see I, iv, xi, 6. (14)—32; see I, iv, xi, 8. (15)—33; see I, iv, xi, 4. (16)—35; see I, iv, xi, 10. (17)—38. (18)—65. (19)—81. (20)—80. (21)—77. (22)—78. (23)—86. (24)—87. (25)—88. (26)—82. (27)—68. (28)—69. (29)—73. (30)—70, 71. (31)—B. San 83a. (32)—72. (33)—163. (34)—164. (35)—91. (36)—92. (37)—93. (38)—94. (39)—96; see VIII, iv, i, 6. (40)—97. (41)—113. (42)—114. (43)—98. (44)—124. (45)—99. (46)—100. (47)—102. (48)—103. (49)—104. (50)—105. (51)—112. (52)—106. (53)—130. (54)—140. (55)—145. (56)—148. (57)—144. (58)—137. (59)—137. (60)—145; cf. VIII, v, xi, 4. (61)—147. (62)—144. (63)—141, 142, 143. (64)—149. (65)—149. (66)—150. (67)—150. (68)—151. (69)—135. (70)—138. (71)—139. (72)—115. (73)—121, 122. (74)—123. (75)—123. (76)—125. (77)—146. (78)—153. (79)—188. (80)—172. (81)—174. (82)—173. (83)—175. (84)—176. (85)—179. (86)—177. (87)—178. (88)—180. (89)—181. (90)—182. (91)—183. (92)—187. (93)—186. (94)—189. (95)—192. (96)—193. (97)—198. (98)—199. (99)—200, 201. (100)—194. (101)—203–206. (102)—209. (103)—207. (104)—307. (105)—308. (106)—309. (107)—220. (108)—221. (109)—222. (110)—223. (111)—224. (112)—225. (113)—226. (114)—210. (115)—212. (116)—211. (117)—213. (118)—214. (119)—306. (120)—215. (121)—216. (122)—216. (123)—217. (124)—218. (125)—219. (126)—101. (127)—239. (128)—241. (129)—242. (130)—285. (131)—300. (132)—195; see below, iii, vii, 7. (133)—301. (134)—317. (135)—62. (136)—61. (137)—157. (138)—321. (139)—323–329. (140)—43. (141)—44. (142)—45. (143)—171. (144)—41. (145)—42. (146)—57. (147)—40. (148)—39. (149)—166. (150)—158. (151)—160. (152)—159. (153)—162. (154)—356. (155)—357. (156)—355. (157)—354. (158)—360. (159)—361. (160)—358. (161)—359. (162)—353. (163)—52. (164)—53. (165)—53. (166)—364. (167)—363. (168)—365.

(3) "by an overt act"—as when he unveils an idolatrous figure to gaze on it; otherwise he is not liable to flogging. See above xviii, 2.

(6) "a figured stone"—with an idolatrous representation carved on it.

(24) "Ephod"—a tightly fitting garment, bound round the body under the arms, and kept in place by straps over the shoulders (see Exod. 28: 6).

(26) "golden altar"—reserved exclusively for incense (Exod. 30: 9).

(31) "an uncircumcised priest"—one whose brothers died as a result of circumcision and who therefore does not have to be circumcised (see B. Yeb 64b).

(55) "most holy sacrifices"—such as sin offerings, burnt offerings, trespass offerings, etc.

(58) "after her husband's death"—when she is permitted to eat of the heave offering.

(59) "a *ḥălalah*"—literally: "profaned," i.e., the daughter of a marriage forbidden to a priest, or a priest's wife illegitimately married to him.

(60) "in a lesser degree"—such as thanksgiving offerings, peace offerings, etc.

(62) a nonpriest is forbidden to eat of it even in Jerusalem; cf. SM, "Negative Commandments," No. 144.

(63) "within the walls of Jerusalem"—literally: "within sight of the Temple."

(65) "Declaration"—set forth in Deut. 26: 5–10.

(73) "Second Passover"—instituted for those who were prevented by un-

cleanness from participating in the Paschal sacrifice on the eve of the fifteenth of Nisan. They were to sacrifice it on the eve of the fifteenth of Iyyar.

(78) "tithes has not been separated." This, too, is designated as ṭeḇel. But while one who eats ṭeḇel from which either of the priestly shares (i.e., the share due him from Israelites and that due him from Levites) has not been separated incurs the penalty of death by divine intervention—see Sec. 2 (5)—one who eats ṭeḇel from which the priestly dues have already been separated but from which any of the tithes (i.e., the first, the second, or the poor tithe) has not been set apart does not incur that penalty.

(88) *"nĕḇelah"*—an animal that died a natural death or was not slaughtered correctly, i.e., according to the ritual rules.

(89) *"ṭĕrefah"*—an animal torn (by beasts or birds of prey); the prohibition was extended to include an animal afflicted with a fatal organic disease.

(94) *"'omer"*—literally: "sheaf"; see Lev. 23:10.

(95) "first three years." The fruit of young trees was forbidden for use during the first three years (Lev. 19:23).

(98) "after midday"—on the fourteenth of Nisan.

(101) "a nazarite"—one who vows to dedicate himself to the service of God. He is to abstain from intoxicants, to let his hair grow, and to avoid contact with a dead body (Num. 6:1–21).

(114) This is a negative command which is transformed into a positive command. The injunction *Thou shalt not wholly reap the corner of thy field* (Lev. 23:22) is followed by the positive command *Thou shalt leave them for the poor, and for the stranger* (*ibid.*). The transgressor is thus given the opportunity to remedy the wrong he has done in reaping the corner of his field. If he fails to carry out the act of redress enjoined in the positive command, he is flogged. This applies also to (115), (116), (117), (118), and (119).

(122) "in any land"—even outside Palestine.

(127) This too is a negative command transformed into a positive command. The injunction *Thou shalt not go into his house to fetch his pledge* (Deut. 24:10) is followed by the command *Thou shalt surely restore to him the pledge* (Deut. 24:13). If he who took the pledge disobeys the positive command, he is flogged. This applies also to (128).

(130) "not liable to payment of compensation." The rule is: *Whoever is liable to compensation is not flogged* (Mak 1:2). If the injury is estimated at a pĕruṭah or more, the one who inflicts the injury is liable to payment of compensation and is not flogged.

(156) So too, one who has intercourse with a woman whom he did not marry according to Jewish law, that is, by means of a marriage contract and the act of bethrothal, transgresses this negative command (see SM, "Negative Commandments," No. 355). It includes also, according to Maimonides, one who has lifelong relations with a woman, without formal declaration of marriage and a marriage contract (see below, v, iv, 4).

Chapter XX

1. MRSY Exod. 23:7 (cf. MM, p. 125); Mek Exod. 23:7, III, 169–170; San 5:1.

"And the innocent," etc.—i.e., take every precaution not to condemn an innocent person to death.

2. See I, 1, v, 4.

"in those instances"—i.e., idolatry, adultery, and murder.

"has desecrated"—by refusing to endanger his life.

"the damsel"—who has been ravished.

3. B. Yeb 53b; B. Ket 51b.

"is guilty . . . offense." But the penalty is not meted out to him; see KM *ad loc.*

"voluntary act"—depending on one's will.

4. Sif Deut. 19:13, p. 84b (168); 19:21, p. 85a (169); Sif Lev. 19:15, p. 351a; Tos San 6:2.

5. Mek Exod. 23:6, III, 168.

"poor religiously"—literally: "poor in the performance of the comandments."

6. Ab 5:8.

7. Ab 4:7.

8. B. Yeb 109b; B. AZ 19b; Ab 4:7.

"enmity"—of litigants who are disappointed by his decision.

"robbery." He may unintentionally give an incorrect decision and thus make a wrong disposition of money.

"false swearing." He may be the means of causing a litigant to swear falsely.

9. B. San 5b.

"three Persian miles"—24,000 cubits.

10. B. San 8a.

"maneh"—100 zuz, equal in weight to 100 common shekels.

11. B. BM 55b.

12. Sif Deut. 24:17, p. 95b (190).

"two negative commandments"—i.e., the one mentioned before and the one that follows.

Chapter XXI

1. Sif Lev. 19:15, p. 351a; Tos San 6:2.

2. Tos San 6:2.

3. Tos San 6:2; B. Shebu 30b; cf. Tanḥ Deut. 16:19, p. 325a, b (649–650).

4. B. Shebu 30b.

5. "all courts." ṬḤM 17:5 and SA ḤM 17:3 cite this section but omit the phrase "with the academies"; see, however, BY ṬḤM 28:6.

"the Talmud." The Venice edition and all old editions have "Talmud" instead of "Gemara."

"we are powerless," etc. Litigants and witnesses might resent the discomfort of standing during the trial and give vent to their resentment in contention fraught with serious consequences (see BḤ ṬḤM 17:5).

6. B. Yeb 100a.

"Judge the fatherless," etc. First *judge the fatherless,* then *plead for the widow.*

"the humiliation"—of waiting in court.

7. B. San 7b; B. Shebu 31a; Mek Exod. 23:7, III, p. 168.

"a single statement"—so the Venice edition.

"accept a false report," etc. The usual rendering of this injunction is: "Do not utter a false report." In the absence of his opponent, the litigant might feel free to make untrue statements.

8. Mak 1:9, and B. *ibid.,* 6b.

"appoint an interpreter." This translation is based upon ṬḤM 17:9.

9. P. San 3:8, 17b (34); B. San 7b.

10. B. Shebu 30b; Ab 1:9.

"express approval"—literally: "become an advocate," i.e., comment favorably on the arguments given by one of the parties to a suit.

"from a false matter." A favorable comment on the argument of one of the litigants indicates partiality.

"keep silent." The judge should avoid saying anything likely to create the impression that he is biased in favor of one of the litigants.

11. P. San 3:8 17b (34); Ab 1:8.

Chapter XXII

1. B. San 6b; Sif Deut. 1:17, p. 55b (110); 1:16, p. 55a (109); B. Hor 10a, b.

2. Tos San 1:4; see Mek Exod. 23:7, III, 168.

"sitting before his master"—while the latter is trying a case.

"uncultured"—devoid of all knowledge.

"to sit before him." He may express a wrong view, confuse the judge, and cause him to give a wrong decision.

3. B. Shebu 31a.

"give a contrary decision"—literally: "build up (the case)"; cf. B. Shebu 31a.

"Keep thee . . . a false matter"—it is disingenuous to do so.

4. B. San 6b.

"carries peace with it"—arbitration brings peace to both parties, whereas the application of the law may fail to achieve this result.

"justice." The usual rendering of the quotation is: "execute the judgment of . . . and peace."

"the law must take its course"—literally: "let the law cut through the mountain."

5. B. San 6a.

6. B. San 5b.

7. San 3:7; and B. *ibid.,* 31a.

8. B. San 30a.

" 'was acquitted' "—or "was found liable."

9. B. San 30a.

"the judges of Jerusalem"—literally: "the men of Jerusalem." In B. San 23a and 30a, the reading is: "the pure-minded."

10. B. Shebu 30b.

"join him"—in trying a case.

Chapter XXIII

1. Sif Deut. 16:19, p. 80b (160); B. Ket 105a; B. Tem 4b (see BhG ḤM 9:1, n. 2).

"The purport . . . is not," etc. This prohibition is explicitly stated in the negative command *Thou shalt not wrest judgment* (Deut. 16: 19).

2. B. BM 75b.

"The giver." He is on a par with one who lends money on interest; cf. BhG ḤM 9: 1, n. 3.

3. B. Ket 105b.

"stays at home"—unlike Samuel who attended to the spiritual needs of the people in person; see I Sam. 7: 16; also B. Shab 56a.

"bribe of words"—including any favor or courtesy shown to the judge.

"feather"—In the text two words are used for "feather"; namely: *noṣah* and *'eḇrah*. In some Mss. the word noṣah is omitted. It is not unlikely that noṣah was originally placed in the margin to explain the word 'eḇrah and that later it was incorporated in the text; see Job 39: 13.

"mantle." In B. Ket 105b the reading is: "(a bird) from his head."

"spittle in front . . . of a judge." In B. Ket 105b the reading is: "spittle ejected by the judge."

"who presented." He wanted the judge to try a case in which he was interested.

"tenant farmer"—one who receives from the owner a fixed percentage of the crops.

4. B. Ket 105b.

5. Bek 4: 6; B. Ket 105a.

"it is evident." The word "not" is omitted in the Venice edition.

"loss of time"—involved in trying the case.

6. B. Ket 105b.

"his most intimate friend"—literally: "his friend as his own soul" (see Deut. 13: 7).

7. B. San 29a.

8. B. San 6b, 7a.

"think of himself," etc.—i.e., he should feel keenly the responsibility resting upon him.

"Gehenna"—originally a place south of Jerusalem, where children were sacrificed to Molech (II Kings 23: 10). It has become a synonym for "Hell."

9. B. San 6a, b, 7a; B. Shab 10a.

"anxiety"—apprehension of giving a wrong judgment.

10. Ab 1: 6, 8.

"before you"—during the trial.

Chapter XXIV

1. B. Ket 85a.

"unimpaired"—i.e., the validity of which is not questioned.

"against the same defendant"—whose funds are insufficient to meet both claims; cf. Per ṬḤM 15: 4, n. 4.

"throw . . . of court"—literally: "throw it in his face."

"If this be so"—i.e., since such vast discretionary power is given to the judge.

2. Alf, B. Ket 85a.

"qualifications"—for the office they hold.

"understanding"—to exercise the functions of judge.

"that . . . should not be guided." For the correct reading of the text, see ṬḤM 15: 4.

3. B. Shebu 30b, 31a.

"has reason to suspect"—literally: "knows." His suspicion, however, may prove unfounded as a result of the examination which the witnesses undergo. Hence the statement: "If after this thoroughgoing examination, he concludes [that there is nothing fraudulent about the suit, he gives his decision on the evidence]." However, the author of *Děrišah* (ṬḤM 15: 3) takes the word *yoḏea'* literally: "the judge knows." Hence the sole purpose of the examination given the witness is to expose the guilty litigant, i.e., to protect his opponent. It is evident that the edition used by the author of *Děrišah* did not have the bracketed statement quoted above.

"one of the litigants"—either the plaintiff or the defendant.

"bear the responsibility"—literally: "the chain (of guilt) will hang around the neck of the witnesses."

"let another judge . . . pronounce judgment." The fact that he withdraws from the case is no reflection on the judge who takes it over.

"the judgment is God's." The judge must follow the dictates of his conscience.

4. B. San 46a.

"under a fig tree"—an offense which according to the law is not punishable by flogging.

"the days of the Greeks"—the days of Antiochus Epiphanes and his successors, when religious laxity prevailed in Palestine.

"rode a horse on the Sabbath"—riding on Sabbath is a rabbinical prohibition and therefore is not punished by death.

5. B. Ḳid. 81a; B. Yeb 25a; B. Meg 26b; cf. IV, v, ii, 14.

6. B. MḲ 16a.

"or give it away"—omitted in ṬḤM 2: 2.

7. B. MḲ 16a.

"major excommunication." If the offender who is under the ban persists in his disobedience, the major excommunication is pronounced upon him.

"the desired end"—to bring the offender to terms.

"Curse ye Meroz." The curse was by the authority of Barak, who spoke in the name of the angel. Moreover the sin of Meroz was specified and made public.

8. B. MḲ 16a.

9. B. MḲ 16a.

10. B. San 46a; B. Ber 19b; see Ab 4: 6.

"whosoever dishonors"—literally: "despises."

Chapter XXV

1. B. RH 17a.

"he will not see any (sons) . . . *wise of heart."* This sentence is usually translated: "he regardeth not any that are wise of heart."

2. B. San 7b, 8a.

"force his way"—literally: "step over the heads of the holy people." The listeners used to sit on the floor and by his pushing his way through them, it would appear as if he were striding over their heads.

3. B. San 8a; B. Ḳid 70a.

"this command"—to treat the congregation with respect.

4. B. Ḳid 70a.

"lower its standards"—literally: bring it (the Torah) down to the ground (see Isa. 26: 5).

5. B. BḲ 112b.

"banned"—for contempt of court.

"no writ . . . issued." The writ involves expenditure, for the payment of which one is liable only on the evidence of two witnesses.

6. B. MḲ 16a; B. Ḳid 12b.

7. B. San 8a.

"thus speaking." Possibly, two distinct readings were combined in the section: (a) If the messenger says, "So-and-so has sent me." (b) If the messenger speaks in the name of one of the judges.

"on a court day"—Monday or Thursday.

8. B. BḲ 113a.

"as soon . . . 'I accept it' "—a mere promise is enough.

"set a day"—*zĕman;* the word *hay-yom* (a day) is superfluous; it is omitted in the Venice edition.

"the following day"—Tuesday.

9. B. BḲ 113a.

"busy on the eve of the Sabbath"—and may forget about the summons.

10. B. BḲ 112b, 113a.

11. B. MḲ 16a.

Chapter XXVI

1. B. San 66a; Mek Exod. 22: 27, III, p. 152; Sif Lev. 19: 14, p. 350a; cf. Hor 3: 3.

"revile the judges"—literally: "revile God"; see note above, iii, 8.

"who curses a minor." ṬḤM 27: 1 quoting this section has: "one who is asleep" instead of: "a minor"; see, however, the next section.

2. Sif Lev. 19: 14, p. 350a; Mek Exod. 22: 27, III, p. 152.

"a judge, twice"—for transgressing two negative commands, i.e., Lev. 19: 14 and Exod. 22: 27.

"a Naśi, thrice"—for transgressing the above-mentioned injunctions and the injunction *Nor curse a ruler of thy people* (Exod. 22: 27).

"the son of a Naśi." This is the correct reading.

3. Shebu 4: 13, and B. *ibid.*, 36a.

"guard well thy life"—usually translated: "And keep thy soul diligently."

"guard well thy life"—i.e., the duty is enjoined upon every man to preserve and promote his physical life (see B. Ber 32b.).

"an oath"—and is therefore binding.

"a ban." If a sage says to a man, "Thou art *'arur* (cursed)," the latter is under ban.

4. Shebu 4: 13.

"due warning"—flogging is a substitute for a death penalty and requires due warning; see above, xvi, 1, 4.

5. B. MḲ 16a; P. BḲ 8: 6, p. 36b (72); cf. I, III, vi, 12.

"a disciplinary beating"—in addition to the ban.

"the judges fine him"—Sherira Gaon deduces this ruling from B. BḲ 91a; cf. BhG ḤM 27: 2, n. 13.

6. B. Ket 17a; B. San 46a.

7. B. Giṭ 88b; Tanḥ Exod. 21: 1, p. 127b (254); B. BḲ 92b.

Treatise II: Evidence

Chapter I

1. B. BḲ 55b.

"as it is said." In the text the scriptural quotation is at the end of the section. But it belongs to the place given it in the translation.

2. B. Shebu 30b.

"the tribunal"—before whom he is to testify.

"in the case of a prohibition." For example: if a married woman believing her husband to be dead wishes to remarry and the scholar knows that her husband is alive, it is his duty to give evidence and prevent her from remarrying.

"negative command." *If he do not utter it, then he shall bear his iniquity* (Lev. 5: 1).

3. San 2: 1; B. *ibid.*, 18b.

4. San 5: 1; B. *ibid.*, 32b; Ab 1: 9.

"from point to point"—in the evidence submitted by them.

"through the examination"—the line of questioning.

"week of years?"—year of the Jubilee.

"On what day?"—of the week.

"other queries"—which vary with the offense committed.

"there are also other queries." What follows falls under the category of "inquiries," not "queries"; see ii, 1 and iii, 3.

"What did he worship?"—what idol?

"How did he worship it?"—by sacrifice, by offering incense, by libations, or by prostration?

5. B. San 41b.

"the act"—with which the accused is charged.

"the time, and the place"—when and where the act was committed.

6. San 5: 2; B. *ibid.*, 41a.

"the act"—of the murder.

"the stalks"—of the tree.

Chapter II

1. San 5: 2; B. *ibid.*, 41a.

"With what weapon?"—a question which comes under the head of "inquiries" (*dĕrišoṯ*).

2. San 5: 2; B. *ibid.*, 41a.

"his clothes"—the clothes of the slayer or of the slain; see above, i, 6.

"is void." The witnesses thus contradict each other.

3. B. San 41b.
4. San 5: 3; B. *ibid.*, 41 b.
"intercalated"—i.e., the preceding month consisted of thirty days.
5. San 5: 3; B. *ibid.*, 42a.
"during the second hour." The length of the day is counted from sunrise to sunset.
"during the fifth hour." An error of two hours is not likely.

Chapter III

1. San 4: 1, and B. *ibid.*, 32a.
"to shut the door to borrowers"—i.e., make credit difficult.
"zuz"—silver coin, a *denar*, one fourth of the shekel of the sanctuary.
"coinage"—its weight and circulation; cf. B. BḲ 97b, 98a.
"maneh." See note above, I, xx, 10, and Glossary.
2. B. San 32b; see above, I, xxiv, 3.
"enactment"—of the Rabbis.
"admission"—witnesses who testify that the defendant admitted his liability.
"transaction of loans"—witnesses who were present when the loan was made.
"involving fines"—imposed upon offenders.
3. B. San 30b; 31a.
"any of the inquiries"—questions bearing on the main fact, i.e., the debt.
"queries"—questions bearing upon time and place.
4. Sif Deut. 19: 15, p. 84b (168).
5. Shebu 5: 2; Tos San 6: 6; P. Ket 2: 3, p. 11a (21).
"a verbal condition"—and he does not know whether the condition has been complied with.
6. Ket 2: 3; B. *ibid.*, 18b.
"minors." Their evidence is inadmissible; see below, ix, 1.
"kinsmen." They are ineligible as witnesses; see below, ix, 1.
7. B. Ket 18b; 19b.
"no man can incriminate himself." One's testimony against oneself has no legal effect.
"on trust"—that the loan stated in the document would subsequently be consummated.
8. B. Ket 19b.
"verbal protest"—declaration made by seller in the presence of witnesses that he is about to convey under compulsion.
"credence is given." The sale was made under duress. Violence was threatened against the owner and the witnesses had a right to sign the deed.
9. B. Ket 19b.
"upon a condition"—which has not been fulfilled.
"to the purchaser"—literally: "to the litigants." What follows is also in the plural, as it is in B. Ket 19b, where it says: "When they (the purchasers) come before us for judgment, we tell them: fulfill the condition and cite him (the seller) to court."
10. B. Ket 19b.

"(and the deed cannot be authenticated . . .)"—otherwise, the statement of the first witness is disregarded; cf. RaDbeZ *ad loc.;* BY ṬḤM 29: 2.

"one witness." Therefore the defendant is bound to take an oath; cf. LM *ad loc.;* ṬḤM 46: 36; ŠA ḤM 46: 37.

11. B. BḲ 112b.

"If the plaintiff is ill." The above translation is based on BḤ ṬḤM 28: 21; cf. LM *ad loc.*

"documentary evidence"—i.e., witnesses who affixed their signature to the document.

12. B. Ket 27b.

"a difficult man"—literally: "a powerful man."

Chapter IV

1. Mak 1: 9; B. *ibid.*, 6b.

"otherwise"—if they did not see each other.

"if two of them"—literally: "some of them."

"a single body." Hence neither pair can be condemned as plotting witnesses unless all of them are proved to be false witnesses.

"they are put to death." They are found to be plotting witnesses.

2. B. San 30b; cf. ṬḤM 30: 7.

3. B. San 30b.

4. B. San 30b.

5. B. BB 165b.

"set . . . in writing"—an agreement by ḳinyan, unless otherwise specified, is meant to be written out (B. BB 40a).

"and the debtor . . . paid it." But the plaintiff cannot collect from the defendant's alienated property. This is the interpretation given by KM, LM, and ShK ḤM 51: 1.

6. B. BB 165b; B. Ket 21a, b.

"in a third court"—otherwise there would be only two judges left, and two do not constitute a court. The translation is based upon the interpretation suggested in KM; see ṬḤM 30: 12; SA ḤM 30: 12. The same rule obtains if the evidence was given by the witnesses only in two courts, and one of the judges of one court and two of the other have gone abroad. In the latter case, too, the remaining three meet and considered the evidence presented to them.

7. B. BḲ 70b; B. San 30b.

"a matter"—i.e., the whole matter, not when each testifies to only a part of it.

"three (successive) years." If a person enjoys three successive years of undisturbed possession of an estate, his title to it is established.

"maturity." The majority of a person begins from the time when two hairs appear in the region of the pubes.

"But if one witness testifies." The translation is based upon the reading given in KM *ad loc.*

"their evidence is combined." The evidence of each is complete.

Chapter V

1. Sif Deut. 19: 15, p. 84b (168); B. Shebu 40a.

"rises . . . an oath"—testimony of one witness renders the defendant liable to an oath.

"Treatise on Pleading"—XIII, IV, i, 1.

2. So 6: 2; 9: 8; B. *ibid.*, 47b; Sif Deut. 19: 15, p. 84b (168); B. Yeb 117b.

"not made to drink." If there is one witness who testifies that she has been defiled, she is divorced and forfeits her marriage settlement; otherwise she has to undergo the "ordeal of jealousy" described in Num. 5: 21–31.

"not broken." If there is one witness who states that he saw the murderer, the residents of the city nearest to the place where the slain is found do not have to make atonement for the murder by the ceremony described in Deut. 21: 1–9, the chief feature of which is the breaking of a heifer's neck.

"as has already been stated"—IV, v, i, 14; XI, v, ix, 12.

3. Yeb 16: 7; So 9: 8; B. *ibid.*, 47b; Shebu 4: 1; Mak 1: 7, 8.

4. B. Mak 6a.

"witnessing"—the word *ha-'am* (the people) after "witnessing" should be omitted.

5. B. Mak 6a.

6. B. BB 162b. This ruling is given by Alf, B. Mak 6a.

"otherwise"—if conclusive evidence is lacking.

7. "the first signatory," etc.—for the reason given before, i.e., the prominent man was to be the first signatory.

8. San 5: 4; B. *ibid.*, 33b; B. BḲ 90b.

"any further statement"—either for acquittal or for condemnation.

9. B. Ket 21b; B. Giṭ 5b.

Chapter VI

1. B. BB 39b, 40a; B. Ket 22a; see above, I, iii, 4; II, iii, 4.

"rabbinical ordinance . . . of credit." According to scriptural law, no documentary evidence is admitted (see above, I, iii, 4); however, for the benefit of those in need of credit, the Rabbis ordained that it be accepted (B. Ket 28a), provided that the document is certified.

2. Ket 2: 3, 4; B. *ibid.*, 21a, b.

3. B. Ket 20a.

4. B. Ket 21a.

5. B. BB 138b.

6. B. Ket 22a.

"writ of certification"—i.e., legal attestation signed by the judges stating, "We were in a session of three when So-and-so and So-and-so (the witnesses) appeared before us and their signatures were attested" (Rashi on Ket 85a).

"indication." If the writ contains some such phrase as, "So-and-so (mentioning the name of the third judge) said to us," or "We said to So-and-so" (ṬḤM 46: 23).

7. B. Ket 21b, 22a.

"returned in repentance." A dishonest person who undergoes a change of heart is reinstated only after the change wrought in him has become known.

"three (competent) judges"—i.e., at the time when they sign the writ, his eligibility is no longer open to question.

"nonexistent." The change in him was not known.

"at the outset"—at the time when his eligibility was questioned.

8. B. Ket 85a, 109b.

Chapter VII

1. Ket 2: 10.

"kinsman." The certification of documents is a rabbinical enactment and therefore the handwriting of the witnesses may be identified even by kinsmen.

2. Ket 2: 10.

3. B. Ket 19b, 21a.

4. B. Ket 21a; B. BB 57a.

"three quarters"—one half on his own signature which he identifies, and one quarter on the signature of the second witness identified by him and the other man.

5. B. Ket 21a.

"even on a piece of clay." It goes without saying that he may write his signature on the top of a sheet of paper (see Tosafoṯ on Ket 21a).

6. B. Ket 21b.

"as was already stated." See above, v, 9.

"rabbinical derivation." The certification of documents is a rabbinical enactment (see above, vi, 1).

7. B. Ket 19b, 20a.

"does not collect his claim." The money remains in the possession of the defendant.

Chapter VIII

1. B. Ket 20a.

2. B. Ket 20a.

3. B. Ket 20a, b; cf. S. Asaf, ThG, p. 96.

4. B. Ket 20a; P. Ket 2: 4, p. 11b (22).

"the sole significance"—literally: "since the matter is so."

5. B. Ket 20a; Alf, B. *ibid.*

Chapter IX

1. Shebu 4: 1; B. BḲ 88a; RH 1: 8; Giṭ 2: 5; San 3: 3, 4; B. *ibid.*, 27b; B. Ḳid 40b; B. BB 43a.

2. Shebu 4: 1.

3. BḲ 3: 11.

"*ṭumṭum*"—one whose sex is unknown.

"transferred"—from the defendant to the plaintiff.

"passed"—upon the accused.

"change hands"—on the principle that the burden of proof is upon the claimant.

4. B. BḲ 88a; B. Ḥag 4a.
"a heathen"—who is not subject to any of the commandments.
6. B. Giṭ 39a.
7. B. BB 155b.
"the greater part"—thirty-five years and one day.
"Treatise on Marriage"—IV, 1, ii, 11.
8. Nid 6: 1; B. *ibid.*, 48b; B. BB 155b.
"age of maturity"—thirteen years and one day.
"further investigation"—to ascertain that the lower tokens have appeared.
9. Tos Shebu 3: 6; B. BB 128a; B. Ḥag 3b, 4a; B. RH 28a.
10. *Responsum* by Alf cited in *'Iṭṭur* under the letter *Ḳof*.
11. Tos Shebu 3: 6; Giṭ 7: 1, B. Giṭ 71a: B. Ar 18a.
"that he give oral testimony." In the text, this is followed by the phrase: "or that he be able to give oral evidence." ṬḤM 35: 12 and ŠA ḤM 35: 11 omit it; BḤ and Der (*ad loc.*) delete it; see above, iii, 4.
"although . . . tested." If one who has lost his speech wishes to divorce his wife, he is tested three times whether for "no" he says "no" and for "yes" he says "yes" (Giṭ 7: 1).
"*'ăgunah*"—a woman whose husband has disappeared, and who cannot remarry so long as there is no evidence of his death.
12. Tos Shebu 3: 6.

Chapter X

1. B. San 27a; B. Shebu 30b.
"the latter's testimony is accepted"—whereas there is really but one witness, i.e., the other is ineligible.
"that the other is a false witness"—that he knows nothing about the case concerning which he is about to testify. Cf. ShK ḤM 34: 1, n. 3.
2. B. San 26b.
"*wicked deserving of death.*" The usual rendering of this phrase is: "that is guilty of death."
3. B. San 25a, b, 27a; Kil 9: 8; B. Be 4b; B. Nid 61b.
"nĕbelah." See note above, 1, xix, 4 (88), and Glossary.
"to satisfy his appetite"—because it is cheaper.
"in a spirit of defiance"—to show his contempt for the law.
"*ša'aṭnez*"—a garment of wool and linen.
"*šua'*," etc.—a fanciful explanation of the consonants of the word *ša'aṭnez*.
"We have already enumerated"—above, 1, xix.
4. B. San 25b, 26b, 27a; San 3: 3; B. *ibid.*, 25a; RH 1: 8; B. *ibid.*, 22a; Tos San 5: 2.
"from the time . . . stolen or robbed." All the evidence given by them in the meantime is invalid.
"direct"—fixed, stipulated.
"indirect"—literally: dust of usury, i.e., not fixed.
"of small cattle"—i.e., shepherds.
"or large"—i.e., cowherds.

"their own." If the herdsmen or cowherds are hired by others, it is presumed that they will not allow the cattle to graze on other people's lands, on the principle that no man will commit a transgression if he personally stands to gain nothing by it.

"herdsmen . . . are disqualified"—because of the damage they do to the fields.

"small cattle . . . are ineligible." Small cattle cannot be tethered.

"tax farmers"—who pay the government a fixed amount for the right to collect taxes and are invested with discretionary power to decide how much each is to pay.

"tax collectors"—literally: collectors of the portion due to the king, i.e., salaried officials who are expected to turn over the revenue they raise to the king's treasury.

"seventh year produce." The law declares it ownerless (Lev. 25: 2–7).

"the presumption is." There is no conclusive proof that the crop is the produce of the Sabbatical year.

"form of robbery"—literally: the dust of robbery.

5. B. San 26b.

"tenant farmer"—an arrangement whereby the owner agrees to pay the tenant a certain proportion of the yield of the land or orchard; see note above, I, xxiii, 3.

"Nisan"—the month when cereals ripen.

"Tishri"—the month when fruits ripen.

"his work." This is the correct reading.

Chapter XI

1. Ḳid 1: 10; B. *ibid.*, 40b.

2. B. Pes 49b.

"*'am ha-'areṣ*"—an ignorant person, untrustworthy in religious observance; see Glossary.

"the Mishnah." See note above, I, vi, 1.

4. B. Pes 49b.

"*hedyoṭ*"—ordinary, common.

5. B. Ḳid 40b; B. San 26b.

6. B. San 26b.

7. B. Ḥul 3a, b; B. Yo 78a.

"trustworthy if it concerns others"—on the principle that no man will sin to benefit others (B. Shebu 42b).

8. Bek 5: 4.

"'am ha-'areṣ." He is suspected of eating ṭebel, i.e., crops from which the levitical dues have not been separated.

"firstling." See note above, I, iv, 8.

"fear, not so in monetary matters"—i.e., he will not sin, unless he personally will benefit by it.

9. San 2: 1, 2, B. *ibid.*, 18b (see above, I, ii, 5).

"kings of Israel"—i.e., not of the House of David.

"as was stated before"—I, ii, 4.

10. B. AZ 26a, b; Tos San 13; and B. *ibid.*, 105a; see below, V, viii, 11.

"epicureans"—heretics or unbelievers, whether Jewish or non-Jewish. Maimonides (I, v, iii, 16) speaks of three classes of epicureans: (a) those who deny the reality of prophecy in general; (b) those who deny the prophecy of Moses; (c) those who assert that God has no knowledge of the deeds of man.

"rescue . . . cast them." No effort is to be made to save them from death, nor is their death to be designed.

Chapter XII

1. San 3: 3, and B. *ibid.*, 26b.

"nĕḇelah"—see note above, 1, xix, 4 (88), and Glossary.

"in error"—i.e., he was unaware that he was committing an offense.

"habitual dice player"—i.e., one who has no other occupation.

2. B. San 9b, 10a.

"contracted a loan on interest." The injunction against usury extends also to the borrower (B. San 25a).

"to convict *her*"—on the principle that a man is considered a relative to his wife (B. San 10a).

3. B. Ket 21b, 22a; Alf, B. *ibid.*, 21b.

"money is not made over." There are two witnesses against two. Therefore the possessor is given the benefit of the doubt.

4. Mak 3: 15.

"as soon as he repents"—if the penalty of flogging cannot be inflicted upon him, e.g., if no warning was given him or no witnesses were present when the offense was committed by him.

"but . . . are not reinstated." While those who incur the penalty of flogging are rehabilitated as soon as they are flogged, those guilty of extortion or robbery are not rehabilitated unless, in addition to making restitution, they repent.

The reading of the first part of this section is uncertain. Some editions have the reading: "whoever is guilty of an offense involving the penalty of flogging regains his status . . . as soon as he is flogged." The latter reading brings into clear relief the difference between those who are liable to the penalty of flagellation and those who are liable to make restitution. Cf. PhM San 3: 3.

5. B. San 25b.
6. B. San 25b.
7. B. San 25b.
8. B. San 25b.

"they are put to the test"—i.e., whether they leave the produce for the poor. Cf. P. San 3: 5, p. 15a (29); the word used by Maimonides was also the reading of R. Hananel *ad loc.*

"setting down in writing." The reading in B. San 25b is: "he declares."

9. P. Shebu 7: 4, p. 36b (72).

"tĕrefah." See note above, 1, xix, 4 (89).

"let him don"—as in earnest of genuine repentance.

"meat"—belonging to himself.

10. P. Shebu 7: 4, p. 36b (72).

Chapter XIII

1. B. San 27b, 28a.
2. B. Yeb 48b.

3. B. BB 128a.

4. B. BB 128a.

"Certain it is"—i.e., the opinion to the contrary notwithstanding; cf. B. San 28a.

5. B. BB 128a.

"a grandfather and his son's son." Their relationship is one in the first degree to one in the second degree.

6. B. San 28b.

"the husband is as his wife." Hence her evidence concerning him is inadmissible.

7. Alf, B. San 28b.

"their husbands may testify." The rule that the husband is as his wife does not apply if the kinship of the two women is one in the second degree.

9. P. San 3:6, p. 17a (33): Alf, B. *ibid.*, 28b.

The kinship of the wife to her nephew is one in the first degree to one in the second degree; the same relationship obtains between the wife and her niece.

11. B. San 28b.

12. B. San 28b.

13. San 3:4; B. *ibid.*, 28a, b.

14. B. San 28b.

"One's betrothed wife." In talmudic times betrothal bound the bridal couple as husband and wife save for conjugal relations and minor details.

"it is not invalidated"—i.e., after he has given evidence, but he has no direct permission to do so; see KM *ad loc.*

15. B. BB 159a; San 3:5.

Chapter XIV

1. San 3:5.

2. B. BB 128a.

"his daughter"—i.e., the wife of the man who was in possession of evidence concerning his father-in-law.

"at the beginning"—when he witnessed the occurrence or transaction.

"at the end"—when he submits his evidence.

3. Ket 2:10; cf. VII, III, 1:26.

"This is the handwriting." The signature was affixed to the document while the witness was still a minor.

"virgins." The kĕṯubbah of a virgin is 200 zuz (denar) while that of a widow is only 100 zuz.

"a grave area." A field wherein a grave has been ploughed up, the uncleanness whereof is communicated to a distance of one hundred cubits in each direction (Oh 17:1).

"Sabbath limit"—beyond which locomotion is prohibited.

"two thousand cubits." By biblical law the Sabbath limit is set at 24,000 cubits; see III, I, XXVII, 1, 2.

"to eat of the heave offering"—showing that he is a priest.

"*ḥallah.*" See note above, I, XIX, 2 (4), and Glossary.

"severance party"—disowning him for marrying a woman beneath his priestly rank.

"heave offering instituted by the Rabbis"—literally: "rabbinical heave offering." According to Maimonides (VII, III, i, 26), the duty of separating heave offering even during the period of the Second Temple was of rabbinical derivation (see B. Ket 28b).

4. B. Ket 28b.

5. B. BB 159a.

6. B. San 28b.

"is worthless"—literally: "a sherd," i.e., valueless.

"bears its own disqualification." In the first instance, the witnesses are incompetent because of kinship; in the second, one witness is ineligible on religious grounds.

7. P. Giṭ 1: 1, p. 1b (2).

"the deed"—stating: "All my possessions are to go to A and B."

"one body of testimony"—i.e., only one set of witnesses.

"field" (*ḥaṣer*)—literally: "yard, court, ground." ṬḤM 51: 6, citing the ruling in this section, has the word "field" (*śaḏeh*).

Chapter XV

1. B. BB 43a.

"in his own behalf." He is an interested party.

"town square"—where public gatherings for funeral services, and prayer meetings on fast days, were held (see L. Ginzberg, *A Commentary on the Palestinian Talmud,* II, 71).

"by a perfect ḳinyan"—not merely the semblance of it, as by a kerchief.

2. B. BB 43a.

"no one can relinquish his duty." All are therefore interested parties.

3. B. BB 43a.

"to the poor"—and the heirs contest the will or the money is stolen.

"will derive satisfaction." They are interested parties.

4. B. BB 42b, 43a.

5. B. BB 46b, 29a.

"if the crop . . . removed." He has nothing to gain by giving false evidence.

6. B. BB 46b.

"to take it away from him." This is the correct reading; see ṬḤM 37: 1, and ŠA ḤM 37: 1. The creditor has a lien upon the debtor's landed property. If he produces a bond duly attested by the signatures of at least two witnesses, he can recover the debt out of the landed property sold by the debtor after the loan had been made. If the debtor sold two parcels of land, the creditor's first lien is upon the parcel sold to the second purchaser. If that is unavailable, he can seize for the debt the parcel sold to the first.

Chapter XVI

1. B. BB 43b.

2. B. BB 44a.

"the purchaser has acquired it," etc. Renunciation of hope of recovery on the part of B, the original owner, and change of possessory domain vest title to the garment in C, the purchaser. This is effective only in chattels (movables), but is inoperative in landed property (immovables). The latter, unless it is legally transferred, is deemed to be in the possessory domain of the owner, even if it passses through many hands.

3. B. BB 44b, 45a.

"a guarantee"—that if the field be seized by a creditor, the seller would make restitution to the buyer.

"responsible to him"—in case of seizure by a creditor.

"be branded"—i.e., be a defaulter.

4. B. BB 44b; P. San 3: 9, p. 18a, b (35, 36).

"cannot seize chattel." The creditor has no lien on movables. Hence A has nothing to gain by his evidence, and is therefore a disinterested party.

"Furthermore"—even if B states definitely that A was the original and lawful owner of the cow or garment.

"mortgaged . . . along"—literally: "mortgaged it by dint." While chattel cannot be mortgaged directly, it can be mortgaged along with landed property.

"This applies . . . other ineligibles"—whether they are ineligible as witnesses on account of religious delinquency or of kinship.

5. See above, I, xi, 9.

"to serve in the same Sanhedrin." This applies also to a court-of-three. The members thereof must not be related to one another.

6. Nid 6: 4; San 3: 5; B. *ibid.*, 34b; see above, I, ii, 9, and xi, 11.

"The latter class . . . slave." These are precluded from trying even civil cases.

"an emancipated slave"—disqualification predicated of proselytes applies also to emancipated slaves.

"ineligible to try capital cases"—but are eligible to try civil suits.

Chapter XVII

1. B. Shebu 33b.

"seeing (without knowing)"—i.e., he saw money turned over by one man to another, without knowing the nature of the transaction, whether it was a loan, a gift, or payment of a debt.

"knowing (without seeing)"—i.e., the witness did not see the lender give money to the borrower, but the latter admitted the loan.

2. San 3:6.

"the far-reaching consequences"—the evil that follows in its wake.

"all the people." The litigants, however, remain (B. San 30a); cf. TYṬ, San 3: 6.

"The judges address him." The correct reading is: "they address him."

3. B. San 29a.

"lest . . . go to court." The word "tomorrow" is to be omitted. It occurs in B. San 29a. But there it belongs to the sentence which follows.

4. San 3: 6; B. *ibid.*, 29b.

"ḳinyan." See note above, I, vi, 5, and Glossary.

5. Mek Exod. 23: 1, III, 160–161; B. Shebu 31a.

"maneh." See note above, I, xx, 10, and Glossary.

"join him"—in testifying in my behalf.

6. B. Shebu 31a.
7. B. BḲ 55b.
"judgment of the court"—i.e., the court does not punish him.

Chapter XVIII

1. San 11:6; Mak 1:2, 3.
"to do . . . as he purposed"—i.e., the law of retaliation is applied to plotting witnesses.
2. Mak 1:4; B. *ibid.*, 5a.
"he borrowed money *from* So-and-so." This is the correct reading.
"or ordered to pay compensation"—if the question of a loan is involved.
3. B. San 27a; Mak 1:7.
4. B. BḲ 73b.
"No previous warning." Capital and corporal cases require previous warning. But no warning is required in the case of plotting witnesses (see B. Ket 33a; see below, xx, 4).
"executed . . . compensation"—depending upon the nature of the offense with which the accused was charged.
5. B. Ket 20a.
6. B. BḲ 74b.
"the negative command (contravened)," etc. *Thou shalt not bear false witness against thy neighbor* (Exod. 20:13).
"disciplinary flogging"—i.e., lashing for disobedience.
"left to its discretion." In disciplinary lashing the number of strokes is subject to the discretion of the court.
7. B. San 89a.
"public announcement"—to act as a deterrent.
8. B. Mak 2b, 3a.
"on their own admission"—on the principle that no fine is payable on one's own admission.
"their admission . . . indemnity." As soon as they are sentenced to make payment, the compensation is no longer regarded as penal.

Chapter XIX

1. B. Mak 5a.
"they are not accounted plotting witnesses"—i.e., their evidence is not refuted.
"in half the (usual) time"—literally: "doubled the way," i.e., the speed.
2. B. Mak 5a.
"both the slayer." He is condemned to death on the evidence of the second pair of witnesses.
"had not yet been passed." At that time, he was presumed to be innocent and they plotted against him. They are therefore subject to the law of retaliation; see below, xx, 1.
"cases involving fines"—fourfold and fivefold restitution.
"whatever the actual day"—literally: "at all events, in any case."
3. B. San 32a (cf. Alf, B. BḲ 72b), 27a.

"the bond is valid." A postdated bond is valid.

"the first of Adar"—a month earlier than the date on the bond.

Chapter XX

1. Mak 1: 6, 7, 8.

2. B. Mak 5b.

"the strength of a logical deduction"—on an argument from the minor to the major; i.e., if witnesses whose plot failed are put to death, does it not stand to reason that they should be put to death if their plot succeeded?

"has not yet done it"—i.e., their plot failed.

"are flogged." The rule: "as he had purposed to do but has not yet done it" does not obtain in cases involving either corporal punishment or payment of restitution.

3. Mak 1: 7; B. *ibid.,* 6a.

"given by each pair"—i.e., if there are more than three witnesses.

"a disciple to greet his master"—saluting him with the words: "Peace be unto thee, my master, my teacher." (See note above, 1, xii, 2.) In the Hebrew text, this phrase occurs in the third sentence. Logically, it belongs to the second, to which the translation transposes it.

4. B. San 60a; B. Ket 33a.

"or uses a similar expression"—so according to the Venice edition.

"declaring 'Yea' "—or a like term affirming the evidence of the other witness.

"does not involve action." The Bible says *who doeth aught in error* (Num. 15: 29). The emphasis is upon *doeth;* mere speech is not considered an act.

"as has already been stated"—above, xviii, 4.

5. Mak 1: 5.

"even fifty sets." Probably the original reading was: "even a hundred sets." Therefore the section continues: "even as many as a hundred (sets)," unless the word "hundred" refers not to sets but to the number of witnesses who are confuted, i.e., a hundred witnesses, comprising fifty sets.

6. This logically follows from the preceding section.

"one pair following the other"—literally: "one coming, the other going."

7. B. San 78a.

"slay him"—the person charged with murder.

"they would not be executed." Since he is suffering from an incurable disease, he is already regarded as dead.

"would not suffer death"—i.e., they are not subject to the law of retaliation.

8. Mak 1: 1; B. *ibid.,* 2b.

"was divorced"—i.e., when his father married her.

"released from levirate marriage"—rite prescribed for a woman whose husband died without issue (Deut. 25: 5–10). She is forbidden to a priest. If she or a divorced woman is married again to a priest, the son is a *ḥalal* (profaned).

"banished (. . . refuge)"—punishment prescribed for accidental homicide (Num. 35: 11–12).

"sold as a slave"—to make restitution for theft (see Exod. 22: 2).

9. B. Mak 2b.

"on the authority of Scripture"—i.e., no tradition is required for that.

10. San 11: 6; B. *ibid.*, 90a.

"by strangulation"—mode of death prescribed for an adulterer.

"by burning"—mode of death for an adulteress who is a priest's daughter.

Chapter XXI

1. Mak 1: 1; B. *ibid.*, 3a.

"kĕṯubbah"—amount stipulated in the marriage contract.

"today or tomorrow"—i.e., sooner or later.

"one would be prepared to offer." The buyer is taking a chance; for should she die first, the husband would inherit her.

"zuz"—see note above, II, iii, 1.

"it will sell . . . for less." The amount is too paltry to take a chance on it.

2. Mak 1: 1.

3. BḲ 1: 4.

"its own body"—the body of the goring animal.

"the ox has consumed," etc. The owner stands forewarned with regard to such damage (BḲ 1: 4).

4. B. BḲ 73b.

"had knocked out," etc. Brutal treatment by the master resulting in the loss of a limb, gives the slave his freedom (Exod. 21: 26–27).

"the value of the slave . . . eye." Had the evidence not been refuted, the master would have lost his slave and would have had to pay the latter for blinding his eye.

"it is found that he had first." The slave at all events gains his freedom.

"for the loss of his eye"—i.e., the difference between the value of a tooth and that of an eye.

5. P. So 1: 1, p. 1b, 2a (2, 3).

"has warned"—telling her not to meet clandestinely the man with whom she is suspected of having relations.

"has warned . . . secreted herself." Two witnesses are required to testify to the husband's warning as well as to her seclusion with her paramour.

"If one . . . committed adultery." Only one witness is required to testify to her defilement, in which case she is not subjected to the ordeal described in Num. 5: 12–31, but is divorced and forfeits the marriage settlement provided in the kĕṯubbah.

"to pay . . . in the kĕṯubbah"—which she would have lost had his evidence not been refuted.

"not subject to flagellation"—because they have to pay compensation; see above, I, xviii, 2.

"Did they not . . . defiled herself?"—an offense punishable by death.

6. BḲ 7: 3.

"pay in full"—fourfold for a sheep, fivefold for an ox (Exod. 21: 37).

"twofold restitution"—penalty for stealing (Exod. 22: 3).

"twofold or threefold"—penalty for killing or selling a stolen animal (Exod. 21: 37).

"the thief . . . twofold restitution." The evidence of the first pair is not refuted.

"twofold or threefold restitution to the thief." The text reads: "fourfold or fivefold." This is manifestly an error. It should read: "twofold or threefold."

7. BB 3: 4; see above, iv, 7.

"three (successive) years"—thus establishing the possessor's title to the field.

"payment . . . is divided." Each pair pays one third.

"as one testimony." The evidence of one pair without that of the other is incomplete.

"for one of the years"—i.e., for a different year.

"three distinct testimonies"—therefore the evidence given by the three brothers (kinsmen) is accepted.

8. B. BḲ 24a, b.

"declared 'forewarned.'" An ox is declared noxious, i.e., the owner stands "forewarned," if it has gored three times. If it has gored less than three times, it is *tam* (innocuous).

"three sets"—each set testifying to a different goring.

"they . . . are exempt." With respect to proving them false witnesses, their evidence is accounted one testimony and none of them is declared a plotting witness unless all of them are adjudged plotting witnesses.

"(the additional half)." If their evidence had not been refuted, the owner would have been "forewarned," i.e., he would have had to pay full damage for the fourth goring (see KM *ad loc.*)

"As to the first half"—which the owner has to pay even if the goring animal is still tam, i.e., in an innocuous state.

"are motioning to one another,"—i.e., to testify, even if each pair gives evidence on a different day but they appear together, and are motioning to one another, which proves conspiracy on their part.

"simultaneously." All give evidence on the same day, which indicates collusion.

"cannot identify." It is manifest therefore that their intention is to declare the owner "forewarned." For the half, damage is paid from the body of the goring ox (Sec. 3), and since the evidence is with regard to an ox which the witnesses are unable to identify, the owner is exempt from paying the damage.

9. B. San 86b.

"only the penalty of flogging." On the evidence submitted by the first two witnesses, i.e., at the first trial, the stubborn and rebellious son is flogged.

"solely"—after the evidence given by the first two witnesses.

"death by strangulation"—the penalty which would have been inflicted upon the accused had not the evidence been refuted (Exod. 21: 16).

"the first step"—part of a capital offense.

"made signs." In capital cases, signaling or motioning on the part of witnesses is not regarded as evidence of collusion.

10. B. San 9b, 10a.

"the fine to the husband"—the hundred shekels of silver which the husband would have had to pay had not the father's witnesses been confuted (Deut. 22: 19).

"exempt . . . fine"—on the principle that no monetary fine is incurred for an offense which carries with it the death penalty (Ket 3: 2).

"they are put to death"—in retaliation for death intended for the woman.

"ordered to pay the fine." The fine is due to the father and is therefore not remitted.

Chapter XXII

1. B. Shebu 47b.
"each is accepted"—neither set is disqualified.
2. B. Shebu 47b.
"pays only one maneh"—the lesser amount. The borrower has the right to say that the witnesses on the other note are the false witnesses.
"a sacred object"—such as the scroll of the Law.
"as was stated before"—XIII, IV, iv, 10.
3. B. Shebu 7:5 and B. *ibid.*, 47b.
"a rabbinical oath." According to Scriptures an oath is to be taken only by the defendant to exempt him from paying the creditor. In any case where the creditor is ordered to take an oath to enforce his claim, the oath is of rabbinical derivation.
"a shopkeeper"—who, authorized by the householder to advance small change to his employee, or to give his son goods on credit, swears to the correctness of his account book and collects what is due him.
4. B. Shebu 47b.
"consuetudinal oath." See note above, I, vii, 4.
"same borrower"—named in the first note. The text reads: "from the lender." The correct reading is: "from the borrower."
5. B. Mak 5b; B. Ket 36b.
"no claim . . . on such a note"—he himself may have forged the signatures.

Treatise III: Rebels

Chapter I

1. Sif Deut. 17:8, 10, 11, p. 81b (162).
2. Sif Deut. 17:11, p. 81b (162).
"Thou shalt not turn aside from." In our text the word: "any" (*kol*) is added, i.e., *from any sentence which they shall declare*. But the word "any" does not occur in the sentence in Deuteronomy.
3. Tos San 7:1; P. *ibid.*, 1:4, p. 8b (16).
4. Tos San 7:1; P. *ibid.*, 1:4, p. 8b (16); B. *ibid.*, 88b. The reading in B. San is: "Originally there were not *many* controversies."
"their deputies"—i.e., a committee appointed by the court.
"court meeting . . . Court." This was a higher court than the one at the Temple Mount; see note above, I, ii, 8.
5. B. AZ 7a; P. Giṭ 1:2, p. 5a (9).
"had not yet reached"—and the matter was pressing, brooking no delay. The translation is based upon the reading in the Venice edition.

Chapter II

1. B. RH 25b; cf. Sif Deut. 17:9, p. 81b (162).
"it may do so," etc. This applies only to a decision derived from the applica-

tion of the hermeneutical rules. It does not apply to decrees, ordinances, and customs instituted by the Supreme Court; see Sec. 2.

2. Ed 1: 5.

"We include . . . the wise men"—who are not members of the Supreme Court.

3. B. AZ 36a.

4. B. San 46a.

"on his account"—i.e., to save a man's life.

5. B. AZ 36a.

6. B. AZ 35a.

7. B. AZ 36a.

"the doings of Israel"—i.e., the spiritual conditions.

8. Ed 8: 4; B. AZ 37a.

9. "binding upon succeeding generations"—if the decree is designed to safeguard religion; see above, Sec. 3.

"or the Oral Law"—i.e., a law learned by tradition.

"harmful results"—to the cause of religion.

Chapter III

1. "epicureans." See note above, II, xi, 10; see B. San 99b.

The bracketed phrases in Secs. 1 and 2 are found in most editions.

2. "cast into the pit." See note above, II, xi, 10.

"heretics"—Jewish infidels, members of the sect of the early Jewish-Christians. Cf. I, v, iii, 15.

3. "Zadok and Boethus"—The former was the founder of the Sadducean sect, the latter of the Boethusean—a sect closely related to, if not a development of, the Sadducean sect. Cf. L. Ginzberg, *J.E.,* III, 284–285.

"who went astray." The Hebrew word signifying "after him" is omitted in Mss.

"Karaites"—members of a sect founded in the eighth century C.E. by Anan who revolted against the Talmud. The Venice edition has "heretics" instead of "Karaites."

"raised in their religion." The Venice edition has "their religion" instead of "their view."

4. B. San 87a; San 11: 2; *ibid.,* 6: 2; B. *ibid.,* 88a, b.

The definition given in this section of a rebellious elder is developed below, Secs. 5–8.

5. San 11: 2, 3; B. *ibid.,* 87a, 88b.

"phylacteries"—i.e., the number of compartments the head phylacteries are to contain.

"one who finds . . . hard matter." One who is not qualified to render decisions will find it hard to decide even questions which are not difficult.

6. San 11: 2.

"outstanding member." Cf. L. Ginzberg, *A Commentary on the Palestinian Talmud,* III, 212–219.

7. B. San 14b; Ed 5: 6.

"assigned for their sessions"—namely, the Hall of Hewn Stones.

8. San 11: 2, 4; B. *ibid.*, 88a, b; 89a.
"Temple Mount . . . If he accepts," etc.—literally: "if they accept."
"witnesses see"—so according to the reading in the Venice edition.
"the local court"—the Small Sanhedrin.
"the following festival"—i.e., one of the three Pilgrim Festivals.
"And all the people shall hear." The text in this section reads: *And all Israel shall hear*. In the Bible, however, the word "people" is used.

Chapter IV

1. B. San 88a.
"sixth hour"—11:00 A.M.
"fifth hour"—10:00 A.M.

2. B. San 87a, b, 88a; (see Lev. 19: 9; 27: 2 ff.; 27: 14 ff.; 27: 28; Deut. 24: 19–20).

"a certain color of blood"—i.e., a greenish discharge. If the rebellious elder contrary to the ruling of the Supreme Court declares that a greenish discharge is to be regarded as blood and that the days when a woman has such discharges are included in the seven days of uncleanness, the husband who has marital relations with her after the seven days commits an offense the deliberate transgression of which involves the penalty of excision, and the unwitting transgression a sin offering.

"(. . . after) childbirth"—i.e., in case the woman after giving birth to a female child (see Lev. 12: 3), has a continuous discharge of blood either from the end of the fourteenth into the beginning of the fifteenth day, or from the eightieth into the eighty-first day. If the rebellious elder, defying the ruling of the Supreme Court, maintains that the flow from the end of the fourteenth into the fifteenth renders her unclean and the flow from the eightieth to the eighty-first day does not render her unclean, the husband who has marital relations with her on the latter day, when on the view of the Supreme Court she is unclean, violates a law the wanton infraction of which entails the penalty of excision, and the unwitting infraction a sin offering.

"(during a certain period)"—i.e., within the eleven days between the menses. If the elder disregards the ruling of the Supreme Court, the husband who has relations with her during the period, when according to the Supreme Court the discharge of blood is symptomatic of a running issue, commits a transgression the deliberate violation whereof carries with it the penalty of excision and the unwitting violation a sin offering.

"eating of leaven during the Passover." Whatever decision the Supreme Court makes with regard to the intercalation of the year, if the rebellious elder dissents from it and acts upon his own decision, Passover, according to his calculation, will occur either before or after the Passover fixed by the Supreme Court. He will thus cause the people to eat leaven on the real Passover—an offense the deliberate commission of which entails the penalty of excision and the unwitting commission a sin offering.

"monetary case"—i.e., if they differ on a point of law with respect to a civil suit.

"number of judges"—whether a judgment given by two judges is valid.

"on the view that the defendant is in debt to the claimant"—i.e., if the dispute between them is with regard to the question whether the defendant is in debt to the plaintiff. It holds good also in case the dispute between them is with regard to the number of judges, e.g., if only two tried the case. For on the view that the judgment given by those who tried the case is valid, the claimant obtained what rightfully belonged to him (the argument is continued in the text on page 147 f.

"according to the first opinion," etc. No matter what the ruling of the elder is, if it runs counter to that of the Supreme Court, it may lead to an offense the wanton commission of which involves the penalty of excision and the unwitting commission a sin offering. Thus if he insists that A, the plaintiff, was entitled to his claim and A betroths a woman with the money awarded to him and later C betroths the same woman, the latter betrothal is on his view void. If A subsequently dies, she is, according to the position taken by the elder, a widow; whereas according to the Supreme Court she is married to C and in case another man has relations with her in the absence of witnesses or without previous warning, he is guilty of an offense punishable by excision. On the other hand, if the elder affirms that A was not entitled to the money claimed by him and A betroths a woman with this money, the betrothal, according to the opinion of the elder, is invalid; whereas on the view of the Supreme Court it is valid; and in the event another man has relations with her in the absence of witnesses or without due warning, he incurs the penalty of excision.

"not liable to flogging"—i.e., if the question is whether the accused is liable to the penalty of flagellation. If the question is one bearing on the number of judges to decide cases of flagellation, and the elder acts on the view that a larger number of judges is required to decide such cases, the one who suffered the flogging is entitled to compensation.

"the valuation of a human being"—i.e., the valuation of an infant less than a month old.

"he . . . to pay the valuation"—i.e., in case of valuation. So, too, in case of undesignated devotion, the elder is culpable if he rejects the ruling of the Supreme Court. If he avers that undesignated devotions are to be applied to the needs of the Temple and the priest betroths a woman with them, and later C betroths the same woman, her betrothal to C would according to the elder be valid; whereas on the ruling of the Supreme Court, if C has relations with her in the absence of witnesses or without due warning, he is guilty of an offense punishable by excision. On the other hand, if he maintains that undesignated devotions go to the priest and the latter betroths a woman with them and later C betroths the same woman, excision may be involved (cf. above, in this section, the note under "according to the first opinion").

"the redemption is invalid"—i.e., the dedicated object retains its sanctity.

"(dedicated) object, the betrothal is null." See the note under "according to the first opinion."

"heifer . . . betrothal is null." See the note under "according to the first opinion."

"*'orlah*"—the fruit a tree yields in the first three years (Lev. 19:23). If the point at issue between the rebellious elder and the Supreme Court is whether the owner may make use of it, the ruling given by the elder might lead to a transgression the wanton commission of which involves excision, and the unwitting transgression a sin offering.

"leprosy in man"—i.e., if there is a doubt whether the bright spot came before the white hair or the white hair before the bright spot; according to R. Joshua, he is clean; according to the Rabbis, he is unclean (Neg 4: 11).

"in houses"—i.e., if the leprosy does not appear at the corner of two walls (Neg 12: 3).

"in garments"—i.e., if the leprosy is spread over the whole garment.

"the person"—who shows those symptoms of leprosy or who enters the house or touches the garment in question.

"(with certain physical defects)"—if he lacks the thumb of the right hand, the big toe of his right foot, or the right ear (see Neg 14: 9). Should, e.g., the elder in defiance of the ruling of the Supreme Court, maintain that such a leper can fulfill the requirements of purification, the latter would be permitted to enter the sanctuary or eat of holy things; whereas, according to the ruling of the Supreme Court, he would, on entering the sanctuary or eating of holy things, be guilty of an offense the deliberate commission of which entails the penalty of excision and the unwitting commission a sin offering.

"*soṭah*"—a woman suspected of infidelity to her husband (Num. 5: 11–31).

"bound to her brother-in-law"—if the husband dies childless (Deut. 25: 5–10).

3. San 11: 3; B. *ibid.*, 88b, 89a.

"so grave a consequence"—eventuating in an offense the deliberate commission of which carries with it the penalty of excision, and the unwitting commission a sin offering.

"(head) tĕfillin"—phylacteries put on the head. It contains four compartments, with inscriptions in each.

"according to the law"—i.e., each shut off from the next.

"the outer compartment"—i.e., the fourth.

Chapter V

1. San 7: 4; 11: 1; B. *ibid.*, 66a.

"Whether he curses them"—either of them.

"ṭumṭum." See note above, II, ix, 3.

2. San 7: 8; cf. I, xxvi, 3.

"special Names"—such as *YH*, God, Almighty (see above, I, xxvi, 3).

"attribute"—such as the Merciful, the Jealous, etc. (see above, I, xxvi, 3).

3. Sif Lev. 20: 9, p. 365b.
4. Sif Lev. 20: 9, p. 368a.

"explicitly stated." Exod. 21:17; Lev. 20: 9.

5. San 11: 1.

"by strangulation." Whenever Scripture decrees the death penalty without specifying the mode, strangulation is meant; see above, I, xiv, 1.

6. B. BḲ 86a.
7. B. San 84b.
8. Mek Exod. 21: 15, III, p. 44.

"explicitly stated"—Exod. 21: 15.

9. Sif Lev. 20: 9, p. 365b; Yeb 2: 5; B. BB 149a.

"*šeṯuḳi*"—one who knows his mother but does not know his father, i.e., his paternity is not known (Ḳid 4: 2).

"not stoned"—for cursing him.

"or strangled"—for striking him.

"either offense." His status is that of his mother.

"in an unhallowed condition." His mother was not Jewish at that time.

"in a hallowed condition." His mother had in the meantime embraced the Jewish religion.

10. Sif Lev. 20: 9, p. 365b.

"the last three"—whose paternity is known.

11. B. Yeb 22a; B. BḲ 88a.

"they were manumitted"—i.e., he and his father.

12. B. San 85a; B. Yeb 22b.

"one's father and mother"—i.e., either of them.

"if a stranger . . . strikes." So far as a stranger is concerned, the culprit is regarded as a dead person, since he has already been condemned to death. The son, however, is bound to honor his father even after the latter's death.

"he is liable." He thus insults the family of the culprit.

13. B. San 85a.

14. B. San 85b.

"save . . . is an enticer." The Hebrew text adds: "and a seducer." But the additional word *u-maddiaḥ* (and a seducer) does not occur in B. San 85b.

15. ThG (quoted in ṬZ YD 241, n. 2).

"We have already stated"—XI, v, i, 3.

Chapter VI

1. Sif Lev. 19: 3, p. 343a.

"concerning the duty . . . to parents." The same expression is used in both instances.

2. Sif Lev. 19: 3, p. 343a; B. Ḳid 30b, 31a.

3. "Reverence requires"—Sif Lev. 19: 3, pp. 343a, 344a; B. Ḳid 31b.

"decide against his opinion"—cf. Per ṬYD 240, n. 3.

"designate them by another name"—possibly we have here a hint at the talmudic sage "Abbayyi," whose real name appears to have been "Naḥmani" (cf. *Aruch Completum, s.v. Abbayyi*).

4. B. Ḳid 33b, 31b.

5. B. Ḳid 31b.

"may I be an atonement"—i.e., for the judgment he may be visited with in the hereafter.

"[for a blessing]." The bracketed words are part of the deferential term to be used; see B. Ḳid 31b.

6. Ḳid 1: 7; Sif Lev. 19: 3, p. 343a; P. Pe 1: 1, p. 3b (6).

"dependent on others"—i.e., her husband.

7. B. Ḳid 31a, 32a.

"presiding over the congregation." It is possible that we have here another instance of two readings which were combined: (a) "presiding over the congregation"; (b) "sitting in the presence of the congregation."

8. B. Ḳid 32a.

"to stumble." They might resent the treatment accorded them.

"shut his eyes"—to their failure to pay him the honor due him.

9. B. MḲ 17a.

"Nor put a stumbling block." The son might be tempted to resist the father.

10. B. Ḳid 31b.

11. Yeb 2: 5; B. Ḳid 32a.

12. Sif Lev. 19: 3, p. 344a.

"for it is said." The two precepts are placed in juxtaposition, implying that duty to parents does not take precedence over duty to God.

13. B. Ḳid 32a; B. Meg 16b.

14. Sif Lev. 19: 3, p. 343a; B. Ḳid 31a.

15. B. Ket 103a.

"But after her death." Likewise, after the death of his father, he is no longer bound to honor his stepmother.

Chapter VII

1. B. Zeb 106b; B. San 63a; Sif Deut. 21: 20, p. 88b (176).

"spoken of in Scripture"—Deut. 21: 18–21.

2. San 8: 2, 3; B. *ibid.,* 70b, 71a; Tos *ibid.,* 11: 2.

"he steals (money) from his father." What belongs to his father is within his reach, making it easy for him to become addicted to gluttony.

"buys meat and wine cheaply." If he has to pay a high price, he will find it hard to procure them.

"outside his father's premises." He is afraid to consume them in his father's domain.

"raw." Thieves, afraid of detection, do not wait long enough to cook their meat properly.

"[partially] diluted." This is the correct reading. The words *wĕlo mazuḡ* have been inadvertently omitted.

"fifty denar"—i.e., half a maneh, the equivalent of 6¼ ounces according to some; about 3 ounces according to others. See Glossary.

"loḡ"—a liquid measure equal to the space occupied by six eggs.

"involves the infraction." The above translation is based upon the correction made by KM *ad loc.*

"a religious festivity"—e.g., the eating of the Paschal lamb.

"second tithe"—to be eaten by the owners in Jerusalem; he steals money of the second tithe, purchases meat and wine, which he consumes in Jerusalem.

3. San 8: 2; B. *ibid.,* 70a, b.

4. B. San 70a.

"no attraction." It will not lead him to intemperance.

"from the third day it was salted." Before that time it is still regarded as fresh meat.

"vat"—in its first stage of fermentation.

5. B. San 68b.

"scope of the commandments"—i.e., thirteen years and one day.

"the hair . . . entire membrum"—i.e., the hair of the genitals.
"independent"—i.e., he is regarded as a man.

6. B. San 69a.
"a father." Since his wife is pregnant, he is fit to be called a father.
"he is exempt from punishment." He is past the age limit.

7. San 8:4; B. *ibid.*, 71b; Tos *ibid.*, 11:3.
"flog him"—literally: "chasten him."
"second testimony"—literally: "final testimony."
"three months"—from the time he produced two hairs.
"the first three"—the members of the first court.

8. B. San 88b.

9. San 8:4.

10. San 8:4.
"This our son"—i.e., they can see him.
"He doth not hearken"—i.e., they can hear his reply.

11. Sif Deut. 21:18, p. 88b (176).
"a daughter"—who is stubborn and rebellious.
"ṭumṭum"—see note above, II, ix, 3.

12. B. BB 126b.
"his birth"—so the Venice edition; see B. BB 126b.

13. B. San 89a; Tos *ibid.*, 11:3.

Treatise IV: Mourning

Chapter I

1. Alf, B. MḲ 19b; P. MḲ 3:5, p. 14b (28); P. Ket 1:1, p. 2b (4).
"if I had eaten." Eating by the priests of the flesh of a sin offering is a positive command (Lev. 6:19, 22), yet this command is set aside in the case of a priest who is in mourning.
"seven days of feasting"—on the occasion of a wedding.

2. B. MḲ 27a.
"David washed," etc.—II Sam. 12:20.

3. Sem 2:11.
"the thirty days." See below, vi, 1.
"hope of stealing them"—a hope not likely to be realized.

4. Sem 2:12.

5. B. MḲ 22a.
"their faces away"—to return home.

6. B. Shab 135b; B. Bek 49a.

7. B. Nid 44b; B. Shab 135b.

8. Sem 1:7.
"last rites performed"—literally: "occupy (themselves) with," i.e., attend to their bodies. But this does not imply that the relatives should not provide for their funeral (Rashba cited by BY ṬYD 345). It refers only to funeral rites, such as the rending of clothes, making lamentations, etc.

9. San 6: 5, 6; Tos *ibid.,* 4: 3.

"observe mourning"—i.e., the seven days, the thirty days, and the twelve months of mourning.

10. Sem 2: 10.

"epicureans." See note above, II, xi, 10.

"white garments"—sign of joy.

11. Sem 2: 1, 2.

"lamentation"—includes funeral oration, selections from the Book of Lamentations, etc., dirges by professional wailers (see below, xii, 1, 4).

"Mourner's Benediction." See below, xii, 7.

"climbing to the top." In Sem 2: 2, the additional sentence occurs: "I will cast myself down and die"; Alf, MḲ 18a quotes Sem 2: 2, and he too omits this sentence.

Chapter II

1. B. MḲ 20b.

"by the same father." The scriptural text (Lev. 21: 2) implies only a paternal brother or sister.

3. B. Yeb 29b.

"he does not observe," etc. The child has the status of the mother.

"*'ăninuṭ.*" The laws prescribed for a mourner between death and burial of a kinsman.

4. B. MḲ 20b.

"his son's brother"—i.e., by another father.

"his son's mother"—whom he divorced.

5. B. MḲ 20b.

"overturns his couch." See below, v, 1.

"or her son"—by a previous marriage.

"do not mourn one with the other." The Hebrew text has: "one for the other." This obviously is a mistake.

6. Sem 4: 8; So 3: 7 (cf. RaDbeZ *ad loc.*).

7. Sem 4: 8; B. Yeb 89b; Sif Lev. 21: 3, p. 377a; see above, Sec. 1.

"a religious duty." See below, iii, 8.

"sole heir." According to scriptural law, the property of the wife passes to the husband on her death.

8. Sif Lev. 21: 4, p. 378a; 21: 2, p. 376a.

9. Sif Lev. 21: 4, p. 378a; 21: 2, p. 376a; Yeb 10: 1; B. *ibid.,* 22b.

10. Sif Lev. 21: 3, p. 377a.

"is a priest"—even if she was divorced from him.

"violated or seduced." She is no longer a virgin.

"caused by a man." This refers only to a sister who has lost her virginity through an accident. That a sister who is of age is included among those for whom a priest may defile himself is derived from the word *'elaw* (unto him); see Sif Lev. 21: 3, p. 377a; B. Yeb 60a.

11. B. Yeb 60a.

12. Sif Lev. 21: 2, p. 376a.

"his heirs"—i.e., a paternal brother or sister.

13. Sif Lev. 21: 3, p. 377a.

"whether the child"—if the wife he divorced married soon after procuring her divorce.

14. B. Naz 33b.

"the bones . . . are gathered." In talmudic times the dead were first given a temporary burial, and after the flesh had been decomposed the bones were transferred in a cedar coffin to a permanent burial place. (P. MḲ 1: 5, p. 5a [9]; see ṬYD 362.)

15. Sif Lev. 21: 3, p. 377a; B. Naz 33b.

Chapter III

1. Sif Lev. 21: 1, pp. 375–376; X, I, i, ii, iii, v, vi, ix.

"overshadows it"—literally: "forms a tent over it," i.e., it is under the same roof. Both what overshadows a corpse, what a corpse overshadows, and what is overshadowed by something which also overshadows a corpse communicate uncleanness (see Oh 3: 1; see also X, I, i, 10).

"which exudes"—e.g., blood.

3. "to enter or to go out"—X, I, xiv, xvii; xiii, 2; xii–xiii, xv; xviii–xix; ix, 4.

4. Naz 6: 4; Shebu 2: 3; B. *ibid.*, 16b; see VIII, III, iii, 21–23.

"to prostrate oneself"—i.e., long enough to recite the passage: *And they bowed themselves with their faces to the ground upon the pavement, and prostrated themselves, and gave thanks to the Lord: "for he is good, for His mercy endureth forever"* (II Chron. 7: 3).

5. Tos Mak 3: 7 (cf. BhG YD 303: 2, n. 3).

6. B. Naz 42b.

"someone tears open the top"—so that the box, chest, or turret is part of the house.

7. B. Naz 42b.

"he is also flogged"—in addition to the flogging for defiling himself.

8. Naz 7: 1; B. Yeb 89b.

"meṯ miṣwah"—literally: "a corpse whose burial is a religious duty."

9. Naz 7: 1.

"nazarite." See note above, I, xix, 4 (101), and Glossary.

"not a lifelong sanctity." It lasts only during the period for which he has consecrated himself or till he seeks absolution of his vow.

10. P. Naz 7: 1, p. 33b (66).

"as a meṯ miṣwah." See note above, Sec. 8.

"'onen"—status of mourner between death and burial of a kinsman.

11. Sif Lev. 21: 1, p. 375a.

"retained their priestly status"—i.e., who are the sons of Aaron in the full sense of the word.

12. B. Yeb 114a.

13. So 7: 3; B. *ibid.*, 44a; Sem 4: 20 (see NhG *ad loc.*); see X, I, ii, 15.

"a grave area." See note above, II, xiv, 3.

"outside Palestine." The land of the heathens defiles (Naz 7: 3).

"buttressing stone"—side stone which supports the top stone.

14. B. AZ 13a; B. Ber 19b.

Chapter IV

1. Sem 1: 2; Shab 23: 5; B. *ibid.*, 151b; B. MḲ 27b.

"zuz." See note above, II, iii, 1.

"the poor"—who cannot afford to buy an expensive shroud.

2. B. MḲ 27b; Tos Nid 9: 11.

3. P. Ber 3: 1, p. 24a (47).

4. BB 6: 8; B. *ibid.*, 73b, 74a; P. Naz 9: 3, p. 45a (89); B. MḲ 29a; P. *ibid.*, 1: 5, p. 5a (9); Sheḳ 1: 1; P. *ibid.*, 2: 5, p. 11a (21); Gen. R 35: 14, p. 155b (310).

"It is permissible"—Cf. RaDbeZ *ad loc.*

"one need not . . . too frequently"—i.e., one can find ample inspiration in contemplating their deeds, which is their most abiding memorial. This is the explanation given in Res. RIbeSh 421, which offers a variant reading: "One need not turn for (inspiration) to their graves."

5. Sem 1: 2, 3.

6. Sem 10; B. MḲ 23b.

"room"—literally: house.

"partition"—ten handbreadths high.

"recline"—as was the custom to do while eating.

"others"—who partake of the meal.

"join him." Three or more partaking of a meal join as a group in saying grace.

"Shema"—so called from the first word (*šĕma'*, "hear"). It consists of three passages from the Pentateuch (Deut. 6: 4–9; 11: 13–21; Num. 15: 37–41) and is recited daily in the morning and in the evening.

"'Ămidah"—"standing,' designated *tĕfillah,* i.e., the prayer par excellence, the Eighteen Benedictions obligatory on every Jew, to be recited in a standing posture three times a day: morning, afternoon, and evening.

7. B. MḲ 22a.

8. Sem 9; B. MḲ 22a; San 6: 5.

9. B. MḲ 15a, 21a, 27b; P. *ibid.*, 3: 5, p. 16b (32).

"to sit on"—the reading of ṬYD, 387, is "to sleep on."

"sit on an overturned couch"—as a sign of mourning (see below, v, 1).

"It is written." Ezekiel was then in mourning for his wife (Ezek. 24: 18).

"thy headtire"—literally: "thy ornament," which is interpreted to mean the phylacteries.

Chapter V

1. "mourner's headdress"—a wrap which covered the chin and the mouth, leaving only the nose and eyes exposed.

2. B. MḲ 14b, 18a; Sem 7; 5: 8.

"be finished"—out of regard for his personal appearance.

"an instrument"—i.e., nail-cutters or scissors.

3. B. MḲ 15a, b; 23a.

"mourning apparel"—which proves prohibition of washing one's clothes while in mourning.

4. B. Ta 13b.

5. B. MḲ 15b; B. Ket 4b.

"before that time"—before the expiration of the (seven) days of mourning.

6. B. MḲ 15b; Sem 5: 10.

7. B. MḲ 15b; P. *ibid.*, 3: 8, p. 19a (37).

"intimated"—i.e., it is no conclusive proof.

8. B. MḲ 21b.

9. P. MḲ 3: 5, p. 14a (27).

10. MḲ 2: 1; Sem 5: 2. The text in Sem reads: "to apply the pressing beam to his olives which have been turned over." Maimonides' version was also that of R. Hananel. Cf. PhM, MḲ 2: 1.

"to turn over his olives"—to soften them.

"they spoil"—i.e., great loss of money is involved.

"[his] turn." The word "his" is supplied in the Venice edition.

11. B. MḲ 11b.

"'ărisuṯ"—the owner paying the tenant for his work a certain proportion of the produce of the land; see note above, 1, xxiii, 3, and Glossary.

"ḥăḳiruṯ"—the tenant paying the owner a certain quantity, regardless of the yield of the crop; see Glossary.

"ḳabbělanuṯ"—the tenant paying the owner a stipulated amount of money; see Glossary.

"may do . . . as usual"—if the owner suffered bereavement. They carry on their work even if the lease expired, because the presumption is that it will be renewed.

"unless," etc.—so that they be not the losers.

12. B. MḲ 11b.

"may not work"—if his employer suffers bereavement.

"in another town"—where he is not known.

13. B. MḲ 11b.

14. "involve a heavy loss"—e.g., if he has made preparation to go abroad or his witnesses are seriously ill.

15. B. MḲ 15a.

"in silence"—i.e., he was to keep silent, refrain from study (see Tosafoṯ B. MḲ 15a).

16. B. MḲ 21a.

"Mishnah"—see note above, 1, vi, 1, and Glossary.

"Midrash"—"the higher exegesis of Scriptures" (see Moore, *Judaism,* I, 319).

"Halakhah"—matters of legal import.

"interpreter"—who expounded the discourse to the listeners in the vernacular.

17. B. MḲ 21a (cf. LM on iv, 9 of this Treatise); P. MḲ 3: 5, p. 16b (32).

18. Sem 11; B. MḲ 27a.

"all the beds"—used by the members of the family.

"in ten houses"—if they are all occupied by him (Sem 11).

"they all overturn"—if they sleep in their own homes.

"couch of leather"—its strappings consisted of leather instead of ropes. It stood very low, because it was not supported by long legs (see PhM Ned 7: 5).

"the two poles whereof protrude downward." It had two poles, one at the head and one at the foot of the bed; the two poles were connected by a crosspole over which a net was spread to form a slanting cover (M. Jastrow, *s.v. naḵliṭin*).

"cannot be overturned"—on account of the protruding poles.

19. B. MḲ 15a; see above, n. 1.

20. B. MḲ 15a, 21b.

"in silence"—i.e., keep silent, do not salute anyone.

Chapter VI

1. P. Naz 1: 3, p. 4a (7).

2. Sem 7; B. MḲ 22b; P. *ibid.*, 3: 8, p. 19a (37).

3. B. MḲ 22b; Sem 7 (see NhG n. 14); P. MḲ 3: 8, p. 19a (37). Alf, B. MḲ 22b.

"chide him"—i.e., call his attention to the neglect of his personal appearance.

4. B. MḲ 23a, 18a.

"forbidden . . . new and white"—i.e., woolen clothes.

"After the thirty days," etc.—even if they are new and white.

5. Sem 7; P. Yeb 4: 11, p. 28b (56).

"marry her forthwith"—lest a rival suitor marry her.

6. B. MḲ 22b.

"his turn to entertain"—i.e., a group of friends meeting from time to time for social purposes, each taking his turn in acting as host to the others.

7. B. MḲ 22b.

"under no circumstances"—even if it is his turn to entertain others.

8. P. MḲ 3: 8, 19a (37).

"a (long) business trip"—usually an occasion for joviality.

9. B. MḲ 22a, b.

"less attention"—between the seven and the thirty days of mourning.

10. B. MḲ 26b, 27a.

11. Sem 2: 13.

"is forbidden to reside." The survivor's presence in the city will remind the inhabitants of the execution and the dead will thus be disgraced.

"decomposed"—by that time the incident of the execution will have been forgotten.

"as large as Antioch"—where the residents of one section may not know those of another.

12. B. MḲ 19b.

13. MḲ 3: 1; B. *ibid.*, 17b; B. Ta 13b.

"in immediate succession"—i.e., a second bereavement occurred before the thirty days of mourning for the first had expired.

"released from a ban." A person under a ban is forbidden to cut his hair or to wash his clothes.

"from a vow"—not to cut his hair.

"application to a sage." A sage is authorized under certain circumstances to absolve a person from a vow rashly made; cf. Ned 9: 1 ff.

"uncleanness to cleanness." He has to cut his hair and to wash his clothes (Lev. 14: 8–9).

Chapter VII

1. B. MḲ 20a; Alf, *ad loc.*

"the seventh and the thirtieth"—i.e., the first part of the day is regarded as the seventh, the rest as the thirtieth. See next section.

2. B. MḲ 20b.
3. B. MḲ 20b.
4. B. MḲ 21b.

"(the time of the burial)"—which is on the day of the death (see above, i, 1).

"a distant place"—more than ten Persian miles, i.e., more than a day's journey.

5. B. MḲ 21b; Sem 10.
6. Hor 3:5; San 2:1; see Lev. 21:10.

"to follow the bier"—that he become not levitically impure.

"mourner's meal"—the meal of comfort given mourners after the funeral.

"between [himself] and the people"—i.e., the deputy is on the right of the High Priest and the people on the left.

7. San 2:3; see II Sam. 3:31.
8. San 2:3.

Chapter VIII

1. B. MḲ 24a, 20b, 26b, see above, vii, 6.

"that ye die not." These words were addressed to Aaron and his surviving sons, when Nadab and Abihu died.

2. B. MḲ 22b.

"on the inside"—of the garment.

3. B. MḲ 24a, 22b.

"his chest"—literally: "heart."

"undershirt"—literally: "the shirt that absorbs the sweat."

4. B. MḲ 26b.

"not . . . to rend his clothes." The reading in the talmudic text before us is: "in his presence"; i.e., no rending is to take place in the presence of a kinsman who is ill. See Alf, B. MḲ 26b and R. Hananel *ad loc.*

5. B. MḲ 26b.
6. B. MḲ 20b, 26b.

"no cloak to rend"—i.e., he is clad in rags or in borrowed clothes (ShK YD 340:18, n. 26).

7. B. MḲ 26b.
8. B. Ned 87a, 86b; see above, II, xx, 3.
9. B. MḲ 26b.
10. B. MḲ 26b; see below, ix, 1.

Chapter IX

1. B. MḲ 22b.
2. B. MḲ 26a; cf. Sem 9.

"his teacher"—i.e., his chief teacher to whom he is indebted for most of what he knows (see I, III, v, 9).

" 'Aḇ beṯ din." See note above, I, i, 3.

"slaying (that affected)"—i.e., even if the number of the slain was not large. See B. MḲ 26a; ṬYD 340; YD 340: 36.

3. B. MḲ 26a, b.

"Alexandrian mending"—so sewn together that the rent was invisible.

4. B. MḲ 26b.

5. B. MḲ 26a.

"to sever the stiff border." The passage cited proves (a) that a disciple must tear his clothes for a teacher; (b) that the disciple does not discharge his duty of rending for his teacher unless he severs the stiff border—the rent required in the case of the death of a father (see above, viii, 3).

6. B. MḲ 26a.

7. B. MḲ 26a.

"with their clothes rent." Rab-shakeh had blasphemed the name of God (II Kings 18: 22 ff.).

8. B. MḲ 26a.

9. B. MḲ 26a.

"nor rent their garments." They failed to do their duty.

"an act of violence"—i.e., not the result of an accident.

"for the parchment." Sanctity attaches to the parchment on which the Law is written.

10. B. MḲ 26a.

"their clothes rent." They had just learned of the destruction of the Temple.

11. B. MḲ 25a, 22b; Sem 10.

"not related to the deceased." It is as though he witnessed the burning of a scroll (B. MḲ 25a).

"his school"—the House of Study where he imparted instruction.

12. B. MḲ 25a.

13. B. MḲ 25a.

14. B. MḲ 22b; cf. Sem 10.

"The (steady) attendants"—e.g., the ten men of leisure, appointed in every community to attend services in the Synagogue (see note above, I, i, 10; cf. NY on Alf, B. MḲ 22b, 23a). Many of the people would attend services at the house of the deceased 'Aḇ beṯ din.

15. Sem 10; B. MḲ 22b, 23a.

"come to Synagogue"—to read the weekly portion, but they pray at home even on the Sabbath (Rashi, B. MḲ 23a).

Chapter X

1. MḲ 3: 5; B. *ibid.*, 24a.

"mourner's hood"—in the home.

2. B. MḲ 27a.

"Afternoon Service"—from 3:30 P.M. (See NY on Alf, B. MḲ 27a.)

3. MḲ 3: 5, 6; B. *ibid.*, 24b.

"(Pilgrim) Festivals"—i.e., Passover, Pentecost, and Tabernacles.

"Hence," etc. New Year and the Day of Atonement, like the Pilgrim Festivals, interrupt the seven days of mourning; that is, they annul the restrictions appertaining to those days; but unlike the Pilgrim Festivals, New Year, and the Day of Atonement do not count each as seven days.

"he counts"—to complete the thirty days.

"twenty-three days." If this reading is correct, it would mean that the New Year and the Day of Atonement are regarded as blank days; i.e., while they annul the restrictions prescribed for the seven days, they do not enter into the count of the thirty days; otherwise, the mourner would have to observe only twenty-one days after the (two days) of the New Year and twenty-two days after the Day of Atonement. It seems, however, that the reading of RaDbeZ (*ad loc.*) was "twenty-one days," that is, after the New Year only twenty-one days are counted.

"counts as seven days." It is allowed an extension of seven days, i.e., if one is unable to offer the sacrifice ordained for Pentecost on the Festival, he is given seven days of grace to do it.

4. B. MḲ 24b.

5. B. MḲ 19b.

"part of the day . . . full day." The first part brings the seven days to a close, and the remainder concludes the thirty days (see R. Hananel on B. MḲ 19b).

"chide him"—for the neglect of his personal appearance.

6. B. MḲ 19b.

"the five things." See above, vi, 2.

7. B. MḲ 17b.

"during the festival"—i.e., the intermediate days of the festival.

"have been annulled"—by the festival or the New Year or the Day of Atonement.

8. B. MḲ 19b; Alf *ad loc.*

9. Alf, B. MḲ 19b.

"as was stated before"—Sec. 8.

10. Alf, B. MḲ 19b; cf. III, VIII, iii, 1; see above, i, 1.

"the last day thereof"—i.e., the last day of Passover or Tabernacles.

Chapter XI

1. MḲ 3:7.

2. MḲ 3:7; B. *ibid.*, 25a.

3. MḲ 3:7; 3:8; 1:5; 3:9.

"the bones . . . gathered." See note above, ii, 14.

"Ḥanukkah"—the Feast of Dedication. Beginning on the 25th of Kislew, it lasts eight days.

4. MḲ 3:9.

5. MḲ 3:9; B. *ibid.*, 27b.

"in his presence"—i.e., where the body lies.

6. MḲ 1:5; B. *ibid.*, 8a, b.

"a woman"—the same stricture applies to a man.

"(avail herself . . .)"—whenever a wailer came around, the people said, "Let all who are of a bitter heart weep with him," i.e., engage him for wailing (B. MḲ 8a).

7. See the next section.

8. B. Ket 3b, 4a.

"the father . . . the mother"—on whom preparations for the wedding feast devolve.

Chapter XII

1. B. San 47a; P. Naz 7: 1, p. 33a (65).
"Funeral services"—i.e., funeral address, dirges, etc.; see note above, i, 11.
2. B. Shab 105b.
3. B. MḲ 25a.
"scroll . . . on the bier"—to indicate that the deceased had fulfilled the commandments enjoined in the scroll (see B. BḲ 17a).
4. B. BB 100b; Meg 4: 3.
"halts"—literally: "standing and sitting." It was the practice on the return from a funeral to stop seven times and make lamentation for the dead (B. BB 100b).
"who conducts the service." See PhM Meg 4: 3.
5. B. BB 100b; B. Meg 28b; MḲ 3: 8.
6. P. MḲ 1: 5, p. 5b (10).
7. B. MḲ 25a.
8. B. MḲ 8a.
9. B. MḲ 24b.
"poor or elderly parents." Poor or elderly people feel the loss of a child more keenly than the rich, because the child is their only joy.
10. B. MḲ 24a, b.
11. B. MḲ 24b; B. San 20a.
12. B. Ber 16b.

Chapter XIII

1. B. San 19a; B. Ket 8a.
2. B. San 19a.
"one by one"—i.e., Indian file.
3. "most prominent place"—B. MḲ 28b.
"The comforters . . . sit only on the ground." This statement, attributed to R. Juda in the name of Raḇ, is part of B. Mak 28a in Alfasi's text (cf. Alf, B. Mak 18a).
4. B. Shab 152a, b.
"ten worthy people"—so that there be daily services in the house of mourning.
"in his place"—i.e., in the place where he died.
5. B. MḲ 27b.
6. B. MḲ 27a.
"perfumes and spices"—to avoid all pleasure (NY on Alf, B. MḲ 27a).
7. MḲ 3: 7; B. *ibid.*, 27a.
"be not put to shame." The poor do not possess expensive receptacles.
8. B. Ket 8b.
"None (of the consolers . . .)"—cf. L. Ginzberg, *A Commentary on the Palestinian Talmud*, II, 77.
9. B. Ber 3b; B. Mak 23a.
"halakhic"—themes dealing with legal matters.

"aggadic"—themes dealing with nonjuridic matters, e.g. homiletical.

10. B. MḲ 27b; B. Meg 6a; B. Ket 103b; B. Yeb 78b, 79a.

"our Teacher, the saint"—R. Judah Hannaśi (the Patriarch), the redactor of the Mishnah. He is generally cited as "Rabbi."

11. B. MḲ 27b.

"the way of the world"—i.e., the law of nature.

"other four things." The text says "five." It includes cutting the hair (see above, vi, 2).

12. B. MḲ 27b; B. Shab 106a.

"Reflections . . . moved"—omitted in the Venice edition.

Chapter XIV

1. B. Shab 127a; B. So 14a, 46b; B. Suk 49b; Ket 6: 5; Tos *ibid.*, 6: 7; B. Ber 6b; PRE XVI, XVII; Pe 1: 1; Tos *ibid.*, 4: 19; P. *ibid.*, 1: 1, p. 2b (4).

"no fixed measure is prescribed." The extent of the practice of these benevolent acts depends solely upon man's kindly feeling and generous impulse.

2. Gen. R 21: 33, p. 111b (222); B. Shab 127a; B. So 46b.

"ran to meet them." The verse following it reads *And (he) said: "My Lord, if now I have found favor in Thy sight, pass not away, I pray Thee, from Thy servant"* (Gen. 18: 3). Abraham was addressing these words to God, who had communed with him, not to leave him till he had discharged the duty of hospitality to the strangers (B. Shebu 35b).

3. B. So 46b.

"outskirts of the city"—seventy cubits and two-thirds beyond the houses of the city.

"Sabbath limit"—2,000 cubits.

4. B. Ned 39b. The talmudic text reads: *It is as though he would take away a sixtieth of his pain.*

5. P. Pe 3: 7, p. 18a (35); B. Ned 40a.

6. B. Shab 12b.

"wrap himself up"—sit in a prayerful mood, because the Divine Presence is above the head side of the patient.

8. Sem 11; B. Ket 17a.

9. B. Meg 29a.

10. B. MḲ 27b.

"others who will attend"—e.g., an organization that does it.

11. B. Ket 17a, b.

12. Tos Giṭ 3: 18; B. *ibid.*, 61a.

13. B. Meg 29a; B. Ber 18a.

14. B. Ber 18a.

15. Sem 13.

"on his own ground"—the family plot of the deceased.

16. Sem 13.

17. B. San 47b.

"a built grave"—a grave elevated above the ground or one erected within the excavation.

18. B. San 47b.

"not forbidden"—although it was designated for the burial of a particular person.

19. B. San 48a.

20. B. San 48a.

21. B. AZ 29b; B. Ar 7b; B. San 47b.

22. B. San 48b.

"garments thrown"—out of grief.

"lest confusion arise." It might be concluded that since the garments thrown upon the bier are permitted for use, the shroud, too, is permitted.

23. B. San 48a.

"no effort . . . to save them"—since they are already forbidden for use; see the preceding section.

24. Sem 9.

25. B. AZ 11a, b; B. BḲ 16b; B. Ket 103b.

26. B. AZ 11a.

"'the way . . . Amorites'"—which is forbidden (see Shab 6: 10).

Treatise V: Kings and Wars

Chapter I

1. B. San 20b.

"set him king"—i.e., whom God will choose.

2. Sif Deut. 17: 14, p. 81b (162); Tos San 4: 3.

3. Tos San 3: 2; Sif Deut. 17: 15, p. 81b (162).

"seventy(-one)"—Venice edition; see Tos San 3: 2.

4. B. Yeb 45b; B. Ḳid 76b.

"a Jewess by descent." So too, if his father is a Jew by descent, he is eligible. Cf. KM *ad loc.*

5. Sif Deut. 17: 15, p. 81b (162).

6. B. Ḳid 82a.

7. B. Ker 5b; Sif Deut. 17: 20, p. 82a (163); B. Ket 103b; Mek Exod. 12: 1, I, p. 5.

"as Jehoiada acted"—II Kings 11: 4, 19.

8. "rules . . . king"—I Sam. 8: 11–17.

"wilt hearken"—actually: "diligently hearken." The quotation is inaccurate.

10. B. Hor 11b.

"Only the descendants," etc. In the text this is the last sentence; logically, however, it belongs to the place given it in the translation. See LM *ad loc.*

11. B. Hor 11b.

"at a spring"—to symbolize the hope that their government be prolonged.

12. B. Hor 11b.

"the claim of Jehoiakim"—who was two years older than his brother.

Chapter II

1. San 2: 5; Tos *ibid.*, 4: 2; B. *ibid.*, 19b, 22a.
"these objects." As to the disposition of the horse he rode and the calf which drew his carriage, see above, IV, xiv, 25.
"would have been permitted"—i.e., had he desired to marry her.
2. San 2: 2.
3. San 2: 2, 5; B. *ibid.*, 19b.
"ḥălișah"—release from levirate marriage described in Deut. 25: 7–10.
4. San 2: 3; Tos *ibid.*, 4: 2; see above, IV, vii, 7.
5. B. San 22b; Sif Zut Num. 27: 21, p. 321 (see L. Finkelstein, JQR [1934–35], p. 485); B. Ket 103b.
"the Urim." The Urim and the Tummim put in the High Priest's breastplate "were used for the purpose of ascertaining the divine will on questions of national importance." (Driver on Exod. 28: 30.)
"by means of the Urim." See Num. 27: 21; I Sam. 28: 6.
6. *"humbled within me."* The usual translation is: "wounded within me."
"as did David"—Tos San 4: 2.
"not against us"—i.e., we are but the servants of God. Cf. B. San 110a.
"[as it is written]"—the Venice edition supplies the word meaning "as it is said" or "written."

Chapter III

1. San 2: 4; B. *ibid.*, 21b; P. *ibid.*, 2: 6, p. 13a (25).
2. San 2: 4; B. *ibid.*, 21a.
3. San 2: 4; B. *ibid.*, 21b.
4. San 2: 4; B. *ibid.*, 21b.
"It is commendable." See I Chron. 29: 2–5.
5. See B. San 70b; Sif Deut. 17: 19, p. 82a (163); Tos San 4: 5.
6. B. San 21a.
7. See above, I, ii, 5.
8. B. San 49a; Tos *ibid.*, 9: 3.
"as did Shimei"—II Sam. 16: 5, 7.
9. B. San 49a.
10. B. Yeb 79a.

Chapter IV

1. B. San 20b.
"section . . . king"—I Sam. 8: 11–17.
"the section relating to the king"—describing the methods he will resort to.
4. "Wives . . . contract," etc.—B. San 21a.
"acquire his maidservant"—Exod. 21: 7–11.
8. B. BB 122a.
9. San 2: 4; Tos *ibid.*, 4: 3; B. *ibid.*, 20b, 48b.
"one half thereof"—in addition to the royal treasures of the kingdom he conquers. Cf. PhM San 2: 4.
"baggage"—the implements and supply of war.

Chapter V

1. So 8:7; B. *ibid.,* 44b.

"the seven nations"—that occupied Canaan before Israel conquered it.

"to deliver Israel"—i.e., a defensive war.

"enhance," etc.—and thus protect Israel from all attacks.

2. San 1:5.
3. San 2:4.
4. "has long perished"—Yad 4:4.

"has long perished"—i.e., their identity has been destroyed. The conquests of Sennacherib, King of Assyria, led to a commingling of races and nations.

5. Sif Deut. 25:17, 19, p. 98a (195).
6. Sif Deut. 11:24, p. 68a (135); B. Giṭ 46b.

"court"—the Supreme Court; see Sec. 2.

"national conquest"—in contradistinction to conquest by an individual (see B. Giṭ 8b).

7. Mek Exod. 14:13, I, 213; B. Suk 51b.

"Great Sea"—the Mediterranean.

8. P. San 10:8, p. 54b (108).
9. B. AZ 13a; B. Ket 111a; B. BB 91a.

"Mahlon and Chilion"—Ruth 1:2–5; cf. B. BB 91a.

10. B. Ket 112a, b.
11. B. Ket 111a.

"make expiation for His people." The usual rendering is: "and doth make expiation for the land of His people."

"unclean land"—in exile.

"whom Palestine receives," etc.—i.e., one who settles in Palestine, or one whose remains are transferred there for burial.

"Jacob"—Gen. 50:13.

"Joseph"—Gen. 50:25; Josh. 24:32.

12. B. Ket 110b, 111a; Sif Lev. 25:38, p. 443a.

Chapter VI

1. Sif Deut. 20:10–11, p. 86a (171).

"an inferior status"—literally: "that they be despised and degraded" (Mal. 2:9). The word "beneath" is omitted in some editions.

"with their body"—i.e., that they do task work. The rest of the section sets forth the nature of the task work.

"their money." See the following section.

3. See Josh. 9:18.
4. *"But the women."* The quotation in the text is inaccurate.

"the (above-cited) command"—Deut. 20:16.

5. P. Shebi 6:1, p. 16b (32); B. Giṭ 46a.

"resort to stratagem"—pretending that they were not inhabitants of Canaan. They should have sued for peace and it would have been granted to them (see Josh. 9:9–13).

"but for the oath"—to let the Gibeonites live (Josh. 9: 15).

"error"—due to the deceit of the Gibeonites.

"desecration." The heathens would have said that the Israelites violated an oath made by them.

6. Sif Deut. 23: 7, p. 92b (184).

7. Sif Num. 31: 7, p. 49a (97).

8. Sif Deut. 20: 19, p. 86b (172); B. BḲ 91b, 92a; ḆB 2: 11.

9. B. BḲ 91b.

"*ḳaḇ*"—measure of capacity, four loḡ; its space is 416⅔ square cubits.

10. B. Shab 105b.

11. Sif Deut. 20: 19, p. 86b (172).

"What has been said"—in Secs. 7–11.

12. B. Er 17a; see above, IV, iii, 8.

"acquires the right"—even if he has someone to attend to his remains.

"lying in the road"—with none to attend to the body (see above, IV, iii, 8).

13. Er 1: 10; P. *ibid.*, 1: 10, p. 13a (25).

" 'dubious' produce"—produce bought from those suspected of neglecting to set apart the tithes.

"detached . . . dry"—and therefore belongs to the owner.

" '*eruḇ* of courtyards"—literally: combination of (houses with common) courtyards. The Bible forbids carrying things on the Sabbath from one house to another. If, however, the occupants of separate houses around a court prepare, before the Sabbath sets in, a meal to which each contributes something and to which all of them have access, all the houses are by this act considered as common to all, and the inmates thereof are permitted to carry objects from one house to another.

"the Treatise on the Sabbath"—III, I, xvi, 15.

14. Sif Deut. 23: 13, p. 93a (185).

15. Sif Deut. 23: 14, p. 93a (185).

"[What has been said . . .]"—in Secs. 12–15. In the Hebrew text the bracketed sentence is the opening sentence of Chap. vii. It should be the concluding sentence of Chap. vi; see Heller, SM, "Positive Commandments," No. 191, p. 83, n. 8.

Chapter VII

1. So 8: 1.

"to address the troops." This refers to an optional war only; see Heller, p. 83, n. 8.

"the troops"—literally: "the people."

2. Sif Deut. 20: 2, p. 85b (170); B. So 42a, b.

"on the frontier." It is perfectly clear from Sif Deut. 20: 2, p. 85b (170), that even at the frontier the entire part of the proclamation set forth in Deut. 20: 5–7—the part assigned to the "priest anointed for war"—was made by him. The passage in Sifre reads: *When they reach the frontier, the priest enumerates the circumstances under which one is sent back home.*

3. B. So 43a.

4. So 8: 6, 7.

5. So 8: 2; P. *ibid.*, 8: 4, p. 37a (73); B. *ibid.*, 43b; B. Suk 3b.

"[or a straw magazine]." In the text as we have it, the bracketed phrase occurs in the last part, that is, "one who has built a straw magazine is not sent back home." This is contrary to the ruling in So 8: 2. The bracketed words, as Rabbi S. Strashun (*ad loc.*) suggests, have been misplaced and belong to the place given them in the translation.

6. So 8: 2; B. *ibid.*, 43b.

" 'orlah." See note above, III, iv, 2, and Glossary.

"subject . . . 'orlah"—i.e., they are regarded as newly planted vines, since they are subject to 'orlah.

7. So 8: 2 and B. *ibid.*, 44a; P. *ibid.*, 8: 6, p. 38a (75).

"one of them dies"—leaving no issue.

8. So 8: 3.

"ḥăliṣah." See note above, ii, 3, and Glossary.

"Nethinah"—a female descendant of the Gibeonites.

"Nathin"—a male descendant of the Gibeonites.

9. So 8: 2.

10. So 8: 4.

11. So 8: 4; B. *ibid.*, 44a.

"municipal . . . duties." In the text these words come at the end of the section. But since these are intended as an explanation of the Deuteronomy quotation, they are placed in the translation immediately after the quotation.

"two negative commands"—i.e., *He shall not go out in the host* and *Neither shall he be charged with any business.*

12. P. So 8: 4, p. 37a (73).

"already dedicated it." He is exempt from joining the army.

"the expiration of the twelve months"—when the rent is paid. He is then sent back home.

13. P. So 8: 4, p. 37b (74).

14. P. So 8: 4, p. 37a (73).

15. So 8: 5.

Chapter VIII

1. B. Ḥul 17a.

"nĕḇelah." See note above, I, xix, 4 (88), and Glossary.

"ṭĕrefah." See note above, I, xix, 4 (89), and Glossary.

2. B. Ḳid 21b.

3. Sif Deut. 21: 11, p. 87b (174); B. Ḳid 22a.

"force her"—to have relations with him the first time when he is permitted to do it.

4. B. Ḳid 21b.

"a proselyte." A priest is not permitted to marry a proselyte.

5. B. Yeb 47b, 48a, b; Sif Deut. 21: 13, p. 87b (174); 21: 12, p. 87b (174).

"to accept Judaism"—literally: "to enter under the wings of the Divine Presence."

6. Sif Deut. 21: 13, p. 87b (174); 21: 14, p. 87b (174).

"two months thereafter"—i.e., three months in all, to make certain that the child that will be born was conceived by the mother after her conversion and marriage to her erstwhile captor.

7. Mek on Deut. 21: 14 (see L. Finkelstein, JQR [1934–35], p. 494; see also Kasher, *op. cit.*, p. 148).

8. "But the court," etc.—B. Ket 11a; B. San 21a.

"first intercourse"—with David.

"married to Amnon." Amnon was her brother by the same father, but she was not regarded as David's daughter.

9. Mek on Deut. 21: 14 (see n. 7).

10. B. San 59a; B. AZ 64b, 65a.

"for the resident alien"—literally: "for the stranger."

"associates"—punctilious Jews, who observe scrupulously the rules of tithing, and of cleanness and uncleanness.

11. B. San 105a; cf. B. Meg 16a.

"but . . . wise men." The word *'ella,* "but," should be inserted.

Chapter IX

1. Gen. R 2: 16, p. 38b (76).

"In Egypt," etc. Some commandments were given to the Israelites in Egypt (Mek Exod. 19: 10, ii, p. 211); Amram is said to have been the president of the Sanhedrin (Exod. R 1: 16, p. 4b [8]; B. So 12a).

2. B. San 56b.

"imposes . . . (upon a Jew)"—if he is the offender.

3. B. San 56a.

"ineffable"—i.e., the Tetragrammaton.

"a Jew." He is liable only if he employs the ineffable Name; cf. I, iv, ii, 7.

4. B. San 57b.

"In none of these cases." Cf. B. Nid 44a; XI, v, ii, 2, 6, 8; i, 13.

5. B. San 58a.

6. B. San 58a, 54b, 55b.

"their son is liable"—though she was never made his father's wife.

7. B. San 58b.

"by the Jewish law." Heathens do not consider it a capital offense.

"a married heathen woman." Heathens, too, consider it a capital offense.

8. B. San 58b; Gen. R 2: 24, p. 41a; P. Ḳid 1: 1, p. 2a (3).

"the wife of"—Maimonides' reading of B. San 58b was "the wife of," whereas the ordinary reading is "the girl of."

"she goes bareheaded."—literally: "she uncovers."

9. B. San 57a; B. AZ 71b.

"pĕruṭah." See note above, I, xvi, 12.

10. B. San 59a.

"fixed measures"—with regard to size, quantity, etc.

11. B. Ḥul 121b.

"It makes no difference"—in any of these instances, he is culpable.

12. B. Ḥul 121b.

13. B. Ḥul 102a, 121a.

"is culpable." A Jew, however, is culpable only if the limb or flesh he eats is of a clean cattle or beast of chase.

"forbidden to a Noahide." A Jew, however, is permitted to eat of an animal the organs whereof have been properly cut, even if it is still jerking.

14. B. San 56a, b, 57a, b.

"Shechem"—Gen. 34: 1–23.

"because Shechem"—the son of Hamor, the prince of the land (Gen. 34: 2).

Chapter X

1. B. Mak 9a.

"A Noahide"—who has not accepted the seven commandments enjoined upon Noahides, i.e., he is a heathen. Translation is based upon LM *ad loc.*

"do not offer him an asylum." The cities of refuge sheltered an involuntary homicide who was an Israelite or a resident alien, but did not protect an involuntary homicide who was a heathen. See B. Mak 9a; cf. XI, v, v, 4.

"condemn him"—i.e., the accidental slayer.

2. B. San 74b; P. Shebi 4: 2, p. 10b (20).

3. B. Yeb 47b; B. Ket 11a.

4. B. San 71b.

"blasphemed . . . idol." Conversion effects a change in (a) his legal status and (b) the mode of his execution. A Noahide is tried by one judge, and is condemned to death on the testimony of one witness even if no warning has been given him (see above, ix, 14); whereas a Jew is tried by a court of twenty-three, is condemned to death only on the testimony of at least two witnesses after warning has been given him. Moreover, a Noahide who blasphemes God or worships an idol is punished by decapitation with the sword; whereas a Jew who is guilty of this offense incurs the penalty of stoning—a severer mode of execution than the former.

"relations . . . killed a Noahide." Were he to commit either of the offenses after accepting the Jewish religion, he would not be liable to death.

"he is liable." Were he to commit either of the two offenses after embracing Judaism, he would be liable to death.

"decapitated . . . a Jew"—i.e., the punishment which he would have suffered had he remained a heathen.

"status has changed." As a heathen he would have been liable to decapitation, a severer mode of death than strangulation. Since his status has changed, the lighter punishment—that prescribed by the Jewish law—is meted out to him. Cf. KM and RaDbeZ *ad loc.*

5. See above, ix, 14.

6. B. San 56b, 58b.

"are forbidden only." They are permitted, however, to wear garments of wool and linen and to sow diverse seeds together.

"(by the court)." His punishment is death by divine intervention.

7. B. San 59b.

8. B. San 59b.

9. B. San 58b, 59a.

"deserves death"—but is not put to death; see the end of this section.

10. See Eccles. R 1: 9, p. 4b (8); B. Pes 21b; B. BB 10b (cf. VII, II, viii, 9).

"any other commandment"—other than the seven enjoined upon him.

12. B. BḲ 113a; cf. Sif Deut. 1:16, p. 55a, b (109, 110); B. Giṭ 61a, 62a.
"a resident alien"—i.e., in a suit in which he and a Jew are involved.

Chapter XI

1. "believe in a restoration"—literally: "believe in him."
"section . . . Balaam"—Num. 22–24.
"And all the Edomites." The quotation is inaccurate (see II Sam. 8:14; I Chron. 18:13).
2. Sif Deut. 19:9, p. 84a (167); cf. XI, v, viii, 4.
3. "affirmed . . . was King Messiah"—Lam R 2:2, p. 21 (41); P. Ta 4:5, p. 24a (47).
"Ben Kozba"—literally: the son of Kozba. His full name was Simeon bar Kozba (Kozeḇa[?]) or bar Kokhba. He was the leader of the last Jewish War of Independence (132 C.E.).
"all the wise men." This does not agree with what is recorded in P. Ta 4:5, pp. 24a, 24b: that not all the wise men of that generation acclaimed Ben Kozba as the Messiah.
"The general principle is." It is difficult to find any connection between the last three sentences in this section and what precedes them.
"[is not subject to change] . . . [Whoever adds . . .]." The Venice edition and all older prints contain the bracketed passages.

Chapter XII

1. "with Israel." The reading is uncertain; a variant reading is: "like Israel."
2. "Gog and Magog"—who, prior to the coming of the Messiah, will invade the land of Israel and be exterminated by God (see B. Ber 13a; see also Ezek., 38 f.).
"will come . . . clean"—Ed 8:7.
"Blasted be." The talmudic text reads: "Blasted be the bones of those," etc.
3. B. Ḳid 71a.
"its status"—of purity, literally: "it remains intermingled."
4. See I, v, ix, 8.

LIST OF ABBREVIATIONS

Sources and Commentaries

Alf—Alfasi (Vilna, 1891)
B.—Babylonian Talmud
BḤ—*Beṯ Ḥaḏaš* (on ṬḤM and ṬYD)
BhG—*Be'ur ha-GRA* (on ŠA)
BY—*Beṯ Yosef* (on ṬḤM and ṬYD)
Der—*Dĕrišah* (on ṬḤM and ṬYD)
GRA—Gaon R. Elijah
Heller—see SM
ḤM—*Ḥošen ha-Mišpaṭ* (Lemberg, 1898)
ḤMḤ—*Ḥidduše Mayim Ḥayyim* (on *Mishneh Torah*)
JE—*Jewish Encyclopedia*
JQR—*Jewish Quarterly Review*
KM—*Kesef Mišneh* (on *Mishneh Torah*)
LhR—*Lĕšonoṯ ha-Rambam* (Venice, 1743)
LM—*Leḥem Mišneh* (on *Mishneh Torah*)
MB—*Minḥaṯ Biḵḵurim* (on *Tosefta*)
Mek—*Mĕḵilta* (ed. Lauterbach, Jewish Publication Society, 1933)
MM—M. M. Kasher, *Maimonides and the Mĕḵilta of Rabbi Simeon ben Yoḥai* (New York, 1943)
MRSY—*Mĕḵilta of Rabbi Simeon ben Yoḥai* (ed. Hoffman)
NhG—*Nusaḥ ha-GRA* (on Sem)
NY—*Nimmuḵe Yosef* (on Alf)
P.—Palestinian Talmud
Per—*Pĕrišah* (on ṬḤM and ṬYD)
PhM—*Peruš ha-Mišnayoṯ* (Maimonides' commentary on the Mishnah)
PRE—*Pirḵe de-Rabbi Eliezer*
R.—*Midrash Rabba* (Romm and Brothers, Vilna, 1887)
RaDbeZ—Rabbi David ben Zimra (16th century)
RaSHbA—Rabbi Solomon ibn Adret (13th century)
RIbeSh—Rabbi Isaac ben Shesheth (14th century)
ŠA—*Šulḥan 'Aruḵ* (Lemberg, 1898)
ShK—*Šifṯe Kohen* (on ḤM and YD)
Sif—*Sifra* (Malbim, Warsaw, 1875)
Sif—*Sifre* on Deuteronomy (Finn and Rosenkranz, Vilna, 1866)
Sif—*Sifre* on Numbers (Finn and Rosenkranz, Vilna, 1866)

Sif Zut—*Sifre Zuṭa* on Numbers (ed. Horovitz)
SM—*Sefer ha-Miṣwot̲* (ed. Heller, Jerusalem, 1946)
SME—*Sefer Mĕ'irat̲ 'Enayim* (on ḤM)
Tanḥ—*Tanḥuma* (ed. Ḥoreb, New York–Berlin, 1927)
ThG—*Tĕšub̲ot̲ ha-Gĕ'onim* (Jerusalem, 1929)
ṬḤM—*Ṭur Ḥošen ha-Mišpaṭ* (Vilna, 1900)
Tos—*Tosefta* (Vilna, 1891)
ṬYD—*Ṭur Yore De'ah* (Warsaw, 1878)
TYṬ—*Tosafot̲ Yom Ṭob̲* (Vilna, 1910)
ṬZ—*Ṭure Zahab̲* (on ḤM and YD)
YD—*Yore De'ah* (Lemberg, 1876)

Tractates of Mishnah and Talmud

Ab—*Ab̲ot̲*
Ar—*'Ărak̲in*
AZ—*'Ăb̲od̲ah Zarah*
BB—*Bab̲a Bat̲ra*
Be—*Beṣah*
Bek—*Bĕk̲orot̲*
Ber—*Bĕrak̲ot̲*
Bik—*Bik̲k̲urim*
BḲ—*Bab̲a Ḳamma*
BM—*Bab̲a Mĕṣi'a*
Ed—*'Ed̲uyyot̲*
Er—*'Erub̲in*
Giṭ—*Giṭṭin*
Ḥag—*Ḥăgig̲ah*
Hor—*Horayot̲*
Ḥul—*Ḥullin*
Ker—*Kĕrit̲ot̲*
Ket—*Kĕt̲ubbot̲*
Ḳid—*Ḳiddušin*
Kil—*Kil'ayim*
Mak—*Mak̲k̲ot̲*
Meg—*Mĕg̲illah*
Men—*Mĕnaḥot̲*
Mid—*Middot̲*
MḲ—*Mo'ed̲ Ḳaṭan*
Naz—*Nazir*
Ned—*Nĕd̲arim*
Neg—*Nĕg̲a'im*
Nid—*Niddah*
Oh—*'Ohalot̲*
Pe—*Pe'ah*
Pes—*Pĕsaḥim*
RH—*Roš Haššanah*
San—*Sanhed̲rin*
Shab—*Šabbat̲*
Shebi—*Šĕb̲i'it̲*
Shebu—*Šĕb̲u'ot̲*
Sheḳ—*Šĕḳalim*
So—*Soṭah*
Suk—*Suk̲k̲ah*
Ta—*Ta'ănit̲*
Ter—*Tĕrumot̲*
Yad—*Yad̲ayim*
Yeb—*Yĕb̲amot̲*
Yo—*Yoma*
Zeb—*Zĕb̲aḥim*

Minor Tractates

ARN—*Ab̲ot̲ de-Rabbi Nathan*
Sem—*Šĕmaḥot̲*

GLOSSARY

'Ab̲ bet̲ din (literally: father of the court)
vice-president of the Great Sanhedrin

'Ad̲ar
the twelfth month of the Jewish calendar, counting from the month of *Nisan*

'Aggad̲ah
rabbinic literature of a nonjuristic character

'Āgunah
a woman the whereabouts of whose husband is unknown, and who cannot remarry as long as there is no evidence of his death

'Am ha-'areṣ (literally: the people of the land)
it signifies in rabbinic literature: a. an ignorant person (II, xi, 2); b. one who is lax in the observance of the commandments, untrustworthy in fulfilling the obligations relating to priestly and levitical dues (II, xi, 8); Maimonides uses it once (II, ix, 10) in the sense of people in general

'Ămid̲ah (literally: standing)
the Eighteen Benedictions (seven on Sabbaths and festivals) recited thrice daily in a standing position

'Ămora'im
expounders, expositors; talmudic authorities who flourished from about 220 C.E. to 500 C.E. and whose discussions are embodied in the Gemara part of the Talmud

'Ăninut̲
the laws of mourning observed between the death and the burial of a kinsman

'Anus
a. one who acts under duress; b. one who abjures the Jewish religion under compulsion

'Ărisut̲
tenancy, the owner paying the tenant a fixed proportion for cultivating the land

Barait̲a (literally: extraneous)
traditions and teachings of the *Tanna'im* not embodied in the Mishnah but incorporated in later collections

Bĕd̲ik̲ot̲
investigation, cross-examination

Boethus

an alleged disciple of Antigonus of Sokḥo and founder of a sect similar to the Sadducean (see ARN 5: 2)

Denar (denarius)

a. coin, silver or gold; b. weight, about 1/8 of an ounce, according to some; 3/50 of an ounce, according to others.

'Ĕlohim (literally: God)

a term applied to judges ordained in Palestine

'Efod̲

a short close-fitting coat worn by the High Priest round the body under the arms and held in place by two shoulder pieces or straps (see Exod. 28: 4)

Epicurean

a heretic or unbeliever, whether Jewish or non-Jewish; see C. Taylor, *Sayings of the Jewish Fathers,* p. 40, n. 45; see also R. Travers Herford, *Christianity in Talmud and Midrash,* p. 120; Maimonides I, v, iii, 16 defines an epicurean as one who either denies the reality of prophecy in general or the prophecy of Moses, or one who maintains that God has no knowledge of the deeds of man

'Erub̲ of courtyards (literally: mixture or combination of courtyards)

pertaining to the prohibition of carrying objects from one house to another on the Sabbath (see Jer. 17: 22): if the inmates of separate houses with a common courtyard prepare before the Sabbath a meal to which each contributes something and to which all of them have access, all the houses are by this act regarded as common to all, and the residents thereof are permitted to carry objects from one house into another

Gehenna

originally a place south of Jerusalem where children were sacrificed to Molech (see II Kings 23: 10); the word has become a synonym for Hell

Gemara

the part of the Talmud that contains comments, discussions, and opinions of the *Amora'im* upon the Mishnah

Geonim (singular: *Ga'on,* Excellency; plural: *Gĕ'onim*)

the title borne by the heads of the two Babylonian Academies at Sura and Pumbeditha; these rabbinical authorities flourished from the seventh century to 1038 C.E.

Ḥăḵirot
queries

Ḥăḵirut
tenure on rent in kind, the tenant paying the owner of the land a fixed quantity of the produce regardless of the yield of the crop

Halakhah
rules, laws, final decisions; legal elements, as opposed to *'Aggaḏah*

Ḥălalah (literally: profaned)
the daughter of a priest and a woman forbidden to him, or a priest's wife illegitimately married to him

Ḥăliṣah (literally: the act of taking off)
the rite whereby a woman is released from levirate marriage, if the husband died childless (see Deut. 25: 5–10)

Ḥallah
the priest's share of the dough (see Num. 15: 20)

Ḥanuḵḵah
the Feast of Dedication instituted in the year 165 B.C.E. by Judas Maccabeus and his brothers; beginning on the 25th day of Kislew, it is observed eight days (I Macc. 4: 53, 59)

Heḏyoṭ
an ordinary man, a commoner, an ignorant person, mediocre (I, xxiv, 8), ill mannered

'Iyyar
the second month of the Jewish calendar

Israelite
a. a Jew, in contradistinction to a heathen or a Gentile; b. a Jew who is neither a priest nor a levite

Jubilee
the fiftieth year, the year following the succession of seven Sabbatical years (see Lev. 25: 8–16)

Ḳaḇ
measure of capacity equal to four loḡ, ⅙ of a *se'ah,* or 416⅔ sq. cubits

Ḳabbĕlanuṯ
a. work on contract; b. tenancy at a fixed rent, the tenant paying the owner a stipulated sum of money; it is in the latter sense that the term is used in IV, V, 11

Karaites (Hebrew *ḳara'im*)
the name given to the followers of Anan (eighth century C.E.); they revolted against the Talmud and rested their practices exclusively on the Bible

Kareṯ (literally: cutting off)
opinions differ as to the exact nature of this punishment; some construe it to mean dying prematurely at the age of 50 or between 50 and 60 (B. MḲ 25a); according to others, it implies dying childless (B. Yeb 55a); still others interpret it to mean the extirpation of the soul in the world to come (B. San 64b); Maimonides (I, v, viii, 2) favors the last explanation

Kĕṯubbah
a. marriage contract, in which the husband pledges himself to assign to the wife a certain sum in the event of his death or in case he divorces her; b. the sum settled on her

Ḳinyan (literally: acquisition, proprietary rights)
it designates: a. a symbolic conveyance as by a kerchief (*suḏar*), the assignee or transferee giving a kerchief to the assignor or transferring party; b. a pledge to carry out a promise or an agreement, the one who makes the pledge handing to the other party a kerchief or any other object

Levite
a. a descendant of the tribe of Levi (see Num. 3: 5 ff); b. as contrasted to "priest" and "(lay) Israelite"

Loḡ
a. a liquid measure equal to a quarter of a *ḳaḇ;* b. the space occupied by six eggs, i.e., 104⅙ sq. cubits

Maneh
one hundred zuz

Meṯ miṣwah (literally: a corpse, the burial of which is a religious duty)
a corpse lying in the road, with no one to attend to it

Midrash
exposition or exegesis of the Scriptures

Mishnah (literally: teaching)
the traditional laws codified by Rabbi Judah Hannaśi about 200 C.E.

Molech
the fire-god of the Canaanites worshiped by child sacrifice

Mufle (literally: outstanding member)
the president of the Great Sanhedrin (PhM Hor 1: 4); it would seem

that Maimonides applies the title also to the head of the Small Sanhedrin (III, iii, 6); thus the *mufle* is described in I, iv, 8 as a sage who is competent to give an authoritative opinion on all questions of law: i.e., he is the foremost member of the Small Sanhedrin (I, i, 5) and, therefore, the head of that body (I, i, 3)

Mumḥe (literally: one who is skilled, an expert)
a competent, well-qualified judge: i.e., one who is ordained and is both erudite and resourceful (see PhM San 1: 1; 3: 1)

Naśi (literally: prince)
the Patriarch, the head or president of the Great Sanhedrin; the head of the Jewish people after the fall of Jerusalem

Nathin (see I Chron. 9: 2; Ezra 2: 43; 8: 20)
a descendant of the Gibeonites (see Josh. 9: 27)

Nazarite
one who vows to dedicate himself to the service of God; his vow implies a. abstention from intoxicants; b. letting his hair grow; c. avoidance of contact with a dead body (see Num. 6: 2–8)

Nĕḇelah
an animal a. that dies a natural death; b. that was not slaughtered according to ritual rules

Nethinah
a female descendant of the Gibeonites

Nisan
the first month of the Jewish calendar

Noahide (literally: a descendant of Noah)
the term signifies: a. a non-Jew who adheres to the seven commandments enjoined upon the descendants of Noah; b. a heathen (see v, x, 1)

'Omer (literally: sheaf)
the first sheaf of barley presented at the sanctuary on the sixteenth day of *Nisan* (see Lev. 23: 10)

'Onen
a mourner in the interval between the death and the burial of a kinsman

'Orlah (literally: uncircumcision)
the fruit of young trees forbidden for use during the first three years (see Lev. 19: 23)

Pĕruṭah
the smallest copper coin

Purim

the Feast of Lots, observed on the fourteenth day of *'Ădar* in commemoration of the salvation of the Jews in Persia; the full story about it is recorded in the Book of Esther

Ša'aṭnez

material of wool and linen interwoven (see Lev. 19: 19)

Sanhedrin

council, high court; the Great Sanhedrin, the Supreme Court consisting of seventy-one members; a Small Sanhedrin, a high court consisting of twenty-three members

Šĕma'

portions of Scripture appointed to be read morning and evening; these comprise three sections: Deut. 6: 4–9; 11: 13–21; Num. 15: 37–41; the first verse (Deut. 6: 4) is often designated as "Israel's Confession of Faith"

Šĕṯuḵi

one whose paternity is not known

Šofar

ram's horn sounded during the services of the New Year, at the conclusion of the Day of Atonement, and on other prescribed occasions

Soṭah

a woman suspected of infidelity to her husband (see Num. 5: 12–31)

Tam (literally: innocuous)

an ox that has done injury (with the horn) less than three times

Tanna'im

authorities cited in the Mishnah or the *Baraiṯa;* these teachers flourished from approximately 10 C.E. to 200 C.E.

Ṭeḇel

produce from which the priestly dues, or any of the tithes, have not been given (see Lev. 27: 30; Num. 18: 26; Deut. 14: 28–29; 18: 4–5)

Tĕfillin

phylacteries; small square boxes of black leather cases enclosing scrolls of parchment on which are written four sections from the Bible: Exod. 13: 1–10, 11–16; Deut. 6: 4–9; 11: 13–21; these boxes are bound on the head and arm by a strap

Ṭĕrefah (literally: torn by a beast or bird of prey)

the prohibition in Exod. 22: 30 was extended to include beasts affected with a fatal organic disease

Tišri
the seventh month of the Jewish calendar

Ṭumṭum
one whose sex is physiologically uncertain

'Urim
see "the judgment of Urim" in Num. 27: 21

Zadok
a disciple of Antigonus of Sokho (Ab 1: 3) and alleged founder of the Sadducean sect (see ARN 5: 2)

Zuz
a coin of the value of a *denar*

INDEX

AARON, 76; sons of, 172; daughters of, 172
'Aḇ beṯ din (*see* Glossary), 5, 13, 187, 188, 189; when, dies, all rend their clothes for him, and all Houses of Study in his city are closed, 189; *see also* Baring the shoulder
Abandonment, of hope of recovering stolen property, 117; of search for a dead body, 163
Abishag, 210
Abner, 184
Abortives, 165; *see* Mourning
Abraham, 200, 231; instituted the Morning Service, 231; was commanded to practice circumcision, 231; hospitality extended by, to wayfarer, 200; children of, 75
Absalom, 229
Absolution. *See* Vows
Academy, of Safed, Introduction xviii; set up near the grave of *Naśi,* 204; academies outside Palestine, 20, 64
Achan, 52
Adam, 230 f.; six commandments given to, 230
Adar (*see* Glossary), 126, 147
Admission, of debts, 18, 86, *passim;* what constitutes, 120; of guilt, 52 f.; none put to death or flogged on one's own, 52 f.; none ordered to pay fine on one's own, 124; none disqualified as witness on one's own, of religious delinquency, 108; *see* Self-incrimination
Admonition, 46, *passim; see* Charge, Warning
Adonijah, 210
'Ăḡunah (*see* Glossary), 102; evidence of one witness accepted in the case of, 92; evidence of one who has lost his speech accepted in the case of, 102; evidence of women accepted in the case of, 92
Ahijah, the Shilonite, 209
Akiba, Rabbi, 239
Alexandria, 218; Alexandrian mending, 187
'Am ha'areṣ (*see* Glossary), 105, 106
Amalek, to destroy the seed of, 207; Amalekite, 52
'Ămiḏah (*see* Glossary), 175
Ammon, 222; Ammonite, 59, 222
Amnon, 229
Amora'im (*see* Glossary), 21
Amram, 231
Antioch, 181
Apostates, 107, 143, 165
Arbitration, in preference to legal adjudication, 66 f.; power of, 67
Army, those eligible for discharge from, 225 f.; provision and maintenance of, 226; exemption from joining, 226; things permitted to soldiers in the invading, 228